W9-AAV-648

Child Growth and Development

Fourteenth Edition

07/08

EDITORS

Ellen N. Junn
California State University, Fullerton

Ellen Junn is a professor of child and adolescent studies and associate dean of the College of Health and Human Development at California State University, Fullerton. She received her B.S. with distinction in psychology and with high honors from the University of Michigan and her M.A. and Ph.D. in cognitive and developmental psychology from Princeton University. Dr. Junn's areas of research include college teaching effectiveness, educational equity, faculty development, and public policy as it affects children and families.

Chris J. Boyatzis
Bucknell University

Dr. Chris Boyatzis is an associate professor of psychology at Bucknell University. He received a B.A. with distinction in psychology from Boston University and his M.A. and Ph.D. in developmental psychology from Brandeis University. His primary research focus is religion and spiritual development across the lifespan but especially during childhood, adolescence, and the college years. He is on the editorial boards of several psychology journals.

 **Contemporary Learning Series**

2460 Kerper Blvd., Dubuque, IA 52001

Visit us on the Internet
http://www.mhcls.com

Credits

1. **Conception to Birth**
   Unit photo—© Royalty-Free/CORBIS.
2. **Cognition, Language, and Learning**
   Unit photo—Banana Stock/PunchStock.
3. **Social and Emotional Development**
   Unit photo—Digital Vision/PunchStock.
4. **Parenting and Family Issues**
   Unit photo—© Royalty-Free/CORBIS.
5. **Cultural and Societal Influences**
   Unit photo—Courtesy of Tara McDermott.

Copyright

Cataloging in Publication Data
Main entry under title: Annual Editions: Child Growth and Development. 2007/2008.
1. Child Growth and Development—Periodicals. I. Junn, Ellen N. and Boyatzis, Chris J., *comp.* II. Title: Child Growth and Development.
ISBN-13: 978–0–07–351616–5   ISBN-10: 0–07–351616–3   658'.05   ISSN 1075–5217

Fourteenth Edition

Cover image © S. Wanke/PhotoLink/Getty Images and Dave J. Anthoy/Getty Images
Printed in the United States of America   1234567890QPDQPD9876   Printed on Recycled Paper

Editors/Advisory Board

Members of the Advisory Board are instrumental in the final selection of articles for each edition of ANNUAL EDITIONS. Their review of articles for content, level, currentness, and appropriateness provides critical direction to the editor and staff. We think that you will find their careful consideration well reflected in this volume.

Staff

Preface

In publishing ANNUAL EDITIONS we recognize the enormous role played by the magazines, newspapers, and journals of the public press in providing current, first-rate educational information in a broad spectrum of interest areas. Many of these articles are appropriate for students, researchers, and professionals seeking accurate, current material to help bridge the gap between principles and theories and the real world. These articles, however, become more useful for study when those of lasting value are carefully collected, organized, indexed, and reproduced in a low-cost format, which provides easy and permanent access when the material is needed. That is the role played by ANNUAL EDITIONS.

We are delighted to welcome you to this fourteenth volume of *Annual Editions: Child Growth and Development 07/08*. The amazing sequence of events of prenatal development that lead to the birth of a baby is an awe-inspiring process. Perhaps more intriguing is the question of what the future may hold for this newly arrived baby. For instance, will this child become a doctor, a lawyer, an artist, a beggar, or a thief? Although philosophers and prominent thinkers such as Charles Darwin and Sigmund Freud have long speculated about the importance of infancy on subsequent development, not until the 1960s did the scientific study of infants and young children flourish. Since then, research and theory in infancy and childhood have exploded, resulting in a wealth of new knowledge about child development.

Past accounts of infants and young children as passive, homogeneous organisms have been replaced with investigations aimed at studying infants and young children at a "microlevel" as active individuals with many inborn competencies, who are capable of shaping their own environment, as well as at a "macrolevel" by considering the larger context surrounding the child. In short, children are not "blank slates" and development does not take place in a vacuum; children arrive with many skills and grow up in a complex web of social, historical, political, economic, and cultural spheres.

As was the case for previous editions, we hope to achieve at least four major goals with this volume. First, we hope to present you with the latest research and thinking to help you better appreciate the complex interactions that characterize human development in infancy and childhood. Second, in light of the feedback we received on previous editions, we have placed greater emphasis on important contemporary issues and challenges, exploring topics such as understanding development in the context of current societal and cultural influences. Third, attention is given to articles that also discuss effective, practical applications. Finally, we hope that this anthology will serve as a catalyst to help students become more effective future professionals and parents.

To achieve these objectives, we carefully selected articles from a variety of sources, including scholarly research journals and texts as well as semi-professional journals and popular publications. Every selection was scrutinized for readability, interest level, relevance, and currency. In addition, we listened to the valuable input and advice from members of our advisory board, consisting of faculty from a range of institutions of higher education, including community and liberal arts colleges as well as research and teaching universities. We are most grateful to the advisory board as well as to the excellent editorial staff of McGraw-Hill Contemporary Learning Series.

Annual Editions: Child Growth and Development 07/08 is organized into five major units. Unit 1 focuses on conception, prenatal development, and childbirth. Unit 2 presents information regarding developments in cognition, language, learning, and school. Unit 3 focuses on social and emotional development, while Unit 4 is devoted to parenting and family issues such as parenting and the roles of mothers and fathers, sibling interactions, and discipline. Finally, Unit 5 focuses on larger cultural and societal influences (e.g., media and marketing, the effects of affluence on development, and fathering in other cultures) and on special challenges (such as child abuse, ADHD, treatment of emotional and mental disorders in children, autism, abhorrent conditions for children living in very poor nations).

Instructors for large lecture courses may wish to adopt this anthology as a supplement to a basic text, whereas instructors for smaller sections might also find the readings effective for promoting student presentations or for stimulating discussions and applications. Whatever format is utilized, it is our hope that the instructor and the students will find the readings interesting, illuminating, and provocative.

As the title indicates, *Annual Editions: Child Growth and Development* is by definition a volume that undergoes continual review and revision. Thus, we welcome and encourage your comments and suggestions for future editions of this volume. Simply fill out and return the *Article Rating Form* found at the end of this book. Best wishes, and we look forward to hearing from you!

Ellen N. Junn
Editor

Chris J. Boyatzis
Editor

Contents

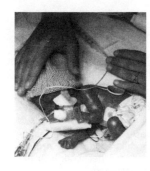

UNIT 1
Conception to Birth

UNIT 2
Cognition, Language, and Learning

The concepts in bold italics are developed in the article. For further expansion, please refer to the Topic Guide and the Index.

UNIT 3
Social and Emotional Development

The concepts in bold italics are developed in the article. For further expansion, please refer to the Topic Guide and the Index.

UNIT 4
Parenting and Family Issues

The concepts in bold italics are developed in the article. For further expansion, please refer to the Topic Guide and the Index.

UNIT 5
Cultural and Societal Influences

The concepts in bold italics are developed in the article. For further expansion, please refer to the Topic Guide and the Index.

The concepts in bold italics are developed in the article. For further expansion, please refer to the Topic Guide and the Index.

The concepts in bold italics are developed in the article. For further expansion, please refer to the Topic Guide and the Index.

Topic Guide

This topic guide suggests how the selections in this book relate to the subjects covered in your course. You may want to use the topics listed on these pages to search the Web more easily.

On the following pages a number of Web sites have been gathered specifically for this book. They are arranged to reflect the units of this *Annual Edition.* You can link to these sites by going to the student online support site at *http://www.mhcls.com/online/.*

ALL THE ARTICLES THAT RELATE TO EACH TOPIC ARE LISTED BELOW THE BOLD-FACED TERM.

Aggression
6. Gender Bender
13. Friendship Quality and Social Development
17. Taming Wild Girls
19. A Profile of Bullying at School
23. Physical Discipline and Children's Adjustment: Cultural Normativeness as a Moderator
25. Why Our Kids Are Out of Control
35. Childhood's End

Aging
1. Brave New Babies

Attachment
4. Brain Research and Early Childhood Development: A Primer for Developmentally Appropriate Practice
13. Friendship Quality and Social Development
21. Contemporary Research on Parenting: The Case for Nature *and* Nurture

Birth and birth defects
1. Brave New Babies
2. Treating the Tiniest Patients
39. Savior Parents

Child abuse
27. The Environment of Childhood Poverty
31. Forensic Developmental Psychology: Unveiling Four Common Misconceptions
35. Childhood's End

Classroom management
8. A Deeper Sense of Literacy
9. Parental School Involvement and Children's Academic Achievement
10. The Trouble with Boys
17. Taming Wild Girls
19. A Profile of Bullying at School

Cognitive development
3. Reading Your Baby's Mind
4. Brain Research and Early Childhood Development: A Primer for Developmentally Appropriate Practice
5. Culture and Language in the Emergence of Autobiographical Memory
7. Language and Children's Understanding of Mental States
9. Parental School Involvement and Children's Academic Achievement
15. The Power of Make-Believe
27. The Environment of Childhood Poverty
30. Watch and Learn
37. When Does Autism Start?

Cross-cultural issues
5. Culture and Language in the Emergence of Autobiographical Memory
6. Gender Bender
23. Physical Discipline and Children's Adjustment: Cultural Normativeness as a Moderator

25. Why Our Kids Are Out of Control
27. The Environment of Childhood Poverty
29. The Culture of Affluence: Psychological Costs of Material Wealth
32. How Many Fathers Are Best for a Child?
35. Childhood's End

Culture
5. Culture and Language in the Emergence of Autobiographical Memory
8. A Deeper Sense of Literacy
23. Physical Discipline and Children's Adjustment: Cultural Normativeness as a Moderator
29. The Culture of Affluence: Psychological Costs of Material Wealth
32. How Many Fathers Are Best for a Child?
36. Children of the Fallen

Development
2. Treating the Tiniest Patients
3. Reading Your Baby's Mind
4. Brain Research and Early Childhood Development: A Primer for Developmentally Appropriate Practice
26. Siblings' Direct and Indirect Contributions to Child Development
27. The Environment of Childhood Poverty

Developmental disabilities
34. Attention Deficit Hyperactivity Disorder in Very Young Children: Early Signs and Interventions
37. When Does Autism Start?
38. Three Reasons Not to Believe in an Autism Epidemic
39. Savior Parents

Discipline
9. Parental School Involvement and Children's Academic Achievement
17. Taming Wild Girls
19. A Profile of Bullying at School
23. Physical Discipline and Children's Adjustment: Cultural Normativeness as a Moderator
24. A Nation of Wimps
25. Why Our Kids Are Out of Control
26. Siblings' Direct and Indirect Contributions to Child Development

Drug abuse
2. Treating the Tiniest Patients
29. The Culture of Affluence: Psychological Costs of Material Wealth
33. The Pediatric Gap

Drug use
29. The Culture of Affluence: Psychological Costs of Material Wealth
34. Attention Deficit Hyperactivity Disorder in Very Young Children: Early Signs and Interventions

Economic issues
27. The Environment of Childhood Poverty
28. Childhood for Sale

Internet References

The following Internet sites have been carefully researched and selected to support the articles found in this reader. The easiest way to access these selected sites is to go to our student online support site at *http://www.mhcls.com/online/*.

AE: Child Growth and Development 07/08

The following sites were available at the time of publication. Visit our Web site—we update our student online support site regularly to reflect any changes.

General Sources

American Academy of Pediatrics
http://www.aap.org

This organization provides data for optimal physical, mental, and social health for all children.

CYFERNet
http://www.cyfernet.mes.umn.edu

The Children, Youth, and Families Education Research Network is sponsored by the Cooperative Extension Service and USDA's Cooperative State Research Education and Extension Service. This site provides practical research-based information in areas including health, child care, family strengths, science, and technology.

KidsHealth
http://kidshealth.org

This site was developed to help parents find reliable children's health information. Enter the Parents site to find such topics as: General Health, Nutrition and Fitness, First Aid and Safety, Growth and Development, Positive Parenting, and more.

National Institute of Child Health and Human Development
http://www.nichd.nih.gov

The NICHD conducts and supports research on the reproductive, neurobiological, developmental, and behavioral processes that determine and maintain the health of children, adults, families, and populations.

UNIT 1: Conception to Birth

Babyworld
http://www.babyworld.com

Extensive information on caring for infants can be found at this site. There are also links to numerous other related sites.

Children's Nutrition Research Center (CNRC)
http://www.bcm.tmc.edu/cnrc/

CNRC, one of six USDA/ARS (Agricultural Research Service) facilities, is dedicated to defining the nutrient needs of healthy children, from conception through adolescence, and pregnant and nursing mothers. The *Nutrition and Your Child* newsletter is of general interest and can be accessed from this site.

Zero to Three: National Center for Infants, Toddlers, and Families
http://www.zerotothree.org

This national organization is dedicated solely to infants, toddlers, and their families. It is headed by recognized experts in the field and provides technical assistance to communities, states, and the federal government. The site provides information that the organization gathers and disseminates through its publications.

UNIT 2: Cognition, Language, and Learning

Educational Resources Information Center (ERIC)
http://www.ed.gov/about/pubs/intro/pubdb.html

This Web site is sponsored by the U.S. Department of Education and will lead to numerous documents related to elementary and early childhood education, as well as other curriculum topics and issues.

I Am Your Child
http://iamyourchild.org

Information regarding early childhood development is provided on this site. Resources for parents and caregivers are available.

National Association for the Education of Young Children (NAEYC)
http://www.naeyc.org

The National Association for the Education of Young Children provides a useful link from its home page to a site that provides resources for "Parents."

Project Zero
http://pzweb.harvard.edu

Harvard Project Zero, a research group at the Harvard Graduate School of Education, has investigated the development of learning processes in children and adults for 30 years. Today, Project Zero is building on this research to help create communities of reflective, independent learners, to enhance deep understanding within disciplines, and to promote critical and creative thinking. Project Zero's mission is to understand and enhance learning, thinking, and creativity in the arts and other disciplines for individuals and institutions.

Vandergrift's Children's Literature Page
http://www.scils.rutgers.edu/special/kay/sharelit.html

This site provides information about children's literature and links to a variety of resources related to literacy for children.

UNIT 3: Social and Emotional Development

Max Planck Institute for Psychological Research
http://www.mpg.de/english/institutesProjectsFacilities/instituteChoice/psychologische_forschung/

Results from several behavioral and cognitive development research projects are available on this site.

National Child Care Information Center (NCCIC)
http://www.nccic.org

Information about a variety of topics related to child care and development is available on this site. Links to the *Child Care Bulletin,* which can be read online, and to the ERIC database of online and library-based resources are available.

Serendip
http://serendip.brynmawr.edu/serendip/

Organized into five subject areas (brain and behavior, complex systems, genes and behavior, science and culture, and science education), Serendip contains interactive exhibits, articles, links to other resources, and a forum area for comments and discussion.

UNIT 4: Parenting and Family Issues

Facts for Families

http://www.aacap.org/publications/factsfam/index.htm

The American Academy of Child and Adolescent Psychiatry here provides concise, up-to-date information on issues that affect teenagers and their families. Fact sheets include issues concerning teenagers, such as coping with life, sad feelings, inability to sleep, getting involved with drugs, or not getting along with family and friends.

The National Association for Child Development

http://www.nacd.org

This international organization is dedicated to helping children and adults reach their full potential. Its home page presents links to various programs, research, and resources in topics related to the family and society.

National Council on Family Relations

http://www.ncfr.com

This NCFR home page will lead you to articles, research, and a lot of other resources on important issues in family relations, such as stepfamilies, couples, and divorce.

Parenting and Families

http://www.cyfc.umn.edu

The University of Minnesota's Children, Youth, and Family Consortium site will lead you to many organizations and other resources related to divorce, single parenting, and step-families, as well as information about other topics of interest in the study of children's development and the family.

Parentsplace.com: Single Parenting

http://www.parentsplace.com/family/archive/0,10693,239458,00.html

This resource focuses on issues concerning single parents and their children. Although the articles range from parenting children from infancy through adolescence, most of the articles deal with middle childhood.

Stepfamily Association of America

http://www.stepfam.org

This Web site is dedicated to educating and supporting stepfamilies and to creating a positive family image.

UNIT 5: Cultural and Societal Influences

Association to Benefit Children (ABC)

http://www.a-b-c.org

ABC presents a network of programs that includes child advocacy, education for disabled children, care for HIV-positive children, employment, housing, foster care, and day care.

Children Now

http://www.childrennow.org

Children Now uses research and mass communications to make the well-being of children a top priority across the nation. Current articles include information on the influence of media on children, working families, and health.

Council for Exceptional Children

http://www.cec.sped.org

This is the home page for the Council for Exceptional Children, a large professional organization that is dedicated to improving education for children with exceptionalities, students with disabilities, and/or the gifted child. It leads to the ERIC Clearinghouse on disabilities and gifted education and the National Clearinghouse for Professions in Special Education.

Prevent Child Abuse America

http://www.preventchildabuse.org

Dedicated to their child abuse prevention efforts, PCAA's site provides fact sheets and reports that include statistics, a public opinion poll, a 50-state survey, and other resource materials.

We highly recommend that you review our Web site for expanded information and our other product lines. We are continually updating and adding links to our Web site in order to offer you the most usable and useful information that will support and expand the value of your Annual Editions. You can reach us at: *http://www.mhcls.com/annualeditions/*.

UNIT 1
Conception to Birth

Unit Selections

1. **Brave New Babies**, Claudia Kalb
2. **Treating the Tiniest Patients**, Claudia Kalb

Key Points to Consider

- Given the new technologies in sex selection, would you consider paying for these tests to choose the sex of your children? Do you agree with some other countries that sex selection of babies should be banned? Why or why not? Some countries, such as China and India, are experiencing widespread sex selection, so much so that girl babies are being aborted or killed at birth. Ultimately, this will result in a skewed, imbalanced adult population with many potentially negative societal implications. What suggestions do you have in terms of dealing with this culturally defined priority for the relative worth of boys versus girls?

- If someone you knew was pregnant and the baby was experiencing a life-threatening condition, do you think that person should consent to experimental fetal surgery? Why or why not? Should fetal surgeries only involve life-threatening conditions or be expanded to other less threatening conditions? Justify your answer. What if prenatal surgery is not covered by your medical insurance? Should it be covered by insurance even if the outcomes are very poor?

Student Website

www.mhcls.com/online

Internet References

Further information regarding these websites may be found in this book's preface or online.

Babyworld
http://www.babyworld.com

Children's Nutrition Research Center (CNRC)
http://www.bcm.tmc.edu/cnrc/

Zero to Three: National Center for Infants, Toddlers, and Families
http://www.zerotothree.org

Our understanding of conception and prenatal development is not what it used to be. We are now witnesses to dramatic changes in reproductive technology. Advances in this new "prenatal science" include fertility treatments for couples who have difficulty conceiving and a host of prenatal diagnostic tests, such as amniocentesis and alpha-fetoprotein testing, which assesses the well-being of the fetus as well as detect genetic or chromosomal problems, not to mention in utero surgery.

In announcing the birth of a baby, perhaps the single most commonly asked question is, "Is the baby a boy or a girl?" Historically, and even today, parental and societal preferences for boys or girls continues to run strong. The authors of "Brave New Babies" report that parents now have the power to select the sex of their children with the advent of new reproductive technologies. Unfortunately, these new medical techniques have now opened up thorny ethical dilemmas and questions, so much so that a handful of European and Asian countries have already banned sex selection. As some countries face increasingly biased sex ratios of boys and girls, larger sociological and societal problems may loom ahead.

Recent research on prenatal development continues to yield new and startling data. "Treating the Tiniest Patients" documents some of these amazing medical advances. If serious conditions arise for a baby in utero, dramatic new surgical techniques now exist to intervene even before the baby is born. This article includes information about some of these amazing medical advances and discusses the potential ethical and medical complications using real-life examples from parents faced with these complex ethical issues

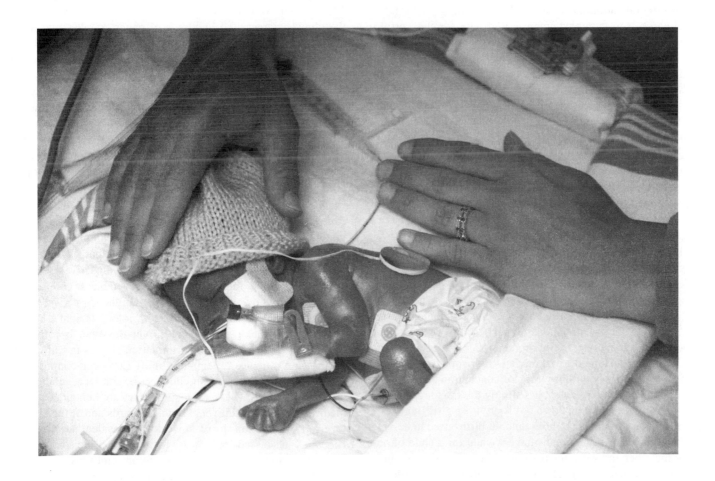

Brave New Babies

Parents now have the power to choose the sex of their children. But as technology answers prayers, it also raises some troubling questions.

CLAUDIA KALB

SHARLA MILLER OF GILLETTE, WYO., ALWAYS wanted a baby girl, but the odds seemed stacked against her. Her husband, Shane, is one of three brothers, and Sharla and her five siblings (four girls, two boys) have produced twice as many males as females. After the Millers' first son, Anthony, was born in 1991, along came Ashton, now 8, and Alec, 4. Each one was a gift, says Sharla, but the desire for a girl never waned. "I'm best friends with my mother;' she says. "I couldn't get it out of my mind that I wanted a daughter." Two years ago Sharla, who had her fallopian tubes tied after Alec's birth, began looking into adopting a baby girl. In the course of her Internet research, she stumbled upon a Web site for the Fertility Institutes in Los Angeles, headed by Dr. Jeffrey Steinberg, where she learned about an in vitro fertilization technique called preimplantation genetic diagnosis. By creating embryos outside the womb, then testing them for gender, PGD could guarantee with almost 100 percent certainty—the sex of her baby. Price tag: $18,480, plus travel. Last November Sharla's eggs and Shane's sperm were mixed in a lab dish, producing 14 healthy embryos, seven male and seven female. Steinberg transferred three of the females into Sharla's uterus, where two implanted successfully. If all goes well, the run of Miller boys will end in July with the arrival of twin baby girls. "I have three wonderful boys," says Sharla, "but since there was a chance I could have a daughter, why not?"

The brave new world is definitely here. After 25 years of staggering advances in reproductive medicine—first test-tube babies, then donor eggs and surrogate mothers—technology is changing babymaking in a whole new way. No longer can science simply help couples have babies, it can help them have the kind of babies they want. Choosing gender may obliterate one of the fundamental mysteries of procreation, but for people who have grown accustomed to taking 3-D ultrasounds of fetuses, learning a baby's sex within weeks of conception and scheduling convenient delivery dates, it's simply the next logical step. That gleeful exclamation, "It's a boy!" or "It's a girl!" may soon just be a quaint reminder of how random births used to be.

Throughout history, humans have wished for a child of one sex or the other and have been willing to do just about anything to get it. Now that gender selection is scientifically feasible, in-terest in the controversial practice (banned, except for medical reasons, in the United Kingdom) is exploding. Despite considerable moral murkiness, Americans are talking to their doctors and visiting catchy Web sites like www.choosethesexofyourbaby.com and myboyorgirl.com—many of them offering money-back guarantees. In just the last six months, Steinberg's site has had 85,000 hits. At the Genetics and IVF Institute (GIVF) in Fairfax, Va., an FDA clinical trial of a sophisticated sperm-sorting technology called MicroSort is more than halfway to completion. Through radio, newspaper and magazine ads ("Do you want to choose the gender of your next baby?"), the clinic has recruited hundreds of eager couples, and more than 400 babies out of 750 needed for the trial have been born. Other couples continue to flock to older, more low-tech and questionable sperm-sorting techniques like the Ericsson method, which is offered at about two dozen clinics nationwide. By far, the most provocative gender-selection technique is PGD. Some clinics offer the procedure as a bonus for couples already going through fertility treatments, but a small number are beginning to provide the option for otherwise healthy couples. Once Steinberg decided to offer PGD gender selection to all comers, he says, "word spread like wildfire."

The ability to create baby Jack or baby Jill opens a high-tech can of worms. While the advances have received kudos from grateful families, they also raise loaded ethical questions about whether science is finally crossing a line that shouldn't be crossed. Even fertility specialists are divided over whether choosing a male or female embryo is acceptable. If couples can request a baby boy or girl, what's next on the slippery slope of modern reproductive medicine? Eye color? Height? Intelligence? Could picking one gender over the other become the 21st century's form of sex discrimination? Or, as in China, upset the ratio of males to females? Many European countries already forbid sex selection; should there be similar regulations in the United States? These explosive issues are being debated in medical journals, on university ethics boards and at the highest levels in Washington. Just last week the President's Council on Bioethics discussed proposals for possible legislation that would ban the buying and selling of human embryos and far-out reproductive experimentation, like creating human-animal hybrids. While the recommendations—part of a report due out this spring—do not suggest limiting IVF or gender selection, the goals are clear: the government should clamp down before technology goes too far. "Even though people have strong differences of opinion on some issues," says council chair and leading bioethieist Leon Kass, "all of us have a stake in keeping human reproduction human."

After their first son, Jesse, was born in 1988, Mary and Sam Toedtman tried all sorts of folksy remedies to boost their chances of having a girl. When Jesse was followed by Jacob, now 10, and Lucas, 7, it seemed clear that boys would be boys in the Toedtman family. Sam has two brothers and comes from a line of boys 70 years long. So, after a lot of serious thinking, the Toedtmans decided to enroll in GIVF's clinical trial of MicroSort for "family balancing." That's the popular new term for gender selection by couples who already have at least one child and want to control their family mix. Since MicroSort's family balance trial began in 1995, more than 1,300 couples have signed on—almost 10 times more than joined a companion trial aimed at avoiding genetic illnesses that strike boys. GIVF is actively recruiting new candidates for both trials. In 2003 a second MicroSort clinic was opened near Los Angeles, and a third is planned for Florida this year. GIVF hopes MicroSort will become the first sperm-sorting device to receive the FDA's stamp of approval for safety and effectiveness. "This will completely change reproductive choices for women, and that's very exciting," says MicroSort's medical director, Dr. Keith Blauer. "We hope to make it available to as many couples as possible."

The MicroSort technology—created originally by the Department of Agriculture to sort livestock sperm—works by mixing sperm with a DNA-specific dye that helps separate X's from Y's.The majority of couples who use MicroSort for gender selection have no fertility problems and use standard artificial insemination to conceive. The technique is far from perfect: most participants have to make more than one attempt, each costing at least $2,500, to get pregnant. And not all end up with the gender of choice. At last count, 91 percent of couples who requested an "X sort" gave birth to a baby girl and 76 percent who chose a "Y sort" produced a boy. It worked for the Stock family. Six-month-old Amberlyn was spared the debilitating neuromuscular disorder that plagues her brother, Chancellor, 7. The Toedtmans were lucky, too. Though it took three tries to get pregnant, Mary finally delivered a girl, Natalie, last April. "She's a total joy," she says.

Determined as she was, Toedtman says she would not have felt comfortable creating embryos to ensure that Natalie was Natalie and not Nathaniel. But a small number of others, knowing that their chance of success with PGD is exponentially better, are becoming pioneers in the newest form of family planning. Available at a limited number of clinics nationwide, PGD was designed and originally intended to diagnose serious genetic diseases in embryos, like Tay-Sachs and cystic fibrosis, before implantation. Over the last decade the technology has allowed hundreds of couples, many of whom have endured the death of sick children, to have healthy babies. Today, some doctors are using PGD to increase the odds of successful IVF pregnancies by screening out chromosomally abnormal embryos.

Some of those patients are asking about gender—and it's their right to do so, many doctors say. After an embryo screening, "I tell them it's normal and I tell them it's male or female," says PGD expert Yury Verlinsky of the Reproductive Genetics Institute in Chicago. "It's their embryo. I can't tell them which one to transfer."

It's one thing to allow infertile couples to choose gender after PGD. Creating embryos solely to sort boys from girls sets off ethical and moral alarm bells. In the last year or so, several clinics have begun to offer the procedure for gender balance without restrictions. Steinberg, of Fertility Institutes, says his team methodically debated the pros and cons before doing so. The logic, he says, is simple: "We've been offering sperm sorting for 20 years without any stipulations. Now, in 2004, I can offer almost 100 percent success with PGD. Why would I make it less available?" Steinberg's clinic, which also has offices in Las Vegas and Mexico, will soon perform its 100th PGD sex-selection procedure. So far, about 40 babies have been born, every one of them the desired sex. It's unclear how many couples will actually want to endure the hefty cost, time commitment and physical burden of fertility drugs and IVF just to ensure gender. But the idea is intriguing for a lot of couples. "I've had friends and neighbors discreetly inquire," says Dr. David Hill, head of ART Reproductive Center in Beverly Hills, Calif., where about 5 to 10 percent of patients are requesting PGD solely for sex selection. Hill has no problem offering it, but he respects colleagues who say no. "This is a really new area," he says. "It's pretty divided right now as to those who think it's acceptable and those who don't."

Dr. Mark Hughes, a leading PGD authority at Wayne State University School of Medicine in Detroit, is one of the latter. "The last time I checked, your gender wasn't a disease," he says. "There is no illness, no suffering and no reason for a physician to be involved. Besides, we're too busy helping desperate couples with serious disease build healthy families." At Columbia University, Dr. Mark Sauer balks at the idea of family balance. "What are you balancing? It discredits the value of an individual life." For those few patients who ask for it, "I look them straight in the face and say, 'We're not going to do that'." And at Northwestern, Dr. Ralph Kazer says bluntly: " 'Gattaca' was a wonderful movie. That's not what I want to do for a living."

One of the most vexing concerns is what some consider gender selection's implicit sexism. When you choose one sex, the argument goes, you reject the other. In Asia girls have been aborted or killed, and populations skewed, because of favoritism toward boys. Could the same thing happen here? GIVF's Blauer says the vast majority of MicroSort couples want girls, not boys, though that could change if Y-sort statistics improve. At Hill's clinic, about 65 percent request boys; at Steinberg's, 55 percent. "It's not going to tip the balance one way or the other," he says. But what if a couple doesn't get the boy or girl they desire? PGD comes as close as it gets to guaranteeing outcome, but there remains the thorny question of what to do with "wrong sex" embryos. Opponents worry that they'll be destroyed simply because they're male or female, but the options are identical for everyone going through IVF: discard the extras, freeze them for later use, donate them or offer them up for scientific research. As for MicroSort, of the more than 500 pregnancies achieved so far, four have been terminated at other facilities (GIVF won't perform abortions) because of "non-desired gender," says Blauer. "It's important to realize that couples have reproductive choice in this country," he says, but "the vast majority of patients want another healthy child and are happy with either gender."

Just beyond these clinical worries lies a vast swamp of ethical quandaries and inherent contradictions. People who support a woman's right to choose find themselves cringing at the idea of terminating a fetus based on sex. Those who believe that embryos deserve the status of personhood decry their destruction, but gender selection could result in fewer abortions. Choosing sex can skew male-female ratios, but it might also reduce overpopulation. Requesting a girl could mean she will be more desired by her parents, but it's also possible she'll grow up and decide she'd rather have been a boy. "Children are going to hold their parents responsible for having made them this way," says bioethicist Kass, "and that may not be as innocent as it sounds."

And then there is the most fundamental conflict of all: science versus religion. One Korean-American couple, with two daughters has been on both sides. Feeling an intense cultural pressure to produce a son, the woman, 31, attended a MicroSort information session, where Blauer reviewed the technique. Intrigued, she went back for a second session and convinced her husband to come along. When it was time to move forward, though, a greater power took over. "I don't think God intended us to do that," she says. "We decided we should just pray about it and leave it up to God."

There are no laws against performing gender selection in the United States. Many people believe that the safety and effectiveness of reproductive technologies like PGD should be regulated, says Kathy Hudson, of the Genetics and Public Policy Center at Johns Hopkins, which recently polled 1,200 Americans on the topic. But, she says, many Americans "are uncomfortable with the government being the arbiter of how to use these technologies." Meanwhile, fertility doctors look to the American Society for Reproductive Medicine for professional standards. John Robertson, head of ASRM's ethics committee, says preconception techniques like MicroSort "would be fine once safety is established." So far, MicroSort reports, 2.4 percent of its babies have been born with major malformations, like Down syndrome, compared with 3 to 4 percent in the general population. But until the trial is completed, there are no definitive data. As for PGD, the ASRM currently discourages its use for sex selection, but Robertson says he wouldn't rule out the possibility that it might become acceptable in the future.

So what, in the end, should we make of gender selection? Will programming of human DNA before birth become inevitable? "I learned a long time ago never to say never," says Rick Myers, chief of Stanford's genetics department. Still, he says, traits we're all worried about, like height, personality and intelligence, aren't the products of single genes. They're cooked in a complex stew of DNA and environment—a stew that boggles scientists, even those with IQs so high you'd swear they were bioengineered. And even if we could create designer Uma Thurmans, would we want to? Sharla Miller and Mary Toedtman say absolutely not. "That's taking it too far," says Miller.

We wouldn't be human if we didn't fantasize about the sci-fi universe around the corner. Steinberg, who has worked in IVF since its conception in the 1970s, remembers finding notes on his windshield in the early days that said, TEST-TUBE BABIES HAVE NO SOUL. The very idea of creating life outside the womb "was unthinkable," he says. And yet, some 1 million test-tube babies later, the practice has become routine. The same will likely be true of gender selection, says Robin Marantz Henig, author of the new book "Pandora's Baby," a history of IVF "The more it's done," she says, "the less you're going to see concerns."

Lizette Frielingsdorf doesn't have any. She and her husband have three boys—Jordan, 8, Justin, 6, and Jake, 5—and one MicroSort girl, Jessica, who just turned 2. "I call her my $15,000 baby. We felt like we won the lottery," says Frielingsdorf "Probably once a week someone will say, 'You got your girl. How did you do that?' and I'll say, 'Here's the number.' I want others to experience the same joy we have." No doubt, many will.

From *Newsweek*, January 26, 2004, pages 45-53. Copyright © 2004 by Newsweek, Inc. All rights reserved. Reprinted by permission. **www.newsweek.com**

Treating the Tiniest Patients

Dramatic advances in fetal medicine—especially in utero surgery—have changed what we know and how we think about the unborn

CLAUDIA KALB

SAMUEL ARMAS, A CHATTERING, brown-eyed 3 1/2-year-old, has no idea what "fetus" means. Nor does he realize that he was one of the most celebrated in medical history. At a mere 21 weeks of gestational age—long before it was time to leave his mother's womb—Samuel underwent a bold and experimental surgical procedure to close a hole at the bottom of his spinal cord, the telltale characteristic of myelomeningocele, or spina bifida. Samuel's parents, Julie and Alex, could have terminated Julie's pregnancy at 15 weeks when they learned about their son's condition, which can result in lifelong physical and mental disabilities. But the Armases do not believe in abortion. Instead, in August 1999, they drove 250 miles from their home in Villa Rica, Ga., to Nashville, Tenn., where Dr. Joseph Bruner, of Vanderbilt University, performed a surgery bordering on the fantastical. Bruner cut into Julie's abdomen, lifted her balloonlike uterus out of her body, made an incision in the taut muscle, removed the fetus, sewed up the spinal defect and tucked him back inside. Fifteen weeks later Samuel Armas "came out screaming," says Julie.

Modern medicine has already granted unborn babies a unique form of personhood—as treatable patients.

That scream became a rallying cry for fetal-rights groups, which seized on a stunning photograph of Samuel's tiny hand emerging from his mother's uterus during surgery. Since then, anti-abortion activists have posted the image on dozens of Web sites to show just how real human fetuses are—even those that aren't yet viable. And that's just fine with the Armases. "We're very glad it's gotten visibility," says Alex. "That wasn't our fetus, that was Samuel."

No matter what legislators, activists, judges or even individual Americans decide about fetal rights, medicine has already granted unborn babies a unique form of personhood—as patients. Twenty-five years ago scientists knew little about the molecular and genetic journey from embryo to full-term fetus. Today, thanks to the biomedical revolution, they are gaining vast new insights into development, even envisioning a day when gene therapy will fix defects in the womb. Technology is introducing parents to their unborn children before they can see their toes. Expecting couples can now have amazing 3-D ultrasound prints made in chain stores like Fetal Fotos. "Instead of some mysterious thing inside her belly, a mother and her family can now identify a little human being," says Bruner. In any other field of medicine, the impact of these dramatic improvements in treatment and technology would be limited largely to doctors, patients and their families. But 30 long and contentious years after *Roe v. Wade*, science that benefits fetuses cannot help but fuel ongoing political, moral and ethical debates.

Fetal surgery has raised the stakes to a whole new level. The very same tools—amniocentesis and ultrasound—that have made it possible to diagnose deformities early enough to terminate a pregnancy are now helping doctors in their quest to save lives. While fetal surgery is still rare and experimental, the possibility that a fetus that might have died or been aborted 10 years ago might now be saved strikes at the core of the abortion debate. And these operations also raise a fundamental question: whose life is more important—the mother's or the child's? While reluctant to take a stand in the political arena, doctors know they are players, like it or not. "We can be a lightning rod used to further a cause, either pro or con," says Diana Farmer, a fetal surgeon at the University of California, San Francisco, "but you can't let that deter you from your mission as a physician."

For decades pediatric surgeons like Michael Harrison, head of UCSF's Fetal Treatment Center, agonized over their inability to save babies from deadly defects after birth. Since 1981, when Harrison performed a pioneering in utero procedure to treat a fetal urinary-tract obstruction, hundreds of fetuses have undergone treatments ranging from tumor removal to spinal-cord repair. Some operations have been dramatic successes, saving the lives of babies who would otherwise have died. Others have been heart-wrenching failures. In no other medical area are the stakes—two patients, not just one—so high. Now the first rigorous National Institutes of Health-sponsored trials will put prenatal medicine, including the spina bifida procedure, to the test. "If there's not a clear advantage," says Farmer, "it's not worth putting the mother at risk."

On the streets, the womb has become a political battlefield. In the OR, it is a medical mine field. Fetuses are moving targets—just locating and positioning them is like trying to catch fish underwater. The placenta, the fetal lifeline, can develop anywhere in the uterus, obstructing access to the fetus. A single nick in the tissue can put the lives of both fetus and mother in danger. Amniotic fluid, the liquid that cushions the growing fetus, can leak to perilously low levels. And preterm delivery, which inevitably occurs because of the disruption to the uterus, is the Achilles' heel of fetal surgery, increasing a baby's likelihood of everything from lung problems to learning disabilities down the road. Bold and entrepreneurial by nature, fetal surgeons have endured the skepticism, even hostility, of colleagues for years. Early on, "folks thought we were nuts," says Dr. Scott Adzick, head of the Center for Fetal Diagnosis and Treatment at the Children's Hospital of Philadelphia (CHOP). "Some still do."

Fetal medicine has been tangled with politics from its inception. Harrison's predecessor in the field, New Zealander A. William Liley, is credited with the first successful fetal intervention in 1963, when he performed an in utero transfusion to treat Rh disease, a deadly blood incompatibility between mother and baby. But over the course of his career, he became as much activist as physician. Ardently opposed to abortion, Liley described the fetus as "a young human," and rallied for fetal rights until his death in 1983. While most doctors keep their beliefs private, the volatile confluence of politics and medicine has led some to join politically aligned groups like Pro-Life Maternal-Fetal Medicine, or Physicians for Reproductive Choice and Health. But those views can sway. In the past, right-to-life groups criticized surgeons for violating the sanctity of the womb. Now many support medical efforts to treat fetuses as patients. Such oscillations mean little to UCSF's Harrison. His goal from the beginning has been to deal with "the practical real problems of real people."

SUSAN AND JEFF DEZURICK ARE two such people. In October 1999, the couple learned that the twins Susan was carrying had a potentially deadly condition called Twin-Twin Transfusion syndrome, in which one fetus floods the other with fluid through a shared blood vessel in the placenta. In a procedure called amnio reduction, the Dezuricks' doctors in Oakland, Calif., removed excess fluid from the saturated twin, hoping to ward off a buildup of pressure on his heart and lungs. But the technique, performed repeatedly on Susan, ultimately failed. With one of the twins on the verge of death, the Dezuricks arrived at UCSF. In a minimally invasive procedure, doctors located the culprit vessel, zapped it with a laser and cut off the faulty connection. (The two techniques—amnio reduction and laser—are now being compared in trials worldwide.) For the Dezuricks, the outcome was happy. Ten weeks after surgery, Sean and Christopher were born, premature but healthy. Today, lightly freckled 4-year-olds with impish grins, the boys spin around their living room, hugging each other on their tippy-toes. "Thank God for technology," says Susan.

As fetal science advances, the critical question remains: is the benefit to the fetus worth the risk to the mother? Ethicists can debate it all they like, but for Kristin Garcia, the answer was undeniably yes. In her 20th week of pregnancy, Garcia's doctor told her that her baby had a severe defect called congenital diaphragmatic hernia. "He told me that most women choose to terminate, because there's absolutely no way the baby would survive," says Garcia. At UCSF, doctors warned, as they do routinely, that they could not guarantee a positive outcome. In any procedure, risks to the fetus—which is usually operated on between 18 and 26 gestational weeks—include brain damage, physical deformities and death. The mother can suffer excessive blood loss or a permanently scarred uterus that could rupture in future pregnancies (C-sections are done to avoid the problem), and, as with any major surgery, there is always the risk of death. For Garcia, the treatment was a success, but it was by no means easy. Fluid backed up into Garcia's lungs after the operation. "I couldn't breathe," she says. "I felt like I was dying." And little Analisa needed several surgeries to patch up her diaphragm. Today Analisa is "perfect and full of life," says Garcia. The physical and emotional tolls, however, were enormous. "I'm glad I did it for my first baby," says Garcia. "But I don't know if I could do it again."

As a lone female voice among fetal surgeons, Farmer is working hard to put the health of the mother front and center. Although fetal surgeries are rare—no more than about 600 patients are candidates in the United States in a given year—interest in the field is growing around the globe. At this year's annual fetal-surgery meeting, Farmer presented the first guidelines for maternal health, including a strict patient-consent process, counseling on nonsurgical alternatives and a fetal-oversight committee.

Even the best intentions for mother and baby cannot always save lives. Sherry Nicholson was almost 29 weeks pregnant when she and her husband, Phil, learned that their baby, Sean, had a lung mass that would almost certainly kill him in utero. The decision to try experimental surgery was "the only thing we would do," says Sherry. "I never wanted to wonder later 'what if?'" The operation went well, but 10 and a half weeks after delivery, Sean's healthy lung gave out and he died. Despite the tragic loss, Sherry is grateful for the outcome. "We got to know him and his personality," says Sherry. "He touched a lot of lives."

Of all of the fetal surgeries performed, the spina bifida operation is the most controversial. The disease, which affects one in 1,000 births every year, is the first and only condition surgeons have attempted to treat that is not life-threatening. And the advantages to going in so early are still unclear. Vanderbilt's Bruner has performed about 200 procedures since 1997 and his own results are mixed, but encouraging. Bladder and bowel function, vexing lifelong problems, do not appear to improve after intervention. But he says babies' brains show a clear benefit. Only about half need shunts—implantable devices that divert fluid from the brain—after birth, compared with the majority of babies operated on as newborns. Samuel Armas, who will soon have bladder surgery, cannot move his feet and toes, but he gets around fine with small leg braces. Not having a shunt, says Julie, "made the surgery worth it." The NIH trial, launched this spring at UCSF, CHOP and Vanderbilt, will recruit some 200 patients who will be observed until the age of 3.

Doctors hope key questions will be answered: Is fetal surgery better than an operation after birth? And just how much benefit justifies the surgical risk?

In the end, no matter what the data show or the politicians decide, some fetuses will still turn out to be imperfect, and some parents will make choices they never thought possible. "I've had patients say to me, 'I marched up and down in front of [abortion] clinics, but I'm terminating my pregnancy,'" says Dr. Mary Norton, head of prenatal diagnosis at UCSF. Andrea Merkord and her husband, Sean, do not believe in abortion. But last year Andrea had laser surgery to cut off the blood supply to a pair of conjoined babies in her uterus. The twins were unviable, but were threatening the life of a healthy triplet. That baby, Thomas, is now 7 months old and healthy. Andrea doesn't doubt her decision for a minute—but it continues to overwhelm her. "Obviously the twins were terminated and that is hard to say," she says in tears. "Until you've been in the situation, you don't know what decision you'll make."

For Vanderbilt's Bruner, operating on the tiniest patients has had a profound effect on his professional and personal life. Initially the experience was one of pure wonderment. "We would open the uterus and everything in the OR would stop. Everyone was just standing there looking." Now, Bruner says, he feels a deep and personal connection with every fetus. "I'm the first human being who will ever touch them," he says. "I speak to every one."

With MARY CARMICHAEL

UNIT 2
Cognition, Language, and Learning

Unit Selections

Key Points to Consider

- Recently, researchers have shown the importance of supporting early interactions and experiences during infancy and preschool to support brain development. How has this information changed or not changed your perceptions and interactions with babies? Given that the infancy and early childhood period is so crucial for the attainment of social-emotional, linguistic, and cognitive development milestones, what specific modifications would you take as a potential parent to support these developments? For example, the research highlights the need for parents and teachers to be emotionally responsive to babies and to engage in rich conversations with preschoolers about people with other views and different emotions. Why are these behaviors beneficial in the development of social and linguistic skills?

- What is your earliest memory as a child? How old were you? Early childhood memories have been shown to be very prone to confabulation, so can you verify the accuracy of this memory with a parent or someone else who was there at the time? Do you remember discussing your early childhood memories more with your mother or father? Do you think there were differences in the way your mother reminisced with you or your siblings as a result of being male or female? Why do you think the research seems to show that children from non-Western families seem to have more elaborate early autobiographical memories than those children from Eastern cultures? What implications does this research have for adult memories?

- Recently, the media has broadcast headlines warning of the decline of boys' achievements in school—ranging from lower grades than girls in school to the decreasing numbers of boys graduating from college. In addition, far more boys are diagnosed with learning disabilities than girls. What factors might account for these trends? Do you think boys are having a harder time in school than girls today? Why or why not? Should corrective measures, if any, be undertaken to address these potential problems? If you had a son, what steps would you take to ensure his success? If you had a daughter, would the steps you take be the same or different than what you would do for your son? Explain.

Student Website
www.mhcls.com/online

Internet References
Further information regarding these websites may be found in this book's preface or online.

Educational Resources Information Center (ERIC)
http://www.ed.gov/about/pubs/intro/pubdb.html

I Am Your Child
http://iamyourchild.org

National Association for the Education of Young Children (NAEYC)
http://www.naeyc.org

Project Zero
http://pzweb.harvard.edu

Vandergrift's Children's Literature Page
http://www.scils.rutgers.edu/special/kay/sharelit.html

We have come a long way from the days when the characterization of cognition of infants and young children included phrases like "tabula rasa" and "booming, buzzing confusion." Infants and young children are no longer viewed by researchers as blank slates, passively waiting to be filled up with knowledge. Today, experts in child development are calling for a reformulation of assumptions about children's cognitive abilities, as well as calling for reforms in the ways we teach children in our schools. Hence, the articles in the first subsection highlight some of the new knowledge of the cognitive abilities of infants and young children, while the second subsection focuses on schooling and learning.

Researchers today continue to discover that babies are developing an impressive array of early social, emotional, and cognitive skills during infancy. In both "Reading Your Baby's Mind" and "Brain Research and Early Childhood Development: A Primer for Developmentally Appropriate Practice," the authors describe new findings showing that infants' earliest interactions and experiences are critical in helping them develop normal social-emotional milestones and other linguistic and cognitive skills. From this perspective, babies are not as passive as once thought, and parents and teachers can provide environments that nurture and support their babies' developing abilities.

Why can't most people seem to recall many specific memories in early childhood? This effect known by researchers as childhood amnesia is discussed in "Culture and Language in the Emergence of Autobiographical Memory." The researchers in this fascinating article present evidence that early autobiographical memory is dependent on the emergence of language during the preschool years and influenced by cultural and gender differences in the extent to which mothers and parents actively reminisce with their preschool children when discussing and reviewing past autobiographical events. For example, the research suggests that children from Western cultures are more likely to recall early autobiographical memories than Eastern children, leading to interesting implications for adult memories.

Similarly, we learn from research in "Language and Children's Understanding of Mental States" that maternal conversation and language interventions play a key role in helping children develop a theory of mind or the ability to understand other people's points of view and emotional states. When parents and teachers engage in rich conversations with their preschool children about others who have varying points of view and different emotions, they help children advance in their understanding of mental states—a critical ingredient for building appropriate social skills.

If you dressed a baby boy in little girl's clothing would that baby be upset? How old were you when you knew you were a boy or a girl? Is your sense of being male or female dependent on genetics, socialization, or prenatal hormones? In the article "Gender Bender," author Sadie Dingfelder presents new research showing that all three factors play complex roles in determining an individual's gender identity and gender-related behaviors.

Another gender-related issue that has drawn more recent public and media attention focuses on challenges facing boys in terms of their decreasing levels of academic performance and adjustment relative to girls. The author of "The Trouble with Boys" chron-

icles some of these developments and raises awareness of the factors that may be contributing to some of these negative trends.

With the explosion of the Internet and the powerful influences of media today, the authors of "A Deeper Sense of Literacy" assert that it may be just as important to teach students media literacy in addition to learning to read. Students today need to have the ability to critically evaluate and analyze the wealth of information from the media and from the Internet in order to make informed decisions.

When debates rage about the schools failing our children, the focus is most often on inadequacies among teachers and our educational system. However, in "Parental School Involvement and Children's Academic Achievement" the researchers acknowledge a third critical partner in the education question—namely the parents. In this article, they examine parental interactions with their children's schools and communities and they identify factors and make policy recommendations that would enhance children's academic success.

Given all of the research showing that the preschool years represent ripe and fertile grounds for the development of fundamental skills for children, it comes as no surprise that children who attend high-quality, developmentally appropriate preschool programs show significant gains and promise in terms of improving their school readiness for kindergarten as well as in terms of long-term outcomes. The authors of "The Preschool Promise" address these effects and summarize recent legislative efforts to increase preschool availability to all children across the United States.

Reading Your Baby's Mind

New research on infants finally begins to answer the question: what's going on in there?

PAT WINGERT AND MARTHA BRANT

LITTLE VICTORIA BATEMAN IS BLOND and blue-eyed and as cute a baby as there ever was. At 6 months, she is also trusting and unsuspecting, which is a good thing, because otherwise she'd never go along with what's about to happen. It's a blistering June afternoon in Lubbock, Texas, and inside the Human Sciences lab at Texas Tech University, Victoria's mother is settling her daughter into a high chair, where she is the latest subject in an ongoing experiment aimed at understanding the way babies think. Sybil Hart, an associate professor of human development and leader of the study, trains video cameras on mother and daughter. Everything is set. Hart hands Cheryl Bateman a children's book, "Elmo Pops In," and instructs her to engross herself in its pages. "Just have a conversation with me about the book," Hart tells her. "The most important thing is, do not look at [Victoria.]" As the two women chat, Victoria looks around the room, impassive and a little bored.

After a few minutes, Hart leaves the room and returns cradling a lifelike baby doll. Dramatically, Hart places it in Cheryl Bateman's arms, and tells her to cuddle the doll while continuing to ignore Victoria. "That's OK, little baby," Bateman coos, hugging and rocking the doll. Victoria is not bored anymore. At first, she cracks her best smile, showcasing a lone stubby tooth. When that doesn't work, she begins kicking. But her mom pays her no mind. That's when Victoria loses it. Soon she's beet red and crying so hard it looks like she might spit up. Hart rushes in. "OK, we're done," she says, and takes back the doll. Cheryl Bateman goes to comfort her daughter. "I've never seen her react like that to anything," she says. Over the last 10 months, Hart has repeated the scenario hundreds of times. It's the same in nearly every case: tiny babies, overwhelmed with jealousy. Even Hart was stunned to find that infants could experience an emotion, which, until recently, was thought to be way beyond their grasp.

And that's just for starters. The helpless, seemingly clueless infant staring up at you from his crib, limbs flailing, drool oozing, has a lot more going on inside his head than you ever imagined. A wealth of new research is leading pediatricians and child psychologists to rethink their long-held beliefs about the emotional and intellectual abilities of even very young babies. In 1890, psychologist William James famously described an infant's view of the world as "one great blooming, buzzing confusion." It was a notion that held for nearly a century: infants were simple-minded creatures who merely mimicked those around them and grasped only the most basic emotions—happy, sad, angry. Science is now giving us a much different picture of what goes on inside their hearts and heads. Long before they form their first words or attempt the feat of sitting up, they are already mastering complex emotions—jealousy, empathy, frustration—that were once thought to be learned much later in toddlerhood.

They are also far more sophisticated intellectually than we once believed. Babies as young as 4 months have advanced powers of deduction and an ability to decipher intricate patterns. They have a strikingly nuanced visual palette, which enables them to notice small differences, especially in faces, that adults and older children lose the ability to see. Until a baby is 3 months old, he can recognize a scrambled photograph of his mother just as quickly as a photo in which everything is in the right place. And big brothers and sisters beware: your sib has a long memory—and she can hold a grudge.

Babies yet to utter an INTELLIGENT SYLLABLE are now known to feel a range of COMPLEX EMOTIONS like envy and empathy.

The new research is sure to enthrall new parents—See, Junior *is* a genius!—but it's more than just an academic exercise. Armed with the new information, pediatricians are starting to change the way they evaluate their youngest patients. In addition to tracking physical development, they are now focusing much more deeply on emotional advancement. The research shows how powerful emotional well-being is to a child's future health. A baby who fails to meet certain key "emotional milestones" may have trouble learning to speak, read and, later, do well in school. By reading emotional responses, doctors have begun to discover ways to tell if a baby as young as 3 months is showing early signs of possible psychological disorders, including depression, anxiety, learning disabilities and perhaps autism. "Instead of just asking if they're crawling or sitting, we're asking more questions about how they share their world with their caregivers," says Dr. Chet Johnson, chairman of the American Academy of Pediatrics' early-childhood committee. "Do they point to things? When they see a new person, how do they react? How children do on social and emotional and language skills are better predictors of success in adulthood than motor skills are." The goal: in the not-too-distant future, researchers hope doctors will routinely identify at-risk kids years earlier than they do now—giving parents crucial extra time to turn things around.

One of the earliest emotions that even tiny babies display is, admirably enough, empathy. In fact, concern for others may be hard-wired into babies' brains. Plop a newborn down next to another crying infant, and chances are, both babies will soon be wailing away. "People have always known that babies cry when they hear other babies cry," says Martin Hoffman, a psychology professor at New York University who did the first studies on infant empathy in the 1970s. "The question was, why are they crying?" Does it mean that the baby is truly concerned for his fellow human, or just annoyed by the racket? A recent study conducted in Italy, which built on Hoffman's own work, has largely settled the question. Researchers played for infants tapes of other babies crying. As predicted, that was enough to start the tears flowing. But when researchers played babies recordings of their own cries, they rarely began crying themselves. The verdict: "There is some rudimentary empathy in place, right from birth," Hoffman says. The intensity of the emotion tends to fade over time. Babies older than 6 months no longer cry but grimace at the discomfort of others. By 13 to 15 months, babies tend to take matters into their own hands. They'll try to comfort a crying playmate. "What I find most charming is when, even if the two mothers are present, they'll bring their own mother over to help," Hoffman says.

Part of that empathy may come from another early-baby skill that's now better understood, the ability to discern emotions from the facial expressions of the people around them. "Most textbooks still say that babies younger than 6 months don't recognize emotions," says Diane Montague, assistant professor of psychology at LaSalle University in Philadelphia. To put that belief to the test, Montague came up with a twist on every infant's favorite game, peekaboo, and recruited dozens of 4-month-olds to play along. She began by peeking around a cloth with a big smile on her face. Predictably, the babies were delighted, and stared at her intently—the time-tested way to tell if a baby is interested. On the fourth peek, though, Montague emerged with a sad look on her face. This time, the response was much different. "They not only looked away," she says, but wouldn't look back even when she began smiling again. Refusing to make eye contact is a classic baby sign of distress. An angry face got their attention once again, but their faces showed no pleasure. "They seemed primed to be alert, even vigilant," Montague says. "I realize that's speculative in regard to infants … I think it shows that babies younger than 6 months find meaning in expressions."

This might be a good place to pause for a word about the challenges and perils of baby research. Since the subjects can't speak for themselves, figuring out what's going on inside their heads is often a matter of reading their faces and body language. If this seems speculative, it's not. Over decades of trial and error, researchers have fine-tuned their observation skills and zeroed in on numerous consistent baby responses to various stimuli: how long they stare at an object, what they reach out for and what makes them recoil in fear or disgust can often tell experienced researchers everything they need to know. More recently, scientists have added EEGs and laser eye tracking, which allow more precise readings. Coming soon: advanced MRI scans that will allow a deeper view inside the brain.

When infants near their first birthdays, they become increasingly sophisticated social learners. They begin to infer what others are thinking by following the gaze of those around them. "By understanding others' gaze, babies come to understand others' minds," says Andrew Meltzoff, a professor of psychology at the University of Washington who has studied the "gaze following" of thousands of babies. "You can tell a lot about people, what they're interested in and what they intend to do next, by watching their eyes. It appears that even babies know that . . . This is how they learn to become expert members of our culture."

Meltzoff and colleague Rechele Brooks have found that this skill first appears at 10 to 11 months, and is not only an important marker of a baby's emotional and social growth, but can predict later language development. In their study, babies who weren't proficient at gaze-following by their first birthday had much less advanced-language skills at 2. Meltzoff says this helps explain why language occurs more slowly in blind children, as well as children of depressed mothers, who tend not to interact as much with their babies.

In fact, at just a few months, infants begin to develop superpowers when it comes to observation. Infants can easily tell the difference between human faces. But at the University of Minnesota, neuroscientist Charles Nelson (now of Harvard) wanted to test how discerning infants really are. He showed a group of 6-month-old babies a photo of a chimpanzee, and gave them time to stare at it until they lost interest. They were then shown another chimp. The babies perked up and stared at the new photo. The infants easily recognized each chimp as an individual—they were fascinated by each new face. Now unless you spend a good chunk of your day hanging around the local zoo, chances are you couldn't tell the difference between a roomful of chimps at a glance. As it turned out, neither could babies just a few months older. By 9 months, those kids had lost the ability to tell chimps apart; but at the same time, they had increased their powers of observation when it came to human faces.

Nelson has now taken his experiment a step further, to see how early babies can detect subtle differences in facial expressions, a key building block of social development. He designed a new study that is attempting to get deep inside babies' heads by measuring brain-wave activity. Nelson sent out letters to the parents of nearly every newborn in the area, inviting them to participate. Earlier this summer it was Dagny Winberg's turn. The 7-month-old was all smiles as her mother, Armaiti, carried her into the lab, where she was fitted with a snug cap wired with 64 sponge sensors. Nelson's assistant, grad student Meg Moulson, began flashing photographs on a screen of a woman. In each photo, the woman had a slightly different expression—many different shades of happiness and fear. Dagny was given time to look at each photo until she became bored and looked away. The whole time, a computer was closely tracking her brain activity, measuring her mind's minutest responses to the different photos. Eventually, after she'd run through 60 photos, Dagny had had enough of the game and began whimpering and fidgeting. That ended the session. The point of the experiment is to see if baby brain scans look like those of adults. "We want to see if babies categorize emotions in the ways that adults do," Moulson says. "An adult can see a slight smile and categorize it as happy. We want to know if babies can do the same." They don't have the answer yet, but Nelson believes that infants who display early signs of emotional disorders, such as autism, may be helped if they can develop these critical powers of observation and emotional engagement.

Halfway across the country, researchers are working to dispel another baby cliché: out of sight, out of mind. It was long believed that babies under 9 months didn't grasp the idea of "object permanence"—the ability to know, for instance, that when Mom leaves the room, she isn't gone forever. New research by psychologist Su-hua Wang at the University of California, Santa Cruz, is showing that babies understand the concept as early as 10 weeks. Working with 2- and 3-month-olds, she performs a little puppet show. Each baby sees a duck on a stage. Wang covers the duck, moves it across the stage and lifts the cover. Sometimes the duck is there. Other times, the duck disappears beneath a trapdoor. When they see the duck has gone missing, the babies stare intently at the empty stage, searching for it. "At 2½ months," she says, "they already have the idea that the object continues to exist."

A strong, well-developed ability to connect with the world—and with parents in particular—is especially important when babies begin making their first efforts at learning to speak. Baby talk is much more than mimickry. Michael Goldstein, a psychologist at Cornell University, gathered two groups of 8-month-olds and decked them out in overalls rigged up with wireless microphones and transmitters. One group of mothers was told to react immediately when their babies cooed or babbled, giving them big smiles and loving pats. The other group of parents was also told to smile at their kids, but randomly, unconnected to the babies' sounds. It came as no surprise that the babies who received immediate feedback babbled more and advanced quicker than those who didn't. But what interested Goldstein was the way in which the parents, without realizing it, raised the "babble bar" with their kids. "The kinds of simple sounds that get parents' attention at 4 months don't get the same reaction at 8 months," he says. "That motivates babies to experiment with different sound combinations until they find new ones that get noticed."

A decade ago Patricia Kuhl, a professor of speech and hearing at the University of Washington and a leading authority on early language, proved that tiny babies have a unique ability to learn a foreign language. As a result of her well-publicized findings, parents ran out to buy foreign-language tapes, hoping their little Einsteins would pick up Russian or French before they left their cribs. It didn't work, and Kuhl's new research shows why. Kuhl put American 9-month-olds in a room with Mandarin-speaking adults, who showed them toys while talking to them. After 12 sessions, the babies had learned to detect subtle Mandarin phonetic sounds that couldn't be heard by a separate group of babies who were exposed only to English. Kuhl then repeated the experiment, but this time played the identical Mandarin lessons to babies on video- and audiotape. That group of babies failed to learn any Mandarin. Kuhl says that without the emotional connection, the babies considered the tape recording just another background noise, like a vacuum cleaner. "We were genuinely surprised by the outcome," she says. "We all assumed that when infants stare at a television, and look engaged, that they are learning from it." Kuhl says there's plenty of work to be done to explain why that isn't true. "But at first blush one thinks that people—at least babies—need people to learn."

So there you have it. That kid over there with one sock missing and smashed peas all over his face is actually a formidable presence, in possession of keen powers of observation, acute emotional sensitivity and an impressive arsenal of deductive powers. "For the last 15 years, we've been focused on babies' abilities—what they know and when they knew it," says the University of Washington's Meltzoff. "But now we want to know what all this predicts about later development. What does all this mean for the child?"

Some of these questions are now finding answers. Take shyness, for instance. It's long been known that 15 to 20 percent of children are shy and anxious by nature. But doctors didn't know why some seemed simply to grow out of it, while for others it became a debilitating condition. Recent studies conducted by Nathan Fox of the University of Maryland show that shyness is initially driven by biology. He proved it by wiring dozens of 9-month-olds to EEG machines and conducting a simple experiment. When greeted by a stranger, "behaviorally inhibited" infants tensed up, and showed more activity in the parts of the brain associated with anxiety and fear. Babies with outgoing personalities reached out to the stranger. Their EEG scans showed heightened activity in the parts of the brain that govern positive emotions like pleasure.

Just because your baby is MORE PERCEPTIVE than you thought doesn't mean she'll be DAMAGED if she cries for a minute.

But Fox, who has followed some of these children for 15 years, says that parenting style has a big impact on which kind of adult a child will turn out to be. Children of overprotective parents, or those whose parents didn't encourage them to overcome shyness and childhood anxiety, often remain shy and anxious as adults. But kids born to confident and sensitive parents who gently help them to take emotional risks and coax them out of their shells can often overcome early awkwardness. That's an important finding, since behaviorally inhibited kids are also at higher risk for other problems.

Stanley Greenspan, clinical professor of psychiatry and pediatrics at George Washington University Medical School, is one of the leaders in developing diagnostic tools to help doctors identify babies who may be at risk for language and learning problems, autism and a whole range of other problems. He recently completed a checklist of social and emotional "milestones" that babies should reach by specific ages (graphic). "I'd like to see doctors screen babies for these milestones and tell parents exactly what to do if their babies are not mastering them. One of our biggest problems now is that parents may sense intuitively that something is not right," but by the time they are able to get their child evaluated, "that family has missed a critical time to, maybe, get that baby back on track."

So what should parents do with all this new information? First thing: relax. Just because your baby is more perceptive than you might have thought doesn't mean she's going to be damaged for life if she cries in her crib for a minute while you answer the phone. Or that he'll wind up quitting school and stealing cars if he witnesses an occasional argument between his parents. Children crave—and thrive on—interaction, one-on-one time and lots of eye contact. That doesn't mean filling the baby's room with "educational" toys and posters. A child's social, emotional and academic life begins with the earliest conversations between parent and child: the first time the baby locks eyes with you; the quiet smile you give your infant and the smile she gives you back. Your child is speaking to you all the time. It's just a matter of knowing how to listen.

With T. Trent Gegax, Margaret Nelson, Karen Breslau, Nadine Joseph and Ben Whitford

Brain Research and Early Childhood Development

A Primer for Developmentally Appropriate Practice

In the infant room, Sophia cruises, holding on to the edge of a table. At the end of the table she stops. The three-foot gap to the closest piece of furniture looks scary. Sophia, a bit anxious and wondering what to do, looks to Mia, her caregiver. Mia moves slowly to Sophia and looks into her eyes. "What are you going to do, Sophia?" she asks gently. The caregiver watches and waits, ready to help if Sophia is unable to resolve the dilemma without becoming distressed or ready to rescue Sophia if she takes a fall. Either way, Mia's warm smile and her eye contact with the child say, "I am here for you, Sophia, you can do it."

In the preschool room, Azim is building an amazing structure—a cardboard and block tower he has been working on for quite a while. His friend Frank approaches. Indicating a particularly vulnerable section of the structure, he says, "Azim, I think that might fall." Azim looks up: "Yeah, it might." Frank offers to hold the base while Azim fixed the problem. "Miss Nancy," the boys call out, "look at our amazing tower." Miss Nancy, watching from several feet away, realizes that what is amazing are the cognitive and social abilities Azim and Frank used to avert a block center crisis. "Frank and Azim, you solved a tough problem together!" she responds.

KATHLEEN CRANLEY GALLAGHER

Observe an early childhood program, and evidence of early brain development abounds. Using brain research to inform early childhood education and care is not a new idea. More than 40 years ago, research on brain development suggested that brain growth was most dramatic in the years before children started formal schooling. This knowledge provided a jump start for early childhood education in the United States with the inception of Head Start. Recognizing that the early years were critical for intervention, Head Start programs aimed to increase cognitive and social development for children from families living in poverty (Ramey & Ramey 2004). However, early insights into brain development only touched on the wealth of information scientists are now uncovering.

Research on brain development now provides increased understanding of developmental periods of dramatic brain growth, information about regions of brain growth, and details on brain functions. We know that the brain has growth spurts during certain times of development, such as early childhood and adolescence (Schore 2001). And throughout the lifespan the brain is described as plastic because of its ability to adapt and change when necessary (Shonkoff & Phillips 2000; Bruer 2004). Neural development, stress hormones, and brain specialization are three areas of brain research that inform and support developmentally appropriate practice (DAP) in early childhood.

This article summarizes some key findings from brain research and suggests implications for aspects of children's de-velopment and teachers' developmentally appropriate practice—in particular, creating a caring community of learners, teaching to enhance development and learning, and establishing reciprocal relationships with families (Bredekamp & Copple 1997).

Neural Development and Developmentally Appropriate Practice

Developmentally appropriate practice requires that we consider current, quality scientific knowledge of children's development in our consideration of best practice (Bredekamp & Copple 1997). Brain research constitutes some of the most important research to consider in pursuit of developmental knowledge. This knowledge starts with an understanding of some basic structures and processes of the brain, in particular, neurons and neural development.

Synapse Development and Pruning

Neurons are the basic material of the brain. These cells are responsible for communicating messages in the brain and from the brain to the body (Bloom, Nelson, & Lazerson 2001; Kolb & Whishaw 2001). Most neurons—there are approximately 100 billion in all—are in place before a child is born (Shore 1997).

After birth the synapses, which are the connection points between the neurons, develop rapidly, becoming more numerous and dense. This rapid change is called synaptogenesis. The greater numbers of synapses allow a greater number and variety of messages to travel in the brain, enabling more information to be processed (Bloom, Nelson, & Lazerson 2001).

The brain produces more synapses in an infant than are needed. A one-year-old has 150 percent more synapses than an adult (Bruer 2004). Scientists are not sure why the brain overproduces synapses, but overproduction may increase the likelihood that the brain has enough neuron material to meet whatever demands the environment places on it (Nelson & Bloom 1997). In other words, the brain doesn't know what the child will need until it—the brain—interacts with the environment; so, better to overproduce than underproduce. This may be nature's way of preparing children for many of the potential environments in which they may live (Shonkoff & Phillips 2000).

When neurons are not used, their synapse connections decrease. This decrease of synapse density is known as pruning, and it is a normal, lifelong process of brain neural development. Pruning is not a "use it or lose it" scenario, as it is sometimes described (Cashmore 2001). Unused synapses are pruned, but neurons remain intact for later learning.

Practices That Support Neural Development

As an example, repetition of sensorimotor patterns may help infants and toddlers maintain important synapse linkages. Babies bat objects and mouth toys in exploration, and toddlers dump and refill containers in experimentation. Infants coo and their caregivers coo back, engaging in an oral-auditory dance, accompanied by visual stimulation from the face of the smiling caregiver. Toddlers point to objects, and caregivers name them and may bring the child close to touch and explore the new discovery. New discoveries maintain synapses, and unused neuron synapses are pruned. Together, these early relationships with caregivers, stimulating environments, and an engaged, active child form a system that shapes the brain's growth and development (Shore 1997).

Synaptic pruning doesn't imply that a child who never hears classical music will be unable to play an instrument or that a child who has limited physical abilities will not develop understanding of moving objects. A stimulating environment that engages a child in a variety of interesting activities, however, may improve the quality of brain functioning or at least prevent decreased quality of brain functioning (Bruer 2004).

Under some circumstances, lack of active engagement may limit a child's potential. Consider a child whose motor activity is limited due to a disability or medical condition (Shonkoff & Phillips 2000). The child's inability to experience movement, engage with new objects, or grab and mouth toys may limit his potential to understand how things in the environment work. In this case, *teaching to enhance development and learning* may include repositioning or moving the child frequently and providing assistive technology. For example, a toddler with limited lower body motor abilities may benefit from using a tummy-scooter to simulate the physical, social, and emotional experiences of crawling. In addition to therapies the child may receive, the child's teacher should provide ample opportunity for movement. The child's brain may benefit from frequent stroller trips, an adaptive swing, and riding an adapted tricycle. Teachers and parents can bring objects for interaction to the child and find ways for the child to engage in sensory activities like playing at a sand and water table. A child with limited motor ability needs frequent opportunities and extra adult assistance to experience movement, different views, and spatial relationships.

Fixed pieces of equipment such as playpens, high chairs, and bouncy seats should be used sparingly, as they provide little opportunity for varied and active experiences.

A typically developing child also needs frequent opportunities for movement and interactions with people and objects. Fixed pieces of equipment such as playpens, high chairs, and bouncy seats should be used sparingly, as they provide little opportunity for varied and active experiences. Teaching for enhancing development and learning includes considering the active nature of children's learning, and it requires considerable supervision and safety planning.

Children need many and varied sensory experiences to maintain neural material (Shonkoff & Phillips 2000). It is important that teachers provide a variety of auditory, visual, and tactile experiences. Evidence from animal research supports this point: rats and monkeys raised in restricted, less complex environments developed less dense neural synapse structures. Rats returned to complex environments showed improvement in their synapse structures (Francis et al. 2002). We do not have evidence that complex or stimulating environments increase neural synapse material in humans. However, we do know that deprived environments in childhood, lacking in sufficient nutrition, health care, and/or auditory stimulation, are associated with greater neural pruning (Shonkoff & Phillips 2000; Bruer 2004).

Every new opportunity gives children new ways in which to interpret and understand the world and may help maintain precious neural connections. In some cases, children's sensory problems go undetected. Brain research suggests that it is critical to identify and treat children with early sensory delays, as these sensory deficits could lead to more serious, permanent disabilities (Shonkoff & Phillips 2000).

Stress Hormones and Developmentally Appropriate Practice

A second area of brain research that supports developmentally appropriate practice is the study of stress hormones. The body produces chemicals called hormones that help regulate body functions and reactions to the environment (Gunnar & Cheatham 2003). Many hormones work together to regulate the activities of the brain.

Cortisol, a hormone that increases in response to stress, contributes to the fight-or-flight reflex that helps the body respond to challenging situations (Kolb & Whishaw 2001). Even daily stressors such as being hungry, hearing a loud noise, or solving a difficult problem can cause increases in cortisol levels. In moderate doses cortisol is a good thing—it helps the brain respond to stress and solve problems. However, too much cortisol production over a long period of time is not good and can lead to problems with memory and self-regulation (Gunnar & Cheatham 2003). In other words, frequent and intense stress can harm abilities like remembering important information and controlling negative emotions or behavior. (For example, consider how stress can lead an adult to draw a blank during a test or yell at another driver in heavy traffic.)

Animal research provides some interesting ways to think about the effects of cortisol on the care and education of young children. Mother rats nurture their pups by grooming and licking the pups' fur. Scientists know from years of working with rats that when mothers provide high quality nurturing, defined as frequent grooming, rat pups are healthier and react less to stress (Caldji, Diorio, & Meaney 2000). Animal studies are helpful in considering how important nurturing caregiving and nurturing relationships may be for helping children cope with stress. Research with children also indicates that cortisol production varies in response to stress and is associated with children's behavior and adjustment (Smider et al. 2002; Gunnar et al. 2003).

Too much cortisol production over a long period of time is not good and can lead to problems with memory and self-regulation.

Children respond to stress differently. Early childhood programs may not be able to reduce stressors in home and community settings. However, child-focused settings, such as a child care program, can be oases of security—places where the child feels both protected and autonomous. Research on cortisol and young children supports guidelines for developmentally appropriate practice in teaching to enhance development and learning and for establishing reciprocal relationships with families.

The following research findings provide guidance for supporting transitions, peer play, communicating with families, and development of self-regulation.

Transitions and Stress

Cortisol level can be measured in any body fluid, but it is most easily taken from saliva samples. People have a baseline cortisol level that is typical for their own biology and personality. Cortisol typically fluctuates throughout the day (usually higher

---

Teachers and Family Working Together

In the year my son Jack turned three, he experienced a long-distance move, parents' unemployment, beginning full-day preschool, and the birth of a sibling. His early childhood teachers could see the effects of these stressors on his emotions and behavior. Jack struggled to play with peers and resisted the preschool routine.

The teachers realized that Jack's adjustment, emotions, and behavior at the time were related to the many stressors in his life, and they sensitively guided his behavior, helping Jack to build friendships and learn in a safe comfortable environment. Just as important his teachers sensitively conveyed their concerns to Jack's dad and me, problem solving with us without ever passing judgement.

It is important to communicate and build bridges with families—and to remember that families need our support. Early childhood programs cannot remove the stress from children's lives, but developmentally appropriate practices on the part of professionals may buffer the effects of potentially stressful events.

---

in the morning and lower in the afternoon) and increases in response to stress (Smider et al. 2002).

Researchers studied changes in cortisol levels in 15-month-old toddlers during the transition to formal child care. The children's cortisol levels were double their baseline (home) levels during the first hour of child care, when separated from their mothers (Ahnert et al. 2004). After several days children's distress decreased and their cortisol returned to baseline levels. Mothers remained in the classroom with the children during the transition to child care for several days. When mothers spent more days in the classroom during the transition, children's attachment relationships with mothers remained secure, but when mothers spent less time in the classroom during the transition to care, children were at greater risk for relationship problems with their mothers.

Secure parent-child relationships are essential for children's well-being. Developmentally appropriate practice in this context suggests that early childhood professionals and programs should support families by allowing sufficient time for children and families to negotiate transitions gently to and from early childhood programs (Bredekamp & Copple 1997). Predictable routines help reduce the stress of transitions. When routines are about to change, children need to be notified and prepared. Foreshadowing is a technique in which adults share news of upcoming events with children to help them prepare. Examples of foreshadowing include "Five minutes till cleanup time" and "A guest is visiting today during group time." Foreshadowing of activities and transitions helps children feel in control and reduces stress.

Because children vary in their reactions to changes in routines, it is important also that adults respect children's individual temperaments and needs (Gallagher 2002). For example, a child who adjusts slowly to transitions or who reacts negatively to change may need individualized foreshadowing a few minutes before the group foreshadowing for a transition or small change in routine.

Supporting Families

Research in stress hormones has implications for how we consider the common stressors in children's lives and our relationships with families. In one study (de Haan et al. 1998), stressful home-related life events for two-year-olds (such as the birth of a sibling, parent job changes, and moving) were associated with increased cortisol levels. Teachers reported more shy and anxious behavior in the classroom for children with higher cortisol levels. It is important to recognize times of stress for young children and provide the necessary comfort and attention in the early childhood setting.

Parents share with teachers important and sometimes sensitive details about their lives. Professionals need to withhold judgment about family situations and share their concerns about children in a nonthreatening way, as families cannot always control the stressors.

Children need time to solve problems on their own and opportunities to engage in extended play.

Classroom Climate

Developmentally appropriate practice is effective in helping reduce stress in the early childhood setting (Hart et al. 1998). Positive emotions should dominate an early childhood classroom climate, and interactions should be characteristically calm and positive. Teachers may greet each child and family daily with eye contact, a smile, and a calm and positive manner. When interactions between children are intense, teachers can try to comfort children and provide opportunities for them to return to a calm state as quickly as possible.

Finally, it's not a good idea to rush from activity to activity. Sometimes we feel we must stimulate children constantly or stick to a schedule. Children, however, need time to solve problems on their own and opportunities to engage in extended play. A fast-paced approach may interfere with opportunities for real learning and enjoyment.

Development of Self-Regulation

Children with higher cortisol levels may sometimes be described by their families and early childhood teachers as more anxious, distressed, and socially withdrawn (Smider et al. 2002; Watamura et al. 2003). Teachers can support self-regulation by accepting and guiding children's expression of emotion, talking through their anxieties, and scaffolding children's understanding of their emotions. Using emotion words, accepting emotions that children express, and offering alternatives for dealing with stressful situations are all ways teachers can help

children deal with strong emotions as they experience them (O'Brien 1997). It is important to recognize that children vary in their emotional expression—gender, culture, and genetics all influence how we react to stress and change.

The right side of the brain experiences greater growth during the first 18 months of life and dominated brain functioning for the first three years.

Peer Play

We cannot assume that the path to social play and friendship is the same for all children or that it is without struggles. In one study, children with lower cortisol levels played more cooperatively with other children (Watamura et al. 2003). Children with higher cortisol levels sought out social play, but they were more likely to experience difficult interactions with peers. In a study focusing on the transition to preschool, two-year-olds with higher cortisol levels showed high activity levels and aggressive behavior with peers (de Haan et al. 1998).

Early childhood professionals can help children experience success with their peers. Developmentally appropriate practice requires that teachers join children in their social play, modeling and guiding children's interactions and supporting children in times of conflict. Without interfering or stifling children's play, teachers can help play become more complex and at the same time more collaborative (Gartrell 2004).

Brain Specialization and Developmentally Appropriate Practice

A third area of brain research providing guidance for early care and education is in the area of brain hemisphere specialization. The right and left sides of the brain—or more accurately, of the cerebral cortex—specialize in certain functions (Kolb & Whishaw 2001). Generally, the right side of the brain is more responsible for processing negative emotions, intense emotions, and creativity. The left side of the brain is more responsible for positive emotions, language development, and interest in new objects and experiences (Davidson & Hugdahl 1995).

These brain specializations are not fixed, though. When an individual has brain damage to one side of the brain, the other side often takes over the damaged side's functions (Kolb & Whishaw 2001). Furthermore, the sides of the brain do not develop at the same rate. The right side of the brain experiences greater growth during the first 18 months of life and dominates brain functioning for the first three years (Schore 2001).

So, during the period just before birth and for three years after birth, the right brain experiences a growth spurt. What does this mean for the child's learning and experiences?

Learning to Regulate Emotion

Given that the right brain is responsible for processing and helping to regulate negative emotions, and that it develops rapidly during the first three years of life, learning to regulate emotion plays an extremely important role in early childhood development. Infants and young children rely heavily on adult caregivers to help them regulate emotion and behavior (Landy 2002). When young children become distressed and have difficulty regulating their own behavior, caregivers help to minimize the children's stress and provide comfort. The experience of regulating their distressful emotions helps infants organize their experiences. In the opening vignette, Sophia turns to her caregiver for support in negotiating a cruising gap. Similarly, toddlers point to objects, asking their caregivers, "What's that?" Children learn to stop and assess fearful situations, use expressive language to make their needs known, and apply strategies for managing stress. With repeated, sensitive support, children come to know that they will be "okay," that justice will prevail much of the time, and that, most important, they have some control over their experiences.

Building Relationships

Ongoing interaction between infant and caregiver (especially when face-to-face) forms the basis of an infant-caregiver relationship (Brazelton 1982). The caregiver modulation of an infant's arousal helps the infant focus on and sustain attention to people and objects. The infant-caregiver relationship then forms the basis for the child's ongoing ability to regulate behavior and emotion

In a reciprocal dance, the right brain guides children's expression of emotion, and the quality of the adult-child interactions then guides the development of the child's right brain (Schore 2001). When a caregiver responds quickly and appropriately to a child's distress—rocking, speaking softly, meeting the child's gaze with a reassuring face—the child learns to expect the caregiver's, support and to rely upon it. The expectation of support helps the child manage emotions and deal effectively with challenges (Landy 2002).

Some child or family circumstances may put children at risk for not receiving enough help regulating emotion. Conditions related to prematurity, such as difficulty breathing (Diener 2005), may make it hard for an infant to cry to express her needs. A child's challenging temperament may cause the caregiver so much stress that providing individually appropriate, sensitive care is difficult (Gallagher 2002). When a family member experiences mental illness (Clark, Tluczek, & Gallagher 2004) or a family lives in poverty (Zigler 2004), it can be hard for a parent to provide quality caregiving.

What happens when infants do not receive enough assistance regulating emotion? When infants are frequently overstimulated or when they experience distress and are not comforted, they may withdraw from new experiences and relationships and lose opportunities for interaction and learning (Landy 2002).

Caring, Teaching, and Building Relationships

Using developmentally appropriate guidelines for caring, teaching, and building relationships, early childhood professionals can help children gain emotion regulation in many ways (Landy 2002). It is important to accept children's emotions and teach children coping strategies for dealing with strong feelings. Caregivers can create a safe climate for children's expression of emotion.

Teachers need to plan activities that stimulate, challenge, and soothe a child and are appropriate for the child's age and individual characteristics. Joyful experiences should dominate the early childhood climate. Negative emotions cannot, and should not, be completely avoided, but early childhood professionals can help children develop approaches for dealing with intense negative emotions.

For teachers of infants and toddlers, this means providing comfort when children are distressed. For preschool, kindergarten, and primary teachers, support consists of naming and accepting emotions and modeling strategies for coping. Teachers can help children understand that anger, frustration, sadness, and fear are all part of being a person (Gartrell 2004). Our preschool program displays a poster of emotion words and facial expressions for teachers and children to use as a reference. Teachers encourage children to express their feelings with words, as well as they are able, and they help children negotiate their needs with teachers and other children.

Modeling is also important. Teachers may help children name their emotions and model problem-solving strategies: "When someone takes the toy I'm trying to use, I get really angry. I tell him how angry I am and say that he can use the toy when I am done." When early childhood professionals lose control of their own emotions, they can apologize and explain their feelings and behavior to children.

In a reciprocal dance, the right brain guides children's expression of emotion, and the quality of the adult-child interactions then guides the development of the child's right brain.

Conclusion

Understanding brain research means understanding the importance of positive, supportive relationships in early childhood development (Bredekamp & Copple 1997; Shore 1997; Shonkoff & Phillips 2000; Schore 2002). In its preamble the NAEYC Code of Ethical Conduct calls for decisions about interactions and relationships in early childhood programs to be based on knowledge of child development (NAEYC 2005). In light of our knowledge of brain development, developmentally appropriate practice means keeping these relationships at the forefront of what we do with children and families.

> **Developmentally appropriate practice means creating a caring community of learners, one that is inclusive, safe, and orderly, and emphasizes social relationships.**

Let's consider the children we observed at the beginning of this article. In the case of Sophia, the cruising toddler, using developmentally appropriate practice that is informed by knowledge of the brain development of an 18-month-old means balancing emotional and cognitive support for the toddler as she tries new steps—and comforting her when the steps result in falls. For preschoolers Azim and Frank, it means providing an environment in which problem solving and collaboration can occur and stepping back to allow learning to happen. It also means being ready for setbacks—in this case a fumbling structure—and offering emotional support and problem solving when needed.

Developmentally appropriate practice means creating a caring community of learners, one that is inclusive, safe, and orderly and emphasizes social relationships. It means teaching to enhance development and learning by respecting children's individual differences, fostering collaboration among peers, facilitating development of self-regulation, and structuring an intellectually engaging and varied environment. Finally, it means establishing reciprocal, supportive relationships with families, including sharing information, supporting families in times of stress, linking them with support services, and recognizing the complexity and importance of the shared responsibility in childrearing (Bredekamp & Copple 1997).

It does take a whole village to raise a child—and brain research can guide our use of village resources.

References

Ahnert, L., M. Gunnar, M. Lamb, & M. Barthel. 2004. Transition to child care: Associations with infant-mother attachment, infant negative emotion, and cortisol elevations. *Child Development* 75 (3): 639–50.

Bloom, F.E., C.A. Nelson, & A. Lazerson. 2001. *Brain, mind, and behavior*. 3rd ed. New York: Worth.

Brazelton, T.B. 1982. Joint regulation of neonate-parent behavior. In *Social interchange in infancy: Affect, cognition, and communication*, ed. E.Z. Tronick, 7–22. Baltimore: University Park Press.

Bredekamp, S., & C. Copple, eds. 1997. *Developmentally appropriate practice in early childhood programs*. Rev. ed. Washington, DC: NAEYC.

Bruer, J.T. 2004. The brain and child development: Time for some critical thinking. In *The Head Start debates*, eds. E. Zigler & S.J. Styfco, 423–34. Baltimore: Brookes. Available from NAEYC.

Caldji, C., J. Diorio, & M.J. Meaney. 2000. Variations in maternal care in infancy regulate the development of stress reactivity. *Biological Psychiatry* 48 (12): 1164–74.

Cashmore, J. 2001. Early experience and brain development. *Journal of the HEIA* 8 (3): 16–19.

Clark, R., A. Tluczek, & K.C. Gallagher. 2004. Assessment of parent-child early relational disturbances. In *Handbook of infant, toddler, and preschool mental health assessment*, eds. R. Delcarmen-Wiggins & A. Carter, 25–60. Oxford, UK: Oxford University Press.

Davidson, R.J., & K. Hugdahl, eds. 1995. *Brain asymmetry*. Cambridge, MA: MIT Press.

de Haan, M., M. Gunnar, K. Tout, J. Hart, & K. Stansbury. 1998. Familiar and novel contexts yield different associations between cortisol and behavior among 2-year-old children. *Developmental Psychobiology* 33 (1): 93–101

Diener, P.L. 2005. *Resources for educating children with diverse abilities: Birth through eight*. 4th ed. Clifton Park, NY: Thomson Delmar.

Francis, D.D., J. Diorio, P.M. Plotsky, & M.J. Meaney. 2002. Environmental enrichment reverses the effects of maternal separation on stress reactivity. *Journal of Neuroscience* 22 (18): 7840–43.

Gallagher, K.C. 2002. Does child temperament moderate the influence of parenting on adjustment? *Developmental Review* 22: 623–43.

Gartrell, D. 2004. *The power of guidance: Teaching social-emotional skills in early childhood classrooms*. Washington, DC: NAEYC.

Gunnar, M.R., & C.L. Cheatham. 2003. Brain and behavior interfaces: Stress and the developing brain. *Infant Mental Health Journal* 24 (3): 195–211.

Gunnar, M.R., A.M. Sebanc, K. Tout, B. Donzella, & M.M.H. Dulmen. 2003. Peer rejection, temperament, and cortisol activity in preschoolers. *Development and Psychobiology* 43 (4): 346–58.

Hart, C.H., D.C. Burts, M.A. Durland, R. Charlesworth, M. DeWolf, & P.O. Fleege. 1998. Stress behaviors and activity type participation of preschooler in more and less developmentally appropriate classrooms: SES and sex differences. *Journal of Research in Childhood Education* 12 (2): 176–96.

Kolb, B., & I.Q. Whishaw. 2001. *An introduction to brain and behavior*. New York: Worth.

Landy, S. 2002. *Pathways to competence: Encouraging healthy social and emotional development in young children*. Baltimore: Brookes.

NAEYC. 2005. *Code of ethical conduct and statement of commitment*. Rev. ed. Brochure. Washington, DC: Author. Online: **naeyc.org/about/positions/asp**.

Nelson, C.A., & F.E. Bloom. 1997. Child development and neuroscience. *Child Development* 68 (5): 970–87.

O'Brien, M. 1997. Helping young children deal with anger. ERIC Clearinghouse on Elementary and Early Childhood Education. ED 414077-1997-12-00.

Ramey, C.T., & S.L. Ramey. 2004. Early educational interventions and intelligence: Implications for Head Start. In *The Head Start debates*, eds. E. Zigler & S.J. Styfco, 3–18. Baltimore: Brookes.

Schore, A.N. 2001. Effects of a secure attachment relationship on right brain development, affect regulation, and infant mental health. *Infant Mental Health Journal* 22 (1–2): 7–66.

Schore, A.N. 2002. The neurobiology of attachment and early personality organization. *Journal of Prenatal and Perinatal Psychology and Health* 16 (3): 249–63.

Shonkoff, J.P., & D.A. Phillips, eds. 2000. *From neurons to neighborhoods: The science of early childhood development*. Washington, DC: National Academies Press.

Shore, R. 1997. *Rethinking the brain: New insights into early development*. New York: Families and Work Institute.

Smider, N., M.J. Essex, N.H. Kalin, K.A. Buss, M.H. Klein, R.J. Davidson, & H.H. Goldsmith. 2002. Salivary cortisol as a predictor of socioemotional adjustment during kindergarten: A prospective study. *Child Development* 73 (1): 75–92.

Watamura, S.E., B. Donzella, J. Alwin, & M. Gunnar. 2003. Morning-to-afternoon increases in cortisol concentrations for infants and toddlers at child care: Age differences and behavioral correlates. *Child Development* 74 (4): 1006–20.

Zigler, E. 2004. The environmental mystique: Training the intellect versus development of the child. In *The Head Start debates*, eds. E. Zigler & SJ. Styfco, 449–58. Baltimore: Brookes.

Kathleen Cranley Gallagher, PhD, is an assistant professor in the School of Education at the University of North Carolina at Chapel Hill. Kate's experience includes teaching in an early intervention program and a kindergarten, directing a preschool/child care program, and teaching child care professionals. Her research focuses on children's early relationships and developing social competence.

From *Young Children*, Vol. 60, no. 4, July 2005, pp. 12-18, 20. Copyright © 2005 by National Association for the Education of Young Children. Reprinted by permission.

General Article

Culture and Language in the Emergence of Autobiographical Memory

ABSTRACT—Current conceptualizations of childhood amnesia assume that there is a "barrier" to remembering early experiences that must be overcome in order for one to begin to accumulate autobiographical memories. In contrast, we present a social-cultural-developmental perspective on the emergence of autobiographical memory. We first demonstrate the gradual emergence of autobiographical memories across the preschool years and then relate this developmental process to specific developments in language, narrative, and understanding of self and other that vary among individuals, as well as by culture and gender.

ROBYN FIVUSH[1] AND KATHERINE NELSON[2]
[1]*Emory University and* [2]*City University of New York Graduate Center*

Just over one hundred years ago, Freud (1924/1953) identified the phenomenon of childhood amnesia, adults' inability to recall events that occurred before 3 or 4 years of age. Explanations of childhood amnesia, however, have been more elusive (see Pillemer & White, 1989, and Pillemer, 1998, for excellent reviews). Whether focusing on neurological developments (e.g., Newcombe, Drummey, Fox, Lie, & Ottinger-Alberts, 2000), cognitive-schematic changes (e.g., Neisser, 1962), or the role of self in the development of accessible and durable autobiographical memories (e.g., Howe & Courage, 1993), current explanations assume there is a "barrier" that needs to be overcome, and that once this barrier is crossed, autobiographical memories are possible. Barrier accounts assume that what needs to be explained is the lack of memories before a certain developmental point, and then the offset to childhood amnesia that results in the accumulation of autobiographical memories.

In contrast, we propose that what is in need of explanation is the presence of autobiographical memories at all. How and why do humans have autobiographical memory, and what is the process by which it develops? Although almost all adults recall at least some events from their childhood, the age of earliest memory, density of memories across childhood, and level of detail and coherence of autobiographical memories vary widely across individuals. Some of these differences are related to gender and culture: Adult females and individuals from Western cultures have an earlier age of first memory, and have longer and more detailed memories of their childhood, than adult males and individuals from Asian cultures (see Fivush & Haden, 2003, for an overview). These findings call for a different kind of explanation of childhood amnesia.

In this article, we present a social-cultural-developmental perspective on the emergence of autobiographical memory. We first demonstrate the gradual emergence of autobiographical memories across the preschool years and then relate this developmental process to specific developments in language, narrative, and understanding of self and other that vary among individuals, as well as by culture and gender.

Adults' Recollections of Childhood

Whether adults are asked to recall their earliest memory or to generate childhood memories from a set of cue words, the average age at which the earliest remembered events took place (at least among Western participants) is consistently between 3 and 4 years. However, many people can recall some details about at least some events that occurred as early as age 2, when specific events (e.g., the birth of a sibling, an overnight hospitalization) known to have occurred at specific points in their past are targeted (Usher & Neisser, 1993). When forgetting curves are fitted to adults' recollections of early childhood memories, two points of divergence from the expected linear function are found. First, there are significantly fewer memories from below the age of 7 than would be expected by extrapolation of the forgetting curve, and, second, there are almost no memories before the age of 3 (Wetzler & Sweeney, 1986). Weigle and Bauer (2000) confirmed that memories from the preschool period are sparse; they asked participants for their two earliest memories and found that the earliest memory was from about age 3, with the next earliest memory occurring, on average, a year later.

Bruce, Dolan, and Phillips-Grant (2000) developed a technique for estimating when autobiographical memories become more continuous. By calculating the age at which early childhood events that are "remembered" become more numerous than early childhood events that are "known" to have happened but not personally recalled, they found that autobiographical memory does not become continuous until about age 4 1/2. These results point to the critical fact that childhood amnesia is not an all-or-none phenomenon. At least some fragmentary memories may begin to emerge quite early. Yet early memories are sparsely spaced across time and do not seem to approach a continuous sense of the past until the end of the preschool years. How might developmental research help elucidate the gradual emergence of coherent autobiographical memories across the preschool years?

The Development of Memory

Even before birth, the human child is capable of discriminating incoming information and retaining this information over time. De Casper and Spence (1986) demonstrated that neonates can differentiate their mother's voice from other voices within hours of birth. During the first 6 months of life, infants will habituate to objects and pictures of presented stimuli, and by 6 months of age, infants will continue to show decreased looking times to pictures seen as much as 2 weeks in the past (Fagen, 1973). Infants will also learn to kick their feet in order to get a mobile over the crib to move, and they will remember this contingency over increasing time delays across the first year of life (Rovee-Collier & Hayne, 2000). Between 9 and 12 months of age, infants begin to engage in deferred imitation (Bauer, Wenner, Dropik, & Wewerka, 2000); after seeing a novel action performed on an unusual object, infants will remember and perform this action when presented with that object even several days later. By the end of the first year, infants are able to recall several actions performed on multiple objects for reliably longer periods of time. Between the ages of 1 and 3 years, deferred imitation becomes more reliable, more durable over more extended periods of time, and more temporally organized (Bauer et al., 2000). Finally, across the first few years of life, infants develop reliable memory for routine events in their everyday lives (Nelson, 1986).

As impressive as these early memory abilities are, they do not provide evidence of autobiographical memory. Autobiographical memory requires explicit memory of an event that occurred in a specific time and place in one's personal past (Tulving, 2002). Further, autobiographical memory is referenced to the self and has personal significance as part of an organized "life story" (Conway & Rubin, 1993). The need for repeated learning trials and dependence on environmental cues for memory to be demonstrated in the first 2 years of life suggest a developing ability to recall events, but as yet no sense of a self remembering a specific point in the past, or a past memory being related to current conceptions of self in a continuous self-narrative.

Even when children first begin to refer to the past in language, at about 18 months of age, these references are fleeting and fragmentary (Nelson & Ross, 1980), and usually refer to just-completed actions or familiar routines. At about 20 to 24 months of age, children begin to make more extended references to events that occurred in the more distant past. The emergence of linguistic references to past events raises the thorny issue of the relation between language and autobiographical memory.

Language, Narrative, and Autobiographical Memory

Language appears critical in the development of autobiographical memory for three interrelated reasons. First, language is not simply the way in which memories are expressed, but is instrumental in providing an organizational structure for personal experience. Second, language allows children to enter into dialogues with other people about their experiences, and these dialogues facilitate children's developing abilities to form organized representations of their experiences. Finally, these dialogues highlight for children the fact that memories are representations of events that occurred at specified points in the past and that are evaluated from multiple perspectives.

Language and the Organization of Memory

If language is merely a form for expressing existing memory representations, then existing memories should become expressible in language as it develops. However, there is now substantial evidence that experiences that occurred before the advent of language, and that may be remembered nonverbally, are not easily "translatable" into language. Perhaps the best evidence of this is a recent study by Simcock and Hayne (2002). Two- and 3-year-old children engaged in complex play activities, and memory for these activities was assessed both behaviorally and verbally 6 and 12 months later. Simcock and Hayne also assessed both receptive (comprehension) and productive language skills at both the time of experience and the time of recall. Strikingly, although all children provided verbal recall, "in no instance during test did the child use a word or words to describe the event that had not been part of his or her productive vocabulary at the time of the event" (p. 229). The specific language skills available at the time of an experience affect what can subsequently be verbally recalled about it (see Bauer & Wewerka, 1995, and Peterson & Rideout, 1998, for similar results).

Moreover, even after children become more competent language users, the linguistic structure provided by adults during an experienced event provides the organization for subsequent recall. When a child and adult experience events together, the adult provides a linguistic "scaffold" that helps to focus the child's attention and organize the event into a coherent whole. Several studies have demonstrated that those aspects of an experienced event that were linguistically scaffolded by an adult are better recalled by the child than aspects not scaffolded through an adult's language, even when the child demonstrated interest in those particular aspects of the event (Haden, Ornstein, Eckerman, & Didow, 2001; Tessler & Nelson, 1994). Throughout the preschool years, children remain at least somewhat dependent on adults to structure ongoing events through language to help organize the events for future recall. But recalling an event in retrospect also requires linguistic scaffolding. The ways in which adults and children reminisce about past events influence children's developing ability to organize and recall their personal past, which brings us to the second way in which language and autobiographical memory are interrelated.

Adult-Child Memory Dialogues

Extensive research has documented that parental reminiscing style influences children's developing autobiographical memory skills (see Nelson & Fivush, 2000, for a review). Parents vary along a dimension of elaboration in their reminiscing style; some parents talk a great deal about past events, asking many questions and providing a great deal of embellished detail, whereas other parents are less elaborative, discussing the past in less detail and asking fewer and more redundant questions. Longitudinal research confirms that children of more highly elaborative parents come to tell more richly detailed narratives of their own past than do children of less elaborative parents (Fivush, Haden, & Reese, 1996; Reese, 2002).

Talking about the past involves more than recalling details of what occurred. Children must also learn the canonical narrative structure of autobiographical recall in early parent-guided conversations. Those parents who provide more orienting information, setting past events in time and place, and more evaluative information, placing events in emotional and personally meaningful contexts, have children who, by the end of the preschool years, are recounting more coherent and more evaluative narratives of their own personal past (Haden, Haine, & Fivush, 1997).

Thus, our claim is that an elaborative maternal reminiscing style fosters the development of specific autobiographical memory skills that help the child to organize and elaborate on personally experienced events, both as they are occurring and in reminiscing. Although all children will develop autobiographical memories, children of more highly elaborative mothers will come to have more highly elaborated and coherent autobiographical memories than children of less elaborative mothers. Moreover, as children develop the language and narrative skills to organize and recall their past through participating in adult-guided reminiscing, they are also beginning to differentiate the past as past, that is, to understand time and sequence and how past experiences fit along a developing time line. Through locating past events in time, children begin to develop the idea of a continuous self, a self that exists through time.

Language of the Past

The emergence of autobiographical memory involves at least two orderings of time. The first is the ordering of the sequence within the event recalled, an ordering that includes settings, plans, goals, actions, outcomes, achievements, and the temporal and causal relations among them. Very young children have good command of sequences of familiar routines, or scripts (Nelson, 1986), and are sensitive to order, especially causal order, in brief, newly learned action sequences (Bauer et al., 2000). The second ordering dimension places the event narrative at a specific time in the past. Friedman (1993) showed that the ability to order familiar daily events increases over the preschool period, and that children's understanding of sequence, duration, and distance of events begins during the preschool years but continues to develop in later childhood. Preschool children also begin to mark time through language. For a young child who has no external measures of time, such as days, weeks, months, and years, sequencing of events in past time can be achieved primarily by nominal days, for example, "my birthday" or "Christmas," or times of the year, such as "last summer." Use of labels of this kind indicates that the child is conceiving of an event as having happened at a particular time in the past different from the present. However, the acquisition of relative time markers, such as *yesterday* and *tomorrow*, is typically a late achievement, often not realized until late in the fifth year. At the outset of their use, *yesterday* and *tomorrow* may be used for any day not today, or *yesterday* may be used for any time in the past (Harner, 1982).

The beginning use of temporal language marks children's earliest understanding of a personal past, an awareness that it is the current self that engaged in these past activities. Early research on self highlighted the achievement of self-recognition (Lewis & Brooks-Gunn, 1979). Between 16 and 24 months of age, children will begin to touch that place on their face that has been surreptitiously marked with rouge when they see themselves in a mirror. Howe and Courage (1993) have argued that the achievement of this "cognitive self" heralds the offset of childhood amnesia, as there is now a self-schema around which to organize autobiographical memories. Reese (2002) has shown that early in development, autobiographical skills are related to mirror self-recognition, but that by the end of the preschool years, maternal reminiscing style eclipses mirror self-recognition in predicting the development of autobiographical memory. Thus, we agree with Howe and Courage that mirror self-recognition is critical to the emergence of autobiographical memory, but in contrast to them, we see this as just one component of a more complex understanding of self in time.

Povinelli and his colleagues have studied the understanding of the relation of the present self to the past self in 3- and 4-year-olds by using a delayed-self-recognition paradigm (Povinelli, Landry, Theall, Clark, & Castille, 1999). In this paradigm, while the child engages in a game of sorting cards, the experimenter surreptitiously places a sticker on the child's head; the sticker remains visible in a video record of the game. A few minutes later, the child watches the video recording. Most children spontaneously point to and name their image on the screen. However, whereas most children note the sticker on the child's head in the video, only 4- and 5-year-olds attempt to remove it from their heads; very few 3-year-olds do so. This research indicates that only at about age 4 do children begin to have a temporal sense of self, relating past self to present self, a requirement for autobiographical memory. Welch-Ross (2001) found a strong relation between children's ability to recognize themselves on video and to tell a detailed personal narrative, providing a direct link from awareness of self in time to the construction of autobiographical memory.

Language of the Self and Other

Autobiographical memory depends not only on an awareness of self in the past, but also on an awareness of others with whom one has shared the past, as well as an awareness that others may remember the past differently. Through participating in adult-guided interactions, children may become aware that memories are subjective representations, in the sense that what one person remembers about an event may or may not be the same as what someone else who has experienced that same event remembers (Fivush, 2001). In mother-child reminiscing, there are critical conversational junctures at which mothers and children disagree about what occurred. Sometimes this is at the level of the "facts" of the event—who was there, what objects were present, what activities were engaged in. These kinds of disagreements challenge children to begin to understand that memories are representations of what occurred, and that different people may remember different aspects of experienced events. The same process encourages children to reflect on their own recollection of an event as a unique reexperience unshared by others.

Often, disagreements in recollection are not about facts but about emotions and evaluations. Mothers and children may disagree on whether they felt sad or angry, whether or not they were scared, and whether or not they liked the roller coaster or visiting Santa. These points of conflict highlight for children that they may have a different interpretation of, evaluation of, or emotional reaction to an event than others do. This awareness is clearly related to concomitant developments in children's theory of mind (Perner, 2000), that is, their emerging awareness that they and others have thoughts, feelings, desires, and beliefs, and that these mental states can vary among individuals. Theory of mind develops gradually across the preschool years, and both Perner and Welch-Ross (2001) have shown that developments in theory of mind are related to autobiographical memory. Through negotiating disagreements about the past, children may come to understand that they have a unique perspective on what occurred. Their memory is "owned" in the sense that they have a particular evaluative stance that may or may not be shared with others. Thus, parent-child reminiscing can facilitate children's understanding of a past self as differentiated from others, yet as continuous with the self in the present: "This is what I remember about that past event in contrast to what others may remember, and this is how I evaluate that experience from my current self-perspective."

Culture and Gender in Autobiographical Memory

Thus far, we have presented evidence that autobiographical memories emerge gradually across the preschool years and are related to children's developing abilities in language and in understanding self through time and in relation to others. Each of these skills also develops gradually across the preschool years and shows individual differences in rate of acquisition and achievement. We have further demonstrated that these abilities emerge within the context of social interactions within which adults provide a linguistic scaffold for children to organize memories of the past, and, again, that these interactions show great individual variation. Thus, our approach underscores individual differences. In this section, we consider factors related to culture and gender that may contribute to these individual differences in maternal style and child outcome.

If we assume that a major function of talking about the past is to help construct an understanding of self through time, then the way in which the self is conceptualized will influence the way in which the past is constructed, and, in turn, the way in which the past is constructed will influence the way in which the self is conceptualized, in an ongoing dialectical relation. Several theorists have postulated that Western and Eastern cultures differ along a dimension of individualism-collectivism in defining the self (Markus & Oyserman, 1989). More specifically, they propose that Western cultures define the self as an independent autonomous agent, in control of its own emotions, actions, and outcomes, whereas Eastern cultures define the self as an interdependent part of a social group, regulating its actions, emotions, and outcomes in relation to others. Intriguingly, there are cultural differences in autobiographical memory that mirror these distinctions. Mothers from Western cultures talk about the past in more elaborated and more emotional ways than do mothers from Eastern cultures; Western mothers focus on the child's own activities and emotional reactions, whereas Eastern mothers place the child in a more communal setting, playing down emotions, such as anger, that might separate the child from the group and highlighting moral emotions and lessons (Leichtman, Wang, & Pillemer, 2003).

An elaborative and emotional reminiscing style among mothers would predict more elaborated and more detailed autobiographical memory in their children for several reasons. First, a more elaborated reminiscing style would lead to more organized and detailed, and therefore more accessible, memories. Second, more elaborative reminiscing would facilitate children's developing understanding of time, and especially self in time, through focusing children on details of temporally specified events. Finally, more elaborated reminiscing would allow more opportunities for mothers and children to disagree and negotiate the past, thus facilitating children's developing understanding of memory as representational and of the self as having a unique perspective, thus creating a truly personal past. Indeed, as early as middle childhood, children from Western cultures tell more elaborated, more detailed, and more emotional narratives of their past than do children from Eastern cultures (Han, Leichtman, & Wang, 1998), and this pattern persists through adulthood (Pillemer, 1998). In addition, adults from Eastern cultures have a later age of first memory than do adults from Western cultures and much sparser memories of childhood in general (Pillemer, 1998), again suggesting a less elaborated, less differentiated autobiographical self.

Similar to cultural concepts, gendered self-concepts are also expressed in autobiographical memories. In general, compared with adult males, adult females have longer, more detailed, more vivid, and more emotionally laden autobiographical memories of events from both adulthood and childhood, and females have an earlier age of first memory than do males (Pillemer, 1998). And again, maternal reminiscing style differs by gender;

mothers are more elaborative, more evaluative, and more emotional when reminiscing with daughters than with sons (Fivush & Buckner, 2003). Thus, early culture-and gender-differentiated patterns of maternal reminiscing seem to be related to later culture- and gender-differentiated patterns of autobiographical memory and self-understanding.

Functions of Reminiscing: A Social-Cultural-Developmental Perspective

Given the theoretical perspective we have outlined here, the question changes from why human beings do not have autobiographical memories before the age of about 3 (at least in White, Western cultures) to why they develop an autobiographical memory system at all. Although we agree that developments in neurocognitive functioning and basic memory abilities lay a foundation for autobiographical memory, we argue that autobiographical memory emerges within specific social and cultural milieus, which shape the ways in which individuals may or may not develop memories of a specific personal past. Moreover, the kinds of autobiographical memories that are formed, as well as their content, organization, and temporal density, vary as a function of individual and cultural interactions that help shape autobiography and self-concept. Thus, we expect that historical and cultural constructions of self will be reflected in the way in which individuals construct their own autobiographies (Nelson, 2003).

Thus, we argue that autobiographical memory serves mainly social and cultural functions. Whereas memory for specific episodes is important for anticipating and predicting the environment, autobiographical memory is about defining self in time and in relation to others. These functions allow the individual to create a shared past with others from which an individual personal past emerges. The uniquely human ability to create a shared past allows each individual to enter a community, or culture, in which individuals share a perspective on the kinds of events that make a life and shape a self (Fivush et al., 1996). In some cultures, and to some extent in all, these functions may be served by shared cultural narratives; in other cultures (such as contemporary Western culture), more may depend on the individual's self-definition and self-story (Nelson, 2003). Through the creation of a shared past, individuals gain a sense of who they are in relation to others, both locally within their family and community and more globally within their culture. They also attain a shared perspective on how to interpret and evaluate experience, which leads to a shared moral perspective. In a very real sense, the achievement of an autobiographical memory system sets the stage for the intergenerational transmission of family and cultural history, which is the bedrock of human culture.

References

Bauer, P.J., Wenner, J.A., Dropik, P.L., & Wewerka, S.S. (2000). Parameters of remembering and forgetting in the transition from infancy to early childhood. *Monographs of the Society for Research in Child Development, 65*(4, Serial No. 263).

Bauer, P.J., & Wewerka, S. (1995). One- to two-year-olds' recall of events: The more expressed the more impressed. *Journal of Experimental Child Psychology, 59*, 475–496.

Bruce, D., Dolan, A., & Phillips-Grant, K. (2000). On the transition from childhood amnesia to the recall of personal memories. *Psychological Science, 11*, 360–364.

Conway, M.A., & Rubin, D.C. (1993). The structure of autobiographical memory. In A.F. Collins, S.E. Gathercole, M.A. Conway, & P.E. Morris (Eds.), *Theories of memory* (pp. 103–139). Hillsdale, NJ: Erlbaum.

De Casper, A.J., & Spence, M.J. (1986). Prenatal maternal speech influences newborn's perception of speech sounds. *Infant Behavior and Development, 9*, 133–150.

Fagan, J.F., III. (1973). Infants' delayed recognition memory and forgetting. *Journal of Experimental Child Psychology, 16*, 424–450.

Fivush, R. (2001). Owning experience: The development of subjective perspective in autobiographical memory. In C. Moore & K. Lemmon (Eds.), *The self in time: Developmental perspectives* (pp. 35–52). Hillsdale, NJ: Erlbaum.

Fivush, R., & Buckner, J.P. (2003). Constructing gender and identity through autobiographical narratives. In R. Fivush & C.A. Haden (Eds.), *Autobiographical memory and the construction of a narrative self: Developmental and cultural perspectives* (pp. 149–168). Mahwah, NJ: Erlbaum.

Fivush, R., & Haden, C.A. (Eds.). (2003). *Autobiographical memory and the construction of a narrative self: Developmental and cultural perspectives.* Mahwah, NJ: Erlbaum.

Fivush, R., Haden, C.A., & Reese, E. (1996). Remembering, recounting and reminiscing: The development of autobiographical memory in social context. In D. Rubin (Ed.), *Reconstructing our past: An overview of autobiographical memory* (pp. 341–359). New York: Cambridge University Press.

Freud, S. (1953). *A general introduction to psychoanalysis.* New York: Pocket Books. (Original work published 1924)

Friedman, W.J. (1993). Memory for the time of past events. *Psychological Bulletin, 11*, 44–66.

Haden, C.A., Haine, R., & Fivush, R. (1997). Developing narrative structure in parent-child conversations about the past. *Developmental Psychology, 33*, 295–307.

Haden, C.A., Ornstein, P.A., Eckerman, C.O., & Didow, S.M. (2001). Mother-child conversational interactions as events unfold: Linkages to subsequent remembering. *Child Development, 72*, 1016–1031.

Han, J.J., Leichtman, M.D., & Wang, Q. (1998). Autobiographical memory in Korean, Chinese, and American children. *Developmental Psychology, 34*, 701–713.

Harner, L. (1982). Talking about the past and future. In W.J. Friedman (Ed.), *The developmental psychology of time* (pp. 141–170). New York: Academic Press.

Howe, M., & Courage, M. (1993). On resolving the enigma of childhood amnesia. *Psychological Bulletin, 113*, 305–326.

Leichtman, M., Wang, Q., & Pillemer, D.P. (2003). In R. Fivush & C.A. Haden (Eds.), *Autobiographical memory and the construction of a narrative self: Developmental and cultural perspectives* (pp. 73–98). Mahwah, NJ: Erlbaum.

Lewis, M., & Brooks-Gunn, J. (1979). *Social cognition and the acquisition of self.* New York: Plenum.

Markus, H., & Oyserman, D. (1989). *Gender and thought: The role of the self-concept.* In M. Crawford & M. Gentry (Eds.), *Gender and thought: Psychological perspectives* (pp. 187–220). New York: Springer-Verlag.

Neisser, U. (1962). Cultural and cognitive discontinuity. In T.E. Gladwin & W. Sturtevant (Eds.), *Anthropology and human behavior* (pp. 54–71). Washington, DC: Anthropological Society of Washington.

Nelson, K. (1986). *Event knowledge: Structure and function in development.* Hillsdale, NJ: Erlbaum.

Nelson, K. (2003). Self and social functions: Individual autobiographical memory and collective narrative. *Memory, 11,* 125–136.

Nelson, K., & Fivush, R. (2000). Socialization of memory. In E. Tulving & F.I.M. Craik (Eds.), *Oxford handbook of memory* (pp. 283–295). New York: Oxford University Press.

Nelson, K., & Ross, G. (1980). The generalities and specifics of long term memory in infants and young children. In M. Perlmutter (Ed.), *New directions for child development: Vol. 10. Children's memory* (pp. 87–101). San Francisco: Jossey-Bass.

Newcombe, N.S., Drummey, A.B., Fox, N.A., Lie, E., & Ottinger-Alberts, W. (2000). Remembering early childhood: How much, how, and why (or why not?). *Current Directions in Psychological Science, 9,* 55–58.

Perner, J. (2000). Memory and theory of mind. In E. Tulving & F.I.M. Craik (Eds.), *Oxford handbook of memory* (pp. 297–312). New York: Oxford University Press.

Peterson, C., & Rideout, R. (1998). One- and two-year-olds remember medical emergencies. *Developmental Psychology, 34,* 1059–1072.

Pillemer, D. (1998). *Momentous events, vivid memories.* Cambridge, MA: Harvard University Press.

Pillemer, D., & White, S.H. (1989). Childhood events recalled by children and adults. In H.W. Reese (Ed.), *Advances in child development and behavior, Vol. 22* (pp. 297–340). New York: Academic Press.

Povinelli, D.J., Landry, A.M., Theall, L.A., Clark, B.R., & Castille, C.M. (1999). Development of young children's understanding that the recent past is causally bound to the present. *Developmental Psychology, 35,* 1426–1439.

Reese, E. (2002). A model of the origins of autobiographical memory. In J.W. Fagen & H. Hayne (Eds.), *Progress in infancy research* (Vol. 2, pp. 215–260). Mahwah, NJ: Erlbaum.

Rovee-Collier, C.K., & Hayne, H. (2000). Memory in infancy and early childhood. In E. Tulving & F.I.M. Craik (Eds.), *Oxford handbook of memory* (pp. 267–282). New York: Oxford University Press.

Simcock, G., & Hayne, H. (2002). Breaking the barrier? Children fail to translate their preverbal memories into language. *Psychological Science, 13,* 225–231.

Tessler, M., & Nelson, K. (1994). Making memories: The influence of joint encoding on later recall by young children. *Consciousness and Cognition, 3,* 307–326.

Tulving, E. (2002). Episodic memory: From mind to brain. *Annual Review of Psychology, 53,* 1–25.

Usher, J., & Neisser, U. (1993). Childhood amnesia and the beginnings of memory for four early life events. *Journal of Experimental Psychology: General, 122,* 155–165.

Weigle, T.W., & Bauer, P.J. (2000). Deaf and hearing adults' recollections of childhood and beyond. *Memory, 8,* 293–310.

Welch-Ross, M. (2001). Personalizing the temporally extended self: Evaluative self-awareness and the development of autobiographical memory. In C. Moore & K. Lemmon (Eds.), *The self in time: Developmental perspectives* (pp. 97–120). Hillsdale, NJ: Erlbaum.

Wetzler, S.E., & Sweeney, J.A. (1986). Childhood amnesia: An empirical demonstration. In D. Rubin (Ed.), *Autobiographical memory* (pp. 191–202). New York: Cambridge University Press.

Address correspondence to **ROBYN FIVUSH**, Department of Psychology, Emory University, Atlanta, GA 30322; e-mail: psyrf@emory.edu.

From *Psychological Science,* Vol. 15, no. 9, September 2004, pp. 573-577. Copyright © 2004 by Association for Psychological Science. Reprinted by permission of Blackwell Publishing, Ltd. **www.blackwell-synergy.com**

Gender Bender

New research suggests genes and prenatal hormones could have more sway in gender identity than previously thought.

SADIE F. DINGFELDER
Monitor staff

"It's a boy!" announces the doctor to the exhausted mother, a determination the physician makes instantly. And most of the time, the observed sex of an infant docs match the genetic sex—with two X chromosomes producing a girl, and an X plus a Y resulting in a boy.

But in the rare cases where they do not, when prenatal development goes awry and genetic boys are born looking more like girls or vice versa, physicians and parents generally assign the newborn a sex. Most often the child becomes female, because female genitals are easier to construct, says William G. Reiner, MD, a child psychiatrist and urologist at the University of Oklahoma health services center.

The prevailing theory behind this long-standing practice, says Reiner, has been that a person reared as a girl will eventually embrace that category. Now, however, new research by Reiner suggests that perhaps such assumptions ought not to be made. A study by Reiner and John Gearhart, MD, of Johns Hopkins University, finds that biology—in particular the hormonal influences on developing infants' brains—programs children to eventually identify as either male or female, almost regardless of social influences, at least in the case of the children he's studied.

"It's fair to say that some people in the world of psychology have held that [gender] is socially derived, learned behavior," says Reiner. "But our findings do not support that theory."

However, other researchers, such as Sheri Berenbaum, PhD, a psychologist at Pennsylvania State University, maintain that determinates of gender identity may be more complex than that.

"Genetic and hormonal factors are just two of the many influences on gender identity and gender-typical behavior—social influences are certainly very important as well," she says. "And all of these factors seem to interact throughout a child's development."

New Findings

This isn't the view of Reiner and Gearhart though, who point to the findings of their study, published in the Jan. 22 issue of the *New England Journal of Medicine* (Vol. 350, No. 4). The study found that some infants whose brains were exposed to male hormones in utero later identified as male even though they were raised as female and underwent early-childhood operations. Reiner says that indicates that prenatal sex differentiation can at least sometimes trump social influences.

The study followed 16 genetic males with a rare disorder called cloacal exstrophy. Children with this disorder are born without penises, or with very small ones, despite having normal male hormones, normal testes and XY-chromosome pairs. Fourteen of these children underwent early sex-reassignment surgery and were raised as girls by their parents, who were instructed not to inform them of their early medical histories.

The researchers assessed the gender identities and behaviors of these children when they were anywhere from 5 to 16 years old using a battery of measures including the Bates Child Behavior and Attitude Questionnaire and the Child Game Participation Questionnaire. Researchers also asked the children whether they categorized themselves as boys or girls.

> **"Obviously, gender is both a biological and social phenomenon," says Ruble. "Researchers now really need to look carefully at the unfolding of biologically driven processes in interaction with social influences during the first three years of life and beyond."**
>
> *Diane Ruble*
> *New York University*

Of the 14 children raised as females, three spontaneously declared they were male at the initial assessment. At the most recent follow-up, six identified as males, while three reported unclear gender identity or would not talk with researchers. The two participants raised as males from birth continued to identify as male throughout the study.

All of the participants exhibited male-typical behavior, such as rough-and-tumble play and having many male friends.

"If you are looking at the genetic and hormonal male, [sexual identity may be] not plastic at all," says Reiner. "And it appears to be primarily influenced by biology."

Some researchers, such as Kenneth J. Zucker, PhD, a psychologist and the head of the child and adolescent gender identity clinic at Toronto's Centre for Addiction and Mental Health, applaud Reiner's study for renewing interest in the biological determinants of gender and calling into question the notion of some that gender identity is mainly socially constructed and determined by socialization.

That's not to say, however, that socialization isn't still a major or important factor, Zucker emphasizes. "The debate is still up in the air because there are other centers who have studied kids with the same diagnosis, and the rate of changeover from female to male is nowhere near what Reiner is reporting," he explains. "It must be something about their social experience that is accounting for this difference."

Contradictory Evidence

Backing Zucker's belief that socialization still plays a major role—and biology is only part of the story—is research by Sheri Berenbaum, PhD, a psychologist at Pennsylvania State University, and J. Michael Bailey, PhD, a psychologist at Northwestern University.

In a study published in the March 2003 issue of the *Journal of Clinical Endocrinology & Metabolism* (Vol. 88, No. 3), they investigated the gender identity of genetic girls born with congenital adrenal hyperplasia (CAH). Girls with this disorder do not produce enough of the hormone cortisol, which causes their adrenal glands to produce an excess of male sex hormones. As a result, they develop in a hormonal environment that's between that of typical boys and typical girls. These girls tend to have ambiguous genitals, and like the infants with cloacal exstrophy, they generally undergo surgery to remake their bodies in the mold of typical females.

The researchers recruited 43 girls with CAH ages 3 to 18 and assessed their gender-typical behaviors and gender identities using a nine-item questionnaire. One question, for example, asks the child if she would take the opportunity to be magically turned into a boy.

In comparison with a control group of normal girls, those with CAH answered questions in a more masculine way. However, when compared with hormonally normal girls who identified as tomboys, they scored closer to typical girls. And few, says Berenbaum, actually identified as male.

"They behave in some ways more like boys, but they self-identify as girls," she explains.

According to Berenbaum, this shows that prenatal hormones, while important determinates of gendered behavior, aren't the only ones.

"Social influences are also pretty important," she says. "I think the interesting question is how biological predisposition affects our socialization experiences."

Diane Ruble, PhD, a New York University psychologist specializing in early childhood gender identity, agrees.

"In Sheri's work, the hormonal exposure has some masculinizing influence on their play behavior," says Ruble. "That may feed into difficulties that children have even if the hormonal exposure prenatally did not actually directly affect their identities as girls or boys."

For example, she says, a girl who discovers that her behavior is slightly masculine may feel more like a typical boy than girl. She may then primarily socialize with boys, leading to even more male-typical behavior.

"Obviously, gender is both a biological and social phenomenon," says Ruble. "Researchers now really need to look carefully at the unfolding of biologically driven processes in interaction with social influences during the first three years of life and beyond."

Further Reading

Berenbaum, S.A., & Bailey, J.M. (2003). Effects on gender identity of prenatal androgens and genital appearance: Evidence from girls with congenital adrenal hyperplasia. *Journal of Clinical Endocrinology and Metabolism, 88,* 1102–1106.

Martin, C.L., & Ruble, D.N. (in press). Children's search for gender cues: Cognitive perspectives on gender development. *Current Directions in Psychological Science.*

Martin, C.L., Ruble, D.N., & Szkrybalo, J. (2002). Cognitive theories of early gender development. *Psychological Bulletin, 128*(6), 903–933.

Reiner, W.G., & Gearhart, J.P. (2004). Discordant sexual identity in some genetic males with cloacal exstrophy assigned to female sex at birth. *The New England Journal of Medicine, 350*(4), 333–341.

Zucker, K. J. (1999). Intersexuality and gender identity differentiation. *Annual Review of Sex Research, 10,* 1–69.

Language and Children's Understanding of Mental States

ABSTRACT—Children progress through various landmarks in their understanding of mind and emotion. They eventually understand that people's actions, utterances, and emotions are determined by their beliefs. Although these insights emerge in all normal children, individual children vary in their rates of progress. Four lines of research indicate that language and conversation play a role in individual development: (a) Children with advanced language skills are better at mental-state understanding than those without advanced language skills, (b) deaf children born into nonsigning families lag in mental-state understanding, and (c) exposure to maternal conversation rich in references to mental states promotes mental-state understanding, as do (d) experimental language-based interventions. Debate centers on the mechanism by which language and conversation help children's understanding of mental states. Three competing interpretations are evaluated here: lexical enrichment (the child gains from acquiring a rich mental-state vocabulary), syntactic enrichment (the child gains from acquiring syntactic tools for embedding one thought in another), and pragmatic enrichment (the child gains from conversations in which varying perspectives on a given topic are articulated). Pragmatic enrichment emerges as the most promising candidate.

PAUL L. HARRIS,[1] MARC DE ROSNAY,[2] AND FRANCISCO PONS[3]

In the past 20 years, a large body of research has shown that normal children progress through a series of landmarks in their understanding of mental states. At around 4 years of age, children understand that people's actions and utterances are guided by their beliefs, whether those beliefs are true or false. At around 5 to 6 years of age, they come to realize that people's emotions are also influenced by their beliefs (Pons, Harris, & de Rosnay, 2003). This gradual acquisition of what is now routinely known as a *theory of mind* can be illustrated with the classic fairy tale of Little Red Riding Hood. When 3-year-olds are told that the wolf is waiting for Little Red Riding Hood, they typically fail to realize that she mistakenly expects to be greeted by her grandmother as she knocks at the cottage door. By contrast, 4- and 5-year-olds understand Little Red Riding Hood's false belief. Yet many 4-year-olds and some 5-year-olds say that when she knocks, she must be afraid of the wolf—the very wolf that she does not know about! By the age of 6 years, however, most children fully grasp Little Red Riding Hood's naiveté. They understand not only that she fails to realize that a wolf is waiting to eat her, but also that she feels no fear.

Children's acquisition of a theory of mind emerges in orderly steps (Wellman & Liu, 2004; Pons et al., 2003), but individual children vary markedly in their rate of progress. In this article, we review four lines of evidence indicating that language and conversation play a key role in helping children develop an understanding of mental states. We then ask about the causal mechanism involved.

Children's Language Skill and Mental-State Understanding

Among normal children and children with autism, accuracy in the attribution of beliefs and emotions has been correlated with language skill (Happe, 1995; Pons, Lawson, Harris, & de Rosnay, 2003). It could be argued that this correlation shows that a theory of mind facilitates language acquisition. However, longitudinal research has offered little support for such an interpretation. Astington and Jenkins (1999) found that preschoolers' theory-of-mind performance was not a predictor of subsequent gains in language. Rather, the reverse was true: Language ability was a good predictor of improvement in theory-of-mind performance. Children with superior language skills—particularly in the domain of syntax—made greater progress over the next 7 months than other children did in their conceptualization of mental states.

Restricted Access to Language: The Case of Deafness

Does a child's access to language, as well as a child's own language skill, affect his or her theory of mind? When children are born deaf, they are often delayed in their access to language, including sign language. Late signers are particularly common among deaf children born to hearing parents because the parents themselves rarely master sign language.

---

[1]Harvard University, [2]Cambridge University, and [3]University of Aalborg, Denmark

Late signers—like children with autism—are markedly delayed in their understanding of mental states. By contrast, deaf children who learn to sign in a home with native signers are comparable to normal children in their performance on theory-of-mind tasks (Peterson & Siegal, 2000).

Even when efforts are made to bypass problems that late signers might have in grasping the language of such tasks—for example, by substituting a nonverbal (Figueras-Costa & Harris, 2001) or pictorial (Woolfe, Want, & Siegal, 2002) test of mental-state understanding—late signers still have marked difficulties. By implication, late-signing children are genuinely delayed in their conceptualization of mental states; it is not simply that they have difficulty in conveying their understanding when the test is given in sign language.

Maternal Conversation and Mental-State Understanding

Two recent studies show that, even when children have normal access to language, mothers vary in their language style and this style appears to affect children's mental-state understanding. Ruffman, Slade, and Crowe (2002) studied mother-child pairs on three occasions when the children ranged from 3 to 4 years of age. On each occasion, they recorded a conversation between mother and child about a picture book and measured the child's theory-of-mind performance and linguistic ability. Mothers' use or nonuse of mental-state language-terms such as *think, know, want,* and *hope*—at earlier time points predicted children's later theory-of-mind performance. Moreover, the reverse pattern did not hold.

The experimental design used in this study allowed the role of maternal conversation to be clarified in important ways. First, it was specifically mental-state references that predicted children's theory-of-mind performance; other aspects of maternal discourse, such as descriptive comments (e.g., "She's riding a bicycle") or causal comments (e.g., "They have no clothes on because they're in the water"), had no impact on children's theory-of-mind performance over and above the effect of mental-state utterances. Second, children's earlier language abilities also predicted their later theory-of-mind performance independently of their mothers' mental-state discourse.

The study by Ruffman et al. (2002) focused on false-belief tasks mastered somewhere between 3 and 4 years of age. We investigated whether mothers' mental-state discourse is linked to children's performance on a more demanding task typically mastered at around 5 or 6 years of age. Recall the story of Little Red Riding Hood: Only around the age of 5 or 6 years do many children realize that Little Red Riding Hood feels no fear of the wolf when she knocks at the door of grandmother's cottage. In a study of children ranging from 4½ to 6 years (de Rosnay, Pons, Harris, & Morrell, 2004), we found that mothers' use of mentalistic terms when describing their children (i.e., references to their children's psychological attributes as opposed to their behavior or physical attributes) and their children's own verbal ability were positively associated not only with correct false-belief attributions, but also with correct

emotion attributions in tasks utilizing stories akin to that of Little Red Riding Hood. Moreover, mothers' mentalistic descriptions predicted children's correct emotion attributions even when the sample was restricted to children who had mastered the simpler false-belief task. So, even after children have mastered the false-belief task, there is still scope for maternal discourse to help the child make further progress in understanding mental states.

Four important conclusions emerge from these studies. First, mothers who talk about psychological themes promote their children's mental-state understanding. Second, it is unlikely that psychologically precocious children prompt more mental-state language in their mothers; rather, the direction of causation is from mother to child. Third, mere talkativeness on the part of a mother does not promote mental-state understanding—it is the mother's psychological language that is critical. Fourth, mothers' psychological orientation has sustained influence: This influence is evident among 3-year-olds and 6-year-olds alike. The effect of maternal language is not restricted to false-belief understanding. It also applies to the later understanding of belief-based emotions.

Language-Based Interventions

So far, we have summarized correlational findings demonstrating a link between language and mental-state understanding. However, experimental language interventions also produce gains in mental-state understanding. In one study, Lohmann and Tomasello (2003) pretested a large group of 3-year-olds. Those who failed a standard test of false-belief received various types of intervention and were then retested using other false-belief tasks. The most effective intervention for improving children's understanding of false belief combined two factors: (a) the presentation of a series of objects, some of which had a misleading appearance (e.g., an object that looked initially like a flower but turned out to be a pen); and (b) verbal comments on what people would say, think, and know about the perceptible properties and actual identity of these objects. Hale and Tager-Flusberg (2003) also found that language-based interventions were effective in improving children's false-belief understanding. In one intervention, children discussed story protagonists who held false beliefs. In a second intervention, they discussed story protagonists who made false claims. In each case, the children were given corrective verbal feedback if they misstated what the protagonists thought or said. Both interventions proved very effective in promoting 3-year-olds' grasp of false belief.

These intervention studies confirm that conversation about people's thoughts or statements has a powerful effect on children's understanding of belief. One additional finding underscores the critical role of conversation. When Lohmann and Tomasello (2003) presented children with various misleading objects but offered minimal verbal comment—other than a request to look at the objects—the impact on children's mental-state understanding was negligible.

How Does Language Help?

Given the converging evidence just described, the claim that language makes a difference for children's developing theory of mind is convincing. Not only do children's own language abilities predict their rate of progress in understanding the mind, but their access to conversation, especially conversation rich in mentalistic words and concepts, is an equally potent and independent predictor.

Despite this solid evidence for the role of language, there is disagreement over how exactly it helps. Consider the type of comments that a mother might make as she and her preschool child look at a picture book—"I think it's a cat" or "I don't know whether it's a dog" (Ruffman et al., 2002, p. 740). It could be argued that such comments help the child develop an understanding of mental states because the words think and know draw the child's attention to mental processes. But there are other possible explanations. For example, such comments are also syntactically distinctive: They embed a proposition ("… it's a cat" or "… whether it's a dog") in another clause containing a mental verb ("I think …" or "I don't know… "). Mastery of the way propositions can be embedded in other clauses might help children to conceptualize mental states that take particular states of affairs as their target. Mental-state understanding often calls for an appreciation of the way in which a mental state such as a thought, a belief, or a hope is targeted at a particular state of affairs. But also, such comments play a role in the pragmatics of conversation. More specifically, they set out a claim (e.g., "… it's a cat") and they convey the particular perspective of the speaker toward that claim. Accordingly, such comments might underline the way people can vary in the mental stance or perspective they adopt toward a given claim. In short, mentalistic comments contain distinctive words (e.g., *think* and *know*), grammatical constructions (e.g., embedded propositions), and pragmatic features (e.g., the enunciation of individual perspectives). Which factor is critical? It is too early to draw firm conclusions, but the evidence increasingly points to the importance of pragmatic features.

First, two recent studies with children speaking languages other than English suggest that the syntax of embedded propositions is not the reason why language skill correlates with theory-of-mind understanding. In German, *want* sentences such as "Mother wants George to go to bed" must be rendered with a *that* proposition—"Mutter will, dass George ins Bett geht" (literally, "Mother wants that George into the bed goes"). Perner, Sprung, Zauner, and Haider (2003) studied whether early exposure to, and understanding of, the *want–that* structure is associated with good performance on standard theory-of-mind tasks, but they found no evidence supporting such a relationship. Similarly, a study of Cantonese-speaking children failed to uncover any link between mastery of verbs that can serve to embed another proposition and theory-of-mind understanding, once general language competence had been taken into account (Cheung et al., 2004).

Second, our findings (de Rosnay et al., 2004) make both the lexical and the syntactic explanations problematic. Maternal usage of terms like think and know together with their embedded propositions might plausibly help children to understand false beliefs because when they attribute a false belief to someone

children will need to use the same linguistic constructions. For example, to describe Little Red Riding Hood's mistaken belief, it is appropriate to say: "She thinks that it's her grandmother" or "She doesn't know that it's a wolf." However, the attribution of emotion, including belief-based emotion, does not call for the use of mental-state terms with embedded propositions. It simply calls for appropriate use of particular emotion terms. "Little Red Riding Hood felt happy as she knocked at the cottage." Yet we found that mothers' mental discourse not only helped children understand false beliefs, but also helped them move on to understand belief-based emotions. An emphasis on pragmatics can readily explain this twofold impact: Mothers disposed to talk about varying individual beliefs regarding a given situation will probably also articulate the feelings that flow from those individual beliefs.

Conclusions

People often observe other people's facial expressions and bodily postures for clues to their mental life. Indeed, a great deal of research on the early development of a theory of mind has focused on infants' skill at interpreting these nonverbal clues. However, in contrast to any other species, human beings are also able to talk to each other about their mental lives. They can talk about their feelings, compare their beliefs, and share their plans and intentions.

The research reviewed here shows that such conversations play a key role in helping children to make sense of mental states. We are on the brink of designing longitudinal and intervention studies that will help us determine just how conversation helps children in this endeavor. So far, research on children's mental-state understanding has mainly focused on the milestone of understanding false beliefs. We have shown here, however, that maternal discourse is also linked with how well children attribute belief-based emotions to other people, and specifically that this link holds true even among children who have already mastered false beliefs.

In the future, it will be important to study various other milestones in children's mental-state understanding. For example, only around age 5 or 6 do children understand that the emotions people actually feel may not correspond to the emotions that they express. Also, it is not until middle childhood that children fully understand self-conscious emotions such as guilt—or understand that it is possible to feel conflicting emotions about the same situation. In the future, researchers can focus on these developmental advances to better understand the influence of parents' conversation on children's mental-state understanding. If it is found that the same type of parental conversation style (e.g., coherent psychological discourse) has a pervasive influence across different aspects of mental-state understanding, then it will become less likely that specific lexical or semantic features of discourse are the crucial factor. Instead, as we have noted, it will be more plausible to assume that some parents elucidate a variety of mental states in conversation with their children. That elucidation is not tied to particular lexical terms or syntactic constructions. Instead, it reflects a wide-ranging sensitivity to individual perspectives and nurtures that same sensitivity in children.

Researchers may also consider the implications of mental-state understanding for children's behavior and social relationships. An increasing body of evidence indicates that good performance on theory-of-mind tasks is correlated with the ability to form relationships with peers (Pons, Harris, & Doudin, 2002). A plausible—but as yet untested—interpretation is that children's mental-state understanding helps them both to initiate and to maintain friendships. This hypothesis can be tested by assessing the impact of a discourse-based intervention not just on children's mental-state understanding, but also on their relationships with peers.

Finally, researchers may look forward to an important bridge between developmental and clinical psychology. The mother who is alert to her child's mental states, who accurately puts thoughts and feelings into words, and who nurtures her child's sensitivity to different mental perspectives may have an effect on her child that is not unlike that of a clinician or therapist who fosters a reflective stance in his or her patients.

Recommended Readings

Astington, J.A., & Baird, J. (Eds.). (2005). *Why language matters for theory of mind*. New York: Oxford University Press.

de Rosnay, M., Pons, F., Harris, P.L., & Morrell, J. (2004). (See References)

Harris, P.L. (1996). Desires, beliefs and language. In P. Carruthers & P.K. Smith (Eds.), *Theories of theories of mind* (pp. 200–220). Cambridge, England: Cambridge University Press.

Harris, P.L. (2000). Understanding emotion. In M. Lewis & J. Haviland-Jones (Eds.), *Handbook of emotions* (2nd ed., pp. 281–292). New York: Guildford Press.

Peterson, C.C., & Siegal, M. (2000). (See References)

References

Astington, J.W., & Jenkins, J.M. (1999). A longitudinal study of the relation between language and theory-of-mind development. *Developmental Psychology*, *35*, 1311–1320.

Cheung, H., Hsuan-Chih, C., Creed, N., Ng, L., Wang, S.P, & Mo, L. (2004). Relative roles of general and complementation language in theory-of-mind development: Evidence from Cantonese and English. *Child Development*, *75*, 1155–1170.

de Rosnay, M., Pons, F., Harris, P.L., & Morrell, J. (2004). A lag between understanding false belief and emotion attribution in young children: Relationships with linguistic ability and mothers' mental state language. *British Journal of Developmental Psychology*, *22*, 197–218.

Figueras-Costa, B., & Harris, P.L. (2001). Theory of mind in deaf children: A non-verbal test of false belief understanding. *Journal of Deaf Studies and Deaf Education*, *6*, 92–102.

Hale, C.M., & Tager-Flusberg, H. (2003). The influence of language on theory of mind: A training study. *Developmental Science, 6*, 346–359.

Happé, F.G.E. (1995). The role of age and verbal ability in the theory of mind task performance of subjects with autism. *Child Development*, *66*, 843–855.

Lohmann, H., & Tomasello, M. (2003). The role of language in the development of false belief understanding: A training study. *Child Development, 74*, 1130–1144.

Perner, J., Sprung, M., Zauner, P., & Haider, H. (2003). Want that is understood well before say that, think that, and false belief: A test of de Villiers's linguistic determinism on German-speaking children. *Child Development, 74*, 179–188.

Peterson, C.C., & Siegal, M. (2000). Insights into theory of mind from deafness and autism. *Mind and Language, 15*, 123–145.

Pons, F., Harris, P.L., & Doudin, P.-A. (2002). Teaching emotion understanding. *European Journal of Psychology of Education, 17*, 293–304.

Pons, F., Harris, P.L., & de Rosnay, M. (2003). Emotion comprehension between 3 and 11 years: Developmental periods and hierarchical organization. *European Journal of Developmental Psychology, 2*, 127–152.

Pons, F., Lawson, J., Harris, P.L., & de Rosnay, M. (2003). Individual differences in children's emotion understanding: Effects of age and language. *Scandinavian Journal of Psychology, 44*, 347–353.

Ruffman, T., Slade, L., & Crowe, E. (2002). The relation between children's and mothers' mental state language and theory-of-mind understanding. *Child Development, 73*, 734–751.

Wellman, H.M., & Liu, D. (2004). Scaling of theory of mind tasks. *Child Development, 75*, 523–541.

Woolfe, T., Want, S.C., & Siegal, M. (2002). Signposts to development: Theory-of-mind in deaf children. *Child Development, 73*, 768–778.

From *Current Directions in Psychological Science,* Vol. 14, no. 2, February 2005, pp. 69-73. Copyright © 2005 by Association for Psychological Science. Reprinted by permission of Blackwell Publishing, Ltd. **www.blackwell-synergy.com**

A Deeper Sense of Literacy

Curriculum-Driven Approaches to Media Literacy in the K-12 Classroom

Media literacy can be used effectively as a pedagogical approach for teaching core content across the K-12 curriculum, thus meeting the needs of both teachers and students by promoting critical thinking, communication, and technology skills. This article focuses on the work of Project Look Sharp at Ithaca College, a media literacy initiative working primarily with school districts in upstate New York. Basic principles and best practices for using a curriculum-driven approach are described, with specific examples from social studies, English/language arts, math, science, health, and art, along with methods of assessment used to address effectiveness in the classroom.

CYNTHIA L. SCHEIBE
Ithaca College

One hundred elementary school students are chattering loudly as they walk back up the snowy hill to their school, coming from the local movie theater where they have just been treated to a special holiday showing of the movie *Antz*. The children are not just excited about seeing the movie; they have spent the past 2 weeks in their science class learning about ants and other insects, and now they are calling out examples of ways in which the movie misrepresented true ants. "Ants don't have teeth!" calls one boy. "Who were all those boy ants?" a girl asks. "I thought almost all ants were girls!" Her teacher nods and confirms that nearly all soldier and worker ants are sterile females.

Back in their classrooms, the students and teachers list the ways in which the ants were portrayed correctly (with six legs, three body segments, living in tunneled, communities, carrying large loads) and incorrectly (talking, wearing clothes, with white eyes, etc.). The teachers take time to correct any misperceptions and to reinforce accurate information and then lead a discussion about why the moviemakers showed ants in ways that were not true, "Because they didn't know any better?" proposes one girl. "Because they wanted them to look like people!" suggests another. "It would be boring if they couldn't talk and just ran around like ants!"

This type of curriculum-driven approach to media literacy is at the heart of our work with K-12 teachers at Project Look Sharp, a collaborative initiative of the teacher education, psychology, and communications programs at Ithaca College. As many theorists have noted (e.g., Hobbs, 1997), media literacy is a logical extension of traditional literacy: learning to "read" visual and audiovisual messages as well as text-based ones, recognizing the basic "language" used in each media form, being able to judge the credibility and accuracy of information presented in different formats, evaluating the "author's" intent and meaning, appreciating the techniques used to persuade and convey emotion, and being able to communicate effectively through different media forms. Media literacy, then, incorporates many elements from multiple literacies that are already central to today's education, including information literacy, computer literacy, scientific literacy, and cultural literacy. In addition, media literacy builds critical-thinking, communication, and technology skills and is an effective way to address different learning styles and an appreciation for multiple perspectives.

Before building media literacy into a curriculum unit, it is essential for teachers to have some basic training in media literacy theory and analysis (through staff development workshops and trainings). Project Look Sharp encourages teachers to weave the core elements of media literacy into their teaching practice early in the school year (see Best Practices below). We then work directly with individual teachers (or teams of teachers) to develop unique media literacy lessons that will help teach core content required by their districts and the state. We always start with core content (rather than the media literacy aspects), keeping in mind the teacher's own goals and needs, with a focus on basic learning standards for their grade and curriculum area.

Sometimes we are asked by school administrators to develop a series of lessons or resources to address a particular issue or need. For example, the second-grade social studies curriculum in New York State includes teaching about rural, urban, and suburban communities, and teachers were having a hard time conveying those concepts to 7- and 8-year-old children. Working with the teachers, we developed a series of lessons based on collective reading of historical pictures and short clips from television shows reflecting the three types of communities. Students from rural, urban, and suburban elementary schools then produced digital videos about their own communities and shared them with classes from the other schools. Students were surprised to find that there were many similarities in their videos (they all included lire stations, for example), and that some of the stereotypes they held about different types of communities were not true. Although this was a great deal of work, the unit went far beyond simply teaching the desired social studies and media literacy lessons by building (or reinforcing) a host of other social and organizational skills.

This approach has been surprisingly effective, not just in increasing the students' interest in a particular topic but also in deepening their understanding of the information itself. Teachers who gave a test about insects following the *Antz* movie found that students performed best on questions that related to the discussion of accuracy in the movie (e.g., the physical characteristics of insects), and that even 6 months later—at the end of the school year-most students remembered that information accurately.

By emphasizing media literacy as a pedagogical approach rather than a separate content or skill area, we have been able to help teachers multitask. We have also found that once teachers have developed an awareness themselves of the basic concepts and practices of media literacy, they begin to see opportunities for incorporating media literacy into their classrooms on an ongoing basis. For example, teachers whose classes were going to see *Antz* took a few minutes to explain the concept of "product placements" and told the students that they would be seeing some product placements in the film. When the first bottle of Pepsi appeared in the scene of Insectopia, there was a shout from the children in the audience—"Product placement!"—and students continued to identify product placements in videos and other media for the remainder of the school year.

In using a curriculum-driven approach, teachers sometimes take a narrow focus for a particular topic or lesson (e.g., linking current advertising appeals to a sixth-grade unit on Greek myths) or weave media literacy into ongoing activities in their classrooms (e.g., in a weekly discussion of current events). Sometimes media literacy is used to link several different parts of the curriculum together (e.g., investigating local history and literature through examining original documents at a local museum). And sometimes the production aspect of media literacy is used creatively to convey information to parents and administrators (e.g., fourth-grade students' producing a video to illustrate a typical school day for their parents to watch at open house).

This, of course, is not the only way to approach media literacy education. Students benefit greatly from specific lessons or courses focusing solely on media literacy, media production, and other media-related issues. But our experience has shown that this is rarely possible in the public school system, especially with the increasing focus on tests and a "back to basics" approach. For many teachers, finding even a few days to devote to media literacy is problematic; they are already swamped with core-content requirements they must teach. Even with a growing emphasis on technology skills and critical thinking, there are still only seven states that mandate media literacy as a separate strand in their state standards (Baker, 2004), and even those slates have had difficulty grappling with how to assess media literacy as part of standardized state testing.

Kubey and Raker (2000) have noted, however, that nearly all states do refer to aspects of media literacy education as part of the mandated state standards, although they do not typically use the phrase *media literacy*. In New York, for example, media literacy is clearly reflected in requirements that students "evaluate importance, reliability and credibility of evidence" (Social Studies Standard 1, No. 4) and "comprehend, interpret and critique texts in every medium" (English Standard 2, No. 1). In California, social studies standards for Grades 9 through 12 specifically refer to evaluating "the role of electronic, broadcast, print media, and the Internet as means of communication in American politics" and "how public officials use the media to communicate with the citizenry and to shape public opinion" (Kubey & Baker, 2000, p. 9). Many states include specific references to media issues in their health standards, especially related to tobacco and alcohol use, nutrition, and body image.

In taking a curriculum-driven approach to media literacy integration, it is crucial to explicitly lay out these connections between media literacy and state or district learning standards. Teachers then feel more comfortable about taking class time to teach the basics of media literacy and to weave a media literacy approach into their overall teaching practice. Media literacy can also be used to develop "parallel tasks" for students to build and practice their skills in analyzing information from different sources, listening and taking notes, and supporting their opinions with evidence in written essays—all of which are key components in standardized testing.

Best Practices For Using Media Literacy In the K-12 Classroom

Various writers have described key concepts of media literacy (e.g., Hobbs, 1997) and basic questions to ask about any media message (e.g., Thoman, 1999). We have found the following set of questions to work well with students from elementary school through college:

1. Who made—and who sponsored—this message, and what is their purpose?
2. Who is the target audience and how is the message specifically tailored to that audience?
3. What are the different techniques used to inform, persuade, entertain, and attract attention?
4. What messages are communicated (and/or implied) about certain people, places, events, behaviors, lifestyles, and so forth?
5. How current, accurate, and credible is the information in this message?
6. What is left out of this message that might be important to know?

Introducing these questions at the beginning of the school year as standard practice for evaluating any information or image that is part of the classroom experience promotes general critical-thinking and analysis skills. Other best practices include the following:

- Beginning the school year or the exploration of a new unit by developing an *information plan* in consultation with the students. What types of media and other information sources will the class be using? Where could students go for information on a particular topic, and what might be the strengths and weaknesses of each source? This overlays media literacy questions on the typical K-W-L pedagogical approach to teaching a new topic: What do you already *know* about this topic and where did you learn about it? What do you *want* to know, and where could you find out about it? Reflecting back at the end of the unit, what did you *learn*, and what sources were most (and least) useful?

- Encouraging students to pay attention to both print and visual elements in media sources, noting information that can be learned from the images themselves. This includes, or course, attending to the images in their textbooks. The painting of DeSoto's *Discovery of the Mississippi* shown in Figure 1, for example, is often included in history texts at both the elementary and secondary levels and makes for a fascination collective reading by students in history or art classes. (Which one is DeSoto, and how do you know? What makes him seem powerful? How are the Native Americans portrayed? Who commissioned the painting, and why? Who painted it, and how did they know about the events that took place?)

- For any media source (including textbooks, videos, and Web sites), making sure the students know who wrote or produced it and when it was produced or published. If appropriate, discuss the implications for its usefulness in your current exploration. (What perspectives might be included or left out? What information might be out of date?)

- Training students to learn from videos (and other traditionally entertaining forms of media) in the same way that they learn from teachers, books, and other sources. When showing videos or films in the classroom, show only short segments at a time rather than the full film without interruption, leaving the lights on—if possible—to facilitate active viewing and discussion. Before showing a video, let the students know what things they should he looking and listening for. If appropriate, encourage students to take notes and to raise their hands during a video if they do not understand something they saw or heard.

- Building elements of media production into the classroom experience by

  encouraging students to scan or download images into reports and term papers, making sure that they use images as part of the research process by including captions and citing the appropriate sources.

  providing options for individual or small group presentations such as using PowerPoint, audio or videotape, or desktop publishing.

  emphasizing an awareness of the six media literacy questions as part of the production process (e.g., What is *your* purpose? Who is *your* target audience? What information will *you* leave out, and how will that bias *your* message?).

Basic Principles for Curriculum Integration

In working with a range of teachers and curriculum areas, we have also developed 12 basic principles for integrating media literacy and critical thinking into the K-12 curriculum (Scheibe & Rogow, 2004). Discussions of 4 of these principles follow.

Identify erroneous beliefs about a topic fostered by media content. This is particularly relevant to curricular areas that emphasize "facts," such as science and social studies. Even young students bring existing assumptions and expectations to the classroom situation, and it is critical to examine those assumptions with the students to correct misperceptions and identify the media sources involved. Many adults, for example, believe that tarantulas are deadly or that lemmings follow each other blindly and commit mass suicide by jumping off cliffs into the sea. Both of these erroneous beliefs have been reinforced by the media, such as the 1957 Disney movie *White Wilderness* that showed lemmings falling off cliffs into the sea (they were actually herded off the cliffs by the production crew off camera: see **http://www.snopes.com/disney/films/lemmings.htm**).

Develop all awareness of issues of credibility and bias In the media. This is critical in evaluating how any information is presented and has increased in importance with the rise of the Internet as the dominant source of information students now use in preparing papers and reports. It also applies to math, especially with respect to media reports of statistics (particularly in misleading graphs in advertisements). Although math teachers already emphasize the importance of having both the x-axis and y-axis correctly labeled, for example, a media literacy approach would go beyond that to ask why those producing the graph (or reporting the statistics) would leave out such important information.

Compare the ways different media present information about a topic. Many English/language arts teachers have students compare the same story or play when presented in different media formats or by different directors. Approaching this from a media literacy perspective, the teacher might ask the basic six questions about each presentation, comparing the purposes and target audiences of each and identifying what is left out—and what is added—in each case and why. The same principle can be applied easily to the study of current events at nearly any grade level. Instead of having students cut out newspaper articles reporting three different events, for example, a teacher could have students identify one event that is reported in three different sources (e.g., English language versions of newspapers from different countries). The resulting report about the event would then draw from all three sources and could include an analysis of how the three sources differed and why.

Use media as an assessment tool. There are a number of ways to use media as part of authentic assessment at the end of a curriculum unit. For example, students can be shown an advertisement, a news article, or a short video clip and asked to identify information that is accurate (or inaccurate) in what they see (e.g., showing a clip from the movie *Twister* following a unit on tornadoes or a news report on the results of a political poll following a unit on statistics). Students can also work in small groups to produce their own media messages (e.g., a newspaper article, an advertisement a digital video) illustrating their knowledge and/or opinion on a topic.

Resources and Curriculum Materials

There are many excellent media literacy resources and materials that can be used within the context of teaching core content in K-12 education. Some media literacy curricula are designed with clear links to many subject areas, such as *Assignment: Media Literacy*, which was developed in line with Maryland state learning standards and features connections to language arts, social studies, math, health, and the arts (Hobbs, 2000). Other materials are excellent resources when using a media literacy approach to a specific subject area, such as *Past Imperfect: History According to Movies* (Carnes, 1995). There are several good Web analysis resources. The two we have found most useful for teachers and librarians are both online: Canada's Web-awareness site (**http://www.mediaawareness.ca/english/special_initiatives/web_awareness/**) and Alan November's site (**http://www.ano-vember.com/infolitlindex.html**). One outstanding resource for curriculum-driven media literacy lesson plans and ideas is Frank Baker's Media Literacy Clearinghouse Web site (**http://www.med.sc.edu: 1081/**).

Project Look Sharp has recently begun developing. a series of media literacy kits that take a curriculum-driven approach. The first of these kits, *Media Construction of War: A Critical Reading of History* (Sperry, 2003), uses slides, print, and video materials to teach core historical information about the Vietnam War, the Gulf War of 1991, and the War in Afghanistan following Sept. 11, 2001. After students read short histories of each war, teachers lead collective readings of each image, discussing the overt and implied messages in each and relating the images back to core content that is part of their history curriculum. Among the multiple assessments included in the kit, students are asked to compare these three images of the opposition leaders during each war, discussing who each figure was and how each is portrayed by *Newsweek*.

Evaluation and Assessment

Project Look Sharp has begun conducting empirical studies of the effectiveness of media literacy integration using this type or curriculum-driven approach (reported elsewhere). Some of these studies involve pretest/posttest designs collecting data directly from the students, and some involve assessments of student-produced work. From a program evaluation standpoint, how-

ever, we have found it most useful to solicit qualitative feedback from the teachers themselves. They repeatedly say that media literacy lessons evoke active participation on the part of students, especially students who are nontraditional learners or disenfranchised for other reasons. Teachers also report that after adopting a media literacy approach to teach specific core content, they gradually find themselves weaving media literacy into other aspects of their pedagogy. As one teacher put it, "Oh, I see. You're trying to get us to change teaching practice!"

We also sometimes send home questionnaires to parents of students who have participated in a media literacy lesson or unit to assess what we call the "trickle up" effect—when students come home and talk about what they have learned and even change their behaviors related to media issues. Some parents have said that the "media literacy stuff is the only thing their child has talked about related to school all year; many say their children raise media literacy questions when they are watching television or reading newspapers at home.

We believe that it is this ability for media literacy to empower students in so many ways that, in the end, will lead to its growth and stability in K-12 education. By meeting the needs of teachers and administrators, of parents, and of the students themselves, we can indeed foster a deeper sense of literacy in our children.

References

Baker, F. (2004). State standards, *Media literacy clearinghouse*. Retrieved February 24, 2004, from **http://www.med.sc.edu:1081/statelit.htm**

Carnes, M. C. (Ed.). (1995). *Past imperfect: History according to the movies*. New York: Henry Holt.

Hobbs, R. (1997). Expanding the concept of literacy. In R. Kubey (Ed.), *Media literacy in the information aged* (pp. 163–183). New Brunswick, NJ: Transaction.

Hobbs, R. (2000). *Assignment: Media literacy*. Bethesda, MD: Discovery Communications.

Kubey, R., & Baker, F. (2000). Has media literacy found a curricular foothold? *Telemedium, The Journal of Media Literacy, 46*(Spring), 8–9, 30.

Scheibe, C., & Rogow, F. (2004). *12 basic principles for incorporating media literacy and critical thinking into any curriculum* (2nd ed.). Ithaca, NY: Project Look Sharp—Ithaca College.

Sperry, C. (2003). *Media construction of war: A critical reading of history*, Ithaca, NY: Project Look Sharp—Ithaca College.

Thoman, E. (1999). Skills and strategies for media education, *Educational Leadership, 46*(February), 50–54.

Cynthia L. Scheibe, Ph.D., *is an associate professor in developmental psychology at Ithaca College. She is the director of the Center for Research on the Effects of Television, which she founded with John Condry at Cornell University in 1983. She is also the executive director of Project Look Sharp, a media literacy initiative of Ithaca College, providing support, resources, and training for K-12 teachers and support staff to integrate media literacy and critical thinking across the curriculum.*

From *American Behavioral Scientist*, September 2004, pp. 60–68. Copyright © 2004 by Sage Publications. Reprinted by permission. **www.sagepub.co.uk**

Parental School Involvement and Children's Academic Achievement

Pragmatics and Issues

ABSTRACT—Developing collaborations between families and schools to promote academic success has a long-standing basis in research and is the focus of numerous programs and policies. We outline some of the mechanisms through which parental school involvement affects achievement and identify how patterns and amounts of involvement vary across cultural, economic, and community contexts and across developmental levels. We propose next steps for research, focusing on the importance of considering students' developmental stages, the context in which involvement takes place, and the multiple perspectives through which involvement may be assessed. Finally, we discuss enhancing involvement in diverse situations.

NANCY E. HILL[1] AND LORRAINE C. TAYLOR[2]
[1]*Duke University and* [2]*University of North Carolina*

Families and schools have worked together since the beginning of formalized schooling. However, the nature of the collaboration has evolved over the years (Epstein & Sanders, 2002). Initially, families maintained a high degree of control over schooling by controlling hiring of teachers and apprenticeships in family businesses. By the middle of the 20th century, there was strict role separation between families and schools. Schools were responsible for academic topics, and families were responsible for moral, cultural, and religious education. In addition, family and school responsibilities for education were sequential. That is, families were responsible for preparing their children with the necessary skills in the early years, and schools took over from there with little input from families. However, today, in the context of greater accountability and demands for children's achievement, schools and families have formed partnerships and share the responsibilities for children's education. Parental school involvement is largely defined as consisting of the following activities: volunteering at school, communicating with teachers and other school personnel, assisting in academic activities at home, and attending school events, meetings of parent-teacher associations (PTAs), and parent-teacher conferences.

It is well established that parental school involvement has a positive influence on school-related outcomes for children. Consistently, cross-sectional (e.g., Grolnick & Slowiaczek, 1994) and longitudinal (e.g., Miedel & Reynolds, 1999) studies have demonstrated an association between higher levels of parental school involvement and greater academic success for children and adolescents. For young children, parental school involvement is associated with early school success, including academic and language skills and social competence (Grolnick & Slowiaczek, 1994; Hill, 2001; Hill & Craft, 2003). Head Start, the nation's largest intervention program for at-risk children, emphasizes the importance of parental involvement as a critical feature of children's early academic development because parental involvement promotes positive academic experiences for children and has positive effects on parents' self-development and parenting skills.

Most of the literature focuses on parental school involvement in elementary schools. Parental school involvement is thought to decrease as children move to middle and high school, in part because parents may believe that they cannot assist with more challenging high school subjects and because adolescents are becoming autonomous (Eccles & Harold, 1996). However, few parents stop caring about or monitoring the academic progress of their children of high school age, and parental involvement remains an important predictor of school outcomes through adolescence. For example, one study demonstrated that parental school involvement was associated with adolescents' achievement and future aspirations across middle and high school (Hill et al., in press). Moreover, although direct helping with homework declines in adolescence, parental school involvement during middle and high school is associated with an increase in the amount of time students spend on homework and with an increase in the percentage of homework completed (Epstein & Sanders, 2002).

How Does Parental School Involvement Make A Difference?

There are two major mechanisms by which parental school involvement promotes achievement. The first is by increasing social capital. That is, parental school involvement increases parents' skills and information (i.e., social capital), which makes them better equipped to assist their children in their school-related activities. As parents establish relationships with school personnel, they learn important information about the school's expectations for behavior and homework; they also learn how to help with homework and how to augment children's learning at home (Lareau, 1996). When parents are involved in their children's schooling, they meet other parents who provide information and insight on school policies and practices, as well as extracurricular activities. Parents learn from other parents which teachers are the best and how difficult situations have been handled successfully. In addition, when parents and teachers interact, teachers learn about parents' expectations for their children and their children's teachers. Baker and Stevenson (1986) found that compared with parents who were not involved, involved parents developed more complex strategies for working with schools and their children to promote achievement.

Social control is a second mechanism through which parental school involvement promotes achievement. Social control occurs when families and schools work together to build a consensus about appropriate behavior that can be effectively communicated to children at both home and school (McNeal, 1999). Parents' coming to know one another and agree on goals—both behavioral and academic—serves as a form of social constraint that reduces problem behaviors. When children and their peers receive similar messages about appropriate behavior across settings and from different sources, the messages become clear and salient, reducing confusion about expectations. Moreover, when families do not agree with each other or with schools about appropriate behavior, the authority and effectiveness of teachers, parents, or other adults may be undermined. Through both social capital and social control, children receive messages about the importance of schooling, and these messages increase children's competence, motivation to learn, and engagement in school (Grolnick & Slowiaczek, 1994).

Family and School Characteristics That Influence Parental School Involvement

Parent-school relationships do not occur in isolation, but in community and cultural contexts. One of the biggest challenges schools have today is the increasing diversity among students (Lichter, 1996). Demographic characteristics, such as socioeconomic status, ethnicity, and cultural background, and other parental characteristics are systematically associated with parental school involvement. Overall, parents from higher socioeconomic backgrounds are more likely to be involved in schooling than parents of lower socioeconomic status. A higher education level of parents is positively associated with a greater tendency for them to advocate for their children's placement in honors courses and actively manage their children's education (Baker & Stevenson, 1986). In contrast, parents from lower socioeconomic backgrounds face many more barriers to involvement, including nonflexible work schedules, lack of resources, transportation problems, and stress due to residing in disadvantaged neighborhoods. Finally, because parents in lower-socioeconomic families often have fewer years of education themselves and potentially harbor more negative experiences with schools, they often feel ill equipped to question the teacher or school (Lareau, 1996). It is unfortunate that parents with children who would most benefit from parental involvement often find it most difficult to become and remain involved.

Involvement in school sometimes varies across ethnic or cultural backgrounds as well. Often, teachers who are different culturally from their students are less likely to know the students and parents than are teachers who come from similar cultural backgrounds; culturally different teachers are also more likely to believe that students and parents are disinterested or uninvolved in schooling (Epstein & Dauber, 1991). One study found that teachers believed that those parents who volunteered at school valued education more than other parents, and this belief about parents' values was in turn associated with the teachers' ratings of students' academic skills and achievement (Hill & Craft, 2003). Parental school involvement seems to function differently or serve different purposes in different ethnic and cultural groups. For example, African American parents often are more involved in school-related activities at home than at school, whereas Euro-American parents often are more involved in the actual school setting than at home (Eccles & Harold, 1996). This tendency to be more involved at home than at school may be especially true for ethnic minorities whose primary language is not English. Among African American kindergartners, parental involvement at school is associated with enhanced academic skills, perhaps reflecting the role of social capital (Hill & Craft, 2003), and the influence of parental involvement in schooling on achievement is stronger for African Americans than Euro-Americans among adolescents (Hill et al., in press).

Apart from demographic factors, parents' psychological state influences parental school involvement. Depression or anxiety present barriers to involvement in schooling. Studies consistently show that mothers who are depressed tend to be less involved than nondepressed mothers in preparing young children for school and also exhibit lower levels of involvement over the early years of school.

Self-perceptions also affect parents' school involvement. Negative feelings about themselves may hinder parents from making connections with their children's schools. Parents' confidence in their own intellectual abilities is the most salient predictor of their school involvement (Eccles & Harold, 1996). A factor that may be especially important in this regard is the experience of poverty. Poverty exerts direct effects on parents' mental health and self-perceptions through increased stress resulting from the struggle to make ends meet. Poverty also has indirect effects on children's early school outcomes because its adverse effects on parents are in turn associated with lower parental involvement in school.

Parents' own experiences as students shape their involvement in their children's schooling. As a parent prepares a child to start school, the parent's memories of his or her own school experiences are likely to become reactivated and may influence how the parent interprets and directs the child's school experiences (Taylor, Clayton, & Rowley, in press). Memories of supportive school experiences are likely to enhance parents' involvement and comfort interacting with their children's school.

In addition to characteristics of the parent and family, the school's context and policies influence parental school involvement. Teachers' encouragement of such involvement is associated with greater competence among parents in their interactions with their children and more parental involvement in academic activities at home (Epstein & Dauber, 1991). There is increasing recognition of the importance of promoting *schools'* readiness for children (Pianta, Cox, Taylor, & Early, 1999). "Ready schools" (Pianta et al., 1999) reach out to families, building relationships between families and the school setting before the first day of school. The success of teachers' and schools' efforts to encourage parental school involvement suggests that parents want and will respond to information about assisting their children. For example, LaParo, Kraft-Sayre, and Pianta (2003) found that the vast majority of families were willing to participate in school-initiated kindergarten-transition activities. These practices were associated with greater involvement across subsequent school years, underscoring the importance of school-based activities that encourage family-school links.

Key Issues for Research

The most significant advances in the research on parental school involvement have arisen from the recognition that context is important and there are multiple dimensions to parental school involvement. Whether parental school involvement occurs because a child is having problems in school or because of ongoing positive dialogue between parents and school makes a difference in how involvement influences children's academic outcomes (Hill, 2001). For example, a parent who volunteers in the classroom to learn more about the teacher's expectations for students and a parent who volunteers in the classroom to monitor the teacher's behavior toward her child are both involved in the school, but only the latter parent is likely to create distrust that may impact the children's attitudes toward the school and the teacher.

Parental school involvement does not reflect just one set of activities. Such diverse activities as volunteering in the classroom, communicating with the teacher, participating in academic-related activities at home, communicating the positive value of education, and participating in the parent-teacher relationship are all included in parental school involvement, and each is related to school performance (Epstein & Sanders, 2002; Hill & Craft, 2003). Research on parental school involvement is taking these diverse factors into account.

Despite the recent advances in conceptualizing and studying parental school involvement, there are still challenges. First, the

multidimensional nature of parental school involvement has led to a lack of agreement about definitions and to measurement inconsistencies, making it difficult to compare findings across studies. In addition, whereas research typically examines the relations between types of parental involvement and achievement, the types of parental involvement may influence each other. For example, a high-quality parent-teacher relationship may strengthen the positive impact of a parent's home involvement on achievement. And volunteering at school may lead to an increase in the communicated value of education or change the way parents become involved at home. Issues concerning the reciprocal relations among different types of involvement have yet to be addressed.

The second research challenge is integrating various perspectives. Whom should we survey when assessing parental school involvement? Parents? Teachers? Students? Is one perspective more accurate than another perspective? In fact, multiple perspectives are important for understanding parental school involvement. Although few studies have examined the influence of different perspectives on our understanding of parental school involvement, some studies found that teachers', children's, and parents' reports of parental school involvement were only moderately correlated, but each was related to achievement, suggesting that each perspective is unique and important (Hill et al., in press). The vast majority of research on parental school involvement, like parenting research, is based on mothers' involvement. What are the roles of fathers and other relatives? Does involvement of other family members vary according to demographic background?

Some research suggests that teachers' or parents' perspectives may be biased. Teachers often evaluate African American and low-income families more negatively than Euro-American and higher-income families (Epstein & Dauber, 1991). Moreover, teachers who are not particularly supportive of parental school involvement may tend to prejudge minority or low-income parents (Epstein & Dauber, 1991). Such stereotyping often results in substandard treatment of students and of parents when they do become involved.

Much of our knowledge about parental school involvement is based on research in elementary schools. Parental school involvement declines as children grow up, and middle and high schools are less likely than elementary schools to encourage involvement (Eccles & Harold, 1996). Despite this decline, parental school involvement remains associated with academic outcomes in adolescence (Epstein & Sanders, 2002; Hill et al., in press). Thus, the third research challenge is to take into consideration developmental changes in parental school involvement. Parental school involvement may be different for a 7th-grade student selecting course tracks or 11th-grade student selecting colleges than for a 1st-grade student learning to read. Current measures of parental school involvement do not reflect these developmental variations. In fact, parents' involvement in schooling may not decline during middle and high school; rather, the research may show declining involvement only because the nature of involvement changes in ways that are not reflected in our measures.

From Research to Practice

Evidence strongly supports the potential benefits of policies and programs to increase parental school involvement across the school years and even before children start school. Most parents want information about how to best support their children's education, but teachers have little time or resources to devote to promoting parental school involvement, and some parents are simply "hard to reach." How do we help teachers facilitate parental school involvement? Most teacher training programs do not include courses on how to effectively involve parents. Linking research on parental school involvement to teacher training programs may go far to support family-school collaborations.

When parents cannot become involved, how can schools compensate for the loss of the benefits of involvement? Understanding the mechanisms through which involvement promotes academic achievement would point to logical targets for intervention. For example, if parental school involvement promotes achievement through its effects on the completion and accuracy of homework, then providing home work monitors after school might be an appropriate intervention strategy.

Impoverished families are less likely to be involved in schooling than wealthier families, and schools in impoverished communities are less likely to promote parental school involvement than schools in wealthier communities. Consequently, the children who would benefit most from involvement are those who are least likely to receive it unless a special effort is made. Promoting parental school involvement entails more in disadvantaged schools than in wealthier/schools. Compared with more advantaged parents, parents in impoverished communities often need much more information about how to promote achievement in their children, are overcoming more of their own negative school experiences, and have less social capital. Thus, programs and policies designed to promote parental school involvement in advantaged districts may be ineffective in promoting parental school involvement in high-risk or disadvantaged communities. Understanding each community's unique barriers and resources is important for establishing and maintaining effective collaborations between families and schools.

Recommended Reading

Booth, A., & Dunn, J.F. (Eds.). (1996). *Family-school links: How do they affect educational outcomes?* Mahwah, NJ: Erlbaum.

Epstein, J.L., & Sanders, M.G. (2002). (See References)

National PTA. (2000). *Building successful partnerships: A guide for developing parent and family involvement programs.* Bloomfield, IN: National Education Service.

References

Baker, D.P., & Stevenson, D.L. (1986). Mothers' strategies for children's school achievement: Managing the transition to high school. *Sociology of Education, 59,* 156–166.

Eccles, J.S., & Harold, R.D. (1996). Family involvement in children's and adolescents' schooling. In A. Booth & J.F. Dunn (Eds.), *Family-school links: How do they affect educational outcomes?* (pp. 3–34). Mahwah, NJ: Erlbaum.

Epstein, J.L., & Dauber, S.L. (1991). School programs and teacher practices of parent involvement in inner-city elementary and middle schools. *The Elementary School Journal, 91,* 289–305.

Epstein, J.L., & Sanders, M.G. (2002). Family, school, and community partnerships. In M.H. Bornstein (Ed.), *Handbook of parenting: Vol. 5. Practical issues in parenting* (pp. 407–437). Mahwah, NJ: Erlbaum.

Grolnick, W.S., & Slowiaczek, M.L. (1994). Parents' involvement in children's schooling: A multidimensional conceptualization and motivation model. *Child Development, 65,* 237–252.

Hill, N.E. (2001). Parenting and academic socialization as they relate to school readiness: The role of ethnicity and family income. *Journal of Educational Psychology, 93,* 686–697.

Hill, N.E., Castellino, D.R., Lansford, J.E., Nowlin, P., Dodge, K.A., Bates, J., & Pettit, G. (in press). Parent-academic involvement as related to school behavior, achievement, and aspirations: Demographic variations across adolescence. *Child Development.*

Hill, N.E., & Craft, S.A. (2003). Parent-school involvement and school performance: Mediated pathways among socioeconomically comparable African-American and Euro-American families. *Journal of Educational Psychology, 95,* 74–83.

LaParo, K.M., Kraft-Sayre, M., & Pianta, R.C. (2003). Preschool to kindergarten transition activities: Involvement and satisfaction of families and teachers. *Journal of Research in Childhood Education, 17*(2), 147–158.

Lareau, A. (1996). Assessing parent involvement in schooling: A critical analysis. In A. Booth & J.F. Dunn (Eds.), *Family-school links: How do they affect educational outcomes?* (pp. 57–64). Mahwah, NJ: Erlbaum.

Lichter, D.T. (1996). Family diversity, intellectual inequality, and academic achievement among American children. In A. Booth & J.F. Dunn (Eds.), *Family-school links: How do they affect educational outcomes?* (pp. 265–273). Mahwah, NJ: Erlbaum.

McNeal, R.B., Jr. (1999). Parental involvement as social capital: Differential effectiveness on science achievement, truancy, and dropping out. *Social Forces, 78,* 117–144.

Miedel, W.T., & Reynolds, A.J. (1999). Parent involvement in early intervention for disadvantaged children: Does it matter? *Journal of School Psychology, 37,* 370–402.

Pianta, R.C., Cox, M.J., Taylor, L.C., & Early, D.M. (1999). Kindergarten teachers' practices related to the transition into school: Results of a national survey. *Elementary School Journal, 100,* 71–86.

Taylor, L.C., Clayton, J.D., & Rowley, S.J. (in press). Academic socialization: Understanding parental influences on children's school-related development in the early years. *Review of General Psychology.*

Address correspondence to Nancy E. Hill, Department of Psychology, Duke University, Box 90085, Durham, NC 27708-0085; e-mail: nancy@duke.edu.

From *Current Directions in Psychological Science,* Vol. 13, 2004, pp. 161–165. Copyright ©2004 by Blackwell Publishing, Ltd. Reprinted by permission. www.blackwell-synergy.com

The Trouble with Boys

**They're kinetic, maddening and failing at school.
Now educators are trying new ways to help them succeed.**

PEG TYRE

SPEND A FEW MINUTES on the phone with Danny Frankhuizen and you come away thinking, "What a *nice* boy." He's thoughtful, articulate, bright. He has a good relationship with his mom, goes to church every Sunday, loves the rock band Phish and spends hours each day practicing his guitar. But once he's inside his large public Salt Lake City high school, everything seems to go wrong. He's 16, but he can't stay organized. He finishes his homework and then can't find it in his backpack. He loses focus in class, and his teachers, with 40 kids to wrangle, aren't much help. "If I miss a concept, they tell me, 'Figure it out yourself'," says Danny. Last year Danny's grades dropped from B's to D's and F's. The sophomore, who once dreamed of Stanford, is pulling his grades up but worries that "I won't even get accepted at community college."

44%—The number of male undergraduates on college campuses; 30 years ago, the number was 58%.

His mother, Susie Malcom, a math teacher who is divorced, says it's been wrenching to watch Danny stumble. "I tell myself he's going to make something good out of himself," she says. "But it's hard to see doors close and opportunities fall away."

What's wrong with Danny? By almost every benchmark, boys across the nation and in every demographic group are falling behind. In elementary school, boys are two times more likely than girls to be diagnosed with learning disabilities and twice as likely to be placed in special-education classes. High-school boys are losing ground to girls on standardized writing tests. The number of boys who said they didn't like school rose 71 percent between 1980 and 2001, according to a University of Michigan study. Nowhere is the shift more evident than on college campuses. Thirty years ago men represented 58 percent of the undergraduate student body. Now they're a minority at 44 percent. This widening achievement gap, says Margaret Spellings, U.S. Secretary of Education, "has profound implications for the economy, society, families and democracy."

With millions of parents wringing their hands, educators are searching for new tools to help tackle the problem of boys.

Books including Michael Thompson's best seller "Raising Cain" (recently made into a PBS documentary) and Harvard psychologist William Pollack's definitive work "Real Boys" have become must-reads in the teachers' lounge. The Gurian Institute, founded in 1997 by family therapist Michael Gurian to help the people on the front lines help boys, has enrolled 15,000 teachers in its seminars. Even the Gates Foundation, which in the last five years has given away nearly a billion dollars to innovative high schools, is making boys a big priority. "Helping underperforming boys," says Jim Shelton, the foundation's education director, "has become part of our core mission."

The problem won't be solved overnight. In the last two decades, the education system has become obsessed with a quantifiable and narrowly defined kind of academic success, these experts say, and that myopic view is harming boys. Boys are biologically, developmentally and psychologically different from girls—and teachers need to learn how to bring out the best in every one. "Very well-meaning people," says Dr. Bruce Perry, a Houston neurologist who advocates for troubled kids, "have created a biologically disrespectful model of education."

Thirty years ago it was girls, not boys, who were lagging. The 1972 federal law Title IX forced schools to provide equal opportunities for girls in the classroom and on the playing field. Over the next two decades, billions of dollars were funneled into finding new ways to help girls achieve. In 1992, the American Association of University Women issued a report claiming that the work of Title IX was not done—girls still fell behind in math and science; by the mid-1990s, girls had reduced the gap in math and more girls than boys were taking high-school-level biology and chemistry.

'Often boys are treated like defective girls,' says Thompson.

Some scholars, notably Christina Hoff Sommers, a fellow at the American Enterprise Institute, charge that misguided feminism is what's been hurting boys. In the 1990s, she says, girls were making strong, steady progress toward parity in schools,

Elementary School

Boys start off with lower literacy skills than girls, and are less often encouraged to read, which only widens the gap.

■ Girls ages 3 to 5 are **5%** more likely than boys to be read to at home at least three times a week.

■ Girls are **10%** more likely than boys to recognize words by sight by the spring of first grade.

■ Boys ages 5 to 12 are **60%** more likely than girls to have repeated at least one grade.

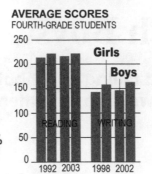

AVERAGE SCORES
FOURTH-GRADE STUDENTS

SOURCES: U.S. DEPARTMENT OF EDUCATION, CENTERS FOR DISEASE CONTROL

■ Girls' reading scores improve **6%** more than boys' between kindergarten and third grade.

■ First- to fifth-grade boys are **47%** more likely than girls to have disabilities such as emotional disturbances, learning problems or speech impediments.

■ Fourth-grade girls score **3%** higher on standardized reading tests than boys.

■ Fourth-grade girls score **12%** higher on writing tests than boys.

but feminist educators portrayed them as disadvantaged and lavished them with support and attention. Boys, meanwhile, whose rates of achievement had begun to falter, were ignored and their problems allowed to fester.

Standardized tests have become common for kids as young as 6.

BOYS HAVE ALWAYS BEEN boys, but the expectations for how they're supposed to act and learn in school have changed. In the last 10 years, thanks in part to activist parents concerned about their children's success, school performance has been measured in two simple ways: how many students are enrolled in accelerated courses and whether test scores stay high. Standardized assessments have become commonplace for kids as young as 6. Curricula have become more rigid. Instead of allowing teachers to instruct kids in the manner and pace that suit each class, some states now tell teachers what, when and how to teach. At the same time, student-teacher ratios have risen, physical education and sports programs have been cut and recess is a distant memory. These new pressures are undermining the strengths and underscoring the limitations of what psychologists call the "boy brain"—the kinetic, disorganized, maddening and sometimes brilliant behaviors that scientists now believe are not learned but hard-wired.

When Cris Messler of Mountainside, N.J., brought her 3-year-old son Sam to a pediatrician to get him checked for ADHD, she was acknowledging the desperation parents can feel. He's a high-energy kid, and Messler found herself hoping for a positive diagnosis. "If I could get a diagnosis from the doctor, I could get him on medicine," she says. The doctor said Sam is a normal boy. School has been tough, though. Sam's reading teacher said he was hopeless. His first-grade teacher complains he's antsy, and Sam, now 7, has been referring to himself as "stupid." Messler's glad her son doesn't need medication, but what, she wonders, can she do now to help her boy in school?

FOR MANY BOYS, THE TROUBLE starts as young as 5, when they bring to kindergarten a set of physical and mental abilities very different from girls'. As almost any parent knows, most 5-year-old girls are more fluent than boys and can sight-read more words. Boys tend to have better hand-eye coordination, but their fine motor skills are less developed, making it a struggle for some to control a pencil or a paintbrush. Boys are more impulsive than girls; even if they can sit still, many prefer not to—at least not for long.

Thirty years ago feminists argued that classic "boy" behaviors were a result of socialization, but these days scientists believe they are an expression of male brain chemistry. Sometime in the first trimester, a boy fetus begins producing male sex hormones that bathe his brain in testosterone for the rest of his gestation. "That exposure wires the male brain differently," says Arthur Arnold, professor of physiological science at UCLA. How? Scientists aren't exactly sure. New studies show that prenatal exposure to male sex hormones directly affects the way children play. Girls whose mothers have high levels of testosterone during pregnancy are more likely to prefer playing with trucks to playing with dolls. There are also clues that hormones influence the way we learn all through life. In a Dutch study published in 1994, doctors found that when males were given female hormones, their spatial skills dropped but their verbal skills improved.

In elementary-school classrooms—where teachers increasingly put an emphasis on language and a premium on sitting quietly and speaking in turn—the mismatch between boys and school can become painfully obvious. "Girl behavior becomes the gold standard," says "Raising Cain" coauthor Thompson. "Boys are treated like defective girls."

Two years ago Kelley King, principal of Douglass Elementary School in Boulder, Colo., looked at the gap between boys and girls and decided to take action. Boys were lagging 10 points behind girls in reading and 14 points in writing. Many more boys—than girls were being labeled as learning disabled, too. So King asked her teachers to buy copies of Gurian's book "The Minds of Boys," on boy-friendly classrooms, and in the fall of 2004 she launched a bold experiment. Whenever possi-

Middle School

Coming of age in a culture that discourages bookishness, boys are more likely to fall victim to drugs and violence.

- Eighth-grade girls score an average of **11 points** higher than eighth-grade boys on standardized reading tests.

- Eighth-grade girls score **21 points** higher than boys on standardized writing tests.

- Between 1993 and 2003, the number of ninth-grade

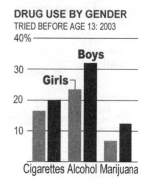

DRUG USE BY GENDER
TRIED BEFORE AGE 13: 2003

boys who skipped school at least once a month because they didn't feel safe increased **22%**.

- Boys between the ages of 5 and 14 are **200%** more likely to commit suicide than girls.

- Ninth-grade boys are **78%** more likely than girls to get injured in a fight at least once a year.

- Between the ages of 5 and 14, boys are **36%** more likely to die than their female counterparts.

ble, teachers replaced lecture time with fast-moving lessons that all kids could enjoy. Three weeks ago, instead of discussing the book "The View From Saturday," teacher Pam Unrau divided her third graders into small groups, and one student in each group pretended to be a character from the book. Classes are noisier, Unrau says, but the boys are closing the gap. Last spring, Douglass girls scored an average of 106 on state writing tests, while boys got a respectable 101.

Boys love video-games because when they lose, the defeat is private.

Primatologists have long observed that juvenile male chimps battle each other not just for food and females, but to establish and maintain their place in the hierarchy of the tribe. Primates face off against each other rather than appear weak. That same evolutionary imperative, psychologists say, can make it hard for boys to thrive in middle school—and difficult for boys who are failing to accept the help they need. The transition to middle school is rarely easy, but like the juvenile primates they are, middle-school boys will do almost anything to avoid admitting that they're overwhelmed. "Boys measure everything they do or say by a single yardstick: does this make me look weak?" says Thompson. "And if it does, he isn't going to do it." That's part of the reason that videogames have such a powerful hold on boys: the action is constant, they can calibrate just how hard the challenges will be and, when they lose, the defeat is private.

When Brian Johns hit seventh grade, he never admitted how vulnerable it made him feel. "I got behind and never caught up," says Brian, now 17 and a senior at Grand River Academy, an Ohio boarding school. When his parents tried to help, he rebuffed them. When his mother, Anita, tried to help him organize his assignment book, he grew evasive about when his homework was due. Anita didn't know where to turn. Brian's school had a program for gifted kids, and support for ones with special needs. But what, Anita asked his teachers, do they do about kids like her son who are in the middle and struggling? Those kids,

one of Brian's teachers told Anita, "are the ones who fall through the cracks."

It's easy for middle-school boys to feel outgunned. Girls reach sexual maturity two years ahead of boys, but other, less visible differences put boys at a disadvantage, too. The prefrontal cortex is a knobby region of the brain directly behind the forehead that scientists believe helps humans organize complex thoughts, control their impulses and understand the consequences of their own behavior. In the last five years, Dr. Jay Giedd, an expert in brain development at the National Institutes of Health, has used brain scans to show that in girls, it reaches its maximum thickness by the age of 11 and, for the next decade or more, continues to mature. In boys, this process is delayed by 18 months.

Middle-school boys may use their brains less efficiently than girls.

Middle-school boys may use their brains less efficiently, too. Using a type of MRI that traces activity in the brain, Deborah Yurgelun-Todd, director of the cognitive neuroimaging laboratory at McLean Hospital in Belmont, Mass., tested the activity patterns in the prefrontal cortex of children between the ages of 11 and 18. When shown pictures of fearful faces, adolescent girls registered activity on the right side of the prefrontal cortex, similar to an adult. Adolescent boys used both sides—a less mature pattern of brain activity. Teenage girls can process information faster, too. In a study about to be published in the journal Intelligence, researchers at Vanderbilt University administered timed tests—picking similar objects and matching groups of numbers—to 8,000 boys and girls between the ages of 5 and 18. In kindergarten, boys and girls processed information at about the same speeds. In early adolescence, girls finished faster and got more right. By 18, boys and girls were processing with the same speed and accuracy.

Scientists caution that brain research doesn't tell the whole story: temperament, family background and environment play

High School and Beyond

Many boys continue to fall behind girls in reading and writing proficiency, and fewer are going to college.

■ Boys are **33%** more likely than girls to drop out of high school.

■ Twelfth-grade girls score **16 points** higher than boys on standardized reading tests.

■ High-school boys are **30%** more likely to use cocaine than high-school girls.

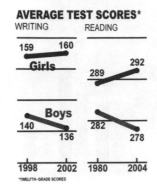

AVERAGE TEST SCORES*

WRITING   READING

Girls: 159 — 160   289 — 292

Boys: 140 — 136   282 — 278

1998 2002   1980 2004

*TWELFTH-GRADE SCORES

■ Twelfth-grade girls score **24 points** higher than boys on standardized writing tests.

■ High-school girls are **36%** more likely to take Advanced Placement or honors biology than high-school boys.

■ **22%** more high-school girls are planning to go to college than boys.

■ The percentage of male undergraduates dropped **24%** from 1970 to 2000.

big roles, too. Some boys are every bit as organized and assertive as the highest-achieving girls. All kids can be scarred by violence, alcohol or drugs in the family. But if your brain hasn't reached maturity yet, says Yurgelun-Todd, "it's not going to be able to do its job optimally."

ACROSS THE NATION, EDUCATORS are reviving an old idea: separate the girls from the boys—and at Roncalli Middle School, in Pueblo, Colo., administrators say, it's helping kids of both genders. This past fall, with the blessing of parents, school guidance counselor Mike Horton assigned a random group of 50 sixth graders to single-sex classes in core subjects. These days, when sixth-grade science teacher Pat Farrell assigns an earth-science lab on measuring crystals, the girls collect their materials—a Bunsen burner, a beaker of phenyl salicylate and a spoon. Then they read the directions and follow the sequence from beginning to end. The first things boys do is ask, "Can we eat this?" They're less organized, Farrell notes, but sometimes, "they're willing to go beyond what the lab asks them to do." With this in mind, he hands out written instructions to both classes but now goes over them step by step for the boys. Although it's too soon to declare victory, there are some positive signs: the shyest boys are participating more. This fall, the all-girl class did best in math, English and science, followed by the all-boy class and then coed classes.

One of the most reliable predictors of whether a boy will succeed or fail in high school rests on a single question: does he have a man in his life to look up to? Too often, the answer is no. High rates of divorce and single motherhood have created a generation of fatherless boys. In every kind of neighborhood, rich or poor, an increasing number of boys—now a startling 40 percent—are being raised without their biological dads. Psychologists say that grandfathers and uncles can help, but emphasize that an adolescent boy without a father figure is like an explorer without a map. And that is especially true for poor boys and boys who are struggling in school. Older males, says Gurian, model self-restraint and solid work habits for younger ones. And whether they're breathing down their necks about grades or admonishing them to show up for school on time, "an older man reminds a boy in a million different ways that school is crucial to their mission in life."

A boy without a father figure is like an explorer without a map.

In the past, boys had many opportunities to learn from older men. They might have been paired with a tutor, apprenticed to a master or put to work in the family store. High schools offered boys a rich array of roles in which to exercise leadership skills—class officer, yearbook editor or a place on the debate team. These days, with the exception of sports, more girls than boys are involved in those activities.

In neighborhoods where fathers are most scarce, the high-school dropout rates are shocking: more than half of African-American boys who start high school don't finish. David Banks, principal of the Eagle Academy for Young Men, one of four all-boy public high schools in the New York City system, wants each of his 180 students not only to graduate from high school but to enroll in college. And he's leaving nothing to chance. Almost every Eagle Academy boy has a male mentor—a lawyer, a police officer or an entrepreneur from the school's South Bronx neighborhood. The impact of the mentoring program, says Banks, has been "beyond profound." Tenth grader Rafael Mendez is unequivocal: his mentor "is the best thing that ever happened to me." Before Rafael came to Eagle Academy, he dreamed about playing pro baseball, but his mentor, Bronx Assistant District Attorney Rafael Curbelo, has shown him another way to succeed: Mendez is thinking about attending college in order to study forensic science.

'An older man reminds a boy that school is crucial to life,' says Gurian.

Colleges would welcome more applications from young men like Rafael Mendez. At many state universities the gender balance is already tilting 60-40 toward women. Primary and secondary schools are going to have to make some major changes, says Ange Peterson, president-elect of the American Association of Collegiate Registrars and Admissions Officers, to restore the gender balance. "There's a whole group of men we're losing in education completely," says Peterson.

For Nikolas Arnold, 15, a sophomore at a public high school in Santa Monica, Calif., college is a distant dream. Nikolas is smart: he's got an encyclopedic knowledge of weaponry and war. When he was in first grade, his principal told his mother he was too immature and needed ADHD drugs. His mother balked. "Too immature?" says Diane Arnold, a widow. "He was six and a half!" He's always been an advanced reader, but his grades are erratic. Last semester, when his English teacher assigned two girls' favorites—"Memoirs of a Geisha" and "The Secret Life of Bees" Nikolas got a D. But lately, he has a math teacher he likes and is getting excited about numbers. He's reserved in class sometimes. But now that he's more engaged, his grades are improving slightly and his mother, who's pushing college, is hopeful he will begin to hit his stride. Girls get A's and B's on their report cards, she tells him, but that doesn't mean boys can't do it, too.

With Andrew Murr, Vanessa Juarez, Anne Underwood, Karen Springen and Pat Wingert

The Preschool Promise

Going to preschool benefits children their entire lives.
Can states afford to provide it to all kids?

JULIE POPPE AND STEFFANIE CLOTHIER

If you walk into a good preschool classroom, you might see a teacher reading to a group of kids, children immersed in an art project, little ones playing on a computer or getting ready for a field trip to a nearby museum or public library.

Those children, mounting research shows, will do better in school and are more likely to attend college. As adults they will have better jobs and pay more taxes. They will even be better parents.

The good news is that more and more children go to preschool; in 2002, 66 percent of 4-year-olds attended. Some schools are government supported, others are private. Today, at least 40 states provide state funding for preschool programs, compared to only 10 in 1980.

Parents from all income ranges send their children to preschool, although better educated parents with higher incomes have the highest participation rate.

Preschools are designed to provide education and a safe caring environment. Some states fund programs that incorporate the needs of working parents, sometimes by coordinating their programs with Head Start and child care subsidy programs to ensure full-day services.

Ready for School

One of the striking findings in early education is the size of the achievement gap at the start of kindergarten between children who have gone to preschool and those who have not. That difference hardly ever goes away. It continues in reading and math achievement in the early grades and throughout school and into the job market. Steve Barnett from the National Institute for Early Education Research—an independent, nonpartisan organization that conducts research and follows state early education policy—says that kids living in poverty are 18 months behind the average kid when they start kindergarten. "This is an incredible amount of

time for a school to catch up," Barnett says. But the achievement gap isn't just a poverty issue. "The gap continues up the income ladder," he says. Because of these findings and recent brain research showing that almost 90 percent of brain growth occurs in children by age 5, more lawmakers, economists, business leaders and parents are supporting early education.

The Right Programs are Key

What makes a good preschool program? Proper teacher qualifications and training, small class sizes and teacher-to-student ratios, stimulating curriculum and other services that support families. A good program can improve a child's achievement over the short and long term. Recent focus on quality has prompted states to consider enhancements. For example, 23 now require preschool teachers to have a bachelor's degree with additional certification and license.

Most states target their state-funded initiatives to children who are in low-income families or at risk of school failure. Some states are looking to expand their preschool programs in response to state litigation, the need to improve test scores due to No Child Left Behind, and the latest research showing early education improves children's school success. Some states have different goals in mind, such as funding and expanding early education programs to reach more working families.

Paying for Quality Preschool

Arkansas has a state-funded preschool program that started in 1991 for low-income children. In recent years, $40 million in funding has allowed more children to attend. Representative LeRoy Dangeau carried a bill this session that resulted in an additional $20 million over the next two years for the continued expansion of the state's program.

THE ACHIEVEMENT GAP AT KINDERGARTEN

Family income has a great deal to do with how well a child does on readiness tests when entering kindergarten. The school readiness gap is steepest for children from families with the lowest incomes and continues through middle income families, gradually decreasing as income rises.

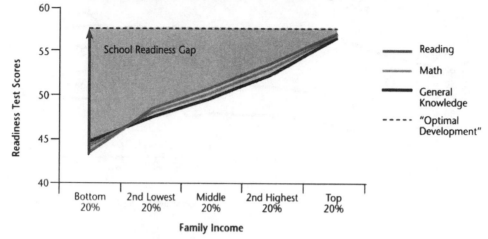

Source: Preschool Policy Matters, April 2004, National Institute for Early Education Research.

Other preschool funding comes from a beer tax (since 2001) that raises about 18 cents on every six-pack, generating $8 million annually for early education. This April, the Legislature passed a bill to extend the beer tax until June 2007.

Dangeau hopes that by the summer of 2007 there will be a total of $100 million dedicated for voluntary preschool for all 3 and 4-year-olds.

"When I became a legislator four years ago," says Dangeau, "I had no clue about the importance of early childhood. But I saw the research, including the benefits of preschool over time, and how it is the best investment of our money," he says.

In a recent Arkansas Supreme Court case on school funding inequity, the court recognized the importance of preschool (but didn't mandate it) as part of its ruling. "I think that the court case had an impact on how the Legislature views preschool," says Dangeau. "We see it as the quickest way to improve test scores. The issue is not whether or not to have preschool. The question is how much money to put into it."

Last year, the National Institute for Early Education Research ranked the quality of Arkansas' preschool program very high.

"I am very proud to say that Arkansas ranked best in terms of quality," says Dangeau. He believes the success is directly tied to legislation passed in 2003 that puts preschool teachers on the same pay scale as K-12 teachers. Any program or school may provide preschool services as long as they meet the state's quality standards, such as one certified teacher per 10 students.

Supporting Working Families

In the mid-'80s, the Illinois legislature established a preschool program for at-risk children. To support working families, the state allows child care centers and Head Start programs that

Preschool Popularity

At least 40 states provide state funding for preschool programs.

- The first to expand preschool to all 4-year-olds were Georgia and then Oklahoma. Florida, Maryland, New York and West Virginia are in the process of phasing in their programs.
- Thirty-six states considered early education bills in 2005. At least 28 states considered expanding preschool programs.
- Florida legislators, responding to a state ballot measure, approved legislation for a voluntary preschool program for all 4-year-olds. New Mexico legislators passed a pilot preschool bill with a $5 million initial appropriation.
- Mississippi, Montana, North Dakota and South Dakota have no state-funded preschool programs, but did consider legislation this session.

meet standards to provide full-day early education services along with public schools. Local communities determine eligibility; there are an estimated 64,000 3- and 4-year-olds enrolled statewide.

The state has significantly increased funding over the past few years. Since 2003, lawmakers have appropriated $30 million annually for early education and are looking to do the same this legislative session.

The National Institute for Early Education Research gave the state high marks for quality. Teachers participating in the program must hold an early childhood teaching certificate to be on the same pay scale as K-12 teachers.

KINDERGARTEN AND PRESCHOOL PARTICIPATION
1965-2002

Over the last several decades, preschool and kindergarten participation has increased steadily for children ages 3 to 5.

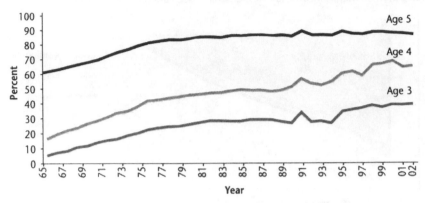

Source: National Institute for Early Education Research.

In 2003, lawmakers created the Illinois Early Learning Council. It builds on the work the state has already done to develop a high-quality early learning system available to all Illinois children up to age 5. Four legislators currently are members of the council, including Representative Elizabeth Coulson.

Coulson, who has a business background, sits on two of the House Appropriation Committee's subcommittees, Human Services and Education, which make funding decisions for early education. She is also a member of the House Human Services Committee. "I'm a link between key committees that focus on early childhood," she says.

She says that Illinois has been concerned for some time about supporting working families and making sure a strong birth-to-age-5 system is in place that nurtures children. In 2003, the legislature increased the percentage of funding for birth-to-age-3 programs from 8 percent to 11 percent of the state's early childhood education block grant. The block grant makes up the state's funding for preschool education, parental training and prevention initiatives. "The formative years have the most impact on education. This is not just a women's issue, but it's also a children's issue and [in terms of economics and business] an important issue for the whole state," she says.

Nearly a third of all Illinois 4-year-olds are in a state-funded preschool program and the number is up from the year before. Coulson says early care is a thriving industry that has an impact on Illinois' economy, and businesses need to be aware of the benefits. Recent research shows that every tax dollar invested in preschool produces $17 for the economy.

"This session, we continue to focus on quality and funding," Coulson says, in the last two years, the state has increased preschool spending by $60 million. "This is a bad budget year for Illinois, but I am optimistic we will find a way to fund another $30 million for early childhood," she says.

Legislative Involvement

During the mid-'80s, Massachusetts set up a state-funded early education program in public schools. Since then, the state has allowed community partnership providers who meet early childhood standards to participate in programs targeting at-risk 3- and 4-year-olds from working families serving almost 16,000 children last year.

During the 2004 session, more than 100 legislators, including leadership in both houses, signed on to a proposal for preschool for all 3-to-5-year-olds to be phased-in over 10 years, at an estimated cost of $1 billion. Two bills that were eventually enacted laid the groundwork for the expansion by reworking state governance of early childhood programs. One law creates a single department to streamline early childhood programs and to expand preschool to all 3- and 4-year-olds. "Hopefully, we will see less duplication of services," says Representative Patricia Haddad.

She co-chairs the legislature's Joint Committee on Education and the state's legislatively created Advisory Committee on Early Education and Care. Nine other legislators participate. They have conducted five public hearings throughout the state. "We had to be a part of the hearings ourselves, because it is nice to read a report, but the passion is different when you are involved," says Haddad. State early childhood advocates also held meetings throughout the state to educate the public on the importance of early childhood education and full-day kindergarten for all.

Last December, the advisory committee completed a report that identified four key components: developing a workforce, defining quality, delivering the system and evaluating progress. Haddad says the next step is providing a good workforce development program for teachers and providers.

The 2004 legislation also created a new board of early education and care, which will start this July. The commissioners from the boards of Higher Education, Education, and Early

Education and Care will each sit on each other's boards. "We want the commissioners to be talking to one another, which will lead to better communication between these three entities," says Haddad.

Representative Haddad says people in Massachusetts are starting to realize the importance of preschool and the role that it might possibly play with No Child Left Behind. "If you do not provide the very best for children in the early years, you will continue to see gaps," she says.

Julie Poppe tracks preschool policy for NCSL. Steffanie Clothier heads NCSL's Child Care and Early Education Project.

UNIT 3
Social and Emotional Development

Unit Selections

Key Points to Consider

- Imagine growing up in a single-parent, homeless family where hunger, violence, drug abuse, and neglect were everyday occurrences. Then imagine trying to walk to school in the same poor, deprived, crime-ridden neighborhood and trying to learn in an inadequate, under-funded school. Most children are permanently scathed by such conditions, but a few prove resilient to even the most severe conditions. How and why does this happen? What factors might help offset these effects? What public policy implications would this have? What could you do to help these children?

- Look at almost any elementary school playground at recess or junior high lunchroom and you will see boys and girls congregating by same-sex groups. Think back to when you were in grade school, what were the rules for girls vs. boys and who enforced these gender-typed behaviors? Did your teachers or parents have different rules for boys and girls? Explain. Do you think girls are more interpersonally and verbally mean than boys? Explain. Do you remember girls having special cliques when you were in school? Will you treat your son and daughter differently? Explain.

Student Website

www.mhcls.com/online

Internet References

Further information regarding these websites may be found in this book's preface or online.

Max Planck Institute for Psychological Research
http://www.mpg.de/english/institutesProjectsFacilities/instituteChoice/psychologische_forschung/

National Child Care Information Center (NCCIC)
http://www.nccic.org

Serendip
http://serendip.brynmawr.edu/serendip/

One of the truisms about our species is that we are social animals. From birth, each person's life is a constellation of relationships, from family at home to friends in the neighborhood and school. This unit addresses how children's social and emotional development is influenced by important relationships with parents, peers, and teachers.

When John Donne in 1623 wrote, "No man is an island, every man is a part of the main," he implied that all humans are connected to each other and that these connections make us who we are. Early in this century, sociologist C. H. Cooley highlighted the importance of relationships with the phrase "looking-glass self" to describe how people tend to see themselves as a function of how others perceive them. Personality theorist Alfred Adler, also writing in the early twentieth century, claimed that personal strength derived from the quality of one's connectedness to others: The stronger the relationships, the stronger the person. The notion that a person's self-concept arises from relations with others also has roots in developmental psychology as Jean Piaget once wrote, "There is no such thing as isolated individuals; there are only relations." The articles in this unit respect these traditions by emphasizing the theme that a child's development occurs within the context of relationships.

Today's society is more complex than ever and children from at-risk families face growing challenges such as acute poverty, homelessness, foster care, illness, alcohol and substance abuse, abandonment, death, and violence in families. Amazingly, in spite of these terrible odds, unlike most children, there are a lucky few who somehow manage to transcend these crushing effects and rise up to bounce back and develop normally. The author of "Children's Capacity to Develop Resiliency" describes how certain key factors such as an understanding of one's strengths and accomplishments, humor, and high, positive expectations can protect children and keep them on the path of normal development.

Another major influence in the landscape of childhood is friendship. When do childhood friendships begin? Friends become increasingly important during the elementary school years. If forming strong, secure attachments with family members is an important task of early childhood, then one of the major psychological achievements of middle childhood is a move toward the peer group. Researcher Thomas J. Berndt, author of "Friendship Quality and Social Development" reviews evidence regarding the quality of childhood friendships and whether or not these early friendships have a lasting influence on the child's future social success. Similarly, in "Loneliness and Peer Relations in Childhood," researchers Steven Asher and Julie Paquette discuss chronic loneliness and how peer rejection and victimization contribute to social maladjustment and other school problems. While in "The Power of Make-Believe," the author explains that children's imaginary playmates may help to resolve emotional issues and promote development.

Reknowned psychologist Eleanor Maccoby reviews emerging research examining how same-sex social groups and group processes influence and socialize children's sex-typed behavior in "Gender and Group Process: A Developmental Perspective." She discusses the role of group size, playtime interactions among all-male and all-female groups, and the formation of sex-distinctive sub-

cultures as powerful forces in shaping children's sex-typed behaviors, values, and interests.

Are girls or boys more aggressive? Typically, most people might nominate boys as being more aggressive. In "Taming Wild Girls," Jeffrey Kluger argues that while boys may be more likely to resort to physical aggression, girls are more likely to engage in relational verbal and interpersonal aggression. With the increasing concerns about bullying, more schools are developing and implementing intervention programs to assist both the bullies and their potential victims. In "A Profile of Bullying at School," researcher Dan Olweus discusses the process of bullying. Given the detrimental effects on children's development and adjustment, the author advocates strongly successful school-bullying prevention programs both in the United States and abroad in countries such as Norway.

Children's Capacity to Develop Resiliency

How to Nurture It

DEIRDRE BRESLIN

Today's world, full of change, uncertainty, and the unexpected challenges everyone's ability to cope. What coping skills must we nurture, enrich, and enhance to help children navigate successfully in a complex society? Resiliency must be primary. Not only is it essential for the children we teach, but it is a vital skill for ourselves as we strive to enable every child to become all that he or she is capable of.

By definition *resiliency* means the capability to rebound or recoil or to spring back, the power of recovery. How can a teacher help young children develop this capacity, the ability to bounce back from set-backs every child experiences in one form or another as a fact of everyday life?

Resiliency is a set of protective mechanisms that modify a person's response to risk situations.

Resiliency is not a fixed attribute. Rather it is a set of protective mechanisms that modify a person's response to risk situations. These mechanisms operate at turning points during the individual's life (Rutter 1984; Garmezy 1991). Resiliency is a valuable coping skill for all young children.

The Defeating Label "At Risk"

"Labeling matters, and the younger the person getting the label is, the more it matters" (Rosenthal & Jacobson 1968, 3). Some educators seek to help a child having difficulty by focusing on the child's inappropriate behavior patterns. The learning approaches and solutions emphasized perpetuate a problem perspective, and children are frequently labeled "at risk." In eradicating behaviors, massive doses of correction are administered to the child. As a result, we minimize or ignore strengths and competencies a child possesses that could promote adaptation and wellness.

Researcher Emmy Werner and her colleague Ruth Smith (1985) document that one in three children considered to be at risk develops into a competent, capable, caring young person by age 18. In their follow-up work (Werner & Smith 1992), they conclude that of the remaining two out of three high-risk adolescents, two-thirds are successful adults by age 32.

The growing body of research about resiliency provides concise information on the ways individuals develop successfully despite adversity and on the lack of predictive power in risk factors (Rutter 1979; Lanni 1989; McLaughlin, Irbey, & Langman 1994; Meier 1995). These facts have profound implications for deciding what approaches to emphasize when helping today's young children develop positive coping skills.

Children's Adaptive Approaches

For two years I systematically interviewed families and young children age five to eight who were identified by the school administration as functioning well in their urban school settings. Each interviewee had three and sometimes more major, ongoing life stressors in their lives: for example, homelessness, foster care, single parent family, alcohol and substance abuse, family problems, abandonment, and death in the family. Despite negative life events and stress, the children and their families seemed to be adapting and surviving. They displayed resilient behavior through their active participation in classroom activities, consistent high attendance, well-developed listening skills, and cooperative child-to-child and teacher-to-child interactions.

No group of families or individual children interviewed showed identical sets of coping behaviors. Although resiliency is an individualized skill, the resiliency of the individuals interviewed revealed some common factors that are important to examine. Four factors of resiliency that I identified are outlined here, with examples of classroom activities to help develop and enrich each aspect.

1. Heightened Sensory Awareness

The kindergarten boy who first alerted me to this quality of re-siliency lived in a very poor area in which the streets contained a great deal of garbage and drug users' paraphernalia. As I walked to his school, I was startled by what I saw and could only focus on the unpleasantness of the journey. On meeting the child, I was so consumed with repugnance from the walk that my first question was, "What is it like coming to school each day?" He looked at me and smiled.

"It's wonderful," he said. "You know, the streets have been 'glassticized,' and all the little pieces of glass that are in the pav-ing material shine and sparkle—it's like finely chopped dia-monds. Every day my grandmother walks with me to school, and we look at the street and count the colors. On sunny days there is silver and gold, but on dark days there are purple and dark colors. We count the colors and name them."

With this boy's positive experience in mind, teachers can trans-form every trip home from school into an opportunity to heighten and enrich sensory awareness no matter where the child lives. The family member or other adult who accompanies the child to and from school can become an integral partner in the experience.

The walk provides a tool for observation as the teacher follows up on it the next day. How many squares did you see on the way home? How many circles? Where were they? Describe the circle. Which vocabulary words can you use in telling about your trip home? What new words can you teach us about your walk? What else do you do/see/feel on the way home from school?

> **The school setting provides many opportunities to encourage high, positive expectations.**

2. High, Positive Expectations

One of the eight-year-old girls interviewed said that she was going to be a female basketball star. "I know I will be a star, be-cause the gym teacher told me how good I am at basketball."

The importance of teacher expectations and feedback has been the focus of much research, starting with the classic study completed by Rosenthal and Jacobson (1968). This study showed that student performance was affected by teachers' ex-pectations of the child. The effect on student performance was called the Pygmalion effect, referring to the growth in motiva-tion that can occur when a teacher believes in and encourages a student. The name Pygmalion comes from the mythological story of a king who creates a female statue and then with the help of the gods brings it to life. The gym teacher's positive ex-pectations and feedback heightened this girl's motivation and helped her to succeed.

Howard Gardner (1983) describes our multiple intelligences and outlines relevant behaviors that accompany each intelli-gence. Bodily kinesthetic intelligence is one of these, and the eight-year-old's performance at basketball indicates strength in that area. The gym teacher was reinforcing one of the intelli-gences this child displayed.

Helping Children Realize Potential through Their Multiple Intelligences

Intelligences	Recognition and reinforcement suggestions
linguistic	Tell stories. Let children dictate their stories to the teacher or an adult volunteer. Transcribers read back each story and give the child his or her own print copy to illustrate. Create poetry orally and in writing. Imagine a character and play-act the role. Play word games and solve puzzles.
spatial	Ask children to describe the physical characteristics they see in a bird, squirrel, cat, dog. Draw visual likenesses of any objects.
logical-mathematical	Use numbers to create calendars. Make itemized, number listcounting anything and everything. Estimate how many of something (pennies, seeds, pebbles, acorns) are in a jar, box, bowl.
musical	Listen to various types of music. Sing songs and clap to the music. Hum, whistle, or use bodily response to the music. Write about whats fun in dancing or playing basketball and other sports. Make up skits or pantomimes in response to literature or music.
bodily-kinesthetic	Dance in all kinds of movement styles. Play pin-the-tail-on-the-donkey. Throw and catch a ball. Try all kinds of sports. Smell flowers and look closely to concentrate on their colors. Names flowers and notice the many differences (reds, pinks, etc.) Takes walks to focus on enhancing and heightening sensory awareness.
interpersonal	Act out situations that children encounter in classroom activities.
intrapersonal	Portray emotions such as sadness, regret, and so forth that everyone experiences.
naturalist	Make books identifying animals, birds, plants, and so on. Write stories and poetry about nature.

Children's self-concepts result partly from the expectations others have for them. Their self-concepts in turn affect the expectations they have for themselves. The school setting provides many opportunities to encourage high, positive expectations.

Gardner (1983) explores intelligence in terms of different "frames of mind." In the chart on the previous page, each of the eight intelligences (including Naturalist, which Gardner proposed later [1998]) is accompanied by suggestions that can be modified and enhanced to match the developmental and unique needs of young children.

3. A clear and developing understanding of one's strengths relating to accomplishment

The most powerful example of this concept came from an eight-year-old who said, "Well, you know I'm not so good at ball games, but I'm an awesome reader." This child understood the concept of knowing one's strengths and ably used his personal interactions with both adults and peers to cast success in the light of what he could accomplish. Developing such a clear understanding supports and reinforces children's high, positive expectations.

4. A heightened, developing sense of humor

All of the children I interviewed seemed to have a well-developed sense of the playful. Humor is not an innate gift, but it can and should be cultivated. It is a frame that can help keep things in perspective. The more children learn about humor, the more they become sensitized to it, and the more humor enters into everyday life (Kozol 2000). Philosopher Reinhold Neibuhr emphasized the importance of humor and the need for using it when trying to make sense out of some of the incongruities of life (Kleinman 2000). Children need this skill more than ever before.

In a second grade classroom I visited, each week the teacher featured an activity that highlighted humor. I joined the children on a humor walk. The teacher asked students to walk silently and listen for any sounds, notice sidewalk cracks, and watch for signs to present to the class in a humorous manner. After the walk the students shared what they saw and heard that was funny for them. One child imitated a bird in a marvelous way. In a few minutes, the entire class was trying to reproduce the sound, laughing and smiling happily.

The walk not only highlighted humor but also developed listening skills, interpersonal communication skills, and having the fun of a shared experience. The children told about another of their humor curriculum stories. For several weeks, children could act out something that happened to them or their family that they found funny. The class voted on the funniest story, and the humor prize of the week went to the winner. This activity enhanced coping skills, built vocabulary, honed presentation skills, and let the children act as critics and judges.

Building Children's Resiliency

One effort that focuses on resiliency in children age two to six is an initiative of the Devereux Early Childhood Foundation in Villanova, Pennsylvania. The Devereux Early Childhood Initiative is a strength-based implemented in Head Start and other early childhood programs. The program consists of an integrated approach that not only provides a tool for assessing children's protective factors and screening challenging behaviors but also suggests strategies for fostering resiliency.

The Devereux Early Childhood Assessment (DECA), a nationally normed assessment of within-the-child protective factors in children age two to five, is the program's assessment tool. Supportive materials provide home and classroom approaches for supporting and enhancing resilient behaviors. An infant/toddler version of the DECA is under development.

More information is available online: **www.devereux-earlychilhood.org.**

The more children learn about humor, the more they become sensitized to it, and the more humor enters into everyday life.

I believe that as part of a humor curriculum, each teacher and his students should develop together the group's criteria for success. This is a meaningful way to introduce the importance of standards. In 2005, standards are critical in every facet of life.

Summary

This look at resiliency development through heightened sensory awareness; high, positive expectations; a clear understanding of one's strengths relating to accomplishment; and a developing sense of humor hopefully can encourage you to foster enriching coping behaviors in children. These four facets of resiliency seem critically important for young children.

But don't be trapped into thinking that there are precisely four resilience factors or seven or three. It is not possible to succinctly categorize human resiliency. Educators today need to help children search for the unique strengths that equip them, no matter the circumstances, to fulfill their individual potential.

However, we must avoid the urge to simplify as we strive to facilitate the resilience of children. Today's teacher must understand that development is part of a very complex unstable phenomenon. Garmezy and Rutter (1983), focusing on the study of competency, give insight into the fact that resiliency may not be fully attainable by all. However, Nobel laureate Albert Camus tells us the worth of trying: "In the midst of winter, I finally learned there was in me an invincible summer."

Educators today need to help children search for the unique strengths that equip them, no matter the circumstances, to fulfill their individual potential.

References

Gardner, H. 1983. *Frames of mind: The theory of multiple intelligences*. New York: Basic.

Gardner, H. 1998. Are there additional intelligences? *In Education, information, and transformation*, ed. J. Kane. Englewood, NJ: Prentice Hall.

Garmezy, N. 1991. Relevance and vulnerability to adverse developmental outcomes with poverty. *Behavioral Scientist* 34 (4): 416–30.

Garmezy, N., & M. Rutter. 1983. *Stress, coping and development in children*. New York: McGraw-Hill.

Kleinman, M.L. 2000. *A world of hope, a world of fear: Henry A. Wallace, Reinhold Neibuhr, and American liberalism*. Columbus: Ohio State University.

Kozol, J. 2000. *Ordinary resurrections*. New York: Crown.

Lanni, F. 1989. *The search for structure: A report on American youth today*. New York: Free Press.

McLaughlin, M., M. Irbey, & J. Langman. 1994. *Urban sanctuaries: Neighborhood organizations in the lives and futures of inner-city youth*. San Francisco: Jossey Bass.

Meier, D. 1995. *The power of their ideas: Lessons for America from a small school in Harlem*. Boston: Beacon.

Rosenthal, R., & L. Jacobson. 1968. *Pygmalion in the classroom*. New York: Rinehart & Winston.

Rutter, M. 1979. *Fifteen thousand hours*. Cambridge: Harvard University Press.

Rutter, M. 1984. Resilient children. *Psychology Today* (March): 57–65.

Werner, E.E., & R.S. Smith. 1985. *Vulnerable but invincible: A study of resilient children*. New York: McGraw-Hill.

Werner, E.E., & R.S. Smith. 1992. *Overcoming the odds*. New York: Cornell University Press.

Deirdre Breslin, PhD, is an urban educator and director of academic programs for Project ReConnect at St. John's University in New York City. Her primary area of research interest is resilient behavior, with a focus on inner-city children.

From *Young Children,* Vol 60, no. 1, January 2005, pp. 47-48, 50-52. Copyright © 2005 by National Association for the Education of Young Children. Reprinted by permission.

Friendship Quality and Social Development

Abstract: A high-quality friendship is characterized by high levels of prosocial behavior, intimacy, and other positive features, and low levels of conflicts, rivalry, and other negative features. Friendship quality has been assumed to have direct effects on many aspects of children's social development, including their self-esteem and social adjustment. Recent research suggests, however, that friendship quality affects primarily children's success in the social world of peers. Friendship quality could also have indirect effects, by magnifying or diminishing the influence of friends on each other's attitudes and behaviors. Having high-quality friendships may lessen children's tendencies to imitate the behavior of shy and withdrawn friends, but little evidence supports the hypothesis that high-quality friendships magnify friends' influence.

Keywords: friendship; social development; peer influence; self esteem

THOMAS J. BERNDT[1]
Department of Psychological Sciences, Purdue University, West Lafayette, Indiana

Do good friendships enhance children's social development? What if those good friendships are with bad friends, friends who often misbehave in school or show other signs of poor social or psychological adjustment? Do good friendships with friends like those have a positive or a negative influence on children?

Similar questions about the effects of friends and friendships have been discussed in theoretical writings for decades. Only in recent years, however, have answers to the questions begun to emerge from empirical research. The recent advances have resulted in part from researchers' success in defining, conceptually and operationally, what a good friendship is. In much of the literature, good friendships are now defined as friendships high in quality (e.g., Berndt, 1996).

High-quality friendships may enhance children's development regardless of the characteristics of those friends. Research on this hypothesis can be described as examining the direct effects of friendship quality. But another possibility is that friendship quality most often has indirect effects on children, effects that depend on the friends' characteristics. For example, when friendships are high in quality, the influence of the friends' characteristics may be magnified. I review evidence for both types of effects in this article, but it is necessary to begin by defining the construct of friendship quality more precisely.

A Definition of Friendship Quality

The old proverb says, "A friend in need is a friend indeed." That is, friends help and share with each other. Children agree with adults that these types of prosocial behavior are expected among friends. Children also agree with adults that good friends praise each other's successes and encourage each other after failures, thereby bolstering each other's self-esteem.

Some features of high-quality friendships are recognized by adolescents but not by young children. Adolescents often say that best friends tell each other everything, or disclose their most personal thoughts and feelings. These personal self-disclosures are the hallmark of an intimate friendship. Adolescents also say that friends will stick up for one another in a fight, demonstrating their loyalty.

A few researchers have described various positive features of good friendships, including prosocial behavior, self-esteem support, intimacy, loyalty, plus others, and investigated the associations between these features by asking questions assessing them. For example, to assess intimacy, researchers have asked children how often they tell a particular friend things about themselves that they would not tell most other people (Berndt & Keefe, 1995). Such research has found that children who say that their friendship has a high level of one positive feature, such as intimacy, typically say that their friendship is high in all other positive features. These results suggest that all positive features are linked to a single dimension of friendship quality.

Even best friendships can have negative features. Most children admit that best friends sometimes have conflicts with each other. In addition, children typically think of themselves as equal to their friends, but equality can be more an ideal than a reality. Children sometimes say that their friends try to boss them around, or dominate them. Children say that their friends "try to prove they're better than me," or engage in rivalry. When asked about actual friendships, children usually report the co-occurrence of conflicts, dominance attempts, and rivalry. Thus, all negative features seem to be linked to a single dimension of friendship quality. Scores on this negative dimension are only weakly correlated with those on the positive dimension (Berndt, 1996), so both dimensions must be considered when defining the quality of a friendship.

Direct Effects of Friendship Quality

Most writers on friendship have assumed that high-quality friendships have positive effects on children: fostering their self-esteem, improving their social adjustment, and increasing their ability to cope with stressors (see Hartup & Stevens, 1999). Moreover, the correlations of friendship quality with indicators of social adjustment are consistent with that assumption. For example, among early adolescents, having friendships with more positive features correlates with greater involvement in school, higher self-perceived social acceptance, and higher general self-esteem (Berndt & Keefe, 1995; Keefe & Berndt, 1996).

Still, a significant correlation between two variables is only weak evidence that one affects the other. To test hypotheses about the effects of friendship quality more conclusively, researchers have assessed children's friendships and their adjustment on two or more occasions months or years apart (e.g., Ladd, Kochenderfer, & Coleman, 1996). Then the researchers have examined whether the quality of children's friendships on the first occasion predicted the changes over time in their adjustment. If so, the researchers tentatively have concluded that friendship quality affected the changes in children's adjustment.

In one study of this type (Ladd et al., 1996), kindergarten children who had high-quality friendships in January of the school year improved by the following May in their liking for school and in their perceptions of their classmates' support. In another study (Berndt, Hawkins, & Jiao, 1999), classmates rated students' sociability and leadership in sixth grade and again in seventh grade. Students whose sixth-grade friendships were high in positive features improved between sixth and seventh grade in peer-rated sociability and leadership, but only if their sixth-grade friendships were stable over time. These findings are consistent with hypotheses about the direct effects of high-quality friendships, but other data are not. In one study (Berndt et al., 1999), my colleagues and I found that friendship quality did not significantly affect the changes over time in students' general self-esteem. In three earlier longitudinal studies (see Keefe & Berndt, 1996), friendship quality also was not significantly related to changes in general self-esteem. These data cast doubt on the hypothesis that good friendships enhance children's self-esteem. Stated more strongly, the repeated failures to confirm the hypothesis that high-quality friendships increase children's self-esteem suggest a need for less sweeping and more specific hypotheses about the benefits of good friendships.

One possibility is that friendships high in positive features affect primarily children's success in the social world of peers. Thus, good friendships can improve children's views of their classmates and improve their classmates' views of them. A speculative explanation for these effects can also be offered. Having a few good friendships may help children make positive

contacts with several other classmates. Those positive contacts may then lead to positive relationships that are not as close as best friendships but that affect the children's attitudes toward their classmates and vice versa.

The effects of negative friendship features have also been examined. In one study (Ladd et al., 1996), kindergarten boys who had many conflicts with friends in the middle of a school year exhibited a decrease by the end of the year in liking for school and engagement in classroom activities, but an increase in loneliness. In another study (Berndt & Keefe, 1995), seventh graders whose friendships were high in negative features in the fall of a year reported increased disruptive behavior at school the following spring. Moreover, those students whose friendships were also high in positive features reported the greatest increase in disruptive behavior.

One possible explanation of these findings focuses on the likely effects of negative interactions between friends. Friends who frequently get into conflicts with each other, or who often try to dominate or assert their superiority over one another, are practicing a repertoire of negative social behaviors that may generalize to interactions with other peers and adults. Moreover, the closer a friendship is, the more the friends interact and the more frequently they practice their negative social repertoire. Naturally, the students' negative behaviors provoke negative reactions from classmates and teachers. Those negative reactions encourage the students to disengage from classmates and classroom activities, to feel more lonely, and to like school less.

These explanations are only possibilities because the recent longitudinal studies do not provide evidence on the processes responsible for the effects of friendship quality. Examining these processes must be a major goal of future research (Hartup, 1999). Information about processes would be especially valuable as researchers seek to replace theories about the general effects of friendship quality with theories that explain the effects of each dimension of friendship quality on specific aspects of social development.

Indirect Effects of Friendship Quality

For decades, researchers from a variety of disciplines have tested the hypothesis that children and adolescents are influenced by the attitudes and behaviors of their peers. Not all studies have provided support for the hypothesis, but the available data convincingly show that close friends influence many facets of children's and adolescents' social behavior and adjustment (Collins & Laursen, 1999). In most studies, researchers have not assessed the quality of the friendships among the peers who were influencing one another. But when the issue has been raised, researchers have often suggested that the magnitude of friends' influence should be affected by the quality of their friendships. In this way, friendship quality can have an indirect effect on children's social development—affecting how much children are influenced by their friends' characteristics.

For example, according to the differential-association theory of delinquent behavior, adolescents who spend time with delinquent friends are expected to commit delinquent acts themselves (see Agnew, 1991). Moreover, delinquent friends are assumed to have more influence the more positive the relationships with those friends are. That is, having high-quality friendships with delinquent friends is assumed to increase the influence of those friends, thereby increasing the degree to which adolescents become like their friends over time.

Many other theories include the hypothesis that friends' influence is magnified when friendships are higher in quality (see Berndt, 1999). For example, social learning theory suggests that observational learning from friends is enhanced when friends have more positive relationships. Other theories suggest that friends' influence should be greater the more friends trust each other, and trust is another facet of the positive dimension of friendship quality.

Given the plausibility of the hypothesis about the magnifying effect of friendship quality, the scarcity of evidence for it is surprising. Some evidence consistent with the hypothesis was obtained in one longitudinal study of adolescents' delinquent behavior (Agnew, 1991). Among all the adolescents whose friends engaged in serious delinquent acts, only those who were closely attached to those friends became more seriously delinquent themselves. However, the comparable effect of attachment to friends who engaged in minor delinquency was nonsignificant. Other studies have yielded equally equivocal support for the hypothesis (Berndt et al., 1999), or no support at all (Berndt & Keefe, 1995; Poulin, Dishion, & Haas, 1999). In short, the general hypothesis that high friendship quality magnifies friends' influence must currently be viewed as doubtful.

Under certain conditions, having high-quality friendships may lessen rather than magnify friends' influence on each other. Consider, in particular, children who have good friendships with peers who are shy and withdrawn. Would those friendships increase the children's tendencies to imitate their friends' shy and withdrawn behavior? Alternatively, would those friendships enhance children's confidence in social situations and make them less prone to social withdrawal?

These questions were addressed in a longitudinal study of early adolescents whose shyness and social withdrawal were judged by their classmates (Berndt et al., 1999). Adolescents whose friends showed above-average shyness and withdrawal became more shy and withdrawn themselves over time only if those friendships were average or low in quality. Having shy and withdrawn friends did not influence changes in students' shyness and withdrawal when those friendships were high in quality. Apparently, the support that the students received from their friends offset any tendencies to imitate the friends' patterns of social behavior.

The hypothesis that variations in friendship quality affect the magnitude of friends' influence on each other can be evaluated only in studies that include measures of friends' characteristics and of friendship quality. Unfortunately, researchers interested in exploring the benefits of friendships have seldom examined what those friends are like, and researchers interested in exploring friends' influence have seldom examined the types of relationships those friends have. Consequently, the evidence necessary for answering questions about indirect effects is very

limited. This gap in the literature creates serious problems, because researchers may misjudge either the effects of friendship quality or the influence of friends by not exploring how friends' influence is moderated by friendship quality.

Understanding of indirect effects would increase if researchers more often probed the processes responsible for those effects (Hartup, 1999). Typically, researchers use interviews or questionnaires to assess friendship quality and the characteristics of children and their friends, without ever seeing how the friends behave toward each other. But a few researchers have shown that rich and compelling data can be obtained by observing the social interactions between friends (e.g., Dishion, Andrews, & Crosby, 1995). These observations can reveal both the features of children's friendships and the relations of those features to the friends' influence on each other. Such observational studies can be a valuable complement to interview-questionnaire studies. When used in combination, the two research strategies should greatly expand knowledge about the indirect effects of friendship quality and the processes responsible for those effects.

Conclusions

Children prize friendships that are high in prosocial behavior, intimacy, and other positive features. Children are troubled by friendships that are high in conflicts, dominance, rivalry, and other negative features. Friendships are high in quality when they have high levels of positive features and low levels of negative features.

High-quality friendships have often been assumed to have positive effects on many aspects of children's social development. However, the direct effects of friendship quality appear to be quite specific. Having friendships high in negative features increases disagreeable and disruptive behaviors, probably because the interactional style that children practice with friends generalizes to interactions with other peers and adults. Having friendships high in positive features enhances children's success in the social world of peers, but it apparently does not affect children's general self-esteem. These findings are surprising because numerous studies with adults suggest that friendships and other supportive relationships enhance many aspects of adults' physical and mental health, including their self-esteem (e.g., Uchino, Uno, & Holt-Lunstad, 1999). If future research confirms that friendship quality has only narrow and specific effects in childhood but has broad and general effects in adulthood, the reasons for this difference should be thoroughly explored.

High-quality friendships may also have indirect effects on children's social development. Most theories of social influence include some form of the hypothesis that children are more strongly influenced by their friends' characteristics the higher the quality of those friendships. An alarming corollary of this hypothesis is that good friendships with bad friends (e.g., friends with poor social or psychological adjustment) should have especially negative effects on children's behavior and development. However, recent research provides equivocal support for this hypothesis. Often, the influence of friends' characteristics has varied little with the quality of these friendships.

More extensive tests of this hypothesis are necessary, for both theoretical and practical reasons. If the hypothesis is not supported in future research, most theories of social influence in childhood will need to be reevaluated. By contrast, if future studies do support the hypothesis, interventions to improve children's friendships will need to be carefully designed to ensure that they do not inadvertently magnify the negative influence of poorly adjusted friends. More generally, a fuller understanding of the joint effects of friendship quality and friends' characteristics will be crucial for enhancing the positive contributions of friendships to children's social development.

Recommended Reading

Bukowski, W. M., Newcomb, A. F., & Hartup, W. W. (Eds.). (1996). *The company they keep: Friendship in childhood and adolescence*. Cambridge, England: Cambridge University Press.

Collins, W. A., & Laursen, B. (Eds.). (1999). (See References)

Hartup, W. W. (1996). The company they keep: Friendships and their developmental significance. *Child Development, 67,* 1–13.

Note

1. Address correspondence to Thomas J. Berndt, Department of Psychological Sciences, Purdue University, W. Lafayette, IN 47907.

References

Agnew, R. (1991). The interactive effects of peer variables on delinquency. *Criminology, 29,* 47–72.

Berndt, T. J. (1996). Exploring the effects of friendship quality on social development. In W. M. Bukowski, A. F. Newcomb, & W. Hartup (Eds.), *The company they keep: Friendship in childhood and adolescence* (pp. 346–365). Cambridge, England: Cambridge University Press.

Berndt, T. J. (1999). Friends' influence on students' adjustment to school. *Educational Psychologist, 34,* 15–28.

Berndt, T. J., Hawkins, J. A., & Jiao, Z. (1999). Influences of friends and friendships on adjustment to junior high school. *Merrill-Palmer Quarterly, 45,* 13–41.

Berndt, T. J., & Keefe, K. (1995). Friends' influence on adolescents' adjustment to school. *Child Development, 66,* 1312–1329.

Collins, W. A., & Laursen, B. (Eds.). (1999). *Relationships as developmental contexts*. Mahwah, NJ: Erlbaum.

Dishion, T. J., Andrews, D. W., & Crosby, L. (1995). Antisocial boys and their friends in early adolescence: Relationship characteristics, quality, and interactional process. *Child Development, 66,* 139–151.

Hartup, W. W. (1999). Constraints on peer socialization: Let me count the ways. *Merrill-Palmer Quarterly, 45,* 172–183.

Hartup, W. W., & Stevens, N. (1999). Friendships and adaptation across the life span. *Current Directions in Psychological Science, 8,* 76–79.

Keefe, K., & Berndt, T. J. (1996). Relations of friendship quality to self-esteem in early adolescence. *Journal of Early Adolescence, 16,* 110–129.

Ladd, G. W., Kochenderfer, B. J., & Coleman, C. C. (1996). Friendship quality as a predictor of young children's early school adjustment. *Child Development, 67,* 1103–1118.

Poulin, F., Dishion, T. J., & Haas, E. (1999). The peer influence paradox: Friendship quality and deviancy training within male adolescent friendships. *Merrill-Palmer Quarterly, 45,* 42–61.

Uchino, B. N., Uno, D., & Holt-Lunstad, J. (1999). Social support, physiological processes, and health. *Current Directions in Psychological Science, 8,* 145–148.

Loneliness and Peer Relations in Childhood

Although loneliness is a normative experience, there is reason to be concerned about children who are chronically lonely in school. Research indicates that children have a fundamental understanding of what it means to be lonely, and that loneliness can be reliably measured in children. Most of the research on loneliness in children has focused on the contributions of children's peer relations to their feelings of well-being at school. Loneliness in children is influenced by how well accepted they are by peers, whether they are overtly victimized, whether they have friends, and the durability and quality of their best friendships. Findings from this emerging area of research provide a differentiated picture of how children's peer experiences come to influence their emotional well-being.

STEVEN R. ASHER[1] AND JULIE A. PAQUETTE
Department of Psychology, Duke University, Durham, North Carolina

The study of children's peer-relationship difficulties has become a major focus of contemporary developmental and child-clinical psychology (see Rubin, Bukowski, & Parker, 1998). As part of this focus, increasing attention is being given to the internal, subjective, and emotional sides of children's social lives. Human beings have fundamental needs for inclusion in group life and for close relationships (e.g., Baumeister & Leary, 1995), so it is fitting to examine what happens when social needs go unmet. It is clear that a variety of strong affective consequences can result. In this article, we focus on one such emotional reaction, loneliness, and we describe what has been learned about the association between loneliness and various indicators of the quality of children's social lives with peers.

Perspectives on Loneliness

Loneliness is typically defined by researchers as involving the cognitive awareness of a deficiency in one's social and personal relationships, and the ensuing affective reactions of sadness, emptiness, or longing. For example, Parkhurst and Hopmeyer (1999) described loneliness as "a sad or aching sense of isolation, that is, of being alone, cutoff, or distanced from others ...associated with a felt deprivation of, or longing for, association, contact, or closeness" (p. 58). Likewise, many other authors emphasize the perceived deficiencies in the qualitative or quantitative aspects of social relationships and the accompanying emotional discomfort or distress that results.

The subjective experience of loneliness should not be viewed as interchangeable with more objective features of children's peer experiences, such as how well accepted they are by peers, whether they have friends, and what their friendships are like. So, for example, it is possible to have many friends and still feel lonely. Likewise, it is possible to be poorly accepted by the peer group or to lack friends and yet to not feel lonely. Loneliness is an internal emotional state that can be strongly influenced by features of one's social life, but it is not to be confused with any particular external condition.

It is also important to note that loneliness in itself is not pathological. Loneliness is actually quite normative in that most people feel lonely at some point during their lives. As social animals who participate extensively in social relationships, humans open themselves up to the possibility of loneliness. This can occur not only when people lack ongoing relationships with others, but even when they have meaningful relationships that take negative turns. For example, loneliness can be a response to separations, such as when a friend is unavailable to play or moves away. These situational or short-term experiences of loneliness are typically not causes for concern. Chronic loneliness, however, is associated with various indices of maladjustment in adolescents and adults, such as dropping out of school, depression, alcoholism, and medical problems. At least 10% of elementary school-aged children report feeling lonely either always or most of the time (Asher, Hymel, & Renshaw, 1984), which suggests a level of loneliness that places children at risk for poor outcomes.

Systematic research on children's loneliness partially grew out of an earlier line of research on the effects of teaching social-relationship skills to children who were highly rejected by their peers. The question that emerged was whether the children who were the focus of these intensive intervention efforts were themselves unhappy with their situation in school. The research was also inspired by very interesting work on adults' loneliness. The study of loneliness in childhood offers unique opportunities that are typically not available to researchers who explore loneliness in adulthood. Much of children's social lives takes place in a "closed" full-time environment, the school, so it is much easier to capture children's peer world. The presence of a child's "colleagues" makes it possible to learn about a child not just by studying that child, but also by querying his or her interactive partners or directly observing the social interactions the child has with peers. By contrast, adults' relationships take place over more contexts, making it harder to get access to most of their social network. Furthermore, it is usually easier to gain research access to schools than the adult workplace.

Can Loneliness Be Meaningfully Studied with Children?

Some people might think that the concept of loneliness does not have much meaning to children or that they cannot give reliable information about their subjective well-being in this regard. Indeed, Harry Stack Sullivan (the famous American psychiatrist who wrote eloquently about the role of "chumship" in middle childhood) argued that children cannot experience true loneliness until early adolescence, when they develop a need for intimacy within the context of close friendships. However, research indicates that children as young as 5 or 6 years of age have at least a rudimentary understanding of the concept of loneliness (Cassidy & Asher, 1992). Their understanding that loneliness involves having no one to play with and feeling sad corresponds fairly well to typical definitions of loneliness in the literature in that children grasp that loneliness involves a combination of solitude and depressed affect. We call this a rudimentary understanding because young children do not yet appreciate that one can be "lonely in a crowd" or even when with a significant other.

Children's basic understanding of loneliness is accompanied by the ability to respond in meaningful ways to formal assessments of loneliness. The most widely used measures have children respond to some items that assess their feelings of loneliness and other items that involve appraisals of whether they have friends, whether they are good at making friends and getting along with others, and whether their basic relationship needs are being met. Because most of these self-report measures for children contain diverse item content that goes beyond loneliness per se (as does the widely used UCLA Loneliness Scale for adults), caution must be used when interpreting results. Some investigators (e.g., Asher, Gorman, Gabriel, & Guerra, 2003; Ladd, Kochenderfer, & Coleman, 1997; Parker & Asher, 1993) have therefore calculated "pure loneliness" scores by using only items that directly assess feelings of loneliness (e.g., "I am lonely at school"; "I feel left out of things at school"; "I feel alone at school").

Researchers in the field have examined whether, within a particular measure, children respond in an internally consistent manner from one loneliness item to another (e.g., Asher et al., 1984). They have also examined whether there is stability in children's reports of loneliness from one time of assessment to another (e.g., Renshaw & Brown, 1993). Several studies indicate that children's reports of loneliness are highly reliable by both of these criteria. Accordingly, researchers have used these methodologically sound measures to examine whether acceptance by peers and friendships influence children's feelings of loneliness.

Peer Acceptance and Loneliness

The preponderance of research on children's loneliness has focused on the influence of acceptance versus rejection by peers. Peer acceptance in school is typically assessed using sociometric measures in which children either nominate schoolmates they like most and like least or use a rating scale to indicate how much they like each of their peers. Regardless of method, there is a consistent association between acceptance by peers and loneliness. Children who are poorly accepted report experiencing greater loneliness. This finding holds whether loneliness is measured in classroom, lunchroom, playground, or physical education contexts (Asher et al., 2003), suggesting that there is no safe haven at school for poorly accepted children. The finding that rejected children experience more loneliness than other children holds for age groups ranging from kindergartners to elementary-school children to middle schoolers. Furthermore, these associations have been found in research in many different countries and for both genders (with mean differences in loneliness between boys and girls rarely significant).

Although rejected children report the most loneliness, there is considerable within-group variability. Researchers have found that there are distinct subgroups of rejected children. Withdrawn-rejected children consistently report greater loneliness than aggressive-rejected children, although in the elementary-school years both groups report more loneliness than children with an average degree of acceptance by their peers. One factor that may account for variability in rejected children's feelings of loneliness is overt victimization. Not all highly disliked children are overtly victimized, but those who are victimized are more likely than others to report elevated loneliness (for relevant research, see Boivin & Hymel, 1997; Ladd et al., 1997)

Friendship and Loneliness

Variability in loneliness among children rejected by their peers also arises from the partial independence of acceptance and friendship. One way researchers assess whether children have friends is by giving them a roster of the names of their classmates and asking them to circle the names of their friends. Researchers typically consider that a friendship exists when two children identify one another as friends. With this mutual-nomination criterion, half of the children who are poorly accepted by their peers prove to have friends, making it possible to learn whether friendship has a buffering effect on the influence of low peer acceptance.

In studies of the connection between friendship and loneliness, children without friends report experiencing more loneliness than children with friends (Parker & Asher, 1993; Renshaw & Brown, 1993). This beneficial effect of friendship occurs for children at all levels of peer acceptance and for both boys and girls. Even children with deviant friends (i.e., friends who participate in delinquent behavior) report less loneliness than friendless children (Brendgen, Vitaro, & Bukowski, 2000).

There is no evidence to date that the number of friends children have (beyond one friend!) relates to loneliness; however, it is important for children to have friendships that endure. In a camp-based study, Parker and Seal (1996) found that children's ability to maintain, as well as form, friendships was related to loneliness. Children who frequently made new friends but who did not maintain their friendships experienced higher levels of loneliness than other children.

The quality of children's friendships also plays an important role in children's feelings of loneliness. Features such as the degree of companionship, help and guidance, intimacy, conflict, and ease of conflict resolution can all be reliably measured among elementary-school children. Children who participate in high-quality friendships experience less loneliness than other children (Parker & Asher, 1993); this result is found even in analyses that statistically control for level of peer acceptance. Furthermore, the effects of friendship quality on loneliness are comparable for boys and girls. One indicator of friendship quality is whether friends engage in relational aggression toward one another. Crick and Nelson (2002) recently found that among both boys and girls, having friends who ignored them when angry or tried to influence them by threatening termination of the friendship was associated with increased loneliness.

There is a need for research on how the influence of specific qualities of friendship might differ for children of different ages. As discussed by Parkhurst and Hopmeyer (1999), the experience of loneliness at different ages might be influenced by cognitive-developmental changes, changes in the kinds of closeness or associations that are meaningful, and changes in the value that children place on certain kinds of relationships. Thus, what causes a 5- or 6-year-old child to feel lonely will likely be different from what causes an adolescent to feel lonely. For example, kindergarteners might feel lonely if there is no one to play with, whereas older youth might feel lonely if they do not have someone with whom to discuss personal thoughts and feelings. These types of developmental predictions need direct tests.

Future Directions

Research to date consistently indicates that both acceptance by peers and friendship processes influence children's feelings of loneliness at school. However, acceptance and friendship variables, as typically measured, still leave much of the variance in loneliness unexplained. Partly this is because of the frequent reliance on singleshot assessments of key constructs. When repeated assessments of rejection or victimization are conducted, the associations with loneliness become stronger. Children who chronically experience negative peer relations are unquestionably at greater risk than children whose adverse circumstances are more short term (e.g., Kochenderfer-Ladd & Wardrop,

2001). Repeated assessments help to account for more of the variance in children's loneliness.

At the same time, psychologists will never fully understand the dynamics of loneliness if they look only at objective indicators of children's adjustment and ignore children's subjective representations of their experiences. Little is known about the role of beliefs and expectations in children's loneliness. For example, children who have idealized views that friends will always "be there for them," will never fail to keep a commitment, or will never hurt their feelings are likely to experience disappointments in their friendships even when other people with different beliefs and expectations might think those friendships are going well. Likewise, children who believe that conflict is a sign of impending dissolution of a friendship are likely to experience higher levels of loneliness than other children because some level of conflict is virtually inevitable in all close relationships. Examining children's beliefs and expectations may shed light on why some children who are highly accepted and have what seem to be high-quality friendships nevertheless are lonely.

Finally, there is a need for intervention research aimed at helping children who experience chronic loneliness. An earlier generation of intervention studies found that teaching children social-relationship skills had beneficial effects on children's peer acceptance (see Asher, Parker, & Walker, 1996, for a review). However, these studies generally predated the more recent research on loneliness in children and therefore did not assess whether the interventions had positive effects on loneliness. Intervention research not only would offer a potential aid to children, but also could be useful for testing specific hypotheses about the processes that lead particular kinds of children to become lonely. For example, intervention research is a way to learn whether increasing the social skills of poorly accepted children who lack friends leads to parallel increases in acceptance and friendship that in turn result in reductions in loneliness. Likewise, for children who are well accepted and have friends yet are lonely, interventions aimed at modifying their thoughts and beliefs about relationships can experimentally test hypothesized linkages between particular representations and loneliness.

Recommended Reading

Asher, S.R., Rose, A.J., & Gabriel, S.W. (2001). Peer rejection in everyday life. In M.R. Leary (Ed.), *Interpersonal rejection* (pp. 105–142). New York: Oxford University Press.

Ernst, J.M., & Cacioppo, J.T. (1999). Lonely hearts: Psychological perspectives on loneliness. *Applied & Preventive Psychology, 8,* 1–22.

Peplau, L.A., & Perlman, D. (Eds.) (1982). *Loneliness: A sourcebook of current theory, research, and therapy.* New York: Wiley.

Rotenberg, K.J., & Hymel, S. (Eds.). (1999). *Loneliness in childhood and adolescence.* New York: Cambridge University Press.

Note

1. Address correspondence to Steven R. Asher, Department of Psychology: Social and Health Sciences, Duke University, Box 90085, Durham, NC 27708-0085; e-mail: asher@duke.edu.

References

Asher, S.R., Gorman, A.H., Gabriel, S.W., & Guerra, V.S. (2003). *Children's loneliness in different school contexts.* Manuscript submitted for publication.

Asher, S.R., Hymel, S., & Renshaw, R.D. (1984). Loneliness in childhood. *Child Development, 55,* 1456–1464.

Asher, S.R., Parker, J.G., & Walker, D.L. (1996). Distinguishing friendship from acceptance: Implications for intervention and assessment. In W.M. Bukowski, A.F. Newcomb, & W.W. Hartup (Eds.), *The company they keep: Friendship during childhood and adolescence* (pp. 366–405). New York: Cambridge University Press.

Baumeister, R.F., & Leary, M.R. (1995). The need to belong: Desire for interpersonal attachments as a fundamental human motivation. *Psychological Bulletin, 117,* 497–529.

Boivin, M., & Hymel, S. (1997). Peer experiences and social self-perceptions: A sequential model. *Developmental Psychology, 33,* 135–145.

Brendgen, M., Vitaro, F., & Bukowski, W.M. (2000). Deviant friends and early adolescents' emotional and behavioral adjustment. *Journal of Research on Adolescence, 10,* 172–189.

Cassidy, J., & Asher, S.R. (1992). Loneliness and peer relations in young children. *Child Development, 63,* 350–365.

Crick, N.R., & Nelson, D.A. (2002). Relational and physical victimization within friendships: Nobody told me there'd be friends like these. *Journal of Abnormal Child Psychology, 30,* 599–607.

Kochenderfer-Ladd, B.J., & Wardrop, J.L. (2001). Chronicity and instability of children's peer victimization experiences as predictors of loneliness and social satisfaction trajectories. *Child Development, 72,* 134-151.

Ladd, G.W., Kochenderfer, B.J., & Coleman, C.C. (1997). Classroom peer acceptance, friendship, and victimization: Distinct relational systems that contribute uniquely to children's school adjustment? *Child Development, 68,* 1181–1197.

Parker, J.G., & Asher, S.R. (1993). Friendship and friendship quality in middle childhood: Links with peer group acceptance and feelings of loneliness and social dissatisfaction. *Developmental Psychology, 29,* 611–621.

Parker, J.G., & Seal, J. (1996). Forming, losing, renewing, and replacing friendships: Applying temporal parameters to the assessment of children's friendship experiences. *Child Development, 67,* 2248–2268.

Parkhurst, J.T., & Hopmeyer, A. (1999). Developmental change in the source of loneliness in childhood and adolescence: Constructing a theoretical model. In K.J. Rotenberg & S. Hymel (Eds.), *Loneliness in childhood and adolescence* (pp. 56–79). New York: Cambridge University Press.

Renshaw, P.O., & Brown, P.J. (1993). Loneliness in middle childhood: Concurrent and longitudinal predictors. *Child Development, 64,* 1271–1284.

Rubin, K.H., Bukowski, W., & Parker, J.G. (1998). Peer interactions, relationships, and groups. In W. Damon (Editor-in-Chief) & N. Eisenberg (Vol. Ed.), *Handbook of child psychology: Vol. 3. Social, emotional, and personality development* (pp. 619–700). New York: Wiley.

The Power of Make-Believe

Parents may worry about a child's imaginary friends, but a new study finds much to love about them

SORA SONG

It's not likely to win any oscars, but the new Robert De Niro thriller, *Hide and Seek*, which revolves around a little girl's obsession with an imaginary friend named Charlie, taps into something quite real: the confusion and fear parents experience when their children start paying more attention to made-up companions than flesh-and-blood friends. Are kids who do so lonely or crazy or crying for help?

In most cases none of the above, says psychologist Marjorie Taylor of the University of Oregon, who with her colleague Stephanie Carlson at the University of Washington has conducted a study of kids and their fictional companions. Not only are such creations common—65% of children up to age 7 played with at least one imaginary friend at some point in their lives, according to a paper Taylor and Carlson published in *Developmental Psychology* late last year—but they may give children who dream them up a developmental advantage.

The first thing to understand about imaginary playmates, says Taylor, is that for most children they are just that: playmates. They're designed to provide companionship and entertainment. Unlike real kids, they don't have to get cranky, throw tantrums or sulk when they lose a game. And they often can do things and go places the child can't. Skateboard Guy, for example, described by one child in Taylor's study, is a tiny, invisible 11-year-old boy who sleeps in the child's shirt pocket and performs amazing skateboard tricks the child wishes he could do.

Of course, not all imaginary friends are so versatile or well behaved. Children often complain about invisible friends who won't share or are too loud, too bossy, too stubborn or too busy to play. One child had a make-believe pal who was such a pill he named her Darn It.

Bad as these friends seem, they are not necessarily signs of a troubled mind. They may, in fact, be stepping stones on the road of emotional development. Negotiating with temperamental imaginary friends can be a way for kids to work out real-life issues. "There are themes that children are mulling over and trying to understand in their play," says Taylor. "Being busy is one of them. Meanness and bossiness are also things children think about when they talk about their real friends."

Indeed, what imaginary friends say and do can be a useful window into a child's mind. Four years ago, Quinn Pascal, 6, a bubbly first-grader from Eugene, Ore., invented Elfie-Welfie, an invisible woman with piles of tie-dyed hair and a menagerie of "dozens of zillions, katrillions" of imaginary animals. Quinn's mother Kate says Quinn uses Elfie-Welfie to play out some very real desires. In Elfie-Welfie's world, Quinn was allowed on the rides at the fair. (In real life, Quinn was too small.) Elfie-Welfie had an orange cat named Stripey. (Quinn desperately wanted a pet.) Elfie-Welfie promised she would give Quinn a little brother or sister. (Quinn is an only child.) "[Elfie-Welfie] was my reality check," says Kate. "There were times I would ask Quinn what she was thinking about, and she would say, 'Oh, I was just thinking about how Elfie-Welfie smiles all the time.' And, sure enough, I'd been having a rough day and grumbling around."

Children who play with imaginary companions may have an edge over their peers. They tend to have better verbal skills and are better at understanding other points of view, according to Taylor and Carlson. Earlier studies suggested that children with imaginary friends may have above-average IQs, be more creative and smile and laugh more on the playground than other kids. "Children with pretend friends are actually less shy and more sociable than children without them," says Taylor. "It's almost the opposite of what you might think."

How far should parents go to accommodate the demands of pretend friends? Taylor recalls one child who forced her family to wait at restaurants for a table big enough to fit her nonexistent companions. Another little girl's imaginary friend was so ill the child wouldn't leave her unsupervised at home. Taylor's advice is to try to find solutions within the boundaries of a child's fantasy. To handle the sick friend, for example, the parents created another imaginary friend specifically to be a caretaker.

The interplay of real and imaginary doesn't have to stop at the end of childhood. In her newest research, Taylor is interviewing fiction writers and finding that they interact with their characters in some ways that parallel children's make-believe play. Authors often report that their characters seem to have autonomous lives, dictating their own dialogue, controlling the plot of stories and sometimes refusing to do what the authors ask of them. Some writers maintain personal relationships with characters outside their fictions. Novelist Alice Walker says she lived with her characters for a year while writing *The Color Purple*, even moving from New York City to Northern California to please them. They didn't like the tall buildings and city congestion, she says.

"Imaginary friends are often seen as a symptom of some illness or malaise, and maybe sometimes they are," says author Ben Rice, whose 2000 novel, *Pobby and Dingan*, is based on his wife's childhood fantasy companions. "But I think sometimes they are just a creative outlet, a way of interpreting the world."

Rice's novel is about a child, Kellyanne, whose two imaginary friends are lost. Set in a mining town in the Australian outback, *Pobby and Dingan* features characters who are all looking for things—missing friends, a mother lode of gems—that seem impossible to find. A movie version of the novel was filmed last year, and producer Lizie Gower says that by the end of the shoot, the imaginary characters had taken on a life of their own. Crew members set places for them at the table and bought them lollipops. The 11-year-old actress who plays Kellyanne kept company with the characters off camera, her own imaginary friends having kindly agreed to step aside while she worked with Pobby and Dingan. "It was extraordinary, watching this girl and seeing the real enjoyment she got from them," says Gower. "It's taught me a lot about being tolerant of other people's thoughts and beliefs."

Of course, adults have a tendency to overthink these things. Taylor says that during interviews in her lab, as researchers peppered the kids with questions and scribbled down notes, some of the children grew concerned that the researchers were getting confused. One of the kids leaned over and reminded her interviewer, "It's just pretend, you know."

Gender and Group Process:
A Developmental Perspective

Abstract: Until recently, the study of gender development has focused mainly on sex typing as an attribute of the individual. Although this perspective continues to be enlightening, recent work has focused increasingly on children's tendency to congregate in same-sex groups. This self-segregation of the two sexes implies that much of childhood gender enactment occurs in the context of same-sex dyads or larger groups. There are emergent properties of such groups, so that certain sex-distinctive qualities occur at the level of the group rather than at the level of the individual. There is increasing research interest in the distinctive nature of the group structures, activities, and interactions that typify all-male as compared with all-female groups, and in the socialization that occurs within these groups. Next steps in research will surely call for the integration of the individual and group perspectives.

Keywords: sex; gender; groups; socialization

ELEANOR E. MACCOBY[1]
Department of Psychology, Stanford University, Stanford, California

Among researchers who study the psychology of gender, a central viewpoint has always been that individuals progressively acquire a set of behaviors, interests, personality traits, and cognitive biases that are more typical of their own sex than of the other sex. And the individual's sense of being either a male or a female person (*gender identity*) is thought to be a core element in the developing sense of self. The acquisition of these sex-distinctive characteristics has been called *sex typing,* and much research has focused on how and why the processes of sex typing occur. A favorite strategy has been to examine differences among individuals in how sex typed they are at a given age, searching for factors associated with a person's becoming more or less "masculine" or more or less "feminine" than other individuals. In early work, there was a heavy emphasis on the family as the major context in which sex typing was believed to take place. Socialization pressures from parents were thought to shape the child toward "sex-appropriate" behaviors, personality, and interests and a firm gender identity.

On the whole, the efforts to understand gender development by studying individual differences in rate or degree of sex typing, and the connections of these differences to presumed antecedent factors, have not been very successful. The various manifestations of sex typing in childhood—toy and activity preferences, knowledge of gender stereotypes, personality traits—do not cohere together to form a cluster that clearly represents a degree of sex typing in a given child. And whether or not a given child behaves in a gender-typical way seems to vary greatly from one situation to another, depending on the social context and other conditions that make an individual's gender salient at a given moment. Only weak and inconsistent connections have been found between within-family socialization practices and children's sex-typed behavior (Ruble & Martin, 1998). And so far, the study of individual variations in sex typing has not helped us to understand the most robust manifestation of gender during childhood: namely, children's strong tendency to segregate themselves into same-sex social groups. Although work on gender development in individual children continues and shows renewed vigor, a relatively new direction of interest is in children's groups. This current research and theorizing considers how gender is implicated in the formation, interaction processes, and socialization functions of childhood social groupings.

In some of this work, the dyad or larger group, rather than the individual child, is taken as the unit of analysis. Through the history of theoretical writings by sociologists and social psychologists, there have been claims that groups have emergent properties, and that their functioning cannot be understood in terms of the characteristics of their individual members (Levine & Moreland, 1998). Accumulating evidence from recent work suggests that in certain gender configurations, pairs or groups of children elicit certain behaviors from each other that are not characteristic of either of the participants when alone or in other social contexts (Martin & Fabes, 2001). Another possibility is that the group context amplifies what are only weak tendencies in the individual participants. For example, in their article "It Takes Two to Fight," Coie and his colleagues (1999) found that the probability of a fight occurring depended not only on the aggressive predispositions of the two individual boys involved, but also on the unique properties of the dyad itself. Other phenomena, such as social approach to another child, depend on the sex of the approacher and the approachee taken jointly, not on the sex of either child, when children's sociability is analyzed at the level of the individual (summarized in Maccoby, 1998). It is important, then, to describe and analyze children's dyads or larger groups as such, to see how gender is implicated in their characteristics and functioning.

Gender Composition of Children's Groups

Beginning at about age 3, children increasingly choose same-sex playmates when in settings where their social groupings are not managed by adults. In preschools, children may play in loose configurations of several children, and reciprocated affiliation between same-sex pairs of children is common while such reciprocation between pairs of opposite sex is rare (Strayer, 1980; Vaughan, Colvin, Azria, Caya, & Krzysik, 2001). On school playgrounds, children sometimes play in mixed-sex groups, but increasingly, as they move from age 4 to about age 12, they spend a large majority of their free play time exclusively with others of their own sex, rarely playing in a mixed-sex dyad or in a larger group in which no other child of their own sex is involved. Best friendships in middle childhood and well into adolescence are very heavily weighted toward same-sex choices. These strong tendencies toward same-sex social preferences are seen in the other cultures around the world where gender composition of children's groups has been studied, and are also found among young nonhuman primates (reviewed in Maccoby, 1998).

Group Size

Naturally occurring face-to-face groups whose members interact with one another continuously over time tend to be small—typically having only two or three members, and seldom having more than five or six members. Some gender effects on group size can be seen. Both boys and girls commonly form same-sex dyadic friendships, and sometimes triadic ones as well. But from about the age of 5 onward, boys more often associate together in larger clusters. Boys are more often involved in organized group games, and in their groups, occupy more space on school playgrounds. In an experimental situation in which same-sex groups of six children were allowed to utilize play and construction materials in any way they wished, girls tended to split into dyads or triads, whereas boys not only interacted in larger groups but were much more likely to undertake some kind of joint project, and organize and carry out coordinated activities aimed at achieving a group goal (Benenson, Apostolaris, & Parnass, 1997). Of course, children's small groups—whether dyads or clusters of four, five, or six children—are nested within still larger group structures, such as cliques or "crowds."

Group size matters. Recent studies indicate that the interactions in groups of four or more are different from what typically occurs in dyads. In larger groups, there is more conflict and more competition, particularly in all-male groups; in dyads, individuals of both sexes are more responsive to their partners, and a partner's needs and perspectives are more often taken into

account than when individuals interact with several others at once (Benenson, Nicholson, Waite, Roy, & Simpson, 2001; Levine & Moreland, 1998). The question of course arises: To what extent are certain "male" characteristics, such as greater competitiveness, a function of the fact that boys typically interact in larger groups than girls do? At present, this question is one of active debate and study. So far, there are indications that group size does indeed mediate sex differences to some degree, but not entirely nor consistently.

Interaction in Same-Sex Groups

From about age 3 to age 8 or 9, when children congregate together in activities not structured by adults, they are mostly engaged in some form of play. Playtime interactions among boys, more often than among girls, involve rough-and-tumble play, competition, conflict, ego displays, risk taking, and striving to achieve or maintain dominance, with occasional (but actually quite rare) displays of direct aggression. Girls, by contrast, are more often engaged in what is called collaborative discourse, in which they talk and act reciprocally, each responding to what the other has just said or done, while at the same time trying to get her own initiatives across. This does not imply that girls' interactions are conflict free, but rather that girls pursue their individual goals in the context of also striving to maintain group harmony (summary in Maccoby, 1998).

The themes that appear in boys' fantasies, the stories they invent, the scenarios they enact when playing with other boys, and the fictional fare they prefer (books, television) involve danger, conflict, destruction, heroic actions by male heroes, and trials of physical strength, considerably more often than is the case for girls. Girls' fantasies and play themes tend to be oriented around domestic or romantic scripts, portraying characters who are involved in social relationships and depicting the maintenance or restoration of order and safety.

Girls' and boys' close friendships are qualitatively different in some respects. Girls' friendships are more intimate, in the sense that girl friends share information about the details of their lives and concerns. Boys typically know less about their friends' lives, and base their friendship on shared activities.

Boys' groups larger than dyads are in some respects more cohesive than girls' groups. Boys in groups seek and achieve more autonomy from adults than girls do, and explicitly exclude girls from their activities more commonly than girls exclude boys. Boys more often engage in joint risky activities, and close ranks to protect a group member from adult detection and censure. And friendships among boys are more interconnected; that is, friends of a given boy are more likely to be friends with each other than is the case for several girls who are all friends of a given girl (Markovitz, Benenson, & Dolenszky, 2001). The fact that boys' friendships are more interconnected does not mean that they are closer in the sense of intimacy. Rather, it may imply that male friends are more accustomed to functioning as a unit, perhaps having a clearer group identity.

How Sex-Distinctive Subcultures are Formed

In a few instances, researchers have observed the process of group formation from the first meeting of a group over several subsequent meetings. An up-close view of the formation of gendered subcultures among young children has been provided by Nicolopoulou (1994). She followed classrooms of preschool children through a school year, beginning at the time they first entered the school. Every day, any child could tell a story to a teacher, who recorded the story as the child told it. At the end of the day, the teacher read aloud to the class the stories that were recorded that day, and the child author of each story was invited to act it out with the help of other children whom the child selected to act out different parts. At the beginning of the year, stories could be quite rudimentary (e.g., "There was a boy. And a girl. And a wedding."). By the end of the year, stories became greatly elaborated, and different members of the class produced stories related to themes previously introduced by others. In other words, a corpus of shared knowledge, meanings, and scripts grew up, unique to the children in a given classroom and reflecting their shared experiences.

More important for our present purposes, there was a progressive divergence between the stories told by girls and those told by boys. Gender differences were present initially, and the thematic content differed more and more sharply as time went on, with boys increasingly focusing on themes of conflict, danger, heroism, and "winning," while girls' stories increasingly depicted family, nonviolent themes. At the beginning of the year, children might call upon others of both sexes to act in their stories, but by the end of the year, they almost exclusively called upon children of their own sex to enact the roles in their stories. Thus, although all the children in the class were exposed to the stories told by both sexes, the girls picked up on one set of themes and the boys on another, and two distinct subcultures emerged.

Can this scenario serve as a prototype for the formation of distinctive male and female "subcultures" among children? Yes, in the sense that the essence of these cultures is a set of socially shared cognitions, including common knowledge and mutually congruent expectations, and common interests in specific themes and scripts that distinguish the two sexes. These communalities can be augmented in a set of children coming together for the first time, since by age 5 or 6, most will already have participated in several same-sex groups, or observed them in operation on TV, so they are primed for building gender-distinct subcultures in any new group of children they enter. Were we to ask, "Is gender socially constructed?" the answer would surely be "yes." At the same time, there may well be a biological contribution to the nature of the subculture each sex chooses to construct.

Socialization Within Same-Sex Groups

There has long been evidence that pairs of friends—mostly same-sex friends—influence one another (see Dishion, Spracklen, & Patterson, 1996, for a recent example). However, only recently has research focused on the effects of the amount of time young children spend playing with other children of their own sex. Martin and Fabes (2001) observed a group of preschoolers over a 6-month period, to obtain stable scores for how much time they spent with same-sex playmates (as distinct from their time spent in mixed-sex or other-sex play). They examined the changes that occurred, over the 6 months of observation, in the degree of sex typing in children's play activities. Martin and Fabes reported that the more time boys spent playing with other boys, the greater the increases in their activity level, rough-and-tumble play, and sex-typed choices of toys and games, and the less time they spent near adults. For girls, by contrast, large amounts of time spent with other girls was associated with increasing time spent near adults, and with decreasing aggression, decreasing activity level, and increasing choices of girl-type play materials and activities. This new work points to a powerful role for same-sex peers in shaping one another's sex-typed behavior, values, and interests.

What Comes Next?

The recent focus on children's same-sex groups has revitalized developmental social psychology, and promising avenues for the next phases of research on gender development have appeared. What now needs to be done?

1. Investigators need to study both the variations and the similarities among same-sex groups in their agendas and interactive processes. The extent of generality across groups remains largely unexplored. The way gender is enacted in groups undoubtedly changes with age. And observations in other cultures indicate that play in same-sex children's groups reflects what different cultures offer in the way of materials, play contexts, and belief systems. Still, it seems likely that there are certain sex-distinctive themes that appear in a variety of cultural contexts.

2. Studies of individual differences need to be integrated with the studies of group process. Within each sex, some children are only marginally involved in same-sex groups or dyads, whereas others are involved during much of their free time. And same-sex groups are internally differentiated, so that some children are popular or dominant while others consistently occupy subordinate roles or may even be frequently harassed by others. We need to know more about the individual characteristics that underlie these variations, and about their consequences.

3. Children spend a great deal of their free time in activities that are not gender differentiated at all. We need to understand more fully the conditions under which gender is salient in group process and the conditions under which it is not.

Recommended Reading

Benenson, J.F., Apostolaris, N. H., & Parnass, J. (1997). (See References)

Maccoby, E. E. (1998). (See References)

Martin, C. L., & Fabes, R. A. (2001). (See References)

Note

1. Address correspondence to Eleanor E. Maccoby, Department of Psychology, Stanford University, Stanford, CA 94305-2130.

References

Benenson, J. F., Apostolaris, N. H., & Parnass, J. (1997). Age and sex differences in dyadic and group interaction. *Developmental Psychology, 33,* 538–543.

Benenson, J. F., Nicholson, C., Waite, A., Roy, R., & Simpson, A. (2001). The influence of group size on children's competitive behavior. *Child Development, 72,* 921–928.

Cole, J. D., Dodge, K. A., Schwartz, D., Cillessen, A. H. N., Hubbard, J. A., & Lemerise, E. A. (1999). It takes two to fight: A test of relational factors, and a method for assessing aggressive dyads. *Developmental Psychology, 36,* 1179–1188.

Dishion, T. J., Spracklen, K. M., & Patterson, G. R. (1996). Deviancy training in male adolescent friendships. *Behavior Therapy, 27,* 373–390.

Levine, J. M., & Moreland, R. L. (1998). Small groups. In D. T. Gilbert, S. T. Fiske, & G. Lindzey (Eds.), *Handbook of social psychology* (Vol. 2, pp. 415–469). Boston: McGraw-Hill.

Maccoby, E. E. (1998). *The two sexes: Growing up apart, coming together.* Cambridge, MA: Harvard University Press.

Markovitz, H., Benenson, J. F., & Dolenszky, E. (2001). Evidence that children and adolescents have internal models of peer interaction that are gender differentiated. *Child Development, 72,* 879–886.

Martin, C. L., & Fabes, R. A. (2001). The stability and consequences of young children's same-sex peer interactions. *Developmental Psychology, 37,* 431–446.

Nicolopoulou, A. (1997). Worldmaking and identity formation in children's narrative play-acting. In B. Cox & C. Lightfoot (Eds.), *Sociogenic perspectives in internalization* (pp. 157–187). Hillsdale, NJ: Erlbaum.

Ruble, D. N., & Martin, D. L. (1998). Gender development. In W. Damon & N. Eisenberg (Eds.), *Handbook of child psychology* (5th ed., Vol. 3, pp. 933–1016). New York: John Wiley & Sons.

Strayer, F. F. (1980). Social ecology of the preschool peer group. In W. A. Collins (Ed.), *Minnesota Symposium on Child Psychology: Vol. 13. Development of cognitions, affect and social relations* (pp. 165–196). Hillsdale, NJ: Erlbaum.

Vaughn, B. E., Colvin, T. N., Azria, M. R., Caya, L., & Krzysik, L. (2001). Dyadic analyses of friendship in a sample of preschool-aged children attending Headstart. *Child Development, 72,* 862–878.

From *Current Directions in Psychological Science,* April 2002, pp. 54–58. © 2002 by American Psychological Society. Reprinted by permission of Blackwell Publishing, Inc.

Taming Wild Girls

**Never mind the gentler gender. Girls, too, can be brawlers.
But parents, teachers and older girls are starting to take control**

JEFFREY KLUGER

YOU CAN TELL THINGS AREN'T GOING to end well the moment the little cluster of girls starts to talk. Amanda, a junior at Lower Dauphin Middle School in Hummelstown, Pa., is in the cafeteria, commiserating with her friends about a monster test they all just took. Her friends are sure they tanked it, but Amanda has no such worries. "I aced it," she says airily, "but that's just me." As she gets up to clear her tray, the other girls exchange narrowed looks. "Let's trip her," one suggests. Another one nods, goes after Amanda and in an instant sends her sprawling.

The scene is a nasty one—or it would be if the girls meant any harm. But they don't. There is no real tray, no real cafeteria, and Amanda's tumble was a planned pratfall. The students are merely role-playing, acting out a Kabuki version of the girl-on-girl aggression they are increasingly finding in their school. The teachers noticed it too and have taken steps to stop it.

THE MENTORS
Positive role models like these student volunteers at a Pennsylvania school help younger girls learn to avoid fights

"O.K.," says Pam Eberly, a health and physical-education teacher who helped the girls stage the exercise. "What happened here? Who was the bully? Who were the bystanders? And what could you have done so that things turned out differently?"

The role playing at Lower Dauphin is part of a new program called Club Ophelia that the school initiated to stem the problem of violence among its girls. And Club Ophelia is just one of a few programs in the U.S. that educators are putting in place to tame a group of girls who—to hear teachers and psychologists tell it have suddenly found their feral side.

The take-no-prisoners pitilessness teenage girls can show one another is nothing new. Pitch-perfect movies such as Mean Girls and Thirteen elevated awareness of the behavior, while shelves of advice books help parents and girls get through those angry years. But while the kids may be acquiring better tools to deal with cliques and cattishness, few are skilled at surviving a darker part of the schoolgirl power struggles: physical violence.

Popular stereotype doesn't always make room for the idea of violent girls, but they are there—and they are acting out. In 2003, according to the Centers for Disease Control, more than 40% of boys admitted to having carried a gun or a knife or been in at least one physical fight in the previous year. But the girls were not far behind, at 25%. And when the violence is girl-on-girl, it can get especially ugly. Deborah Prothrow-Stith, coauthor of *Sugar & Spice and No Longer Nice: How We Can Stop Girls' Violence* and professor of public health at the Harvard School of Public Health, meets with teachers and administrators around the country and is taken aback by what she hears. "Principals talk about not only the increased number of girl fights but also the savagery," she says. "One of them told me, 'We never had to call an ambulance here until girls started fighting.'"

Experts agree that girls can be a handful, but they can't agree on why. One explanation is the *Kill Bill* culture—a reference to the famously bloody movie and its famously lethal female protagonist. If generations of boys found their mojo imitating the likes of Bruce Lee and James Bond, why shouldn't girls be equally juiced at the sight of a jumpsuited, sword-wielding Uma Thurman? ENTERTAINMENT WEEKLY (a sister publication of TIME), recently ran an online list of Hollywood's 15 best "Butt-Kicking Babes," from the pugilistic Hilary Swank to the gun-toting Charlie's Angels. A few of the stars were of older vintage, but most made their screen bones in the last generation.

THE EXERCISES
Trust games, and art projects, like making dream books, help to lower the anger

Then there is the Internet. Girls have traditionally practiced not so much physical aggression as relational aggression—battles of cutting words, frosty looks and exclusion from cliques. E-mail makes it easy for the verbal part of that fragging to go on around the clock. Says Cheryl Dellasega, a humanities professor at Penn State's College of Medicine and creator of the Ophelia clubs:

'They go back and forth on the computer all night, and the next day they're ready to fight."

Whatever the cause of all the combat, it is groups such as Club Ophelia that are making the peace. Dellasega founded the clubs in 2002 after the publication of her first book, *Surviving Ophelia,* about the struggles girls face growing up. One of the principles behind the groups is that girls tend to be tenacious about their anger, with resentments continuing to simmer long after the fisticuffs have ended. Most boys, always thought of as brawlers, are raised from birth on the idea of avoiding fights or at least ending them with a handshake. Girls need to learn the same lessons. More than 400 teachers and guidance counselors have taken Dellasega's workshops, and groups are sprouting up nationwide.

An Ophelia group consists of about 30 girls, two adult counselors and five or six mentors, who are one or two grades above the other girls and sometimes Ophelia graduates themselves. Teachers and administrators pick the participants, looking for girls who are aggressors, victims or enabling bystanders. The groups meet in 12 weekly sessions of 90 min. each. Most meetings begin with cooperation exercises such as forming hand-holding circles with all the girls' arms crisscrossing in the middle, and then trying to untangle without releasing hands. Sullen teens and tweens would not seem the best candidates for such an exercise, but at Lower Dauphin, they go at it gamely. "This is not for speed," Eberly reminds them. "Go slowly and listen to one another."

After the exercise and role playing, the girls retreat to the school's art room, where they work together on creative projects and brainstorm nonviolent solutions to hypothetical situations the instructors present them with. They also discuss powerful—and peaceable—women they admire. The list the teachers compile includes Oprah Winfrey, J. K. Rowling and Laura Bush. The girls' nominees mostly include teachers and guidance counselors and often their mothers.

Ophelia is not the only program doing that work. As long ago as 1986, the Seattle-based Committee for Children introduced its second Step program, a classroom-based regimen that teaches anger management and impulse control. The program, which has been tested in a remarkable 25,000 schools, is aimed at younger kids—ages 4 to 14—and makes no distinction between boys and girls. But nowadays, says Joan Cole Duffell, the Committee's director of partnership development, girls "are beginning to express anger in ways more similar to boys." Other, independent groups are appearing elsewhere, such as Images of Me, a girls-only self-awareness program in District Heights, Md., that teaches mediation and communication skills.

Nobody pretends that programs or mentoring can roll back the girls' behavior all the way—nor should it. Says Erika Karres, a retired teacher who once worked in the North Carolina school system: "You have to teach kids that it's good to have anger because it helps you get things out." The trick, of course, is learning to master the difference between assertiveness and aggressiveness, confidence and swagger.

—With reporting by Melissa August/Washington and Jeanne McDowell/Los Angeles

Girls Just Want to Be Mean

MARGARET TALBOT

Today is Apologies Day in Rosalind Wiseman's class—so, naturally, when class lets out, the girls are crying. Not all 12 of them, but a good half. They stand around in the corridor, snuffling quietly but persistently, interrogating one another. "Why didn't you apologize to me?" one girl demands. "Are you stressed right now?" says another. "I am so stressed." Inside the classroom, which is at the National Cathedral School, a private girls' school in Washington, Wiseman is locked in conversation with one of the sixth graders who has stayed behind to discuss why her newly popular best friend is now scorning her.

"You've got to let her go through this," Wiseman instructs. "You can't make someone be your best friend. And it's gonna be hard for her too, because if she doesn't do what they want her to do, the popular girls are gonna chuck her out, and they're gonna spread rumors about her or tell people stuff she told them." The girl's ponytail bobs as she nods and thanks Wiseman, but her expression is baleful.

Wiseman's class is about gossip and cliques and ostracism and just plain meanness among girls. But perhaps the simplest way to describe its goals would be to say that it tries to make middle-school girls be nice to one another. This is a far trickier project than you might imagine, and Apologies Day is a case in point. The girls whom Wiseman variously calls the Alpha Girls, the R.M.G.'s (Really Mean Girls) or the Queen Bees are the ones who are supposed to own up to having back-stabbed or dumped a friend, but they are also the most resistant to the exercise and the most self-justifying. The girls who are their habitual victims or hangers-on—the Wannabes and Messengers in Wiseman's lingo—are always apologizing anyway.

But Wiseman, who runs a nonprofit organization called the Empower Program, is a cheerfully unyielding presence. And in the end, her students usually do what she wants: they take out their gel pens or their glittery feather-topped pens and write something, fold it over and over again into origami and then hide behind their hair when it's read aloud. Often as not, it contains a hidden or a not-so-hidden barb. To wit: "I used to be best friends with two girls. We weren't popular, we weren't that pretty, but we had fun together. When we came to this school, we were placed in different classes. I stopped being friends with them and left them to be popular. They despise me now, and I'm sorry for what I did. I haven't apologized because I don't really want to be friends any longer and am afraid if I apologize, then that's how it

will result. We are now in completely different leagues." Or: "Dear B. I'm sorry for excluding you and ignoring you. Also, I have said a bunch of bad things about you. I have also run away from you just because I didn't like you. A." Then there are the apologies that rehash the original offense in a way sure to embarrass the offended party all over again, as in: "I'm sorry I told everybody you had an American Girl doll. It really burned your reputation." Or: "Dear 'Friend,' I'm sorry that I talked about you behind your back. I once even compared your forehead/face to a minefield (only 2 1 person though.) I'm really sorry I said these things even though I might still believe them."

Wiseman, who is 32 and hip and girlish herself, has taught this class at many different schools, and it is fair to say that although she loves girls, she does not cling to sentimental notions about them. She is a feminist, but not the sort likely to ascribe greater inherent compassion to women or girls as a group than to men or boys. More her style is the analysis of the feminist historian Elizabeth Fox-Genovese, who has observed that "those who have experienced dismissal by the junior-high-school girls' clique could hardly, with a straight face, claim generosity and nurture as a natural attribute of women." Together, Wiseman and I once watched the movie "Heathers," the 1989 black comedy about a triad of vicious Queen Bees who get their comeuppance, and she found it "pretty true to life." The line uttered by Winona Ryder as Veronica, the disaffected non-Heather of the group, struck her as particularly apt: "I don't really like my friends. It's just like they're people I work with and our job is being popular."

Wiseman's reaction to the crying girls is accordingly complex. "I hate to make girls cry," she says. "I really do hate it when their faces get all splotchy, and everyone in gym class or whatever knows they've been crying." At the same time, she notes: "The tears are a funny thing. Because it's not usually the victims who cry; it's the aggressors, the girls who have something to apologize for. And sometimes, yes, it's relief on their part, but it's also somewhat manipulative, because if they've done something crappy, the person they've done it to can't get that mad at them if they're crying. Plus, a lot of the time they're using the apology to dump on somebody all over again."

Is dumping on a friend really such a serious problem? Do mean girls wield that much power? Wiseman thinks so. In May, Crown will publish her book-length analysis of girl-on-girl nastiness, "Queen Bees and Wannabes: Helping Your Daughter

Survive Cliques, Gossip, Boyfriends and other Realities of Adolescence." And her seminars, which she teaches in schools around the country, are ambitious attempts to tame what some psychologists are now calling "relational aggression"—by which they mean the constellation of "Heathers"-like manipulations and exclusions and gossip-mongering that most of us remember from middle school and through which girls, more often than boys, tend to channel their hostilities.

"My life is full of these ridiculous little slips of paper," says Wiseman, pointing to the basket of apologies and questions at her feet. "I have read thousands of these slips of paper. And 95 percent of them are the same. 'Why are these girls being mean to me?' 'Why am I being excluded?' 'I don't want to be part of this popular group anymore. I don't like what they're doing.' There are lots of girls out there who are getting this incredible lesson that they are not inherently worthy, and from someone— a friend, another girl—who was so intimately bonded with them. To a large extent, their definitions of intimacy are going to be based on the stuff they're going through in sixth and seventh grade. And that stuff isn't pretty."

"Within the hidden culture of aggression, girls fight with body language and relationships instead of fists and knives."
Rachel Simmons, from *Odd Girl Out: The Hidden Culture of Agression in Girls*

This focus on the cruelty of girls is, of course, something new. For years, psychologists who studied aggression among schoolchildren looked only at its physical and overt manifestations and concluded that girls were less aggressive than boys. That consensus began to change in the early 90's, after a team of researchers led by a Finnish professor named Kaj Bjorkqvist started interviewing 11- and 12-year-old girls about their behavior toward one another. The team's conclusion was that girls were, in fact, just as aggressive as boys, though in a different way. They were not as likely to engage in physical fights, for example, but their superior social intelligence enabled them to wage complicated battles with other girls aimed at damaging relationships or reputations—leaving nasty messages by cellphone or spreading scurrilous rumors by e-mail, making friends with one girl as revenge against another, gossiping about someone just loudly enough to be overheard. Turning the notion of women's greater empathy on its head, Bjorkqvist focused on the destructive uses to which such emotional attunement could be put. "Girls can better understand how other girls feel," as he puts it, "so they know better how to harm them."

Researchers following in Bjorkqvist's footsteps noted that up to the age of 4 girls tend to be aggressive at the same rates and in the same ways as boys—grabbing toys, pushing, hitting. Later on, however, social expectations force their hostilities underground, where their assaults on one another are more indirect, less physical and less visible to adults. Secrets they share in one context, for example, can sometimes be used against them in another. As Marion Underwood, a professor of psychology at the

University of Texas at Dallas, puts it: "Girls very much value intimacy, which makes them excellent friends and terrible enemies. They share so much information when they are friends that they never run out of ammunition if they turn on one another."

In the last few years, a group of young psychologists, including Underwood and Nicki Crick at the University of Minnesota, has pushed this work much further, observing girls in "naturalistic" settings, exploring the psychological foundations for nastiness and asking adults to take relational aggression—especially in the sixth and seventh grades, when it tends to be worst—as seriously as they do more familiar forms of bullying. While some of these researchers have emphasized bonding as a motivation, others have seen something closer to a hunger for power, even a Darwinian drive. One Australian researcher, Laurence Owens, found that the 15-year-old girls he interviewed about their girl-pack predation were bestirred primarily by its entertainment value. The girls treated their own lives like the soaps, hoarding drama, constantly rehashing trivia. Owens's studies contain some of the more vivid anecdotes in the earnest academic literature on relational aggression. His subjects tell him about ingenious tactics like leaving the following message on a girl's answering machine—"Hello, it's me. Have you gotten your pregnancy test back yet?"—knowing that her parents will be the first to hear it. They talk about standing in "huddles" and giving other girls "deaths"—stares of withering condescension—and of calling one another "dyke," "slut" and "fat" and of enlisting boys to do their dirty work.

Relational aggression is finding its chroniclers among more popular writers, too. In addition to Wiseman's book, this spring will bring Rachel Simmons's "Odd Girl Out: The Hidden Culture of Aggression in Girls," Emily White's "Fast Girls: Teenage Tribes and the Myth of the Slut" and Phyllis Chesler's "Woman's Inhumanity to Woman."

In her book, the 27-year-old Simmons offers a plaintive definition of relational aggression: "Unlike boys, who tend to bully acquaintances or strangers, girls frequently attack within tightly knit friendship networks, making aggression harder to identify and intensifying the damage to the victims. Within the hidden culture of aggression, girls fight with body language and relationships instead of fists and knives. In this world, friendship is a weapon, and the sting of a shout pales in comparison to a day of someone's silence. There is no gesture more devastating than the back turning away." Now, Simmons insists, is the time to pull up the rock and really look at this seething underside of American girlhood. "Beneath a facade of female intimacy," she writes, "lies a terrain traveled in secret, marked with anguish and nourished by silence."

Not so much silence, anymore, actually. For many school principals and counselors across the country, relational aggression is becoming a certified social problem and the need to curb it an accepted mandate. A small industry of interveners has grown up to meet the demand. In Austin, Tex., an organization called GENaustin now sends counselors into schools to teach a course on relational aggression called Girls as Friends, Girls as Foes. In Erie, Pa., the Ophelia Project offers a similar curriculum, taught by high-school-aged mentors, that explores "how girls hurt each other" and how they can stop. A private Catholic school in Akron, Ohio, and a public-school district near Portland, Ore., have introduced programs aimed at rooting out girl meanness. And Wiseman and her Empower Program colleagues have taught their Owning Up class at 60 schools. "We are currently looking at relational aggression like domestic violence 20 years ago," says Holly Nishimura, the assistant director of the Ophelia Project. "Though it's not on the same scale, we believe that with relational aggression, the trajectory of awareness, knowledge and demand for change will follow the same track."

Whether this new hypervigilance about a phenomenon that has existed for as long as most of us can remember will actually do anything to squelch it is, of course, another question. Should adults be paying as much attention to this stuff as kids do or will we just get hopelessly tangled up in it ourselves? Are we approaching frothy adolescent bitchery with undue gravity or just giving it its due in girls' lives? On the one hand, it is kind of satisfying to think that girls might be, after their own fashion, as aggressive as boys. It's an idea that offers some relief from the specter of the meek and mopey, "silenced" and self-loathing girl the popular psychology of girlhood has given us in recent years. But it is also true that the new attention to girls as relational aggressors may well take us into a different intellectual cul-de-sac, where it becomes too easy to assume that girls do not use their fists (some do), that all girls are covert in their cruelties, that all girls care deeply about the ways of the clique— and that what they do in their "relational" lives takes precedence over all other aspects of their emerging selves.

After her class at the National Cathedral School, Wiseman and I chat for a while in her car. She has to turn down the India Arie CD that's blaring on her stereo so we can hear each other. The girl she had stayed to talk with after class is still on her mind, partly because she represents the social type for whom Wiseman seems to feel the profoundest sympathy: the girl left behind by a newly popular, newly dismissive friend. "See, at a certain point it becomes cool to be boy crazy," she explains. "That happens in sixth grade, and it gives you so much social status, particularly in an all-girls school, if you can go up and talk to boys.

"But often, an Alpha Girl has an old friend, the best-friend-forever elementary-school friend, who is left behind because she's not boy crazy yet," Wiseman goes on, pressing the accelerator with her red snakeskin boot. "And what she can't figure out is: why does my old friend want to be better friends with a girl who talks behind her back and is mean to her than with me, who is a good friend and who wouldn't do that?"

The subtlety of the maneuvers still amazes Wiseman, though she has seen them time and again. "What happens," she goes on, "is that the newly popular girl—let's call her Darcy—is hanging out with Molly and some other Alpha Girls in the back courtyard, and the old friend, let's call her Kristin, comes up to them. And what's going to happen is Molly's going to throw her arms around Darcy and talk about things that Kristin doesn't know anything about and be totally physically affectionate with Darcy so that she looks like the shining jewel. And Kristin is, like, I don't exist. She doesn't want to be friends with the new version of Darcy—she wants the old one back, but it's too late for that."

So to whom, I ask Wiseman, does Kristin turn in her loneliness? Wiseman heaves a sigh as though she's sorry to be the one to tell me an obvious but unpleasant truth. "The other girls can be like sharks—it's like blood in the water, and they see it and they go, 'Now I can be closer to Kristin because she's being dumped by Darcy.' When I say stuff like this, I know I sound horrible, I know it. But it's what they do."

Hanging out with Wiseman, you get used to this kind of disquisition on the craftiness of middle-school girls, but I'll admit that when my mind balks at something she has told me, when I can't quite believe girls have thought up some scheme or another, I devise little tests for her—I ask her to pick out seventh-grade Queen Bees in a crowd outside a school or to predict what the girls in the class will say about someone who isn't there that day or to guess which boys a preening group of girls is preening for. I have yet to catch her out.

Once, Wiseman mentions a girl she knows whose clique of seven is governed by actual, enumerated rules and suggests I talk with this girl to get a sense of what reformers like her are up against. Jessica Travis, explains Wiseman, shaking her head in aggravated bemusement at the mere thought of her, is a junior at a suburban Maryland high school and a member of the Girls' Advisory Board that is part of Wiseman's organization. She is also, it occurs to me when I meet her, a curious but not atypical social type—an amalgam of old-style Queen Bee-ism and new-style girl's empowerment, brimming over with righteous self-esteem and cheerful cattiness. Tall and strapping, with long russet hair and blue eye shadow, she's like a Powerpuff Girl come to life.

When I ask Jessica to explain the rules her clique lives by, she doesn't hesitate. "O.K.," she says happily. "No 1: clothes. You cannot wear jeans any day but Friday, and you cannot wear a ponytail or sneakers more than once a week. Monday is fancy day—like black pants or maybe you bust out with a skirt. You want to remind people how cute you are in case they forgot over the weekend. O.K., 2: parties. Of course, we sit down together and discuss which ones we're going to go to, because there's no point in getting all dressed up for a party that's going to be lame. No getting smacked at a party, because how would it look for the rest of us if you're drunk and acting like a total fool? And if you do hook up with somebody at the party, please try to limit it to one. Otherwise you look like a slut and that reflects badly on all of us. Kids are not that smart; they're not going to make the distinctions between us. And the rules apply to all of us—you can't be like, 'Oh, I'm having my period; I'm wearing jeans all week.'"

She pauses for a millisecond. "Like, we had a lot of problems with this one girl. She came to school on a Monday in jeans. So I asked her, 'Why you wearing jeans today?' She said, 'Because I felt like it.' 'Because you felt like it? Did you forget it was a Monday?' 'No.' She says she just doesn't like the confinement. She doesn't want to do this anymore. She's the rebel of the group, and we had to suspend her a couple of times; she wasn't allowed to sit with us at lunch. On that first Monday, she didn't even try; she didn't even catch my eye—she knew better. But eventually she came back to us, and she was, like, 'I know, I deserved it.'"

Each member of Jessica's group is allowed to invite an outside person to sit at their table in the lunch room several times a month, but they have to meet at the lockers to O.K. it with the other members first, and they cannot exceed their limit. "We don't want other people at our table more than a couple of times a week because we want to bond, and the bonding is endless," Jessica says. "Besides, let's say you want to tell your girls about some total fool thing you did, like locking your hair in the car door. I mean, my God, you're not going to tell some stranger that."

For all their policing of their borders, they are fiercely loyal to those who stay within them. If a boy treats one of them badly, they all snub him. And Jessica offers another example: "One day, another friend came to school in this skirt from Express—ugliest skirt I've ever seen—red and brown plaid, O.K.? But she felt really fabulous. She was like, Isn't this skirt cute? And she's my friend, so of course I'm like, Damn straight, sister! Lookin' good! But then, this other girl who was in the group for a while comes up and she says to her: 'Oh, my God, you look so stupid! You look like a giant argyle sock!' I was like, 'What is wrong with you?'"

Jessica gets good grades, belongs to the B'nai B'rith Youth Organization and would like, for no particular reason, to go to Temple University. She plays polo and figure-skates, has a standing appointment for a once-a-month massage and "cried from the beginning of 'Pearl Harbor' till I got home that night." She lives alone with her 52-year-old mother, who was until January a consultant for Oracle. She is lively and loquacious and she has, as she puts it, "the highest self-esteem in the world." Maybe that's why she finds it so easy to issue dictums like: "You cannot go out with an underclassman. You just cannot—end of story." I keep thinking, when I listen to Jessica talk about her clique, that she must be doing some kind of self-conscious parody. But I'm fairly sure she's not.

On a bleary December afternoon, I attend one of Wiseman's after-school classes in the Maryland suburbs. A public middle school called William H. Farquhar has requested the services of the Empower Program. Soon after joining the class, I ask the students about a practice Wiseman has told me about that I find a little hard to fathom or even to believe. She had mentioned it in passing—"You know how the girls use three-way calling"—and when I professed puzzlement, explained: "O.K., so Alison and Kathy call up Mary, but only Kathy talks and Alison is just lurking there quietly so Mary doesn't know she's on the line. And Kathy says to Mary, 'So what do you think of Alison?' And of course there's some reason at the moment why Mary doesn't like Alison, and she says, Oh, my God, all these nasty things about Alison—you know, 'I can't believe how she throws herself at guys, she thinks she's all that, blah, blah, blah.' And Alison hears all this."

Not for the first time with Wiseman, I came up with one of my lame comparisons with adult life: "But under normal circumstances, repeating nasty gossip about one friend to another is not actually going to get you that far with your friends."

"Yeah, but in Girl World, that's currency," Wiseman responded. "It's like: Ooh, I have a dollar and now I'm more powerful and I can use this if I want to. I can further myself in the social hierarchy and bond with the girl being gossiped about by setting up the conference call so she can know about it, by telling her about the gossip and then delivering the proof."

In the classroom at Farquhar, eight girls are sitting in a circle, eating chips and drinking sodas. All of them have heard about the class and chosen to come. There's Jordi Kauffman, who is wearing glasses, a fleece vest and sneakers and who displays considerable scorn for socially ambitious girls acting "all slutty in tight clothes or all snotty." Jordi is an honor student whose mother is a teacher and whose father is the P.T.A. president. She's the only one in the class with a moderately sarcastic take on the culture of American girlhood. "You're in a bad mood one day, and you say you feel fat," she remarks, "and adults are like, 'Oh-oh, she's got poor self-esteem, she's depressed, get her help!'"

Next to Jordi is her friend Jackie, who is winsome and giggly and very pretty. Jackie seems more genuinely troubled by the loss of a onetime friend who has been twisting herself into an Alpha Girl. She will later tell us that when she wrote a heartfelt e-mail message to this former friend, asking her why she was "locking her out," the girl's response was to print it out and show it around at school.

On the other side of the room are Lauren and Daniela, who've got boys on the brain, big time. They happily identify with Wiseman's negative portrayal of "Fruit-Cup Girl," one who feigns helplessness—in Wiseman's example, by pretending to need a guy to open her pull-top can of fruit cocktail—to attract male attention. There's Courtney, who will later say, when asked to write a letter to herself about how she's doing socially, that she can't, because she "never says anything to myself about myself." And there's Kimberly, who will write such a letter professing admiration for her own "natural beauty."

They have all heard of the kind of three-way call Wiseman had told me about; all but two have done it or had it done to them. I ask if they found the experience useful. "Not always," Jordi says, "because sometimes there's something you want to hear but you don't hear. You want to hear, 'Oh, she's such a good person' or whatever, but instead you hear, 'Oh, my God, she's such a bitch.'"

I ask if boys ever put together three-way calls like that. "Nah," Jackie says. "I don't think they're smart enough."

Once the class gets going, the discussion turns, as it often does, to Jackie's former friend, the one who's been clawing her way into the Alpha Girl clique. In a strange twist, this girl has, as Daniela puts it, "given up her religion" and brought a witch's spell book to school.

"That's weird," Wiseman says, "because usually what happens is that the girls who are attracted to that are more outside-the-box types—you know, the depressed girls with the black fingernails who are always writing poetry—because it gives them some amount of power. The girl you're describing sounds unconfident; maybe she's looking for something that makes her seem mysterious and powerful. If you have enough social status, you can be a little bit different. And that's where she's trying to go with this—like, I am so in the box that I'm defining a new box."

Jackie interjects, blushing, with another memory of her lost friend. "I used to tell her everything," she laments, "and now she just blackmails me with my secrets."

"Sounds like she's a Banker," Wiseman says. "That means that she collects information and uses it later to her advantage."

"Nobody really likes her," chimes in Jordi. "She's like a shadow of her new best friend, a total Wannabe. Her new crowd's probably gonna be like, 'Take her back, pulleeze!'"

"What really hurts," Jackie persists, "is that it's like you can't just drop a friend. You have to dump on them, too."

"Yeah, it's true," Jordi agrees matter-of-factly. "You have to make them really miserable before you leave."

After class, when I concede that Wiseman was right about the three-way calling, she laughs. "Haven't I told you girls are crafty?" she asks. "Haven't I told you girls are evil?"

It may be that the people most likely to see such machinations clearly are the former masters of them. Wiseman's anthropological mapping of middle-school society—the way she notices and describes the intricate rituals of exclusion and humiliation as if they were a Balinese cockfight—seems to come naturally to her because she remembers more vividly than many people do what it was like to be an adolescent insider or, as she puts it, "a pearls-and-tennis-skirt-wearing awful little snotty girl."

It was different for me. When I was in junior high in the 70's—a girl who was neither a picked-on girl nor an Alpha Girl, just someone in the vast more-or-less dorky middle at my big California public school—the mean girls were like celebrities whose exploits my friends and I followed with interest but no savvy. I sort of figured that their caste was conferred at birth when they landed in Laurelwood—the local hillside housing development peopled by dentists and plastic surgeons—and were given names like Marcie and Tracie. I always noticed their pretty clothes and haircuts and the smell of their green-apple gum and cherry Lip Smackers and their absences from school for glamorous afflictions like tennis elbow or skiing-related sunburns. The real Queen Bees never spoke to you at all, but the Wannabes would sometimes insult you as a passport to popularity. There was a girl named Janine, for instance, who used to preface every offensive remark with the phrase "No offense," as in "No offense, but you look like a woofing dog." Sometimes it got her the nod from the Girl World authorities and sometimes it didn't, and I could never figure out why or why not.

Teachers would "guide students to the realization that most girls don't maliciously compete or exclude each other, but within their social context, girls perceive that they must compete with each other for status and power, thus maintaining the status system that binds them all."

Rosalind Wiseman,
Empower Program

Which is all to say that to an outsider, the Girl World's hard-core social wars are fairly distant and opaque, and to somebody like Wiseman, they are not. As a seventh grader at a private school in Washington, she hooked up with "a very powerful, very scary group of girls who were very fun to be with but who could turn on you like a dime." She became an Alpha Girl, but

she soon found it alienating. "You know you have these moments where you're like, 'I hate this person I've become; I'm about to vomit on myself'? Because I was really a piece of work. I was really snotty."

When I ask Wiseman to give me an example of something wicked that she did, she says: "Whoa, I'm in such denial about this. But O.K., here's one. When I was in eighth grade, I spread around a lie about my best friend, Melissa. I told all the girls we knew that she had gotten together, made out or whatever, with this much older guy at a family party at our house. I must have been jealous—she was pretty and getting all this attention from guys. And so I made up something that made her sound slutty. She confronted me about it, and I totally denied it."

Wiseman escaped Girl World only when she headed off to California for college and made friends with "people who didn't care what neighborhood I came from or what my parents did for a living." After majoring in political science, she moved back to Washington, where she helped start an organization that taught self-defense to women and girls. "I was working with girls and listening to them, and again and again, before it was stories about boys, it was stories about girls and what they'd done to them. I'd say talk to me about how you're controlling each other, and I wrote this curriculum on cliques and popularity. That's how it all got started."

Wiseman's aim was to teach classes that would, by analyzing the social hierarchy of school, help liberate girls from it. Girls would learn to "take responsibility for how they treat each other," as Wiseman's handbook for the course puts it, "and to develop strategies to interrupt the cycle of gossip, exclusivity and reputations." Instructors would not let comments like "we have groups but we all get along" stand; they would deconstruct them, using analytic tools familiar from the sociology of privilege and from academic discourse on racism. "Most often, the 'popular' students make these comments while the students who are not as high in the social hierarchy disagree. The comments by the popular students reveal how those who have privilege are so accustomed to their power that they don't recognize when they are dominating and silencing others." Teachers would "guide students to the realization that most girls don't maliciously compete or exclude each other, but within their social context, girls perceive that they must compete with each other for status and power, thus maintaining the status system that binds them all."

The theory was sober and sociological, but in the hands of Wiseman, the classes were dishy and confessional, enlivened by role-playing that got the girls giggling and by Wiseman's knowing references to Bebe jackets, Boardwalk Fries and 'N Sync. It was a combination that soon put Wiseman's services in high demand, especially at some of the tonier private schools in the Washington area.

"I was just enthralled by her," says Camilla Vitullo, who as a headmistress at the National Cathedral School in 1994 was among the first to hire Wiseman. "And the girls gobbled up everything she had to say." (Vitullo, who is now at the Spence School in Manhattan, plans to bring Wiseman there.) Soon Wiseman's Empower Program, which also teaches courses on subjects like date rape, was getting big grants from the Liz Claiborne Foundation and attracting the attention of Oprah Winfrey, who had Wiseman on her show last spring.

Wiseman has been willing to immerse herself in Girl World, and it has paid off. (Out of professional necessity, she has watched "every movie with Kirsten Dunst or Freddie Prinze Jr." and innumerable shows on the WB network.) But even if it weren't her job, you get the feeling she would still know more about all that than most adults do. She senses immediately, for example, that when the girls in her Farquhar class give her a bottle of lotion as a thank-you present, she is supposed to open it on the spot and pass it around and let everybody slather some on. ("Ooh, is it smelly? Smelly in a good way?") When Wiseman catches sight of you approaching, she knows how to do a little side-to-side wave, with her elbow pressed to her hip, that is disarmingly girlish. She says "totally" and "omigod" and "don't stress" and "chill" a lot and refers to people who are "hotties" or "have it goin' on." And none of it sounds foolish on her yet, maybe because she still looks a little like a groovy high-schooler with her trim boyish build and her short, shiny black hair and her wardrobe—picked out by her 17-year-old sister, Zoe—with its preponderance of boots and turtlenecks and flared jeans.

Zoe. Ah, Zoe. Zoe is a bit of a problem for the whole Reform of Girl World project, a bit of a fly in the ointment. For years, Wiseman has been working on her, with scant results. Zoe, a beauty who is now a senior at Georgetown Day School, clearly adores her older sister but also remains skeptical of her enterprise. "She's always telling me to look inside myself and be true to myself—things I can't do right now because I'm too shallow and superficial" is how Zoe, in all her Zoe-ness, sums up their differences.

Once I witnessed the two sisters conversing about a party Zoe had given, at which she was outraged by the appearance of freshman girls—and not ugly, dorky ones, either! Pretty ones!"

"And what exactly was the problem with that?" Wiseman asked.

"As long as education is mandatory, we have a huge obligation to make it socially safe."

Michael Thompson, author of
Best Friends, Worst Enemies

"If you're gonna be in high school," Zoe replied, with an attempt at patience, "you have to stay in your place. A freshman girl cannot show up at a junior party; disgusting 14-year-old girls with their boobs in the air cannot show up at your party going"—her voice turned breathy—"Uh, hi, where's the beer?'"

Wiseman wanted to know why Zoe couldn't show a little empathy for the younger girls.

"No matter what you say in your talks and your little motivational speeches, Ros, you are not going to change how I feel when little girls show up in their little outfits at my party. I mean, I don't always get mad. Usually I don't care enough about freshmen to even know their names."

Wiseman rolled her eyes.

"Why would I know their names? Would I go out of my way to help freshmen? Should I be saying, 'Hey, I just want you to know that I'm there for you'? Would that make ya happy, Ros? Maybe in some perfect Montessori-esque, P.C. world, we'd all get along. But there are certain rules of the school system that have been set forth from time immemorial or whatever."

"This," said Wiseman, "is definitely a source of tension between us."

A little over a month after the last class at Farquhar, I go back to the school to have lunch with Jordi and Jackie. I want to know what they've remembered from the class, how it might have affected their lives. Wiseman has told me that she will sometimes get e-mail messages from girls at schools where she has taught complaining of recidivism: "Help, you have to come back! We're all being mean again"—that kind of thing.

The lunchroom at Farquhar is low-ceilinged, crowded and loud and smells like frying food and damp sweaters. The two teachers on duty are communicating through walkie-talkies. I join Jordi in line, where she selects for her lunch a small plate of fried potato discs and nothing to drink. Lunch lasts from 11:28 to 11:55, and Jordi always sits at the same table with Jackie (who bounds in late today, holding the little bag of popcorn that is her lunch) and several other girls.

I ask Jackie what she remembers best about Wiseman's class, and she smiles fondly and says it was the "in and out of the box thing—who's cool and who's not and why."

I ask Jordi if she thought she would use a technique Wiseman had recommended for confronting a friend who had weaseled out of plans with her in favor of a more popular girl's invitation. Wiseman had suggested sitting the old friend down alone at some later date, "affirming" the friendship and telling her clearly what she wanted from her. Jordi had loved it when the class acted out the scene, everybody hooting and booing at the behavior of the diva-girl as she dissed her social inferiors in a showdown at the food court. But now, she tells me that she found the exercise "kind of corny." She explains: "Not many people at my school would do it that way. We'd be more likely just to battle it out on the Internet when we got home." (Most of her friends feverishly instant-message after school each afternoon.) Both girls agree that the class was fun, though, and had taught them a lot about popularity.

Which, unfortunately, wasn't exactly the point. Wiseman told me once that one hazard of her trade is that girls will occasionally go home and tell their moms that they were in a class where they learned how to be popular. "I think they're smarter than that, and they must just be telling their moms that," she said. "But they're such concrete thinkers at this age that some could get confused."

I think Wiseman's right—most girls do understand what she's getting at. But it is also true that in paying such close attention to the cliques, in taking Queen Bees so very seriously, the relational-aggression movement seems to grant them a legitimacy and a stature they did not have when they ruled a world that was beneath adult radar.

Nowadays, adults, particularly in the upper middle classes, are less laissez-faire about children's social lives. They are more vigilant, more likely to have read books about surviving the popularity wars of middle school or dealing with cliques, more likely to have heard a talk or gone to a workshop on those topics. Not long ago, I found myself at a lecture by the best-selling author Michael Thompson on "Understanding the Social Lives of our Children." It was held inside the National Cathedral on a chilly Tuesday evening in January, and there were hundreds of people in attendance—attractive late-40's mothers in cashmere turtlenecks and interesting scarves and expensive haircuts, and graying but fit fathers—all taking notes and lining up to ask eager, anxious questions about how best to ensure their children's social happiness. "As long as education is mandatory," Thompson said from the pulpit, "we have a huge obligation to make it socially safe," and heads nodded all around me. He made a list of "the top three reasons for a fourth-grade girl to be popular," and parents in my pew wrote it down in handsome little leather notebooks or on the inside cover of Thompson's latest book, "Best Friends, Worst Enemies." A red-haired woman with a fervent, tremulous voice and an elegant navy blue suit said that she worried our children were socially handicapped by "a lack of opportunities for unstructured cooperative play" and mentioned that she had her 2-year-old in a science class. A serious-looking woman took the microphone to say that she was troubled by the fact that her daughter liked a girl "who is mean and controlling and once wrote the word murder on the bathroom mirror—and this is in a private school!"

I would never counsel blithe ignorance on such matters—some children are truly miserable at school for social reasons, truly persecuted and friendless and in need of adult help. But sometimes we do seem in danger of micromanaging children's social lives, peering a little too closely. Priding ourselves on honesty in our relationships, as baby-boomer parents often do, we expect to know everything about our children's friendships, to be hip to their social travails in a way our own parents, we thought, were not. But maybe this attention to the details can backfire, giving children the impression that the transient social anxieties and allegiances of middle school are weightier and more immutable than they really are. And if that is the result, it seems particularly unfortunate for girls, who are already more mired in the minutiae of relationships than boys are, who may already lack, as Christopher Lasch once put it, "any sense of an impersonal order that exists independently of their wishes and anxieties" and of the "vicissitudes of relationships."

I think I would have found it dismaying if my middle school had offered a class that taught us about the wiles of Marcie and Tracie: if adults studied their folkways, maybe they were more important than I thought, or hoped. For me, the best antidote to the caste system of middle school was the premonition that adults did not usually play by the same rigid and peculiar rules—and that someday, somewhere, I would find a whole different mattering map, a whole crowd of people who read the same books I did and wouldn't shun me if I didn't have a particular brand of shoes. When I went to college, I found it, and I have never really looked back.

And the Queen Bees? Well, some grow out of their girly sense of entitlement on their own, surely; some channel it in more productive directions. Martha Stewart must have been a Q.B. Same with Madonna. At least one of the Q.B.'s from my

youth—albeit the nicest and smartest one—has become a pediatrician on the faculty of a prominent medical school, I noticed when I looked her up the other day. And some Queen Bees have people who love them—dare I say it?—just as they are, a truth that would have astounded me in my own school days but that seems perfectly natural now.

On a Sunday afternoon, I have lunch with Jessica Travis and her mother, Robin, who turns out to be an outgoing, transplanted New Yorker—born in Brighton Beach, raised in Sheepshead Bay." Over white pizza, pasta, cannoli and Diet Cokes, I ask Robin what Jessica was like as a child.

"I was fabulous," Jessica says.

"She was," her mother agrees. "She was blond, extremely happy, endlessly curious and always the leader of the pack. She didn't sleep because she didn't want to miss anything. She was just a bright, shiny kid. She's still a bright, shiny kid."

After Jessica takes a call on her pumpkin-colored cellphone, we talk for a while about Jessica's room, which they both describe as magnificent. "I have lived in apartments smaller than her majesty's two-bedroom suite," Robin snorts. "Not many single parents can do for their children what I have done for this one. This is a child who asked for a pony and got two. I tell her this is the top of the food chain. The only place you can go from here is the royal family."

I ask if anything about Jessica's clique bothers her. She says no—because what she calls "Jess's band of merry men" doesn't "define itself by its opponents. They're not a threat to anyone. Besides, it's not like they're an A-list clique."

"Uh, Mom," Jessica corrects. "We are definitely an A-list clique. We are totally A-list. You are giving out incorrect information."

"Soooorry," Robin says. "I'd fire myself, but there's no one else lining up for the job of being your mom."

Jessica spends a little time bringing her mother and me up to date on the elaborate social structure at her high school. The cheerleaders' clique, it seems, is not the same as the pom-pom girls' clique, though both are A-list. All sports cliques are A-list, in fact, except—"of course"—the swimmers. There is a separate A-list clique for cute preppy girls who "could play sports but don't." There is "the white people who pretend to be black clique" and the drama clique, which would be "C list," except that, as Jessica puts it, "they're not even on the list."

"So what you are saying is that your high school is littered with all these groups that have their own separate physical and mental space?" Robin says, shaking her head in wonderment.

When they think about it, Jessica and her mom agree that the business with the rules—what you can wear on a given day of the week and all that—comes from Jessica's fondness for structure. As a child, her mom says she made up games with "such elaborate rules I'd be lost halfway through her explanation of them." Besides, there was a good deal of upheaval in her early life. Robin left her "goofy artist husband" when Jessica was 3, and after that they moved a lot. And when Robin went to work for Oracle, she "was traveling all the time, getting home late. When I was on the road, I'd call her every night at 8 and say: 'Sweet Dreams. I love you. Good Night.'"

"Always in that order," Jessica says. "Always at 8. I don't like a lot of change."

Toward the end of our lunch, Jessica's mother—who says she herself was more a nerd than a Queen Bee in school—returns to the subject of cliques. She wants, it seems, to put something to rest. "You know I realize there are people who stay with the same friends, the same kind of people, all their life, who never look beyond that," she says. "I wouldn't want that for my daughter. I want my daughter to be one of those people who lives in the world. I know she's got these kind of narrow rules in her personal life right now. But I still think, I really believe, that she will be a bigger person, a person who spends her life in the world." Jessica's mother smiles. Then she gives her daughter's hair an urgent little tug, as if it were the rip cord of a parachute and Jessica were about to float away from her.

MARGARET TALBOT, a contributing writer for the magazine, is a fellow at the New America Foundation.

A Profile of Bullying at School

Bullying and victimization are on the increase, extensive research shows. The attitudes and routines of relevant adults can exacerbate or curb students' aggression toward classmates.

DAN OLWEUS

Bullying among schoolchildren is a very old and well-known phenomenon. Although many educators are acquainted with the problem, researchers only began to study bullying systematically in the 1970s (Olweus, 1973, 1978) and focused primarily on schools in Scandinavia. In the 1980s and early 1990s, however, studies of bullying among schoolchildren began to attract wider attention in a number of other countries, including the United States.

What Is Bullying?

Systematic research on bullying requires rigorous criteria for classifying students as bullies or as victims (Olweus, 1996; Solberg & Olweus, in press). How do we know when a student is being bullied? One definition is that

> a student is being bullied or victimized when he or she is exposed, repeatedly and over time, to negative actions on the part of one or more other students. (Olweus, 1993, p. 9)

The person who intentionally inflicts, or attempts to inflict, injury or discomfort on someone else is engaging in *negative actions*, a term similar to the definition of *aggressive behavior* in the social sciences. People carry out negative actions through physical contact, with words, or in more indirect ways, such as making mean faces or gestures, spreading rumors, or intentionally excluding someone from a group.

Bullying also entails an *imbalance in strength* (or an *asymmetrical power relationship*), meaning that students exposed to negative actions have difficulty defending themselves. Much bullying is *proactive aggression*, that is, aggressive behavior that usually occurs without apparent provocation or threat on the part of the victim.

Some Basic Facts

In the 1980s, questionnaire surveys of more than 150,000 Scandinavian students found that approximately 15 percent of students ages 8–16 were involved in bully/victim problems with some regularity—either as bullies, victims, or both bully and victim (bully-victims) (Olweus, 1993). Approximately 9 percent of all students were victims, and 6–7 percent bullied other students regularly. In contrast to what is commonly believed, only a small proportion of the victims also engaged in bullying other students (17 percent of the victims or 1.6 percent of the total number of students).

In 2001, when my colleagues and I conducted a new large-scale survey of approximately 11,000 students from 54 elementary and junior high schools using the same questions that we used in 1983 (Olweus, 2002), we noted two disturbing trends. The percentage of victimized students had increased by approximately 50 percent from 1983, and the percentage of students who were involved (as bullies, victims, or bully-victims) in frequent and serious bullying problems—occurring at least once a week—had increased by approximately 65 percent. We saw these increases as an indication of negative societal developments (Solberg & Olweus, in press).

The surveys showed that bullying is a serious problem affecting many students in Scandinavian schools. Data from other countries, including the United States (Nansel et al., 2001; Olweus & Limber, 1999; Perry, Kusel, & Perry, 1988)—and in large measure collected with my Bully/Victim Questionnaire (1983, 1996)—indicate that bullying problems exist outside Scandinavia with similar, or even higher, prevalence (Olweus & Limber, 1999; Smith et al., 1999). The prevalence figures from different countries or cultures, however, may not be directly comparable. Even though the questionnaire gives a detailed definition of bullying, the prevalence rates obtained may be affected by language differences, the students' familiarity with the concept of bullying, and the degree of public attention paid to the phenomenon.

Boys bully other students more often than girls do, and a relatively large percentage of girls—about 50 percent—report that they are bullied mainly by boys. A somewhat higher percentage of boys are victims of bullying, especially in the junior high school grades. But bullying certainly occurs among girls as well. Physical bullying is less common among girls, who typically use more subtle and indirect means of harassment, such as

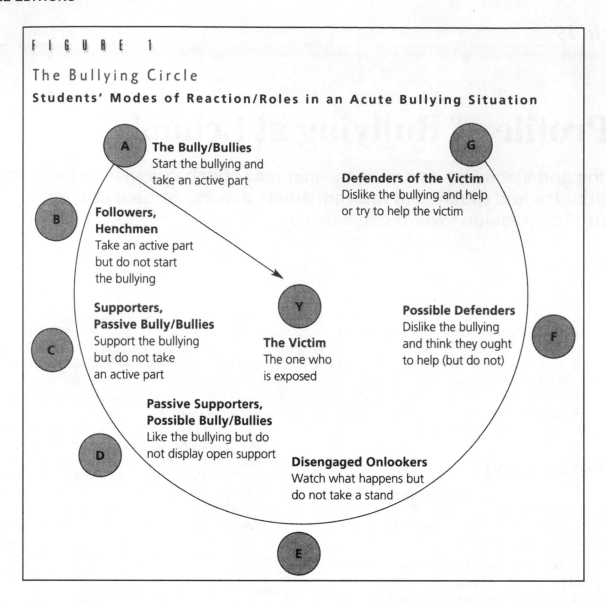

FIGURE 1

The Bullying Circle

Students' Modes of Reaction/Roles in an Acute Bullying Situation

A The Bully/Bullies
Start the bullying and
take an active part

B Followers,
Henchmen
Take an active part
but do not start
the bullying

C Supporters,
Passive Bully/Bullies
Support the bullying
but do not take
an active part

Y The Victim
The one who
is exposed

D Passive Supporters,
Possible Bully/Bullies
Like the bullying but do
not display open support

G Defenders of the Victim
Dislike the bullying and help
or try to help the victim

F Possible Defenders
Dislike the bullying
and think they ought
to help (but do not)

E Disengaged Onlookers
Watch what happens but
do not take a stand

intentionally excluding someone from the group, spreading rumors, and manipulating friendship relations. Such forms of bullying can certainly be as harmful and distressing as more direct and open forms of harassment. Our research data (Olweus, 1993), however, clearly contradict the view that girls are the most frequent and worst bullies, a view suggested by such recent books as *Queen Bees and Wannabes* (Wiseman, 2002) and *Odd Girl Out* (Simmons, 2002).

Common Myths About Bullying

Several common assumptions about the causes of bullying receive little or no support when confronted with empirical data. These misconceptions include the hypotheses that bullying is a consequence of large class or school size, competition for grades and failure in school, or poor self-esteem and insecurity. Many also believe erroneously that students who are overweight, wear glasses, have a different ethnic origin, or speak with an unusual dialect are particularly likely to become victims of bullying.

All of these hypotheses have thus far failed to receive clear support from empirical data. Accordingly, we must look for other factors to find the key origins of bullying problems. The accumulated research evidence indicates that personality characteristics or typical reaction patterns, in combination with physical strength or weakness in the case of boys, are important in the development of bullying problems in individual students. At the same time, environmental factors, such as the attitudes, behavior, and routines of relevant adults—in particular, teachers and principals—play a crucial role in determining the extent to which bullying problems will manifest themselves in a larger unit, such as a classroom or school. Thus, we must pursue analyses of the main causes of bully/victim problems on at least two different levels: individual and environmental.

Victims and the Bullying Circle

Much research has focused on the characteristics and family backgrounds of victims and bullies. We have identified two kinds of victims, the more common being the *passive* or *submis-*

sive victim, who represents some 80–85 percent of all victims. Less research information is available about *provocative victims*, also called *bully-victims* or *aggressive victims*, whose behavior may elicit negative reactions from a large part of the class. The dynamics of a classroom with a provocative victim are different from those of a classroom with a submissive victim (Olweus, 1978, 1993).

Bullies and victims naturally occupy key positions in the configuration of bully/victim problems in a classroom, but other students also play important roles and display different attitudes and reactions toward an acute bullying situation. Figure 1 outlines the "Bullying Circle" and represents the various ways in which most students in a classroom with bully/victim problems are involved in or affected by them (Olweus, 2001a, 2001b).

The Olweus Bullying Prevention Program

The Olweus Bullying Prevention Program,[1] developed and evaluated over a period of almost 20 years (Olweus, 1993, 1999), builds on four key principles derived chiefly from research on the development and identification of problem behaviors, especially aggressive behavior. These principles involve creating a school—and ideally, also a home—environment characterized by

- Warmth, positive interest, and involvement from adults;
- Firm limits on unacceptable behavior;
- Consistent application of nonpunitive, nonphysical sanctions for unacceptable behavior or violations of rules; and
- Adults who act as authorities and positive role models.

We have translated these principles into a number of specific measures to be used at the school, classroom, and individual levels (Olweus, 1993, 2001b). Figure 2 lists the set of core components that our statistical analyses and experience with the program have shown are particularly important in any implementation of the program.

Our research data clearly contradict the view that girls are the most frequent and worst bullies.

The program's implementation relies mainly on the existing social environment. Teachers, administrators, students, and parents all play major roles in carrying out the program and in restructuring the social environment. One possible reason for this intervention program's effectiveness is that it changes the opportunity and reward structures for bullying behavior, which results in fewer opportunities and rewards for bullying (Olweus, 1992).

Research-Based Evaluations

The first evaluation of the effects of the Olweus Bullying Prevention Program involved data from approximately 2,500 students in 42 elementary and junior high schools in Bergen, Norway, and followed students for two and one-half years, from 1983 to 1985 (Olweus, 1991, in press; Olweus & Alsaker, 1991). The findings were significant:

- Marked reductions—by 50 percent or more—in bully/victim problems for the period studied, measuring after 8 and 20 months of intervention.
- Clear reductions in general anti-social behavior, such as vandalism, fighting, pilfering, drunkenness, and truancy.
- Marked improvement in the social climate of the classes and an increase in student satisfaction with school life.

The differences between baseline and intervention groups were highly significant. The research concluded that the registered changes in bully/victim problems and related behavior patterns were likely to be a consequence of the intervention program and not of some other factor. Partial replications of the program in the United States, the United Kingdom, and Germany have resulted in similar, although somewhat weaker, results (Olweus & Limber, 1999; Smith & Sharp, 1994).

In 1997–1998, our study of 3,200 students from 30 Norwegian schools again registered clear improvements with regard to bully/victim problems in the schools with intervention programs. The effects were weaker than in the first project, with averages varying between 21 and 38 percent. Unlike the first study, however, the intervention program had been in place for only six months when we made the second measurement. In addition, we conducted the study during a particularly turbulent year in which Norway introduced a new national curriculum that made heavy demands of educators' time and resources.

Nonetheless, the intervention schools fared considerably better than the comparison schools. Surveys of the comparison schools, which had set up anti-bullying efforts according to their own plans, showed very small or no changes with regard to "being bullied" and a 35 percent increase for "bullying other students" (Olweus, in press). Because we have not yet analyzed the questionnaire information, we cannot fully explain this result, but it is consistent with findings from a number of studies showing that inexpert interventions intended to counteract delinquent and antisocial behavior often have unexpectedly negative effects (Dishion, McCord, & Poulin, 1999; Gottfredson, 1987; Lipsey, 1992).

Most students in a classroom with bully/victim problems are involved in or affected by the problems.

In the most recent (1999–2000) evaluation of the Olweus Bullying Prevention Program among approximately 2,300 students from 10 schools—some of which had large percentages of students with immigrant backgrounds—we found an average reduction by around 40 percent with regard to "being bullied" and by about 50 percent for "bullying other students" (Olweus, in press).

The Need for Evidence-Based Intervention Programs

Coping with bully/victim problems has become an official school priority in many countries, and many have suggested ways to handle and prevent such problems. But because most proposals have either failed to document positive results or have never been subjected to systematic research evaluation, it is difficult to know which programs or measures actually work and which do not. What counts is how well the program works for students, not how much the adults using the program like it.

Recently, when a U.S. committee of experts used three essential criteria (Elliott, 1999) to systematically evaluate more than 500 programs ostensibly designed to prevent violence or other problem behaviors, only 11 of the programs (four of which are school-based) satisfied the specified criteria.[2] The U.S. Department of Justice's Office of Juvenile Justice and Delinquency Prevention and other sources are now providing financial support for the implementation of these evidence-based "Blueprint" programs in a number of sites.

In Norway, an officially appointed committee recently conducted a similar evaluation of 56 programs being used in Norway's schools to counteract and prevent problem behavior (Norwegian Ministry of Education, Research, and Church Affairs, 2000) and recommended without reservation only one program for further use. The Olweus Bullying Prevention Program is one of the 11 Blueprint programs and the program selected by the Norwegian committee.

Norway's New National Initiative Against Bullying

In late 2000, Norway's Department of Education and Research and Department of Children and Family Affairs decided to offer the Olweus Bullying Prevention Program on a large scale to Norwegian elementary and junior high schools over a period of several years. In building the organization for this national initiative, we have used a four-level train-the-trainer strategy of dissemination. At Norway's University of Bergen, the Olweus Group Against Bullying at the Research Center for Health Promotion trains and supervises specially selected *instructor candidates*, each of whom trains and supervises key persons from a number of schools. The key persons are then responsible for leading staff discussion groups at each participating school. These meetings typically focus on key components and themes of the program (Olweus, 1993, 2001b).

The training of the instructor candidates consists of 10–11 whole-day assemblies over 16 months. In between the whole-day meetings, the instructor candidates receive ongoing consultation from the Olweus Group by telephone or through e-mail.

In implementing this train-the-trainer model in the United States with financial support from the U.S. Department of Justice and the U.S. Department of Health and Human Services, we have made some modifications to accommodate cultural differences and practical constraints. In particular, we have reduced

---

Figure 2

The Olweus Bullying Prevention Program

General Prerequisite

- Awareness and involvement of adults

Measures at the School Level

- Administration of the Olweus Bully/Victim Questionnaire (filled out anonymously by students)
- Formation of a Bullying Prevention Coordinating Committee
- Training of staff and time for discussion groups
- Effective supervision during recess and lunch periods

Measures at the Classroom Level

- Classroom and school rules about bullying
- Regular classroom meetings
- Meetings with students' parents

Measures at the Individual Level

- Individual meetings with students who bully
- Individual meetings with victims of bullying
- Meetings with parents of students involved
- Development of individual intervention plans

---

the number of whole-day assemblies to four or five and have granted greater autonomy to individual schools' Bullying Prevention Coordinating Committees than is typical in Norway.

So far, 75 instructor candidates have participated in training, and more than 225 schools participate in the program. Recently, Norway's government substantially increased our funding to enable us to offer the program to more schools starting in 2003.

We see Norway's national initiative as a breakthrough for the systematic, long-term, and research-based work against bully/victim problems in schools. We hope to see similar developments in other countries.

Notes

1. More information about the Olweus Bullying Prevention Program is available at www.colorado.edu/cspv/blueprints/model/BPPmaterials.html or by contacting nobully@clemson.edu or olweus @psych.uib.no.

2. The four school-based programs are Life Skills Training, Promoting Alternative Thinking Strategies (PATHS), the Incredible Years, and the Olweus Bullying Prevention Program. For more information about the Blueprints for Violence Prevention's model programs, visit www.colorado.edu/cspv/blueprints/model/overview.html.

References

Dishion, T. J., McCord, J., & Poulin, F. (1999). When interventions harm: Peer groups and problem behavior. *American Psychologist, 54*, 755–764.

Elliott, D. S. (1999). Editor's introduction. In D. Olweus & S. Limber, *Blueprints for violence prevention: Bullying Prevention Program*. Boulder, CO: Institute of Behavioral Science.

Gottfredson, G. D. (1987). Peer group interventions to reduce the risk of delinquent behavior: A selective review and a new evaluation. *Criminology, 25*, 671–714.

Lipsey, M. W. (1992). Juvenile delinquency treatment: A meta-analytic inquiry into the variability of effects. In T. D. Cook, H. Cooper, D. S. Corday, H. Hartman, L. V. Hedges, R. J. Light, T. A. Louis, & F. Mosteller (Eds.), *Meta-analysis for explanation: A casebook* (pp. 83–125). New York: Russell Sage.

Nansel, T. R., Overpeck, M., Pilla, R. S., Ruan, W. J., Simons-Morton, B., & Scheidt, P. (2001). Bullying behaviors among U.S. youth: Prevalence and association with psychosocial adjustment. *Journal of the American Medical Association, 285*, 2094–2100.

Norwegian Ministry of Education, Research, and Church Affairs. (2000). *Rapport 2000: Vurdering av program og tiltak for å redusere problematferd og utvikle sosial kompetanse.* (Report 2000: Evaluation of programs and measures to reduce problem behavior and develop social competence.) Oslo, Norway: Author.

Olweus, D. (1973). *Hackkycklingar och översittare. Forskning om skolmobbning.* (Victims and bullies: Research on school bullying.) Stockholm: Almqvist & Wicksell.

Olweus, D. (1978). *Aggression in the schools: Bullies and whipping boys.* Washington, DC: Hemisphere Press (Wiley).

Olweus, D. (1983). *The Olweus Bully/Victim Questionnaire.* Mimeo. Bergen, Norway: Research Center for Health Promotion, University of Bergen.

Olweus, D. (1991). Bully/victim problems among schoolchildren: Basic facts and effects of a school-based intervention program. In D. Pepler & K. Rubin (Eds.), *The development and treatment of childhood aggression* (pp. 411–448). Hillsdale, NJ: Erlbaum.

Olweus, D. (1992). Bullying among schoolchildren: Intervention and prevention. In R. D. Peters, R. J. McMahon, & V. L. Quincy (Eds.), *Aggression and violence throughout the life span.* Newbury Park, CA: Sage.

Olweus, D. (1993). *Bullying at school: What we know and what we can do.* Cambridge, MA: Blackwell. (Available from AIDC, P.O. Box 20, Williston, VT 05495; (800) 216-2522)

Olweus, D. (1996). *The Revised Olweus Bully/Victim Questionnaire.* Mimeo. Bergen, Norway: Research Center for Health Promotion, University of Bergen.

Olweus, D. (1999). Norway. In P. K. Smith, Y. Morita, J. Junger-Tas, D. Olweus, R. Catalano, & P. Slee (Eds.), *The nature of school bullying: A cross-national perspective* (pp. 28–48). London: Routledge.

Olweus, D. (2001a). Peer harassment: A critical analysis and some important issues. In J. Juvonen & S. Graham (Eds.), *Peer harassment in school* (pp. 3–20). New York: Guilford Publications.

Olweus, D. (2001b). *Olweus' core program against bullying and anti-social behavior: A teacher handbook.* Bergen, Norway: Research Center for Health Promotion, University of Bergen.

Olweus, D. (2002). *Mobbing i skolen: Nye data om omfang og forandring over tid.* (Bullying at school: New data on prevalence and change over time.) Manuscript. Research Center for Health Promotion, University of Bergen, Bergen, Norway.

Olweus, D. (in press). Bullying at school: Prevalence estimation, a useful evaluation design, and a new national initiative in Norway. *Association for Child Psychology and Psychiatry Occasional Papers.*

Olweus, D., & Alsaker, F. D. (1991). Assessing change in a cohort longitudinal study with hierarchical data. In D. Magnusson, L. R. Bergman, G. Rudinger, & B. Törestad (Eds.), *Problems and methods in longitudinal research* (pp. 107–132). New York: Cambridge University Press.

Olweus, D., & Limber, S. (1999). *Blueprints for violence prevention: Bullying Prevention Program.* Boulder, CO: Institute of Behavioral Science.

Perry, D. G., Kusel, S. J., & Perry, L. C. (1988). Victims of peer aggression. *Developmental Psychology, 24*, 807–814.

Simmons, R. (2002). *Odd girl out.* New York: Harcourt.

Smith, P. K., Morita, Y., Junger-Tas, J., Olweus, D., Catalano, R., & Slee, P. (Eds.). (1999). *The nature of school bullying: A cross-national perspective.* London: Routledge.

Smith, P. K., & Sharp, S. (Eds.). (1994). *School bullying: Insights and perspectives.* London: Routledge.

Solberg, M., & Olweus, D. (in press). Prevalence estimation of school bullying with the Olweus Bully/Victim Questionnaire. *Aggressive Behavior.*

Wiseman, R. (2002). *Queen bees and wannabes.* New York: Crown.

Dan Olweus is Research Professor of Psychology and Director of the Olweus Group Against Bullying at the Research Center for Health Promotion at the University of Bergen, Christies Gate 13, N-5015 Bergen, Norway; olweus@psych.uib.no.

UNIT 4

Parenting and Family Issues

Unit Selections

Key Points to Consider

- Where did you get your ideas, values, and beliefs about how a parent behaves? If you were unsure about how to respond to a particular parenting situation, whom would you consult? Do you think your parents had a significant effect on your growing up? Do you think America is raising more spoiled, overprotected, or anxious children? Explain.

- When you were born, did your mother stay at home or did she work? What are your feelings about your childhood experience as a result? What do you think you would do if you had a child? How would you feel if the father wanted to stay at home with the children? What are the central issues that would be important to consider in making this decision? For example, the research shows that high-quality child care does not disrupt the critical formation of attachment bonds between a baby and a responsive, warm, consistent mother or father.

- Children are not born with a well developed moral consciousness. Think back to your childhood, when do you think you first truly understood the difference between right and wrong? Who or what lessons helped you develop your sense of morality today? What other larger societal influences played a role in your moral consciousness? Do your moral convictions always match your actual behaviors? Explain why or why not.

Student Website

www.mhcls.com/online

Internet References

Further information regarding these websites may be found in this book's preface or online.

Facts for Families
http://www.aacap.org/publications/factsfam/index.htm

The National Association for Child Development
http://www.nacd.org

National Council on Family Relations
http://www.ncfr.com

Parenting and Families
http://www.cyfc.umn.edu

Parentsplace.com: Single Parenting
http://www.parentsplace.com/family/archive/0,10693,239458,00.html

Stepfamily Association of America
http://www.stepfam.org

Few people today realize that the potential freedom to choose parenthood—deciding whether or not to become a parent, deciding when to have children, or deciding how many children to have—is a development due to the advent of reliable methods of contraception and other recent socio-cultural changes. Moreover, unlike any other significant job to which we may aspire, few, if any, of us will receive any formal training or information about the lifelong responsibility of parenting. For most of us, our behavior is generally based on our own conscious and subconscious recollections of how we were parented as well as on our observations of the parenting practices of others around us. In fact, our society often behaves as if the mere act of producing a baby automatically confers upon the parents an innate parenting ability, and furthermore that a family's parenting practices should remain private and not be subjected to scrutiny or criticism by outsiders.

Given this climate, it is not surprising that misconceptions about many parenting practices continue to persist today. Only within the last 40 years or so have researchers turned their lenses on the scientific study of the family. Social, historical, cultural, and economic forces also have dramatically changed the face of the American family today. In fact, most parents never take courses or learn of the research on parenting. In the seminal article "Contemporary Research on Parenting: The Case for Nature *and* Nurture," a distinguished panel of researchers review recent research on parenting and describe the importance of considering the interaction of genetics and environment, a child's temperament, and peer and neighborhood interactions when determining parental influence.

One difficult issue faced by most new parents is the decision whether to have one of the parents (often the mother) elect to leave his or her job and stay at home to raise the new baby. In "The Case for Staying Home," author Claudia Wallis chronicles a recent trend for more women to forego their careers in favor of being a stay-at-home mom and how the business world may or may not be devising alternate work scenarios to help increasingly stressed families cope with the multiple demands of work and family life. In a related vein, fathers, too, face similar challenges as described in "Stress and the Superdad." Conversely however, the author of "A Nation of Wimps" cautions against over-involved parents being over protective of their children.

While a majority of parents in the United States admit to relying on spanking as a form of discipline for their children and do not view spanking as inappropriate, researchers are beginning to amass evidence on the consequences for children. The authors of "Physical Discipline and Children's Adjustment: Cultural Normativeness as a Moderator" present evidence that the mothers' use of physical discipline has differential consequences on children depending on larger cultural factors.

Most children grow up in families with siblings. In "Siblings' Direct and Indirect Contributions to Child Development," researcher Gene Brody chronicles this important research and discusses how parents' differential treatment of their children can affect family dynamics and child outcomes.

Although most Americans picture our nation as one of great possibility and prosperity, recent data shows that more than 19% or 13.4 million of our nation's children live in poverty. Researcher Gary Evans in "The Environment of Childhood Poverty" summarizes the sobering research on poor children showing that for virtually every single quality of life indicator ranging from exposure to violence, family turmoil and instability, educational access, housing and environmental quality, parental involvement, and even child care quality that poor children suffer significant accumulated risks, resulting in an essentially pathogenic existence. In short, the impact of poverty on children profoundly affects every aspect of a child's ecological world and contributes to a host of potential developmental maladjustments among poor children.

The Case for Staying Home

Caught between the pressures of the workplace and the demands of being a mom, more women are sticking with the kids

CLAUDIA WALLIS

It's 6:35 in the morning, and Cheryl Nevins, 34, dressed for work in a silky black maternity blouse and skirt, is busily tending to Ryan, 2 1/2, and Brendan, 11 months, at their home in the leafy Edgebrook neighborhood of Chicago. Both boys are sobbing because Reilly, the beefy family dog, knocked Ryan over. In a blur of calm, purposeful activity, Nevins, who is 8 months pregnant, shoves the dog out into the backyard, changes Ryan's diaper on the family-room rug, heats farina in the microwave and feeds Brendan cereal and sliced bananas while crooning *Open, Shut Them* to encourage the baby to chew. Her husband Joe, 35, normally out the door by 5:30 a.m. for his job as a finance manager for Kraft Foods, makes a rare appearance in the morning muddle. "I do want to go outside with you," he tells Ryan, who is clinging to his leg, "but Daddy has to work every day except Saturdays and Sundays. That stinks."

At 7:40, Vera Orozco, the nanny, arrives to begin her 10 1/2-hour shift at the Nevinses'. Cheryl, a labor lawyer for the Chicago board of education, hands over the baby and checks her e-mail from the kitchen table. "I almost feel apprehensive if I leave for work without logging on," she confesses. Between messages, she helps Ryan pull blue Play-Doh from a container, then briefs Orozco on the morning's events: "They woke up early. Ryan had his poop this morning, this guy has not." Throughout the day, Orozco will note every meal and activity on a tattered legal pad on the kitchen counter so Nevins can stay up to speed.

Suddenly it's 8:07, and the calm mom shifts from cruise control into hyperdrive. She must be out the door by 8:10 to make the 8:19 train. Once on the platform, she punches numbers into her cell phone, checks her voice mail and then leaves a message for a co-worker. On the train, she makes more calls and proof-reads documents. "Right now, work is crazy," says Nevins, who has been responsible for negotiating and administering seven agreements between the board and labor unions.

Nevins is "truly passionate" about her job, but after seven years, she's about to leave it. When the baby arrives, she will take off at least a year, maybe two, maybe five. "It's hard. I'm giving up a great job that pays well, and I have a lot of respect and authority," she says. The decision to stay home was a tough one, but most of her working-mom friends have made the same choice. She concludes, "I know it's the right thing."

THEN, 15 YEARS AGO, IT ALL SEEMED SO DOABLE. Bring home the bacon, fry it up in a pan, split the second shift with some sensitive New Age man. But slowly the snappy, upbeat work-life rhythm has changed for women in high-powered posts like Nevins. The U.S. workweek still averages around 34 hours, thanks in part to a sluggish manufacturing sector. But for those in financial services, it's 55 hours; for top executives in big corporations, it's 60 to 70, says Catalyst, a research and consulting group that focuses on women in business. For dual-career couples with kids under 18, the combined work hours have grown from 81 a week in 1977 to 91 in 2002, according to the Families and Work Institute. E-mail, pagers and cell phones promised to allow execs to work from home. Who knew that would mean that home was no longer a sanctuary? Today BlackBerrys sprout on the sidelines of Little League games. Cell phones vibrate at the school play. And it's back to the e-mail after *Good-night Moon*. "We are now the workaholism capital of the world, surpassing the Japanese," laments sociologist Arlie Hochschild, author of *The Time Bind: When Work Becomes Home and Home Becomes Work.*

Meanwhile, the pace has quickened on the home front, where a mother's job has expanded to include managing a packed schedule of child-enhancement activities. In their new book *The Mommy Myth*, Susan Douglas, a professor of communication studies at the University of Michigan, and Meredith Michaels, who teaches philosophy at Smith College, label the phenomenon the New Momism. Nowadays, they write, our culture insists that "to be a remotely decent mother, a woman has to devote her entire physical, psychological, emotional, and intellectual being, 24/7, to her children." It's a standard of success that's "impossible to meet," they argue. But that sure doesn't stop women from trying.

For most mothers—and fathers, for that matter—there is little choice but to persevere on both fronts to pay the bills. Indeed, 72% of mothers with children under 18 are in the work force—a figure that is up sharply from 47% in 1975 but has held steady since 1997. And thanks in part to a dodgy economy, there's growth in another category, working women whose husbands are unemployed, which has risen to 6.4% of all married couples.

But in the professional and managerial classes, where higher incomes permit more choices, a reluctant revolt is under way. Today's women execs are less willing to play the juggler's game, especially in its current high-speed mode, and more willing to sacrifice paychecks and prestige for time with their family. Like Cheryl Nevins, most of these women are choosing not so much to drop out as to stop out, often with every intention of returning. Their mantra: You can have it all, just not all at the same time. Their behavior, contrary to some popular reports, is not a June Cleaver–ish embrace of old-fashioned motherhood but a new, nonlinear approach to building a career and an insistence on restoring some kind of sanity. "What this group is staying home from is the 80-hour-a-week job," says Hochschild. "They are committed to work, but many watched their mothers and fathers be ground up by very long hours, and they would like to give their own children more than they got. They want a work-family balance."

Because these women represent a small and privileged sector, the dimensions of the exodus are hard to measure. What some experts are zeroing in on is the first-ever drop-off in workplace participation by married mothers with a child less than 1 year old. That figure fell from 59% in 1997 to 53% in 2000. The drop may sound modest, but, says Howard Hayghe, an economist at the Bureau of Labor Statistics, "that's huge," and the figure was roughly the same in 2002. Significantly, the drop was mostly among women who were white, over 30 and well educated.

Census data reveal an uptick in stay-at-home moms who hold graduate or professional degrees—the very women who seemed destined to blast through the glass ceiling. Now 22% of them are home with their kids. A study by Catalyst found that 1 in 3 women with M.B.A.s are not working full-time (it's 1 in 20 for their male peers). Economist and author Sylvia Ann Hewlett, who teaches at Columbia University, says she sees a brain drain throughout the top 10% of the female labor force (those earning more than $55,000). "What we have discovered in looking at this group over the last five years," she says, "is that many women who have any kind of choice are opting out."

Other experts say the drop-out rate isn't climbing but is merely more visible now that so many women are in high positions. In 1971 just 9% of medical degrees, 7% of law degrees and 4% of M.B.A.s were awarded to women; 30 years later, the respective figures were 43%, 47% and 41%.

The Generation Factor

FOR AN OLDER GROUP OF FEMALE PROFESSIONALS who came of age listening to Helen Reddy roar, the exodus of younger women can seem disturbingly regressive. Fay Clayton, 58, a partner in a small Chicago law firm, watched in dismay as her 15-person firm lost three younger women who left after having kids, though one has since returned part time. "I fear there is a generational split and possibly a step backwards for younger women," she says.

Others take a more optimistic view. "Younger women have greater expectations about the work-life balance," says Joanne Brundage, 51, founder and executive director of Mothers & More, a mothers' support organization with 7,500 members and 180 chapters in the U.S. While boomer moms have been reluctant to talk about their children at work for fear that "people won't think you're a professional," she observes, younger women "feel more entitled to ask for changes and advocate for themselves." That sense of confidence is reflected in the evolution of her organization's name. When Brundage founded it in Elmhurst, Ill., 17 years ago, it was sheepishly called FEMALE, for Formerly Employed Mothers at Loose Ends.

The proportion of working married mothers with children under age 3 dropped from 61% in 1997 to 58% in 2002

Brundage may be ignoring that young moms can afford to think flexibly about life and work while pioneering boomers first had to prove they could excel in high-powered jobs. But she's right about the generational difference. A 2001 survey by Catalyst of 1,263 men and women born from 1964 to 1975 found that Gen Xers "didn't want to have to make the kind of trade-offs the previous generation made. They're rejecting the stresses and sacrifices," says Catalyst's Paulette Gerkovich. "Both women and men rated personal and family goals higher than career goals."

A newer and larger survey, conducted late last year by the Boston-area marketing group Reach Advisors, provides more evidence of a shift in attitudes. Gen X (which it defined as those born from 1965 to 1979) moms and dads said they spent more time on child rearing and household tasks than did boomer parents (born from 1945 to 1964). Yet Gen Xers were much more likely than boomers to complain that they wanted more time. "At first we thought, Is this just a generation of whiners?" says Reach Advisors president James Chung. "But they really wish they had more time with their kids." In the highest household-income bracket ($120,000 and up), Reach Advisors found that 51% of Gen X moms were home full time, compared with 33% of boomer moms. But the younger stay-at-home moms were much more likely to say they intended to return to work: 46% of Gen Xers expressed that goal, compared with 34% of boomers.

Chung and others speculate that the attitude differences can be explained in part by forces that shaped each generation. While boomer women sought career opportunities that were unavailable to their mostly stay-at-home moms, Gen Xers were the latchkey kids and the children of divorce. Also, their careers have bumped along in a roller-coaster, boom-bust economy that may have shaken their faith in finding reliable satisfaction at work.

Pam Pala, 35, of Salt Lake City, Utah, is in some ways typical. She spent years building a career in the heavily male construction industry, rising to the position of construction project engineer with a big firm. But after her daughter was born 11 months ago, she decided to stay home to give her child the attention Pala had missed as a kid. "I grew up in a divorced family. My mom couldn't take care of us because she had to work," she says. "We went to baby-sitters or stayed home alone and were scared and hid under the bathroom counter

89

whenever the doorbell rang." Pala wants to return to work when her daughter is in school, and she desperately hopes she won't be penalized for her years at home. "I have a feeling that I'll have to start lower on the totem pole than where I left," she says. "It seems unfair."

Maternal Desire and Doubts

DESPITE SUCH MISGIVINGS, MOST WOMEN who step out of their careers find expected delights on the home front, not to mention the enormous relief of no longer worrying about shortchanging their kids. Annik Miller, 32, of Minneapolis, Minn., decided not to return to her job as a business-systems consultant at Wells Fargo Bank after she checked out day-care options for her son Alex, now 11 months. "I had one woman look at me honestly and say she could promise that my son would get undivided attention eight times each day—four bottles and four diaper changes," says Miller. "I appreciated her honesty, but I knew I couldn't leave him."

Others appreciate a slower pace and being there when a child asks a tough question. In McLean, Va., Oakie Russell's son Dylan, 8, recently inquired, out of the blue, "Mom, who is God's father?" Says Russell, 45, who gave up a dream job at PBS: "So, you're standing at the sink with your hands in the dishwater and you're thinking, 'Gee, that's really complicated. But I'm awfully glad I'm the one you're asking.'"

Psychologist Daphne de Marneffe speaks to these private joys in a new book, *Maternal Desire* (Little Brown). De Marneffe argues that feminists and American society at large have ignored the basic urge that most mothers feel to spend meaningful time with their children. She decries the rushed fragments of quality time doled out by working moms trying to do it all. She writes, "Anyone who has tried to 'fit everything in' can attest to how excruciating the five-minute wait at the supermarket checkout line becomes, let alone a child's slow-motion attempt to tie her own shoes when you're running late getting her to school." The book, which puts an idyllic gloss on staying home, could launch a thousand resignations.

What de Marneffe largely omits is the sense of pride and meaning that women often gain from their work. Women who step out of their careers can find the loss of identity even tougher than the loss of income. "I don't regret leaving, but a huge part of me is gone," says Bronwyn Towle, 41, who surrendered a demanding job as a Washington lobbyist to be with her two sons. Now when she joins her husband Raymond, who works at the U.S. Chamber of Commerce, at work-related dinners, she feels sidelined. "Everyone will be talking about what they're doing," says Towle, "and you say, 'I'm a stay-at-home mom.' It's conference-buzz kill."

Last year, after her youngest child went to kindergarten, Towle eased back into the world of work. She found a part-time job in a forward-thinking architectural firm but hopes to return to her field eventually. "I wish there was more part-time or job-sharing work," she says. It's a wish expressed by countless formerly working moms.

Building On-Ramps

HUNTER COLLEGE SOCIOLOGIST Pamela Stone has spent the past few years interviewing 50 stay-at-home mothers in seven U.S. cities for a book on professional women who have dropped out. "Work is much more of a culprit in this than the more rosy view that it's all about discovering how great your kids are," says Stone. "Not that these mothers don't want to spend time with their kids. But many of the women I talked to have tried to work part time or put forth job-sharing plans, and they're shot down. Despite all the family-friendly rhetoric, the workplace for professionals is extremely, extremely inflexible."

That's what Ruth Marlin, 40, of New York City found even at the family-friendly International Planned Parenthood Federation. After giving birth to her second child, 15 months ago, she was allowed to ease back in part time. But Marlin, an attorney and a senior development officer, was turned down when she asked to make the part-time arrangement permanent. "With the job market contracted so much, the opportunities just aren't there anymore," says Marlin, who hates to see her $100,000 law education go to waste. "Back in the dotcom days, people just wanted employees to stay. There was more flexibility. Who knows? Maybe the market will change."

There are signs that in some corners it is changing. In industries that depend on human assets, serious work is being done to create more part-time and flexible positions. At PricewaterhouseCoopers, 10% of the firm's female partners are on a part-time schedule, according to the accounting firm's chief diversity officer, Toni Riccardi. And, she insists, it's not career suicide: "A three-day week might slow your progress, but it won't prohibit you" from climbing the career ladder. The company has also begun to address the e-mail ball and chain. In December PWC shut down for 11 days over the holidays for the first time ever. "We realize people do need to rejuvenate," says Riccardi. "They don't, if their eye is on the BlackBerry and their hand is on a keyboard."

PWC is hardly alone. Last month economist Hewlett convened a task force of leaders from 14 companies and four law firms, including Goldman Sachs and Pfizer, to discuss what she calls the hidden brain drain of women and minority professionals. "We are talking about how to create off-ramps and on-ramps, slow lanes and acceleration ramps" so that workers can more easily leave, slow down or re-enter the work force, she explains.

"This is a war for talent," says Carolyn Buck Luce, a partner at the accounting firm Ernst & Young, who co-chairs the task force. Over the past 20 years, half of new hires at Ernst & Young have been women, she notes, and the firm is eager not only to keep them but to draw back those who have left to tend their children. This spring Deloitte Touche Tohmatsu will launch a Personal Pursuits program, allowing above-average performers to take up to five years of unpaid leave for personal reasons. Though most benefits will be suspended, the firm will continue to cover professional licensing fees for those on leave and will pay to send them for weeklong annual training sessions to keep their skills in shape. Such efforts have spawned their own goofy jargon. Professionals who return to their ex-employers are known as boomerangs, and the effort to reel them back in is called alumni relations.

One reason businesses are getting serious about the brain drain is demographics. With boomers nearing retirement, a shortfall of perhaps 10 million workers appears likely by 2010. "The labor shortage has a lot to do with it," says Melinda Wolfe, managing director and head of Goldman Sachs' global leadership and diversity.

Will these programs work? Will part-time jobs really be part time, as opposed to full-time jobs paid on a partial basis? Will serious professionals who shift into a slow lane be able to pick up velocity when their kids are grown? More important, will corporate culture evolve to a point where employees feel genuinely encouraged to use these options? Anyone who remembers all the talk about flex time in the 1980s will be tempted to dis-

miss the latest ideas for making the workplace family-friendly. But this time, perhaps, the numbers may be on the side of working moms—along with many working dads who are looking for options.

On-ramps, slow lanes, flexible options and respect for all such pathways can't come soon enough for mothers eager to set examples and offer choices for the next generation. Terri Laughlin, 38, a stay-at-home mom and former psychology professor at the University of Nebraska at Lincoln, was alarmed a few weeks ago when her daughters Erin, 8, and Molly, 6, announced their intentions to marry men "with enough money so we can stay at home." Says Laughlin: "I want to make sure they realize that although it's wonderful staying at home, that's only one of many options. What I hope to show them is that at some point I can re-create myself and go back to work."

Contemporary Research on Parenting

The Case for Nature and Nurture

W. ANDREW COLLINS *University of Minnesota,* ELEANOR E. MACCOBY *Stanford University,*
LAURENCE STEINBERG *Temple University,* E. MAVIS HETHERINGTON *University of Virginia,*
MARC H. BORNSTEIN *National Institute of Child Health and Human Development*

Current findings on parental influences provide more sophisticated and less deterministic explanations than did earlier theory and research on parenting. Contemporary research approaches include (a) behavior-genetic designs, augmented with direct measures of potential environmental influence; (b) studies distinguishing among children with different genetically influenced predispositions in terms of their responses to different environmental conditions; (c) experimental and quasi-experimental studies of change in children's behavior as a result of their exposure to parents' behavior, after controlling for children's initial characteristics; and (d) research on interactions between parenting and nonfamilial environmental influences and contexts, illustrating contemporary concern with influences beyond the parent-child dyad. These approaches indicate that parental influences on child development are neither as unambiguous as earlier researchers suggested nor as insubstantial as current critics claim.

> The heredity and environment of an organism can be completely separated only in analytic thinking, for in actual nature such separation would lead to instant death of the organism, even though the philosopher making the analysis might himself survive. (Gesell & Thompson, 1934, p. 293)

Research on parenting has been the centerpiece of long-standing efforts in psychology to understand socialization processes. As the field moves into its second century, however, this focus on parental influence faces several high-profile challenges. One challenge comes from the charge that there is little compelling evidence of parents' influence on behavior and personality in adolescence and adulthood (Harris, 1995, 1998; Rowe, 1994). Another is the allegation that socialization researchers have neglected significant forces other than parenting—forces that may contribute more extensively than parenting to individual differences in adult behavior. The most commonly cited sources of alternative influences are heredity (Harris, 1995, 1998; Rowe, 1994) and peers (Harris, 1995,

1998), although some writers emphasize the relatively greater importance of concurrent environmental forces more generally (e.g., Lewis, 1997).

These criticisms of socialization research generally invoke studies of parenting published before the early 1980s. Neither the assumptions nor the research paradigms that dominated the field as recently as a decade ago, however, represent research on parenting today. Contemporary students of socialization largely agree that early researchers often overstated conclusions from correlational findings; relied excessively on singular, deterministic views of parental influence; and failed to attend to the potentially confounding effects of heredity. Contemporary researchers have taken steps to remedy many of those shortcomings. Unfortunately, the weaknesses of old studies still permeate presentations of socialization research in introductory textbooks and the mass media, partly because they appeal to preferences for simple generalizations instead of the conditional effects that capture the reality of socialization.

Leading-edge approaches to social development and personality no longer rely exclusively on correlational designs, overly simple laboratory analogs, or additive models for assigning variance to one source or another. Contemporary studies, including research on parenting, turn on complex statistical methods and research designs that capture real-world complexity without sacrificing the rigor necessary to infer causal relations. Moreover, conceptual models increasingly encompass multiple sources of influence. Researchers draw on emerging knowledge in behavior genetics, neuroendocrine studies, studies of animal behavior, and intervention and prevention science to recognize the complex interplay between inherited and experiential components of individual development. The result is both a more complete and a more differentiated picture of parenting and its likely effects (for comprehensive reviews of contemporary socialization research, see Bornstein, 1995b; Eisenberg & Damon, 1998).

One goal of this article is to outline key features of contemporary approaches to studies of parental socialization. We also show how current researchers have, for some time, been identifying and responding to the very challenges pointed to by recent critics.

We pay particular attention to research designs that estimate inherited and other dispositional factors, as well as experiential ones, in estimating influence. We describe several lines of evidence that address issues of causality regarding the scope and nature of parental influences. Finally, we propose that responsible conclusions about the significance of parenting can be based on only the emerging body of research findings that incorporate both individual and social factors and their interrelations.

Contemporary Approaches to Parenting Research

Research during the past two decades has undermined the once tacit assumption that environment should be the sole starting point in explaining individual differences in development. The relevant evidence comes from comparisons of the degree of similarity between individuals who vary in degree of genetic relatedness (e.g., identical vs. fraternal twins). Typical results imply that heredity accounts for a substantial proportion of this similarity, even though a recent meta-analysis (McCartney, Harris, & Bernieri, 1990) concluded that heredity rarely accounts for as much as 50% of the variation among individuals in a particular population, perhaps even less when personality characteristics are the focus. Although these findings also imply that environment contributes substantially to individual differences, behavior-genetics researchers typically infer environmental effects from the residual after estimates of genetic contributions are computed. The sources of the apparent environmental influences are not specified.

Efforts to understand the role of parents in socialization are constrained severely by the traditional analytic model on which the most cited behavior-genetic findings are based. This "additive" model regards hereditary and environmental components as independent and separable and holds that these two components together account for 100% of the variance in a characteristic (Plomin, 1990). Consequently, most behavior-genetic research has allowed for only main effects of genes and environment, ignoring the possibility that genes may function differently in different environments. A primary problem in disentangling heredity and measures of environmental influences, however, is that genetic and environmental factors are correlated (Plomin, 1990). Researchers consistently find that parenting of identical twins is more similar than parenting of fraternal twins and that two biological siblings typically experience more similar parenting than do two adopted children (Dunn & Plomin, 1986; Plomin, DeFries, & Fulker, 1988; Reiss, Niederhiser, Hetherington, & Plomin, in press; Rowe, 1983). Parents' genotypes, as well as children's genotypes, contribute to these contrasting patterns. That individuals who are more closely related genetically also have more similar shared parental environments means that observed associations between parenting and measures of child characteristics cannot be assumed to be either entirely genetic or entirely environmental in origin. As Rose (1995) stated it, the central question in development is "how genetic effects are modulated across lifespans of environmental interactions" (p. 627).

A related problem further limits the usefulness of traditional behavior-genetic approaches to research on parenting. Estimating the effects of heredity versus environment ignores the potential for malleability, even in characteristics heavily influenced by heredity. When environmental conditions change substantially over time, mean levels of a characteristic also may change, although heritability coefficients (which are based on correlations) may or may not change (Plomin & Rutter, 1998). The problem comes from the failure to recognize that means and correlations can vary independently. Thus, although intelligence has been shown to have a high heritability coefficient, individuals' cognitive abilities can improve or decline as a function of experience (for an explanation of this point, see Weinberg, 1989).

Migration studies often reveal similar paradoxes. For example, height is highly heritable, with heritability coefficients in the 90s, showing that within a given population, the variation in children's heights is closely linked with the variations in their parents' heights. By inference, very little variance remains to be attributed to environmental factors. At the same time, grandparents born in Japan are, on the average, considerably shorter than their grandchildren born and reared in the United States (Angoff, 1988). In the same way, genetic factors that are highly important in a behavior do not show up in a study of the heritability of that behavior because this genetic factor is uniform for all members of a population. Thus, analyzing the variation of a factor within a population does not provide exhaustive information concerning either the genetic or the environmental contributions to the factor. Large-scale societal factors, such as ethnicity or poverty, can influence group means in parenting behavior—and in the effects of parenting behaviors—in ways that are not revealed by studies of within-group variability. In addition, highly heritable traits also can be highly malleable. Like traditional correlational research on parenting, therefore, commonly used behavior-genetic methods have provided an incomplete analysis of differences among individuals.

To acknowledge the importance of the interplay of heredity and environment, four lines of contemporary research on parenting have emerged. One line of research adopts the additive model of behavior-genetics research but augments it with direct measures of potential environmental influences in an effort to document environmental effects more precisely (Plomin et al., 1988; Reiss et al., in press). A second line of research addresses the insensitivity of additive models to Gene 5 Environment effects (Plomin & Rutter, 1998; Rutter et al., 1997) by distinguishing among children with different genetic predispositions on a characteristic to see whether they respond differently to different environmental conditions. The distinctions among genetically different groups often rely on measures of temperament or the parent's carrying a known genetic risk factor. A third line of research examines the effect of parental practices after controlling for any initial dispositional characteristics of children. This kind of research is intended to permit inferences about the direction of effects when parent and child characteristics are initially correlated. Evidence on this point comes from three types of research designs: (a) longitudinal studies in which child characteristics at Time 1 are controlled statistically,

(b) experiments in which nonhuman animals are exposed to selected rearing environments, and (c) intervention studies either in which "experiments of nature" have resulted in marked changes in parenting experiences or in which families are randomly assigned to different treatment programs designed to improve parenting with resulting changes in child behavior. A fourth line of contemporary studies addresses the possibility that extrafamilial environmental conditions with which parenting is correlated contribute to individual differences in development and behavior.

Augmented Behavior-Genetic Designs

Traditional behavior-genetic designs give primacy to the effects of heredity, relying on a series of computations to reveal which portions of the variance should be labeled as contributions of the shared environment or assigned to nonshared, "other," or "unknown" sources. Although evidence of shared family influences and experiences has appeared for some characteristics such as health habits, alcohol patterns, smoking patterns (McGue, 1994), depression in later life (Gatz, Pedersen, Plomin, Nesselroade, & McLearn, 1992), delinquency as reported by siblings (Rowe, Chassin, Presson, Edwards, & Sherman, 1992), and autonomy and sociability (Reiss et al., in press), the most frequent conclusion has been that shared environments play a small, inconsequential role in children's development.

Many scholars, however, have challenged this inference. One criticism is that the assumptions, methods, and truncated samples used in behavior-genetic studies maximize the effects of heredity and features of the environment that are different for different children and minimize the effects of shared family environments (Goodman, 1991; Hoffman, 1991; Patterson, 1999; Rose, 1995; Stoolmiller, 1999). For example, Stoolmiller (1999) noted that recent adoption studies have been impaired by pronounced range restrictions (about 67%) in the family environments sampled. Stoolmiller argued that the estimated contribution of shared environment likely would be as much as 50% higher if appropriate corrections for range restriction were applied to data from such studies.

A second criticism is that estimates of the relative contributions of environment and heredity vary greatly depending on the source of data (Turkheimer & Waldron, in press). Twin studies typically yield higher heritability estimates for a trait than adoption studies do (Wachs & Plomin, 1991). Moreover, in both types of studies, heritability estimates vary considerably depending on the measures used to assess similarity between children or between parents and children. The largest effect sizes for environmental influences on social development are found with the relatively rarely used method of direct behavioral observations, whereas the smallest effect sizes for environmental influences are found with parental reports, which are the most commonly used measure in behavior-genetic studies of behavioral outcomes (Emde et al., 1992; Ghodsion-Garpey & Baker, 1997; Miles & Carey, 1997; Rutter et al., 1997; Wachs, 1992). The sizable variability in estimates of genetic and environmental contributions depending on the paradigms and measures used means that no firm conclusions can be drawn about the relative strength of these influences on development.

Traditional twin and adoption studies have been criticized on the grounds that they estimate environmental effects only as a residual: the effects remaining after genetic effects have been estimated and subtracted from 100%. Efforts to rectify this problem by measuring environment directly, however, have failed to clarify the contributions of environment relative to heredity. Most such efforts were stimulated by Plomin and Daniels's (1987) proposal that the environmental variance in behavior-genetic studies emanates largely from experiences that differ for children in the same family. By measuring such differences, researchers hoped to better understand the portion of the variance in behavior-genetic studies not attributed specifically to genetic relatedness. Behavior-genetic analyses, however, can establish that nonshared environment contributes to individual differences in a domain but cannot document the connections between objectively measured nonshared environmental events and development (Turkheimer & Waldron, in press). Most studies with direct measures of the environment and of the development of multiple siblings within a family, moreover, have not used designs that permit heritability estimates (e.g., Brody & Stoneman, 1994; Tejerina-Allen, Wagnere, & Cohen, 1994).

Thus, researchers' attempts to work within the traditional additive model, while augmenting it with direct measures of environment, have yielded findings that are conditional on a series of methodological problems in assessing the relevant environmental factors and in the inherent limitations of the additive model for identifying Gene X Environment interactions. The remainder of this article is devoted to recent investigations of how processes of influence operate and interact.

The Search for Gene X Environment Effects

Traditional behavior-genetic models do not afford comparisons of the effects of differing environments on individuals who vary on genetically influenced characteristics. For example, in twin and adoption studies, degree of biological relatedness between individuals, not specific markers of genetically linked characteristics in the two individuals, is the primary focus, and variations in environments are rarely assessed. The most likely possibility is that the forced estimates of main effects for genetic relatedness and environment in the additive model mask virtually ubiquitous correlations and statistical interactions between the two in existing research. Such interactions are notably difficult to detect because of low statistical power in most relevant studies (McCall, 1991; McClelland & Judd, 1993; Wahlsten, 1990). Although some writers (e.g., Harris, 1998) have elected to subsume evidence of Gene X Environment correlations and interactions under genetic contributions to behavioral development, responsible scholarship requires closer attention to emerging evidence that these effects involve direct parental influences as well (O'Connor, Deater-Deckard, Fulker, Rutter, & Plomin, 1998; Plomin & Rutter, 1998).

The search for Gene X Environment effects often takes the form of using measures of temperament for the purpose of distinguishing among children with different genetic predispositions to see whether they respond differently to given environmental conditions (Bornstein, 1995b; Plomin & Rutter, 1998; Rutter et al., 1997). Studies that pool parenting effects across children with very different temperaments inevitably obscure actual parental effects. Even when parenting effects are apparent, it is not reasonable to expect that a given style or quality of parenting would have the same effect on every child. Moreover, different parental strategies or degrees of parental effort may be required to bring about the same outcome in different children. Two types of recent studies attempt to disentangle individual children's heredity and the nature of their rearing experiences: (a) studies of the effect of rearing experiences on the behavior of children who differ on measures of temperament and (b) studies comparing the effect of high- versus low-risk environments on children of differing vulnerability.

Temperament and parenting. Temperamental characteristics, defined as "constitutionally based individual differences in reactivity and self-regulation" (Rothbart & Ahadi, 1994, p. 55), are thought to emerge early, to show some stability over time, but to be modifiable by experience. In general, statistical associations between early temperamental characteristics and later adjustment are modest (see Rothbart & Bates, 1998, for a review), suggesting that these associations also may be moderated by environmental factors. A difficult temperament, characterized by intense negative affect and repeated demands for attention, is associated with both later externalizing and internalizing disorders (Bates & Bayles, 1988; Bates, Bayles, Bennett, Ridge, & Brown, 1991). Early resistance to control, impulsivity, irritability, and distractibility predicts later externalizing and social alienation (Caspi, Henry, McGee, Moffitt, & Silva, 1995; Hagekull, 1989, 1994), whereas early shy, inhibited, or distress-prone behaviors predict later anxiety disorders, harm avoidance, and low aggression and social potency (Caspi & Silva, 1995).

Correlations between temperamental characteristics and parental behavior reflect bidirectional interactive processes, as well as genetic linkages between parent and child characteristics. Temperamental characteristics may set in motion a chain of reactions from others that put children at risk or protect them from developing behavior and psychological problems (Caspi & Elder, 1988; Hetherington, 1989, 1991; Quinton, Pickles, Maughan, & Rutter, 1993; Rutter, 1990; Rutter & Quinton, 1984; Werner, 1990). Difficultness, irritability, and distress proneness in infants evoke hostility, criticism, a tendency to ignore the child, avoidance, coercive discipline, and a lack of playfulness in mothers (Lee & Bates, 1985; Rutter & Quinton, 1984; Van den Boom, 1989). These reactions, in turn, are associated with avoidant (Grossman, Grossman, Spangler, Suess, & Unzner, 1985; Van den Boom, 1989) or insecure-ambivalent attachment (Goldsmith & Alansky, 1987; Miyake, Chen & Campos, 1985). Bates, Pettit, and Dodge (1995), in a longitudinal study, found that infants' characteristics (e.g., hyperreactivity, impulsivity, and difficult temperament) significantly predicted externalizing problems 10 years later. Although this finding at first seems to support the lasting effects of physiologically based characteristics, Bates et al.

(1995) also showed that predictive power increased when they added information about parenting to the equation. Infants' early characteristics elicited harsh parenting at age 4, which in turn predicted externalizing problems when the children were young adolescents, over and above the prediction from infant temperament. Similarly, this and other findings imply that even though parental behavior is influenced by child behavior, parents' actions contribute distinctively to the child's later behavior. For example, in a longitudinal adoption design, O'Connor et al. (1998) confirmed that children at genetic risk for antisocial behavior elicited more negative parenting from adoptive parents than did children not at risk. They also found, however, that "most of the association between negative parenting and children's externalizing behavior was not explicable on the basis of an evocative gene-environment correlation and that an additional environmentally mediated parental effect on children's behavior was plausible" (p. 970).

Bidirectional and interactive effects of this kind now appear to carry significant implications for distinctive effects of parenting variations on children who differ in temperamental characteristics. In longitudinal work on the socialization of "conscience," Kochanska (1995, 1997) found that maternal use of gentle childrearing techniques that deemphasized power assertion was more effective with temperamentally fearful children than with bolder, more exploratory children in promoting the development of conscience. With bolder children, maternal responsiveness and a close emotional bond with the child were more important in fostering conscience. Similarly, the quality of parenting to some extent moderates associations between early temperamental characteristics of difficultness, impulsivity, and unmanageability and later externalizing disorders (Bates, Pettit, Dodge, & Ridge, 1998; Rothbart & Bates, 1998). Firm, restrictive parental control has been linked to lower levels of later externalizing in early difficult, unmanageable children (Bates et al., 1998). Although only a few studies have examined the moderating effects of parenting on the links between temperamental predispositions and later adjustment, and although not all of these studies have had positive results (Rothbart & Bates, 1998), the evidence nevertheless suggests that parenting moderates these associations.

Studies of risk and resiliency. Parallels to these differential relations between parenting and child behavior can be found in studies of risk and resiliency. Children who showed early developmental problems because of risk factors such as perinatal damage (Werner & Smith, 1992) improved in adjustment under authoritative parenting. Parenting, moreover, appears to play a mediating role between parental psychopathology and child symptoms of disorder (R. Conger, Ge, Elder, Lorenz, & Simons, 1994; Ge, Conger, Lorenz, Shanahan, & Elder, 1995; Ge, Lorenz, Conger, Elder, & Simons, 1994). For example, Downey and Walker (1992) demonstrated that children with a psychiatrically ill parent who were not exposed to parental maltreatment, in contrast to those who were, showed very low levels of both externalizing and internalizing. That different outcomes for children are associated with differential parental responses to the same risk factor implies parental influence, although Downey and Walker cannot rule out evocative behavior on the part of the child.

A Finnish adoption study (Tienari et al., 1994) further illustrates how a genetic predisposition can either manifest itself or not, depending on whether certain triggering environmental conditions are present. Adoptees who had a schizophrenic biological parent were more likely to develop a range of psychiatric disorders (including schizophrenia) than were adoptees not at genetic risk, but only if they were adopted into dysfunctional families (see also Cadoret, 1985). Similar findings have been reported from studies of adopted children whose biological parents had a history of criminality (Bohman, 1996). If adopted into well-functioning homes, 12% of these children displayed petty criminality in adulthood. However, if adopted into families carrying environmental risk, their rate of petty criminality in adulthood rose to 40%. These findings suggest that well-functioning parents can buffer children at genetic risk and circumvent the processes that might ordinarily lead from genotype to phenotype. The more general point is that genetic vulnerabilities (or strengths) may not be manifested except in the presence of a pertinent environmental trigger such as parenting.

Studies of Parental Influence, Controlling for Initial Child Characteristics

A third line of research attempts to provide a basis for examining instances in which parental behavior may exert a causal influence in changing children's behavior. Studies of this type subsume several research strategies. One strategy is longitudinal research in which children's initial characteristics can be observed to change over time in relation to specific parenting experiences. Even more compelling evidence for determining the causal status of parenting, however, involves experimental manipulations. In some recent experiments, young nonhuman animals were exposed to measurably different rearing conditions. Some experiments of nature with humans also have provided evidence of this kind. The most compelling evidence, however, comes from interventions in which parents are assigned randomly to behavior-change treatment groups, with resulting changes in the behavior of both the parents and their otherwise untreated children. Random assignment is the means for ensuring that treatment groups are not initially different.

Longitudinal studies of parenting and child development. The most widely used strategy in contemporary studies of socialization uses short-term longitudinal designs to better distinguish parenting effects from the characteristics of the child (e.g., Ge et al., 1996; Steinberg, Lamborn, Darling, Mounts, & Dornbusch, 1994). In these studies, aspects of child functioning and development are measured at more than one point in time. Statistical procedures, such as the analysis of covariance or multiple regression, are then used to estimate the relation between parenting at one point in time and child outcomes at some subsequent point, after taking into account characteristics of the child at the time that parenting was assessed. Studies showing that the over-time effect of parenting on child development holds even after controlling for earlier child characteristics are important for several reasons. First, in the absence of a random-

ized experimental design, this strategy provides indirect evidence that parenting conceivably affects—rather than simply accompanying or following from—child adjustment. Such indirect evidence is important because one cannot randomly assign children to different home environments. These analyses do not rule out the possibility that different children elicit different parental responses, but they do provide evidence that the correlation between child adjustment and parenting is not due *solely* to the effect of children on parenting behavior.

Significant longitudinal relations between parenting and child adjustment after taking into account their concurrent relation also help rule out a number of third-variable explanations, including the possibility that the observed association is due to factors that parents and their children share, such as genes or socioeconomic status. To be a viable explanation for the observed association, a third variable would have to be correlated with the measures of child adjustment at the time of the longitudinal follow-up but not correlated with the same measures taken earlier. Any genetically mediated link between parenting and child adjustment, for example, would be taken into account by controlling for the concurrent relation between parenting and child adjustment before examining their relation over time.

Rearing experiments with animals. Recent work with nonhuman animals points clearly to the fact that experience—that is, encountering or engaging with the environment—influences brain development in young organisms and that these changes in the brain are associated with changes in behavior (Greenough & Black, 1992). Although some of the relevant environmental events must occur during a sensitive period to affect development (Bornstein, 1989), the mammalian brain generally remains malleable by environmental inputs well into adulthood (Huttenlocher, 1994; Nelson, in press). Environmental events that have to do with the amount or kind of "parenting" that a young organism receives are essential for survival in all mammalian species. The presence and activities of the infant stimulate a set of maternal behaviors needed by the infant (including but not confined to feeding), and these reciprocal maternal behaviors serve to facilitate the infant's adaptation and development (e.g., Stern, 1985). Studies of higher mammals confirm that, as these interactions continue to occur, an intense emotional bond is formed such that separation of the pair produces distress and behavioral disruption in each member of the pair. Studies in which young animals have been deprived of "mothering" have shown clearly that such deprivation not only disrupts the ongoing behavior of the young animal at the time of deprivation but also leads to dysfunctional outcomes for the offspring in the long term.

Current animal work is addressing implications of naturally occurring variation, within the "normal" range, in maternal behavior. Meaney and Plotsky and their colleagues (Caldji et al., 1998; Liu et al., 1997) have studied styles of mothering in rats, relating variations in these styles to behavioral outcomes in their offspring. Maternal animals differ considerably in the frequency with which they lick and groom their newborn pups and in whether they arch their backs to facilitate nursing or lie passively on top of or next to the pups. Individual differences in these mothering styles have been shown to be quite stable. In adulthood, moreover, the offspring of mothers who had done more licking and grooming and had nursed with arched backs (high LG-ABN mothers, whom we can call *nurturant*) were less timid in leaving their home cages to obtain food or explore a novel environment than were the offspring of low LG-ABN mothers. These outcomes are correlated with neuroendocrine processes. As adults, rats who had experienced high levels of maternal licking and grooming as newborns showed reduced levels of adrenocorticotropic hormone and corticosterone in response to a stressful condition (close restraint). Furthermore, differences emerged in the densities of receptors for stress hormones in several loci in the brains of animals that had experienced the two different kinds of maternal styles in their first 10 days of life. Thus, early mothering styles apparently affected the neural circuitry that governs behavioral stress responses in the offspring as they grow into adulthood.

To determine whether there is an independent effect of maternal styles per se on these outcomes, apart from any genetic mediation, researchers have cross-fostered infants born to a low-nurturant mother to rearing by a high-nurturant mother. Early findings (Anisman, Zaharia, Meaney, & Merali, 1998) show that these infants manifest the benefits of their early rearing in their modified adult stress reactions, by comparison with infants born to low-nurturant mothers and reared by them.

Corroborating evidence comes from studies with non-human primates (Suomi, 1997). Suomi and colleagues initially observed naturally occurring individual differences in "emotional reactivity" among Rhesus monkeys. In early life, some animals are hesitant about exploring new environments and show extreme reactions to separation from their mothers, whereas others characteristically react more calmly. Individual animals' reactivity patterns remain quite stable over many years. These patterns of behavior are accompanied by distinctive neuroendocrine patterns. The behavioral and physiological indicators that distinguish highly reactive animals from less reactive ones are especially apparent under environmentally stressful conditions (Suomi, 1997).

When young Rhesus monkeys with clearly different reactivity patterns are cross-fostered to mothers who are either reactive (easily distressed) or nonreactive (calm), their adult behavior is quite different from that shown by the biological offspring of each type of mother. Genetically reactive young animals that are reared by calm mothers for the first six months of their lives and then placed in large social groups made up of peers and nonrelated older adults develop normally and indeed rise to the top of their dominance hierarchy. Further, these cross-fostered animals are adept at avoiding stressful situations and at recruiting social support that enables them to cope with stress. By contrast, genetically reactive infants who are raised by reactive mothers typically are socially incompetent when placed in the larger living group at the age of six months and are particularly vulnerable to stress. In general, the introduction of stressful conditions seems to make the effects of early rearing experience especially perceptible (Suomi, 1997). Thus, variations in mothering style have a lasting effect on the reactivity of the young animals when they move into new social contexts. Moreover, the quality of early mothering now has been found to affect the

way genetically at-risk females parent their own offspring. If cross-fostered to low-reactive mothers, they are competent parents with their own offspring; if raised by high-reactive mothers, they manifest mothering deficits.

Recent work (Suomi, in press) has shown that the genetic make-up of young monkeys influences how large an effect early rearing conditions will have. A gene has been identified for which one allele is associated with a highly reactive temperament and the other allele with a calmer temperament. Certain aspects of the neuroendocrine system (i.e., serotonergic functioning) are controlled by this gene. Maternal deprivation has a powerful effect on the genetically reactive monkeys, producing deficits in their neuroendocrine functioning and in their behavioral and emotional reactions. For the animals not carrying the genetically risky allele, however, maternal deprivation has little effect.

These recent studies trace some of the complex steps in the long pathway between genes and phenotypic behavior. The findings show that both genes and parenting affect brain processes and neuroendocrine systems. These studies point to a future in which researchers will be able to provide more detailed information about the interplay of heredity and parenting influences than traditional twin and adoption studies can yield.

Experiments of nature. No extensively controlled rearing experiments have been conducted with human children, but several natural experiments have yielded information that is strikingly parallel to the findings of the cross-fostering work. A recent example is found with the children who lived in Romanian orphanages for some months or years in early childhood, during which time they were deprived of the opportunity to form a close bond with a single trusted adult caregiver. Some of these children have been adopted into middle-class homes in other cultures. The effects of the early deprivation appear to depend on its duration. Recent follow-up measures at age six in a group of Romanian orphans adopted by Canadian families show that children adopted during approximately the first half year of life manifest no lasting effects of their early experience. But children adopted later have been found to have abnormally high levels of cortisol during the ordinary daily routine of their adoptive homes, indicating that the neuroendocrine system involved in stress regulation has not developed normally (Chisholm, 1998; Chisholm, Carter, Ames, & Morison, 1995; Gunnar, in press; see also Rutter & the ERA study team, 1998).

An example of variations in parenting that are more within the normal range comes from France, where 20 children were located who had been abandoned in infancy by their low-socio-economic-status parents and adopted by upper-middle-class parents (Schiff, Duyme, Dumaret, & Tomkiewitz, 1982). These children all had biological siblings or half-siblings who remained with the biological mother and were reared by her in impoverished circumstances. The researchers were unable to find any selective factors that might have made the abandoned children more genetically promising than the ones retained at home. When tested in middle childhood, however, the adopted children's IQs averaged 14 points higher than those of their natural siblings. By contrast, children who remained with their biological mothers were four times more likely to exhibit failures in their school performance. These results are consistent with those of several other early adoption studies (e.g., Skodak & Skeels, 1949; Scarr & Weinberg, 1976, 1978) showing that adoption into well-functioning middle-class homes can provide a "bonus" in cognitive functioning for the children involved.

What aspects of living in more advantaged homes were responsible for these children's cognitive and educational gains is not known. Was it the more stimulating, more cultured, more educated environments provided by the adoptive parents, or were there greater amounts of parent-child interaction or more secure attachments? We can only suspect that something about the way these adoptive parents dealt with the children contributed to the effect. Evidence from the Colorado Adoption Project provides some suggestive evidence for a bidirectional process. The Colorado project included data on rates of communicative development in groups of 12-month-olds either born or adopted into intact families (Hardy-Brown, 1983; Hardy-Brown & Plomin, 1985; Hardy-Brown, Plomin, & DeFries, 1981). Biological mothers' verbal intelligence correlated with the language competencies of children they had not seen since birth. Reciprocally, however, adoptive mothers' activities, like imitating their infants' vocalizations and vocalizing responsively and contingently to infants' vocalizations, also predicted child language competencies. Similarly, another comparison of children with their biological and their adoptive parents (Scarr & Weinberg, 1978) showed that correlations between the vocabulary scores of adoptive mothers and children were as high as those between the vocabulary scores of biological mothers and their children. Like other examples cited earlier, these findings clearly show the distinct contribution of parental behavior over and above the contribution of heredity.

Interventions with human parents. Finally, interventions that seek to change the mean level of a behavioral or personality characteristic in children provide additional evidence of the efficacy of parenting. Efforts to manipulate parental behavior for the purpose of influencing child behavior are surprisingly rare. Laboratory analog studies (e.g., Kuczynski, 1984), although documenting short-term effects of specific behaviors of parents, cannot establish that such behaviors significantly influence broadband outcomes for offspring. The primary source of relevant information for human children comes from evaluations of programs designed to remediate or prevent socialization problems. Such programs typically target the behavior of either children alone or both children and parents. Of particular relevance to socialization, however, are studies in which the behavior of parents, but not the children, is the target of the manipulation. If the manipulation produces desired changes in the parent's behavior and if the degree of change, in turn, is associated with changes in the child's behavior, the evidence for the causal influence of parents is compelling. Unfortunately, only a few such programs focus on improving parental behavior, and even fewer estimate the causal influences of changes in parental behavior on child outcomes (for reviews, see Cowan, Powell, & Cowan, 1998; McMahon & Wells, 1998).

An exception is a recent prevention program intended to foster more effective parenting following divorce (Forgatch & De-Garmo, 1999). School-age sons of recently divorced single mothers often manifest increased academic, behavioral, social, and emotional problems relative to sons of nondivorced mothers, and the divorced mothers themselves commonly behave toward their sons in a more coercive and less positive manner than nondivorced mothers do (Chase-Lansdale, Cherlin, & Kiernan, 1995; Hetherington, 1993; Zill, Morrison, & Coiro, 1993). In most reports, however, the direction of causality is unclear. Forgatch and DeGarmo sought both to address the causality issue and to test a method for preventing these apparently negative sequelae of divorce. They designed group-intervention and individual follow-up procedures for 153 recently divorced mothers who met three criteria: they had been separated from their partners within the prior 3 to 24 months, they resided with a biological son in Grades 1 through 3, and they did not cohabit with a new partner. Initial observational, self-report, and teacher report measures of both mothers' parenting and children's behaviors were used to control for possible genetically influenced differences among parent-child pairs. Random assignment ensured that the treatment group was not systematically different from the control group of 85 mothers and sons who also met the screening criteria. No intervention was provided to the children. At the end of 12 months, treatment-group mothers generally showed less coercive behavior toward children and less decline in positive behavior than control-group mothers did (although both treatment- and control-group mothers manifested at least temporary declines in positive behavior during the year following divorce). Moreover, the degree of change in the mothers' behavior over the course of 12 months significantly predicted the degree of change in the children's behaviors. Changes in parenting practices were associated significantly with changes in teacher-reported school adjustment and with changes in both child-reported and parent-reported maladjustment. Estimated effect sizes for these correlated changes ranged from .032 to .144 (M. Forgatch, personal communication, November 1, 1999). These effect sizes are small to medium, according to Cohen's (1988) criteria.

Other intervention attempts with parents have yielded similarly impressive evidence. Cowan and Cowan (in press), in a randomized design, showed that parents' participation in a 16-week series of discussion groups on effective parenting just prior to their children's kindergarten entry resulted in better school adjustment and higher academic achievement for children in kindergarten and first grade, compared with children whose parents attended a series of discussion groups without the effective-parenting emphasis. The relative advantage for the children of intervention-group parents has persisted through age 10, a period of six years. With parents of infants, Van den Boom (1989, 1994) demonstrated that an intervention to train lower-class mothers to respond sensitively to their infants irritability and reduced the extent of avoidant attachment in distress-prone infants. Similarly, Belsky, Goode, and Most (1980) found that interventions to increase mothers' didactic interactions with infants during play resulted in significantly higher exploratory play among infants, compared with a no-treatment control group. In interventions to improve the behavioral-training skills of parents of noncompliant children, Forehand and colleagues demonstrated both improvements in parental behavior and behavioral changes in the children, as well as increased parental perceptions of improved child behavior and decreased parental depression (Forehand & King, 1977; Forehand, Wells, & Griest, 1980). Depending on the content of the maternal training, children have been shown to manifest differing patterns of competence. Riksen-Walraven (1978) showed that infants of mothers trained in responding demonstrated higher levels of exploratory competence, whereas infants of mothers trained on improving sensory stimulation habituated more efficiently. When interventions are effective, behavior change tends to be long-lasting (Patterson, 1975).

Findings from studies of parenting-focused interventions provide the strongest evidence available on the efficacy of parenting behavior in humans. Whether naturally occurring behaviors of the kind encouraged by these experimental programs account for behavioral development is more difficult to establish. Nevertheless, the increasing use of multimethod, multi-informant assessments and structural equation modeling is helping to overcome some of the shortcomings of traditional correlational studies of socialization and behavior-genetic studies using single informants (Rutter et al., 1997). These more methodologically rigorous studies (e.g., R. Conger & Elder, 1994; Forgatch, 1991; Kim, Hetherington, & Reiss, 1999) generally yield associations between parenting and child outcomes, with appropriate controls for Time 1 status on outcome measures, that meet Cohen's (1988) criteria for small or medium effect sizes. Some studies (e.g., Kochanska, 1997) yield impressively large effect sizes. Even small effects of parenting, however, are likely to become large effects over time (Abelson, 1985). Parental behavior has been shown to be highly stable across time (Holden & Miller, 1999). Thus, specific parental influences, consistently experienced, likely accumulate to produce larger meaningful outcomes over the childhood and adolescent years.

Studies of Links Between Parenting and Other Influences

Current investigations address a further challenge from recent critics of parenting research as well: the need to consider environmental influences other than parents in accounting for differences among children. Socialization research today is guided by an ecological perspective on human development (Bronfenbrenner, 1979; for recent reviews, see Bornstein 1995a, 1995b; Bronfenbrenner & Morris, 1998). Families are seen as important influences on children, the effect of which can be understood only in light of the simultaneous influence of social spheres such as peer groups and schools. These influences occur within broad contexts (e.g., neighborhood, cultural context, historical epoch) that add to, shape, and moderate the effect of the family. The ecological perspective not only emphasizes the potential significance of extrafamilial influences on the child's development but also, more importantly, stresses the interactive and synergistic, rather than additive and competitive, nature of the links between the family and other influences. In this section we consider the implications of this view for parenting in relation to two extrafamilial influences on socialization: peers and macrocontexts of parent-child relations.

Relations of parental and peer influence. In an earlier era, socialization researchers cast families and peers as opposing forces vying for influence over the child's behavior. In much the same way that recent developments in behavior genetics have challenged the wisdom of attempting to estimate how much variance in a trait is attributable to genes versus the environment, contemporary models of socialization no longer ask whether children are influenced more by parents or by peers. Today, socialization researchers develop and test models that examine how parents and peers exert conjoint influence on the developing child (e.g., Brown, Mounts, Lamborn, & Steinberg, 1993; Cairns & Cairns, 1994; Kishion, Patterson, Stoolmiller, & Skinner, 1991; Fuligni & Eccles, 1993; Mounts & Steinberg, 1995).

This new direction rests on four findings that have emerged consistently from research on parent and peer influences. The first finding is that the observed similarity between adolescents and their friends across a wide array of variables, including school achievement (Epstein, 1983), aggression (Cairns, Cairns, Neckerman, Gest, & Gariepy, 1988), internalized distress (Hogue & Steinberg, 1995), and drug use (Kandel, 1978), is due mostly to the tendency for individuals to select like-minded friends, as well as to the influence that friends have over each other (Berndt, 1999; Berndt, Hawkins, & Jiao, 1999). Children are not randomly assigned to peer groups. Although unambiguous estimates of the relative effect of selection and influence effects are not available, a child with antisocial inclinations may be far more likely to fall into a similarly inclined peer group than an antisocial peer group is to corrupt a well-behaved youngster. Similarly, an academically oriented child may be more likely to select academically oriented friends than a child who is not interested in school is to develop a passion for achievement because his or her friends are so inclined. Equating peer influence with peer similarity overstates considerably the extent of peer influence, because the equation fails to take account of the selection effect (Bauman & Fisher, 1986).

The second finding is that peer influence often operates with respect to everyday behaviors and transient attitudes, not enduring personality traits or values (Brown, 1990). Most studies examining individuals' religiosity, educational plans, and occupational choices, for example, reveal that parental influence on adolescent personality development is deeper and more enduring than that of peers (Brown, 1990). To be sure, even transient peer influences over day-to-day behaviors can have enduring sequelae that are opposed to what parents might desire (e.g., peer influence to become sexually active can result in an unplanned pregnancy and foreshortened educational attainment; peer influence to engage in criminal activity can result in a jail sentence). However, because peer influence tends to be immediate, its content changes with shifts in friendships. Studies that track individuals through adolescence often reveal that young adults are more similar to their parents than they had appeared to be as teenagers (J. Conger, 1971).

The third finding is evidence of the significance of parents and parent-child relationships in influencing which peers children select. Any psychological snapshot taken during adolescence, when peers are undeniably an important force in children's lives, rightly should be viewed as the end of a long process of socialization that began early in childhood and most likely has its origins in the family. Parke and Bhavnagri (1989) indicated that parents influence children's peer experiences in two general ways. During elementary school parents propel their children toward certain peers by managing their youngsters' social activities (which has the effect of increasing contact with some peers and diminishing it with others); during both childhood and adolescence, parents actively steer children toward certain friends and away from others. In addition, throughout the child's development parents indirectly influence the child's attitudes, values, personality, and motives, which in turn affect the child's interactions and affiliations with particular peers (Brown et al., 1993). For all of these reasons, parental and peer influence tend to be complementary, not antithetical (Brown, 1990).

Finally, and perhaps most importantly, adolescents differ considerably in their susceptibility to peer influence, and one of the most important contributors to this differential susceptibility is the quality of the parent-child relationship. Adolescents whose parents are authoritative (i.e., responsive and demanding) are less swayed by peer pressure to misbehave than are adolescents whose parents are permissive (Devereux, 1970) or authoritarian (Fuligni & Eccles, 1993). Indeed, adolescents from authoritative homes are more susceptible to prosocial peer pressure (e.g., pressure to do well in school) but less susceptible to antisocial peer pressure (e.g., pressure to use illicit drugs and alcohol; Mounts & Steinberg, 1995). In other words, the particular peers a youngster selects as friends and the extent to which he or she is susceptible to their influence are both affected by parenting.

A compelling illustration of indirect effects of parents comes from research on the development of antisocial behavior and aggression (DeBaryshe, Patterson, & Capaldi, 1993; Dishion et al., 1991; Patterson, DeBaryshe, & Ramsey, 1989). Researchers consistently have confirmed that adolescents' involvement in antisocial activity is influenced significantly by their relationships with antisocial peers but that the chain of events that leads some adolescents into antisocial peer groups begins at home during childhood. The links in this chain include exposure to harsh and coercive parenting, which contributes to the development of aggression and to academic difficulties in school; these problems, in late childhood, lead to the selection of antisocial peers. Even when selection effects are controlled, much of what appears to be peer influence is actually the end result of familial influence at an earlier point in the child's development.

Macrocontexts of parenting. Parents also mediate the association between broader social, cultural, economic, and historical contexts and children's behavior and personality. These broad contextual forces affect how parents behave and may accentuate or attenuate the effect of parental behavior on children's development. R. Conger (e.g., R. Conger et al., 1994) and McLoyd (1990), for example, have demonstrated that many of the deleterious effects of poverty on children's development are mediated through the effect of poverty on parenting; economic stress and disadvantage increase parental punitiveness, which in turn adversely affects the child. One implication of this for understanding the results of research on parenting is that estimates of the strength of parental influence are likely specific to particular communities in particular cultures at particular points in time. Many apparent "effects" of social class or economic disadvantage are mediated through the effect of these factors on parenting practices.

An example comes from recent research on the effects of neighborhood contexts on children's behavior and personality (Brooks-Gunn, Duncan, & Aber, 1997; Brooks-Gun, Duncan, Klebanov, & Sealand, 1993; Chase-Lansdale & Gordon, 1996). Neighborhood characteristics have been shown both to influence parents' behavior and to moderate the effect of parenting practices on the child's development (Klebanov, Brooks-Gunn, & Duncan, 1994). The effect of neighborhoods on parental practices is evident in the finding that parents adjust their management strategies to suit the demands of the neighborhood context within which they live (Furstenberg, Eccles, Elder, Cook, & Sameroff, 1997). Parents who live in dangerous neighborhoods tend to be more controlling and restrictive, which protects the child's physical well-being but which also may have the unintended consequence of squelching the child's sense of autonomy. With respect to moderating effects, Darling and Steinberg (1997) have shown that the links between parental involvement in school and children's achievement vary as a function of the behavior of other parents in the neighborhood, with parental involvement having more potent effects within neighborhoods with high concentrations of involved parents. Similarly, the beneficial effects of authoritative parenting are accentuated when adolescents affiliate with peers who themselves have authoritative parents (Fletcheer, Darling, Steinberg, & Dornbusch, 1995).

The documented relations between parental and other influences are consistent with recent criticisms (e.g., Harris, 1995, 1998) that socialization researchers have overemphasized the role of parents and underemphasized the role of nonfamilial influences, most notably, the peer group. Studies of the broader context of parental socialization, however, neither support nor refute claims about the potency of parental influence. These studies do amply illustrate that, far from a myopic focus on the influence of parents, contemporary researchers have for some time amassed evidence that socialization can be fully understood only by examining the role of parents in light of the influence of other settings in which children and families function.

Conclusions

The lines of research just described imply a concept of parenting and parental influence that is more differentiated and complex than the dominant models of earlier eras. Whereas socialization researchers often depicted parents as "molding" children to function adequately in the society (Hartup, 1989; Maccoby, 1992), contemporary evidence clearly points toward multiple roles for parents that often do not imply the deterministic effect once attributed to them. Whereas researches using behavior-genetic paradigms imply determinism by heredity and correspondingly little parental influence (e.g., Rowe, 1994), contemporary evidence confirms that the expression of heritable traits depends, often strongly, on experience, including specific parental behaviors, as well as predispositions and age-related factors in the child. Whereas both older traditions typically limited ideas about environmental effects to parents, contemporary researchers have shown the interrelated effects of parenting, nonfamilial influences, and the role of the broader context in which families live (e.g., Bronfenbrenner, 1979; Bronfenbrenner & Ceci, 1994; Brooks-Gunn et al., 1997; Darling & Steinberg, 1997; Wachs, 1999).

This new generation of evidence on the role of parenting should add to the conviction, long held by many scholars, that broad, general main effects for either heredity or environment are unlikely in research on behavior and personality. Statistical interactions and moderator effects are the rule, not the exception. Information of this kind, unfortunately, fits poorly with the desire of the popular media for facile sound bites about parenting or the yearning of some writers of introductory textbooks for general, causal statements about behavioral development. Contrary to criticisms of socialization research, the difficulty today is not that the evidence is inadequate to show parenting effects but that the evidence has revealed a reality that is far more complex than critics expected or that writers can convey in most popular media outlets. For psychologists, the challenge is to make that reality a compelling foundation for the science and practice of the future and to find ways of disseminating this knowledge to a public eager to understand the forces that shape children's development.

References

Abelson, R. (1985). A variance explanation paradox: When a little is a lot. *Psychological Bulletin, 97,* 129–133.

Angoff, W. H. (1988). The nature-nurture debate, aptitudes, and group differences. *American Psychologist, 43,* 713–720.

Anisman, H., Zaharia, M. D., Meaney, M. J., & Merali, Z. (1998). Do early-life events permanently alter behavioral and hormonal responses to stressors? *International Journal of Developmental Neuroscience, 16,* 149–164.

Bates, J., & Bayles, K. (1988). The role of attachment in the development of behavior problems. In J. Belsky & T. Nezworski (Eds.), *Clinical implications of attachment* (pp. 253–299). Hillsdale, NJ: Erlbaum.

Bates, J., Bayles, K., Bennett, D. S., Ridge, B., & Brown, M. M. (1991). Origins of externalizing behavior problems at eight years of age. In E. J. Pepler & K. H. Rubin (Eds.), *The development and treatment of childhood aggression* (pp. 197–216). New York: Academic Press.

Bates, J., Pettit, G., & Dodge, K. (1995). Family and child factors in stability and change in children's aggressiveness in elementary school. In J. McCord (Ed.), *Coercion and punishment in long-term perspectives* (pp. 124–138). New York: Cambridge University Press.

Bates, J., Pettit, G., Dodge, K., & Ridge, B. (1998). Interaction of temperamental resistance to control and restrictive parenting in the development of externalizing behavior. *Developmental Psychology, 34,* 982–995.

Bauman, K., & Fisher, L. (1986). On the measurement of friend behavior in research on friend influence and selection: Findings from longitudinal studies of adolescent smoking and drinking. *Journal of Youth and Adolescence, 15,* 345–353.

Belsky, J., Goode, M. K., & Most, R. K. (1980). Maternal stimulation and infant exploratory competence: Cross-sectional, correlational, and experimental analyses. *Child Development, 51,* 1168–1178.

Berndt, T. J. (1999). Friends' influence on children's adjustment to school. In W. A. Collins & B. Laursen (Eds.), *Relationships as developmental contexts: The Minnesota Symposia on Child Psychology* (Vol. 30, pp. 85–108). Mahwah, NJ: Erlbaum.

Berndt, T. J., Hawkins, J. A., & Jiao, Z. (1999). Influence of friends and friendship on adjustment to junior high school. *Merrill-Palmer Quarterly, 45,* 13–41.

Bohman, M. (1996). Predispositions to criminality: Swedish adoption studies in retrospect. In G. R. Bock & J. A. Goode (Eds.), *Genetics of criminal and antisocial behavior, Ciba Foundation Symposium 194* (pp. 99–114). Chichester, England: Wiley.

Bornstein, M. H. (1989). Sensitive periods in development: Structural characteristics and causal interpretations. *Psychological Bulletin, 105,* 179–197.

Bornstein, M. H. (1995a). Form and function: Implications for studies of culture and human development. *Culture and Psychology, 1,* 123–137.

Bornstein, M. H. (Ed.). (1995b). *Handbook of parenting.* Mahwah, NJ: Erlbaum.

Brody, G., & Stoneman, Z. (1994). Sibling relations and their association with parental differential treatment. In E. M. Hetherington, D. Reiss, & R. Plomin (Eds.), *Separate social worlds of siblings: The impact of nonshared environment on development* (pp. 129–142). Hillsdale, NJ: Erlbaum.

Bronfenbrenner, U. (1979). *The ecology of human development.* Cambridge, MA: Harvard University Press.

Bronfenbrenner, U., & Ceci, S. J. (1994). Nature-nurture reconceptualized in developmental perspective: A bioecological model. *Psychological Review, 101,* 568–586.

Bronfenbrenner, U., & Morris, P. A. (1998). The ecology of developmental processes. In W. Damon & R. M. Lerner (Eds.), *Handbook of child psychology: Theoretical models of human development* (5th ed., Vol. 1, pp. 993–1028). New York: Wiley.

Brooks-Gunn, J., Duncan, G., & Aber, L. (Eds.). (1997). *Neighborhood poverty: Context and consequences for children.* New York: Russell Sage Foundation.

Brooks-Gunn, J., Duncan, G., Klebanov, P., & Sealand, N. (1993). Do neighborhoods influence child and adolescent development? *American Journal of Sociology, 99,* 353–395.

Brown, B. (1990). Peer groups. In S. Feldman & G. Elliott (Eds.), *At the threshold: The developing adolescent* (pp. 171–196). Cambridge, MA: Harvard University Press.

Brown, B., Mounts, N., Lamborn, S., & Steinberg, L. (1993). Parenting practices and peer group affiliation in adolescence. *Child Development, 64,* 467–482.

Cadoret, R. (1985). Genes, environment and their interaction in the development of psychopathology. In T. Sakai & T. Tsuboi (Eds.), *Genetic aspects of human development* (pp. 165–175). Tokyo: Igaku-Shoin.

Cairns, R., & Cairns, B. (1994). *Lifelines and risks: Pathways of youth in our time.* New York: Cambridge University Press.

Cairns, R., Cairns, B., Neckerman, H., Gest, S., & Gariepy, J. L. (1988). Social networks and aggressive behavior: Peer support or peer rejection? *Developmental Psychology, 24,* 815–823.

Caldjii, C., Tannenbaum, B., Sharma, S., Francis, D., Plotsky, P. M., & Meaney, M. J. (1998). Maternal care during infancy regulates the development of neural systems mediating the expression of fearfulness in the rat. *Proceedings of the National Academy of Science, 95,* 5335–5340.

Caspi, A., & Elder, G. (1988). Emergent family patterns: The intergenerational construction of problem behavior and relationships. *International Journal of Behavioral Development, 5,* 81–94.

Caspi, A., Henry, B., McGee, R. O., Moffitt, T. E., & Silva, P. A. (1995). Temperamental origins of child and adolescent behavior problems: From age 3 to age 15. *Child Development, 66,* 55–68.

Caspi, A., & Silva, P. (1995). Temperamental qualities at age 3 predict personality traits in young adulthood: Longitudinal evidence from a birth cohort. *Child Development, 66,* 486–498.

Chase-Lansdale, P. L., Cherlin, A., & Kiernan, K. (1995). The long-term effects of parental divorce on the mental health of young adults: A developmental perspective. *Child Development, 66,* 1614–1634.

Chase-Lansdale, P. L., & Gordon, R. A. (1996). Economic hardship and the development of five- and six-year-olds: Neighborhood and regional perspectives. *Child Development, 67,* 3338–3367.

Chisholm, K. (1998). A three-year follow-up of attachment and indiscriminate friendliness in children adopted from Romanian orphanages. *Child Development, 69,* 1092–1106.

Chisholm, K., Carter, M., Ames, E. W., & Morison, S. J. (1995). Attachment security and indiscriminately friendly behavior in children adopted from Romanian orphanages. *Development and Psychopathology, 7,* 283–294.

Cohen, J. (1988). *Statistical power analysis for the behavioral sciences* (2nd ed.). Hillsdale, NJ: Erlbaum.

Conger, J. (1971). A world they never knew: The family and social change. *Daedalus, 100,* 1105–1138.

Conger, R., & Elder, G. E. (1994). *Families in troubled times: Adapting to change in rural America.* New York: Aldine.

Conger, R., Ge, X., Elder, G. H., Lorenz, F., & Simons, R. (1994). Economic stress, coercive family process and developmental problems of adolescents. *Child Development, 65,* 541–561.

Cowan, P. A., & Cowan, C. P. (in press). What an intervention design reveals about how parents affect their children's academic achievement and social competence. In J. Borkowski, S. Landesman-Ramey, & M. Bristol (Eds.), *Parenting and the child's world: Multiple influences on intellectual and social-emotional development.* Hillsdale, NJ: Erlbaum.

Cowan, P. A., Powell, D., & Cowan, C. P. (1998). Parenting interventions: A family systems perspective. In W. Damon, I. Sigel, & K. A. Renninger (Eds.), *Handbook of child psychology: Child psychology in practice* (Vol. 4, pp. 3–72). New York: Wiley.

Darling, N., & Steinberg, L. (1997). Community influences on adolescent achievement and deviance. In J. Brooks-Gunn, G. Duncan, & L. Aber (Eds.), *Neighborhood poverty: context and consequences for children: Conceptual, methodological, and policy approaches to studying neighborhoods* (Vol. 2, pp. 120–131). New York: Russell Sage Foundation.

DeBaryshe, B., Patterson, G., & Capaldi, D. (1993). A performance model for academic achievement in early adolescent boys. *Developmental Psychology, 29,* 795–804.

Devereux, E. C. (1970). The role of peer group experience in moral development. In J. P. Hill (Ed.), *Minnesota Symposia on Child Psychology* (Vol. 4, pp. 94–140). Minneapolis: University of Minnesota Press.

Dishion, T., Patterson, G., Stoolmiller, M., & Skinner, M. (1991). Family, school, and behavioral antecedents to early adolescent involvement with antisocial peers. *Developmental Psychology, 27,* 172–180.

Downey, G., & Walker, E. (1992). Distinguishing family-level and child-level influences on the development of depression and aggression. *Development and Psychopathology 4,* 81–96.

Dunn, J., & Plomin, R. (1986). Determinants of maternal behavior toward three-year-old siblings. *British Journal of Developmental Psychology, 57,* 348–356.

Eisenberg, N., & Damon, W. (Eds.), (1998). *Handbook of child psychology: Social, emotional, and personality development* (Vol. 3). New York: Wiley.

Emde, R., Plomin, R., Robinson, J., Corley, R., DeFries, J., Fulker, D., Reznick, J. S., Campos, J., Kagan, J., & Zahn-Waxler, C. (1992). Temperament, emotion, and cognition at fourteen months: The MacArthur longitudinal twin study. *Child Development, 63,* 1437–1455.

Epstein, J. L. (1983). The influence of friends on achievement and affective outcomes. In J. L. Epstein & N. Karweit (Eds.), *Friends in school* (pp. 177–200). New York: Academic Press.

Fletcher, A., Darling, N., Steinberg, L., & Dornbusch, S. (1995). The company they keep: Relation of adolescents' adjustment and behavior to their friends' perceptions of authoritative parenting in the social network. *Developmental Psychology, 31,* 300–310.

Forehand, R., & King, H. E. (1977). Noncompliant children: Effects of parent training on behavior and attitude change. *Behavior Modification, 1,* 93–108.

Forehand, R., Wells, K. C., & Griest, D. L. (1980). An examination of the social validity of a parent training program. *Behavior Therapy, 11,* 488–502.

Forgatch, M. S. (1991). The clinical science vortex: A developing theory of antisocial behavior. In D. Pepler & K. Rubin (Eds.), *The development and treatment of childhood aggression* (pp. 291–315). Hillsdale, NJ: Erlbaum.

Forgatch, M. S., & DeGarmo, D. S. (1999). Parenting through change: An effective prevention program for single mothers. *Journal of Consulting and Clinical Psychology, 67,* 711–724.

Fuligni, A., & Eccles, J. (1993). Perceived parent-child relationships and early adolescents' orientation toward peers. *Developmental Psychology, 29,* 622–632.

Furstenberg, F., Jr., Eccles, J., Elder, G., Jr., Cook, T., & Smaeroff, A. (1997). *Managing to make it.* Chicago: University of Chicago Press.

Gatz, M., Pedersen, N. L., Plomin, R., Nesselroade, J. R., & McLearn, G. E. (1992). Importance of shared genes and shared environments for symptoms of depression in older adults. *Journal of Abnormal Psychology, 101,* 701–708.

Ge, X., Conger, R., Cadoret, R., Neiderhiser, J., Yates, W., Troughton, E., & Stewart, M. (1996). The developmental interface between nature and nurture: A mutual influence model of child antisocial behavior and parent behavior. *Developmental Psychology, 32,* 547–598.

Ge, X., Conger, R., Lorenz, F., Shanahan, M., & Elder, G. (1995). Mutual influences in parent and adolescent psychological distress. *Developmental Psychology, 31,* 406–419.

Ge, X., Lorenz, F., Conger, R., Elder, G., & Simons, R. (1994). Trajectories of stressful life events and depressive symptoms during adolescence. *Developmental Psychology, 30,* 467–483.

Gesell, A., & Thompson, H. (1934). *Infant behavior: Its genesis and growth.* New York: McGraw-Hill.

Ghodsion-Carpey, J., & Baker, L. A. (1997). Genetic and environmental influences on aggression in 4- to 7-year-old twins. *Aggressive Behavior, 13,* 173–186.

Article 21. Contemporary Research on Parenting

Goldsmith, H., & Alansky, J. (1987). Maternal and infant temperamental predictors of attachment: A meta-analytic review. *Journal of Consulting and Clinical Psychology, 55,* 805–816.

Goodman, R. (1991). Growing together and growing apart: The non-genetic forces on children in the same family. In R. McGuffin & R. Murry (Eds.), *The new genetics of mental illness* (pp. 212–224). Oxford, England: Oxford University Press.

Greenough, W., & Black, J. (1992). Induction of brain structure by experience: Substrates for cognitive development. In M. R. Gunnar & C. A. Nelson (Eds.), *Developmental neuroscience: Minnesota Symposia on Child Psychology* (Vol. 24, pp. 155–200). Hillsdale, NJ: Erlbaum.

Grossmann, K., Grossman, K., Spangler, G., Suess, G., & Unzner, L. (1985). Maternal sensitivity and newborns' orientation responses as related to quality of attachment in Northern Germany. *Monographs of the Society for Research in Child Development, 50*(1–2, Serial No. 209), 233–256.

Gunnar, M. (in press). Early adversity and the development of stress reactivity and regulation. In C. A. Nelson (Ed.), *The effects of adversity on neurobehavioral development: Minnesota Symposia on Child Psychology* (Vol. 31). Mahwah, NJ: Erlbaum.

Hagekull, B. (1989). Longitudinal stability of temperament within a behavioral style framework. In G. A. Kohnstamm, J. E. Bates, & M. K. Rothbart (Eds.), *Temperament in childhood* (pp. 283–297). Chichester, England: Wiley.

Hagekull, B. (1994). Infant temperament and early childhood functioning: Possible relations to the five-factor models. In C. J. Halverson, Jr., G. A. Kohnstamm, & R. P. Martin (Eds.), *The developing structure of temperament and personality* (pp. 227–240). Hillsdale, NJ: Erlbaum.

Hardy-Brown, K. (1983). Universals in individual differences: Disentangling two approaches to the study of language acquisition. *Developmental Psychology, 19,* 610–624.

Hardy-Brown, K., & Plomin, R. (1985). Infant communicative development: Evidence from adoptive and biological families for genetic and environmental influences on rate differences. *Developmental Psychology, 21,* 378–385.

Hardy-Brown, K., Plomin, R., & DeFries, J. C. (1981). Genetic and environmental influences on rate of communicative development in the first year of life. *Developmental Psychology, 17,* 704–717.

Harris, J. R. (1995). Where is the child's environment? A group socialization theory of development. *Psychological Review, 102,* 458–489.

Harris, J. R. (1998). *The nurture assumption: Why children turn out the way they do.* New York: Free Press.

Hartup, W. W. (1989). Social relationships and their developmental significance. *American Psychologist, 44,* 120–126.

Hetherington, E. M. (1989). Coping with family transitions: Winners, losers, and survivors. *Child Development, 60,* 1–14.

Hetherington, E. M. (1991). The role of individual differences in family relations in coping with divorce and remarriage. In P. Cowan & E. M. Hetherington (Eds.), *Advances in family research: Family transitions* (Vol. 2, pp. 165–194). Hillsdale, NJ: Erlbaum.

Hetherington, E. M. (1993). A review of the Virginia Longitudinal Study of Divorce and Remarriage: A focus on early adolescence. *Journal of Family Psychology, 7,* 39–56.

Hoffman, L. W. (1991). The influence of the family environment on personality: Accounting for sibling differences. *Psychological Bulletin, 110,* 187–203.

Hogue, A., & Steinberg, L. (1995). Homophily of internalized distress in adolescent peer groups. *Developmental Psychology, 31,* 897–906.

Holden, G. W., & Miller, P. C. (1999). Enduring and different: A meta-analysis of the similarity in parents' child rearing. *Psychological Bulletin, 125,* 223–254.

Huttenlocher, P. R. (1994). Synaptogenesis, synapse elimination, and neural plasticity in human cerebral cortex. In C. A. Nelson (Eds.), *Minnesota Symposia on Child Psychology: Threats to optimal development: Integrating biological, psychological, and social risk factors* (Vol. 27, pp. 35–54). Hillsdale, NJ: Erlbaum.

Kandel, D. (1978). Homophily, selection, and socialization in adolescent friendships. *American Journal of Sociology, 84,* 427–436.

Kim, J. E., Hetherington, E. M., & Reiss, D. (1999). Associations between family relationships, antisocial peers and adolescent's externalizing behaviors: Gender and family type differences. *Child Development, 70,* 1209–1230.

Klebanov, P. K., Brooks-Gunn, J., & Duncan, G. T. (1994). Does neighborhood and family poverty affect mothers' parenting, mental health and social support? *Journal of Marriage and the Family, 56,* 441–455.

Kochanska, G. (1995). Children's temperament, mothers' discipline, and the security of attachment: Multiple pathways to emerging internalization. *Child Development, 66,* 597–615.

Kochanska, G. (1997). Multiple pathways to conscience for children with different temperaments: From toddlerhood to age 5. *Developmental Psychology, 33,* 228–240.

Kuczynski, L. (1984). Socialization goals and mother-child interaction: Strategies for long-term and short-term compliance. *Developmental Psychology, 20,* 1061–1073.

Lee, C. L., & Bates, J. (1985). Mother-child interaction at age two years and perceived difficult temperament. *Child Development, 56,* 1314–1325.

Lewis, M. (1997). *Altering fate: Why the past does not predict the future.* New York: Guilford Press.

Liu, D., Diorio, J., Tannenbaum, B., Caldji, C., Francis, D., Freedman, M. A., Sharma, S., Pearson, P., Plotsky, P. M., & Meaney, M. J. (1997, September 12). Maternal care, hippocampal glucocorticoid receptors and hypothalamic-pituitary-adrenal responses to stress. *Science, 277,* 1659–1662.

Maccoby, E. E. (1992). The role of parents in the socialization of children: An historical overview. *Developmental Psychology, 28,* 1006–1017.

McCall, R. (1991). So many interactions, so little evidence: Why? In T. Wachs & R. Plomin (Eds.), *Conceptualization and measurement of organism-environment interactions* (pp. 142–161). Washington, DC: American Psychological Association.

McCartney, K., Harris, M., & Bernieri, F. (1990). Growing up and growing apart: A developmental meta-analysis of twin studies. *Psychological Bulletin, 107,* 226–237.

McClelland, G., & Judd, C. (1993). Statistical difficulties of detecting interactions and moderator effects. *Psychological Bulletin, 114,* 376–390.

McGue, M. (1994). Genes, environment, and the etiology of alcoholism. In R. Zucker, G. Boyd, & J. Howard (Eds.), *The development of alcohol problems: Exploring the biopsychosocial matrix of risk* (National Institute of Alcohol Abuse and Alcoholism Research Monograph No. 26, pp. 1–40). Rockville, MD: U. S. Department of Health and human Services.

McLoyd, V. (1990). The impact of economic hardship on Black families and children: Psychological distress, parenting, and socioemotional development. *Child Development, 61,* 311–346.

McMahon, R. J., & Wells, K. C. (1998). Conduct problems. In E. J. Mash & R. A. Barkley (Eds.), *Treatment of childhood disorders* (2nd ed., pp. 111–151). New York: Guilford Press.

Miles, D., & Carey, G. (1997). Genetic and environmental architecture of human aggression. *Journal of Personality and Social Psychology, 72,* 207–217.

Miyake, K., Chen, S. J., & Campos, J. (1985). Infant temperament, mother's mode of interaction and attachment in Japan: An interim report. *Monographs of the Society for Research in Child Development, 50* (1–2, Serial No. 209), 276–297.

Mounts, N., & Steinberg, L. (1995). An ecological analysis of peer influence on adolescent grade point average and drug use. *Developmental Psychology, 31,* 915–922.

Nelson, C. A. (in press). The neurobiological bases of early intervention. In S. J. Meisels & J. P. Shonkoff (Eds.), *Handbook of early childhood intervention* (2nd ed.). New York: Cambridge University Press.

O'Connor, T. G., Deater-Deckard, K., Fulker, D., Rutter, M. L., & Plomin, R. (1998). Genotype-environment correlations in late childhood and early adolescence: Antisocial behavioral problems and coercive parenting. *Developmental Psychology, 34,* 970–981.

Parke, R., & Bhavnagri, N. P. (1989). Parents as managers of children's peer relationships. In D. Belle (Ed.), *Children's social networks and social support* (pp. 241–259). New York: Wiley.

Patterson, G. R. (1975). Multiple evaluations of a parent-training program. In T. Thompson & W. S. Dockens (Eds.), *Applications of behavior modification* (pp. 299–322). New York: Academic Press.

Patterson, G. R. (1999). *Recent news concerning the demise of parenting may be a bit premature.* Unpublished manuscript, Oregon Social Learning Center, Eugene, OR.

Patterson, G. R., DeBaryshe, B. D., & Ramsey, E. (1989). A developmental perspective on antisocial behavior. *American Psychologist, 44,* 329–335.

Plomin, R. (1990). *Nature and nurture: An introduction to human behavioral genetics.* Pacific Grove, CA: Brooks/Cole.

Plomin, R., & Daniels, D. (1987). Why are children in the same family so different from each other? *Behavioral and Brain Science, 10,* 1–16.

Plomin, R., DeFries, J., & Fulker, D. (1988). *Nature and nurture during infancy and early childhood.* New York: Cambridge University Press.

Plomin, R., & Rutter, M. (1998). Child development, molecular genetics, and what to do with genes once they are found. *Child Development, 69,* 1223–1242.

Quinton, D., Pickles, A., Maughan, B., & Rutter, M. (1993). Partners, peers, and pathways: Assortative pairing and continuities in conduct disorder. *Development and Psychopathology, 5,* 763–783.

Reiss, D., Niederhiser, J., Hetherington, E. M., & Plomin, R. (in press). *The relationship code: Deciphering genetic and social patterns in adolescent development.* Cambridge, MA: Harvard University Press.

Riksen-Walraven, J. (1978). Effects of caregiver behavior on habituation rate and self-efficacy in infants. *International Journal of Behavioral Development, 1,* 105–130.

Rose, R. (1995). Genes and human behavior. *Annual Review of Psychology, 46,* 625–654.

Rothbart, M., & Ahadi, S. (1994). Temperament and the development of personality. *Journal of Abnormal Psychology, 103,* 55–66.

Rothbart, M., & Bates, J. (1998). Temperament. In W. Damon & N. Eisenberg (Eds.), *Handbook of child psychology: Social, emotional, and personality development* (Vol. 3, pp. 105–176). New York: Wiley.

Rowe, D. (1983). A biometrical analysis of perceptions of family environment: A study of twin and singleton sibling kinship. *Child Development, 54,* 416–423.

Rowe, D. (1994). *The limits of family influence: Genes, experience, and behavior.* New York: Guilford Press.

Rowe, D., Chassin, L., Presson, C., Edwards, D., & Sherman, S. J. (1992). An "epidemic" model of adolescent cigarette smoking. *Journal of Applied Social Psychology, 22,* 261–285.

Rutter, M. (1990). Psychosocial resilience and protective mechanisms. In J. Rolf, A. S. Masten, D. Cicchetti, K. H. Nuechterlein, & S. Weintraub (Eds.), *Risk and protective factors in the development of psychopathology* (pp. 181–214). New York: Cambridge University Press.

Rutter, M., Dunn, J., Plomin, R., Simonoff, E., Pickles, A., Maughan, B., Ormel, H., Meyer, J., & Eaves, L. (1997). Integrating nature and nurture: Implications of person-environment correlations and interactions for developmental psychopathology. *Development and Psychopathology, 9,* 335–364.

Rutter, M., & the English and Romanian Adoptees (ERA) study team. (1998). Developmental catch-up, and deficit, following adoption after severe global early privation. *Journal of Child Psychology and Psychiatry and Allied Disciplines, 39,* 465–476.

Rutter, M., & Quinton, D. (1984). Parental psychiatric disorder: Effects on children. *Psychological Medicine, 14,* 853–880.

Scarr, S., & Weinberg, R. A. (1976). IQ test performance of Black children adopted by White families. *American Psychologist, 31,* 726–739.

Scarr, S., & Weinberg, R. A. (1978). The influence of "family background" on intellectual attainment. *American Sociological Review, 43,* 674–692.

Schiff, M., Duyme, M., Dumaret, A., & Tomkiewitz, S. (1982). How much could we boost scholastic achievement and IQ scores? A direct answer from a French adoption study. *Cognition, 12,* 165–196.

Skodak, M., & Skeels, H. (1949). A final follow-up of one hundred adopted children. *Journal of Genetic Psychology, 75,* 85–125.

Steinberg, L., Lamborn, S., Darling, N., Mounts, N., & Dornbusch, S. (1994). Over-time changes in adjustment and competence among adolescents from authoritative, authoritarian, indulgent, and neglectful families. *Child Development, 65,* 754–770.

Stern, D. N. (1985). *The interpersonal world of the infant.* New York: Basic Books.

Stoolmiller, M. (1999). Implications of the restricted range of family environments for estimates of heritability and nonshared environment in behavior-genetic adoption studies. *Psychological Bulletin, 125,* 392–409.

Suomi, S. J. (1997). Long-term effects of different early rearing experiences on social, emotional and physiological development in nonhuman primates. In M. S. Kesheven & R. M. Murra (Eds.), *Neurodevelopmental models of adult psychopathology* (pp. 104–116). Cambridge, England: Cambridge University Press.

Suomi, S. J. (in press). A biobehavioral perspective on developmental psychopathology: Excessive aggression and serotonergic dysfunction in monkeys. In A. J. Sameroff, M. Lewis, & S. Miller (Eds.), *Handbook of developmental psychopathology.* New York: Plenum.

Tejerina-Allen, M., Wagner, B. M., & Cohen, P. (1994). A comparison of across-family and within-family parenting predictors of adolescent psychopathology and suicidal ideation. In E. M. Hetherington, D. Reiss, & R. Plomin (Eds.), *Separate social worlds of siblings: The impact of nonshared environment on development* (pp. 143–158). Hillsdale, NJ: Erlbaum.

Tienari, P., Wynne, L. C., Moring, J., Lahti, I., Naarala, M., Sorri, A., Wahlberg, K. E., Saarento, O., Seitma, M., Kaleva, M., & Lasky, K. (1994). The Finnish adoptive family study of schizophrenia: Implications for family research. *British Journal of Psychiatry, 23* (Suppl. 164), 20–26.

Turkheimer, E., & Waldron, M. C. (in press). Nonshared environment: A theoretical, methodological, and quantitative review. *Psychological Bulletin.*

Van den Boom, D. C. (1989). Neonatal irritability and the development of attachment. In G. A. Kohnstamm, J. E. Bates, & M. K. Rothbart (Eds.), *Temperament in childhood* (pp. 299–318). Chichester, England: Wiley.

Van den Boom, D. C. (1994). The influence of temperament and mothering on attachment and exploration: An experimental manipulation of sensitive responsiveness among lower-class mothers with irritable infants. *Child Development, 65,* 1457–1477.

Wachs, T. D. (1992). *The nature of nurture.* Newbury Park, CA: Sage.

Wachs, T. D. (1999). Celebrating complexity: Conceptualization and assessment of the environment. In S. Friedman & T. D. Wachs (Eds.), *Measuring environment across the life span: Emerging methods and concepts* (pp. 357–392). Washington, DC: American Psychological Association.

Wachs, T. D., & Plomin, R. (1991). *Conceptualization and measurement of organism–environment interaction.* Washington, DC: American Psychological Association.

Wahlsten, D. (1990). Insensitivity of the analysis of variance to heredity-environment interaction. *Behavior and Brain Science, 13,* 109–161.

Weinberg, R. A. (1989). Intelligence and IQ: Landmark issues and great debates. *American Psychologist, 44,* 98–104.

Werner, E. (1990). Protective factors and individual resilience. In S. Meisels & J. Shonkoff (Eds.), *Handbook of early childhood intervention* (pp. 97–116). Cambridge, MA: Harvard University Press.

Werner, E., & Smith, R. (1992). *Overcoming the odds: High risk children from birth to adulthood.* Ithaca, NY: Cornell University Press.

Zill, N., Morrison, D., & Coiro, M. (1993). Long-term effects of parental divorce on parent-child relationships, adjustment, and achievement in young adulthood. *Journal of Family Psychology, 7,* 91–103.

Editor's note. Jerome Kagan served as action editor for this article.

Authors' note. W. Andrew Collins, Institute of Child Development, University of Minnesota; Eleanor E. Maccoby, Department of Psychology, Stanford University; Laurence Steinberg, Department of Psychology, Temple University; E. Mavis Hetherington, Department of Psychology, University of Virginia; Marc H. Bornstein, Child and Family Research, National Institute of Child Health and Human Development.

Preparation of this article was supported in part by the Rodney S. Wallace Professorship for the Advancement of Teaching and Learning, College of Education and Human Development, University of Minnesota. We thank the following for helpful comments on the manuscript: Marion S. Forgatch, Ben Greenberg, Megan R. Gunnar, Willard W. Hartup, Jerome Kagan, Gerald Patterson, Stephen Suomi, Deborah Vandell, Theodore Wachs, and Richard A. Weinberg.

Correspondence concerning this article should be addressed to W. Andrew Collins, Institute of Child Development, University of Minnesota, 51 East River Road, Minneapolis, MN 55455–0345. Electronic mail may be sent to wcollins@tc.umn.edu.

Stress and the Superdad

Like the supermoms before them, today's fathers are struggling to balance work and home

MICHELE ORECKLIN

THE PAST 30 YEARS HAVE SEEN THE emergence of the working mom, the single mom, the supermom, the soccer mom and—because full-time motherhood is often considered a choice rather than a given—the stay-at-home mom. Yet aside from the recent categorization of NASCAR dads (which more pointedly concerns the significance of NASCAR than parenting), the title of dad has rarely been linked to a modifier. It would be wrong, however, to conclude that the role of fathers has remained unaltered; the majority of men today are vastly more involved in the rearing of their children and maintenance of their households than their fathers ever were. That no phrases have been coined to describe such behavior can probably be attributed to the fact that unlike women, men have not particularly organized, united or even been pro-active to effect these reforms but, in essence, adapted to the changes the women in their lives demanded for themselves.

That is not to say men resent the transformation. Data from focus groups, conversations with men around the country and a poll conducted by the men's cable network Spike TV and shared exclusively with TIME suggest that men, most interestingly those in their early 20s through early 40s—the first generation to come of age in the postfeminist era—are adjusting to their evolving roles, and they seem to be doing so across racial and class lines. But in straining to manage their responsibilities at work and home, many men say they don't feel an adequate sense of control in either realm. "There's a push-pull," says Kevin Lee, 40, a photographer in Salt Lake City, Utah, with two small children and a wife who works part time. "I feel like when I'm with the kids, it's great, and I enjoy that time. But in the back of my mind, I'm always thinking that I've got all these other things to do, like work around the house or job-related work."

As pioneer superdads, these men have few role models. Not terribly long ago, a man went out into the world and worked alongside other men, and when he came home, the rest of the family busied itself with making him comfortable. Now, as with women of a generation ago, men are experiencing the notion of a second shift, and they are doing so at a time when downsizing, outsourcing and other vagaries of the economy have made that first shift feel disquietingly unstable. Says Dr. Scott Haltzman, 44, a psychiatrist in Barrington, R.I., with many male clients un-

der 45: "Historically, men felt that if they applied themselves and worked hard, they would continue to rise within an organization." Now they must contend with a shaky economy, buyouts, layoffs and mergers, not to mention rapidly evolving technological advances. Of the 1,302 men polled, 75% said they were concerned about keeping up with changing job skills, and even among those 25 to 34, a presumably more tech-savvy cohort, 79% admitted to such concerns.

There are things men do that women don't see as contributing

There is also uncertainty in men's roles at home. Says Bob Silverstein, an employment consultant and personal life coach in New York City: "Home has become one more place where men feel they cannot succeed." For as much as women desire and demand their husbands' assistance in floor waxing and infant swaddling, many men complain that their wives refuse to surrender control of the domestic domain and are all too adept at critiquing the way their husbands choose to help out. Haltzman, who gathers research on husbands through his SecretsOfMarriedMen.com website, points out that "there are a lot of things men do that women don't define as contributing to the household. If a man is in the yard and notices that the basketball is flat and he pumps it up, he gets no credit because it's not something that needed to get done in the wife's eyes. But from the man's perspective, it's just as important as picking up an article of clothing or doing the wash."

But even while men chafe at not being appreciated around the house, few of them express a desire to return to the roles defined by previous generations. "I would love a reprieve from all the domestic chores," says Steve McElroy, 35, of Barrington, R.I., a father of two whose wife is a full-time professor. "But I wouldn't want it at the expense of my family and what I have with them." Asked by Spike TV to choose how they measure success, only 3% of men said through their work, while 31% said they did so through their faith in God, 26% through being the best person possible, 22% through their network of family and friends, and 17% through maintaining a balance between home and work.

In calibrating an acceptable balance between the two, men came down decisively on the side of family life, with 72%—including those who are single—saying they would sacrifice advancements at work to spend more time at home and 66% saying they would risk being perceived poorly by a superior to ask for a month's paternity leave. In 2002, Mark Carlton, 33, left his job in mechanical design and moved with his wife and two children from Evansville, Ind., to Minneapolis, Minn., when his wife got a better-paying position. While interviewing for a new job, Carlton told potential employers that he expected a "give and take. I give it my all at work, and in return if I have a family issue, I should be able to have the time."

Despite their best intentions, however, men are not necessarily curtailing their work hours. Nearly 68% of men work more than 40 hours a week, and 62% are working on weekends. And men with children are putting in more hours than those without: 60% of them work 41 to 59 hours a week, whereas only 49% of men without kids rack up that many hours.

Even though men say they spend too much time on the job, they don't seem to care about the gender or race of those they work alongside or below. This would appear to be progress over 10 years ago, when many downsized men channeled their frustration toward minorities and women whom they perceived as threats to their professional advancement. Today, the Spike poll shows that 55% of men profess to have no preference for a male or female boss, while 9% actually prefer a woman. Proof that men may now recognize the advantages of having women in the workplace is evident in another poll number: 55% say they have no problem dating someone who earns significantly more than they do.   **—With reporting by Sonja Steptoe/Los Angeles and Sarah Sturmon Dale/Minneapolis**

Physical Discipline and Children's Adjustment: Cultural Normativeness as a Moderator

JENNIFER E. LANSFORD
Duke University

LEI CHANG
Chinese University of Hong Kong

KENNETH A. DODGE AND PATRICK S. MALONE
Duke University

PAUL OBURU AND KERSTIN PALMÉRUS
Göteborg University

DARIO BACCHINI
University of Naples

CONCETTA PASTORELLI AND
ANNA SILVIA BOMBI
Rome University "La Sapienza"

ARNALDO ZELLI
Istituto Universitario di Scienze Motorie

SOMBAT TAPANYA
Chiang Mai University

NANDITA CHAUDHARY
University of Delhi

KIRBY DEATER-DECKARD
University of Oregon

BETH MANKE
California State University

NAOMI QUINN
Duke University

Interviews were conducted with 336 mother–child dyads (children's ages ranged from 6 to 17 years; mothers' ages ranged from 20 to 59 years) in China, India, Italy, Kenya, the Philippines, and Thailand to examine whether normativeness of physical discipline moderates the link between mothers' use of physical discipline and children's adjustment. Multilevel regression analyses revealed that physical discipline was less strongly associated with adverse child outcomes in conditions of greater perceived normativeness, but physical discipline was also associated with more adverse outcomes regardless of its perceived normativeness. Countries with the lowest use of physical discipline showed the strongest association between mothers' use and children's behavior problems, but in all countries higher use of physical discipline was associated with more aggression and anxiety.

The effects of physical discipline on North American (primarily White, middle class) samples have received a great deal of research attention. Studies that have not taken into account the ethnic or cultural background of the samples have generally found that physical discipline is associated with more child behavior problems such as aggression (Eron, Huesmann, & Zelli, 1991), delinquency (Farrington & Hawkins, 1991), and criminality (McCord, 1991; see Gershoff, 2002, for a review and meta-analysis). However, in a variety of domains, parenting behaviors have been found to relate differently to children's adjustment depending on the contexts in which these behaviors are situated, suggesting that the effects of parental

discipline may not be direct or universal (e.g., Florsheim, Tolan, & Gorman-Smith, 1996; Pinderhughes, Dodge, Bates, Pettit, & Zelli, 2000). In much of the research that has found contextual differences in parenting effects, race or ethnicity in U.S. samples has been examined as a moderator of the link between parents' use of physical discipline and children's adjustment (e.g., Deater-Deckard, Dodge, Bates, & Pettit, 1996; Gunnoe & Mariner, 1997; Polaha, Larzelere, Shapiro, & Pettit, 2004). Although race or ethnicity might be conceptualized as a proxy for culture, and previous research has offered hypotheses about why race or ethnicity might moderate the link between physical discipline and children's adjustment, extant studies have not empirically examined these possible explanations.

If parenting behaviors do relate differently to children's adjustment depending on the contexts in which these behaviors are situated, this seriously challenges many prevailing theories of parent effects. For example, social learning theory would imply direct and universal effects of some parenting behaviors on children's adjustment. According to this theory, parents' use of physical discipline teaches children that aggression is appropriate in some situations (see Maccoby & Martin, 1983) and would thus be expected to be related to higher levels of externalizing behavior problems, regardless of the context in which it is used or children's appraisals of it (e.g., Straus, 1996).

One theory that can account for some apparently discrepant findings across cultures is Rohner's (1986) parental acceptance–rejection theory, which suggests that if children interpret their parents' behavior as rejection, it will have deleterious effects on their adjustment. For example, in one of many empirical tests of the theory Rohner, Kean, and Cournoyer (1991) found that parents' use of physical discipline negatively affects children's adjustment in part through its effect on children's perception of being rejected by their parents. Rohner's acceptance–rejection theory has been examined across several cultures; this research finds that children's perception of parental rejection is the strongest correlate of their maladjustment.

Grusec and Goodnow (1994) provide a useful theoretical framework in which to understand differences in how parents' discipline strategies affect children's adjustment. In particular, Grusec and Goodnow's framework postulates that the extent to which children accurately perceive their parents' disciplinary messages and accept those messages contributes to the impact of the discipline. For example, if children perceive their parents' discipline strategy as being unfair or unreasonable, they are less likely to internalize the message their parents are trying to convey and may show worse long-term adjustment (Grusec & Goodnow, 1994).

Thus, the effect of discipline may depend on the context in which it is used and the meaning it delivers for the parent and child. What is lacking from this research is attention to how culture might affect children's acquired knowledge structures that allow them to make judgments about what constitutes parental rejection or what determines their perceptions of what is fair and reasonable discipline. This study is important because it seeks a description of how cultural contexts moderate the effects of parents' discipline strategies on child adjustment, one that can emerge only from the coordinated study of multiple diverse contexts.

Our primary aim is to test the hypothesis that the association between parents' discipline strategies and child adjustment is moderated by the normativeness of the discipline strategy. This moderation model will help explain why previous research has shown links between particular kinds of parenting behaviors and negative outcomes for children in some but not other cultural groups. We hypothesize that under conditions of cultural normativeness, there is little association between physical discipline and children's adjustment difficulties. Instead, it is only in circumstances where physical discipline is nonnormative that

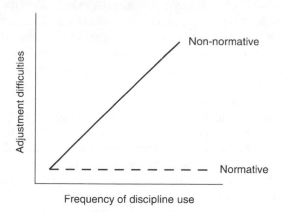

Figure 1 Hypothesized moderating role of normativeness of discipline strategy. We expect normativeness to moderate the link between parents' use of a discipline strategy and children's adjustment because normativeness might affect children's cognitive and emotional appraisals of whether the discipline strategy is fair and just or whether it conveys parental rejection.

an association will be found between more frequent physical discipline and greater adjustment difficulties. These hypotheses are depicted in Figure 1.

There are at least two main ways to conceptualize cultural normativeness. The first involves perceptions of normativeness (i.e., what forms of discipline children and parents believe other parents in their cultural group use). The second involves actual normativeness (i.e., what forms of discipline parents within a cultural group actually use). Frameworks such as Rohner's acceptance–rejection theory emphasize children's interpretation of their parents' behavior as rejection as the key factor that relates to children's adjustment problems; therefore children's perceptions of normativeness might be the most important moderator. However, parents' perceptions of normativeness might be important because parents who use discipline strategies they believe to be normative are more likely to be acting in a controlled manner rather than striking out in anger. That distinction may be important because if parents are out of control and angry when disciplining their child, the message received by the child may be that the experience is scary and unpredictable; however, if parents use discipline strategies as a controlled part of an overall parenting plan, then the message received by the child may be that although the discipline is unpleasant, it is carried out in a careful manner with the child's best interests at heart (e.g., Mosby, Rawls, Meehan, Mays, & Pettinari, 1999). Actual normativeness is also likely to be important because perceptions are derived, at least in part, from how other people in a cultural group actually behave.

To date, hypotheses regarding the moderating role of cultural context have received indirect support in the examination of ethnic differences in the effects of physical discipline within the United States. For example, using a representative community sample of 585 children from Nashville and Knoxville, TN, and Bloomington, IN, Deater-Deckard et al. (1996) found that the experience of physical discipline in the first 5 years of life was associated with higher levels of teacher- and peer-reported externalizing behavior problems for European American children when they were in kindergarten through third grade. However, there was no significant association between the experience of physical discipline and subsequent teacher- and peer-reported externalizing behaviors for African American children. In an extension and expansion of this work, Lansford, Deater-Deckard, Dodge, Bates, and Pettit (2004) found that the experience of physical discipline in the first 5 years of life and in grades 6 and 8 was related to higher levels of externalizing behaviors in grade 11 for European American adolescents but lower levels of externalizing behaviors for African American adolescents. Other investigations using American samples have reported similar ethnicity moderation effects (see Deater-Deckard, Dodge, & Sorbring, in press; Gunnoe & Mariner, 1997). One purported explanation of these ethnic differences is that physical discipline is more normative for African American than for European American families, which alters the meaning of physical discipline to the child (Deater-Deckard & Dodge, 1997).

To test the cultural normativeness explanation explicitly and expand the scope of inquiry beyond ethnic differences in the United States, six countries (i.e., China, India, Italy, Kenya, the Philippines, and Thailand) were selected for inclusion in this study on the basis of the unique contribution that each group could make to understanding how parents' use of physical discipline affects children's adjustment. Several criteria were used to select the participating countries. One dimension was individualistic vs. collectivist orientation, which has been the orienting framework in much cross-cultural research (e.g., Markus & Kitayama, 1991). A second dimension was the culture's predominant religious affiliation, which has been found to be significantly related to parents' discipline behaviors within the United States (e.g., Gershoff, Miller, & Holden, 1999). A third dimension was notable legal action involving parents' discipline, particularly in the selection of Italy, where cases involving parents' use of physical discipline have been brought to trial (see Bitensky, 1998). A fourth dimension was historical, ideological, and other distinctions between groups in these countries. Our overarching goal was to select cultural groups that vary along several dimensions that have been found to affect parent–child relationships in general and parental discipline in particular.

Of the countries included in this study, the use of physical discipline was expected to be most normative in Kenya. High levels of physical discipline, including the frequent use of objects in physical discipline, have been reported in sub-Saharan Africa (e.g., Monyooe, 1996). Palmérus and her colleagues have found that physical discipline is common in Kenya, along with physical restraint and verbal threats of physical discipline (Awuor & Palmérus, 2001; Oburu & Palmérus, 2003). For example, in one study of grandmothers who were parenting their orphaned grandchildren, physical discipline was the most common and frequently mentioned form of discipline, followed by physical restraint (Oburu & Palmérus, 2003). In Oburu and Palmérus's sample, 57% of grandmothers reported caning, pinching, slapping, tying with a rope, hitting, beating, and kicking as forms of discipline they had used with their grandchildren. An additional 36% of grandmothers reported using a combination of physical discipline and reasoning. Only 7% of

grandmothers reported using reasoning without accompanying physical discipline. Similar results were found in another sample of mothers from Kenya (Awuor & Palmérus, 2001).

Although we expected that the use of physical discipline would be the most normative in Kenya, findings from the WorldSAFE study suggest that physical discipline is also used frequently in India and the Philippines (WorldSAFE, 2004). For example, in India, 30% of mothers in the WorldSAFE study reported that their children had been beaten with an object. This sounds like a high percentage, but is actually comparable to the Gallup poll results in the United States that 28% of American parents have used an object to spank their 5- to 12-year-old children in the last year (Straus & Stewart, 1999). In a separate middle-class sample of professionals in India, 57% reported spanking or slapping their children, and 42% reported engaging in more severe forms of physical discipline (e.g., kicking, biting, hitting with an object; Segal, 1995). In early research (Giovannoni & Becerra, 1979), Indians were found to regard physical abuse as the sixth most detrimental form of abuse in relation to children's adjustment, whereas Americans regarded physical abuse as second only to sexual abuse in terms of its relation to children's adjustment. However, India also has a rich tradition of unconditional love and acceptance of the young child, which coexists with firmness and strict discipline (Kakar, 1978). In the Philippines, 75% of mothers in the WorldSAFE study had spanked their child in the last year, and 51% had spanked the child with an object.

In China, as in other countries, previous generations of parents appear to have used more harsh and power-assertive strategies, including physical discipline (e.g., Ho, 1986), than do parents in the present generation. In contrast to early work, recent studies suggest that harsh parenting is consistently low with Chinese parents (Chang, Lansford, Schwartz, & Farver, 2004; Chang, McBride-Chang, Stewart, & Au, 2003; Chang, Schwartz, Dodge, & McBride-Chang, 2003; Tao, Wang, Wang, & Dong, 1998). Furthermore, although 97% of doctors and nurses surveyed at eight hospitals in Eastern China believed that physical discipline was widely used by Chinese parents, 76% of these respondents indicated that they personally disapproved of using physical discipline (Hesketh, Hong, & Lynch, 2000). Thus, we expected physical discipline to be less normative in China than in Kenya, India, and the Philippines.

In this study, Thailand may be at the opposite end of the continuum of physical discipline use from Kenya. The Thai population of 60 million consists of 95% Buddhists (National Identity Board, 1995), and Thai social values are closely related to Buddhist teachings. The virtue of "namchai" (water of the heart), which embodies warmth, compassion, and unrequited kindness to strangers, is emphasized in interpersonal relations. The Buddhist principle emphasizes avoiding any unnecessary friction in interpersonal relations. This cultural and religious theme is also seen in phrases such as "krengchai," which means extreme reluctance to impose on others or disturb interpersonal equilibrium by direct criticism or confrontation. These cultural values are also apparent in parents' socialization of their children, which emphasizes peacefulness and deference (Weisz, Suwanlert, Chaiyasit, & Walter, 1987).

To summarize, our first main hypothesis was that China, India, Italy, Kenya, the Philippines, and Thailand would differ in how frequently mothers used physical discipline and how normative mothers and children perceived the use of physical discipline to be in their country. Our second main hypothesis was that associations between parents' use of physical discipline and child adjustment would be moderated by mothers' and children's perceptions of the normativeness of physical discipline as well as the actual normativeness of physical discipline.

Method

Participants

Children and their mothers were recruited for participation through schools in Beijing, China ($n = 50$; 46% girls); Delhi, India ($n = 46$; 59% girls); Rome and Naples, Italy ($n = 81$; 58% girls); the Rachuonyo District of Nyanza province, Kenya ($n = 49$; 55% girls); Manila, Philippines ($n = 50$; 38% girls); and Chiang Mai, Thailand ($n = 60$; 55% girls; total $N = 336$). Children ranged in age from 6 to 17 years ($M = 10.57$, $SD = 1.86$). Mothers ranged in age from 20 to 59 years ($M = 38.64$, $SD = 5.93$). Although there are ethnic minorities in these countries, the participants did not identify themselves as being members of any ethnic minority groups. In 94% of cases, the biological mother was interviewed; in the remaining cases, an adoptive parent or relative who was the child's primary caregiver was interviewed.

Within each country, the samples were considered primarily middle class and had similar standings in terms of within-country socioeconomic status. However, there were differences in socioeconomic status between countries that were handled by the multilevel aspect of our analysis strategy described below. Income was assessed in local currency using ranges that reflected income distributions within a particular country. The annual median incomes (converted to U.S. dollars) in each country were as follows: (a) China median = $2,172 – $5,796 (which may be an underestimate because it does not include bonuses that many Chinese employees earn in addition to their base salary); (b) India median = $13,728 – $16,464; (c) Italy median = $32,585 – $37,799; (d) Kenya median = $1,560 – $2,352; (e) Philippines median = $3,306 – $4,404; and (f) Thailand median = $3,036 – $15,180.

Measures

To determine whether the types of physical discipline assessed were relevant in each culture and whether we were using the appropriate terms in the culture, we conducted a small number of open-ended, qualitative interviews with mothers and children in the different countries. On completion of the qualitative interviews, we gave mothers and children drafts of measures we were considering using in the quantitative study. In addition to completing these quantitative measures, the mothers and children highlighted and described any ambiguities or sections of the measures they believed were inappropriate. On the basis of this feedback, we made changes to the measures eventually administered in the larger study. In addition, a procedure of translation and back-translation was used to ensure the linguistic equivalence of measures across languages. The translators were fluent in English and the target language. Translators were asked to note places in the research instruments that did not translate well, were inappropriate for the age groups in the study, or were culturally insensitive. Any problems noted were resolved through discussions among the translators and investigators. English versions of the measures were administered in the Philippines and India, where English is an official language. Measures were administered in Mandarin Chinese, Dholuo (Kenya), Italian, and Thai in the other countries. Because not all participants were literate, questions were asked orally and responses were recorded by the interviewer for all participants. Interviews were conducted in participants' homes by a native of the country.

Discipline interview (mother and child reports). This measure was developed for the present study. The parent-report version includes items regarding the frequency (1 = *never*, 2 = *less than once a month*, 3 = *about once a month*, 4 = *about once a week*, 5 = *almost every day*) with which mothers use 17 particular discipline strategies that were adapted from other instruments that assess parents' discipline strategies (Deater-Deckard et al., in press; Straus, 1979) as well as our own pilot studies in the targeted countries. Questions regarding how frequently other parents use each discipline strategy (rated on the same 5-point scale ranging from *never* to *almost every day*) were added to assess perceived cultural normativeness of the behaviors. In the child-report version of the measure, children are not asked about their own parents' use of different types of discipline. Instead, children are asked how frequently parents in general engage in each of the 17 discipline strategies when their children misbehave. For this study, analyses focused on three physical discipline strategies (spank or slap, grab or shake, beat up) that are of particular conceptual relevance to the hypotheses. The three items were averaged to create scales reflecting mothers' use of physical discipline ($\alpha = .60$), mothers' perceptions of how frequently other parents use physical discipline ($\alpha = .73$), and children's perceptions of how frequently other children's parents use physical discipline ($\alpha = .63$). We conducted preliminary analyses using the three individual items separately; the analyses with the individual items showed consistent results across the individual items and results that were consistent with those reported below that use the scales averaging the three items.

Child Behavior Checklist and Youth Self-Report (mother and child reports). The Child Behavior Checklist (CBC; Achenbach, 1991) is a widely used parent-report measure of children's internalizing and externalizing behavior problems. Mothers rate whether each item (e.g., fearful or anxious; cruelty, bullying, or meanness to others) is "not true," "somewhat or sometimes true," or "very true or often true" of their child. Responses are summed to create scale scores. The Youth Self-Report (YSR; Achenbach, 1991) is a widely used measure of children's self-reported internalizing and externalizing behavior problems. Children rate whether each item (e.g., "I worry a lot;" "I get into many fights") is "not true," "somewhat or sometimes true," or "very true or often true" of them. As in the CBC, responses to the YSR questions are summed to create scale scores. For the present study, analyses focused on the aggression and anxiety scales; however, the YSR measure was not administered in Italy.

111

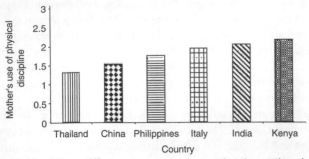

Figure 2 Mean differences among countries in mothers' reports of their own use of physical discipline. For Thailand, China, the Philippines, Italy, India, and Kenya, the 95% confidence intervals for the means were 1.14, 1.48; 1.32, 1.69; 1.53, 1.90; 1.77, 2.08; 1.81, 2.24; and 1.98, 2.42, respectively.

The CBC and YSR have been translated into at least 64 languages, and published studies have used these measures with at least 50 cultural groups. The Achenbach measures have been used previously in all of the countries involved in the present study: China (e.g., Dong, Wang, & Ollendick, 2002), India (Gill & Kang, 1995), Italy (Artigas, 1999), Kenya (Weisz, Sigman,Weiss, & Mosk, 1993), the Philippines (Florencio, 1988), and Thailand (Weisz, Suwanlert, Chaiyasit, Weiss, Achenbach, & Eastman, 1993).

Results

Differences Among Countries in the Use and Normativeness of Physical Discipline

To address our first main hypothesis that the six countries would differ in how frequently mothers used physical discipline and how normative mothers and children perceived the use of physical discipline in their country to be, we conducted a multivariate analysis of covariance (MANCOVA), controlling for child age and gender. The overall MANCOVA was significant, Pillai's $F(15, 915) = 13.20$, $p < .001$. There were significant differences among countries for all three follow-up univariate ANCOVAs, $F(5) = 12.08$, 19.58, and 30.13 for mothers' use of physical discipline, mothers' perceptions of the normativeness of physical discipline strategies, and children's perceptions of the normativeness of physical discipline strategies, respectively, all $p < .001$.

As shown in Figure 2, the rank order (from low to high) of how often mothers reported using physical discipline was Thailand, China, the Philippines, Italy, India, and Kenya. Figure 3 shows that the rank order (from low to high) of mothers' perceptions of how often other parents use physical discipline was China, Thailand, India, the Philippines, Kenya, and Italy. Figure 4 shows that the rank order (from low to high) of children's perceptions of how often other children's parents use physical discipline was Thailand, the Philippines, China, India, Kenya, and Italy.

To summarize, mothers and children in Kenya and Italy generally reported more frequent use and more normative use of

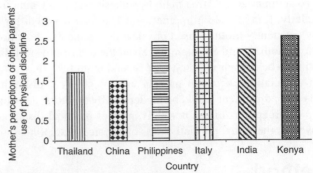

Figure 3 Mean differences among countries in mothers' reports of other parents' use of physical discipline. For Thailand, China, the Philippines, Italy, India, and Kenya, the 95% confidence intervals for the means were 1.48, 1.94; 1.26,1.74; 2.25, 2.73; 2.54, 2.94; 1.96, 2.52; and 2.29, 2.86, respectively.

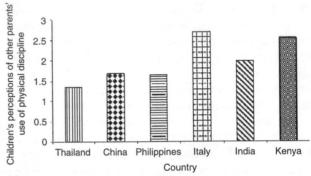

Figure 4 Mean differences among countries in children's reports of other parents' use of physical discipline. For Thailand, China, the Philippines, Italy, India, and Kenya, the 95% confidence intervals for the means were 1.15, 1.54; 1.42, 1.85; 1.40, 1.83; 2.53, 2.89; 1.76, 2.25; and 2.34, 2.85, respectively.

physical discipline than did mothers and children in other countries, mothers and children in China and Thailand generally reported less frequent and less normative use of physical discipline, and mothers and children in India and the Philippines reported moderate levels of frequency and normativeness of use of physical discipline. Overall, there were substantial parallel findings for mothers' reports of their own use of physical discipline and mothers' and children's perceptions about how frequently other parents used physical discipline.

Differences by Normativeness in the Links Between Physical Discipline and Children's Adjustment

Two sets of analyses used PROC MIXED in SAS v9.1.3 to examine our hypothesis that associations between parents' use of physical discipline and child adjustment would be moderated by the normativeness of physical discipline, either by mothers' and children's reports of perceived normativeness or by an aggregate of the mothers' actual use reports. Preliminary tests of gender × mothers' use of physical discipline × normativeness interactions were all nonsignificant. The interactions involving gender were dropped from the analyses reported below, al-

Table 1 Regressions Predicting Aggression and Anxiety from Discipline Frequency and Perceived Norms

Discipline	YSR aggression		YSR anxiety		CBC aggression		CBC anxiety	
Child report of norm								
Frequency of use with child	1.61**	(.54)	0.63	(.49)	3.08***	(.45)	2.17***	(.35)
Child report of norm	2.25***	(.50)	1.56***	(.46)	0.15	(.37)	0.14	(.28)
Interaction	−1.35**	(.51)	−0.85†	(.47)	−0.44	(.40)	−0.80*	(.31)
Mother report of norm								
Frequency of use with child	2.28***	(.56)	1.13*	(.50)	2.89***	(.47)	2.22***	(.35)
Mother report of norm	0.17	(.44)	0.22	(.40)	0.53	(.35)	0.32	(.26)
Interaction	0.10	(.46)	−0.31	(.42)	−0.59	(.40)	−1.17***	(.29)

Note. Analyses control for child age and gender. Tabled values are unstandardized regression coefficients and standard errors (in parentheses).
†$p < .10$. *$p < .05$. **$p < .01$. ***$p < .001$.

though the analyses continue to control for gender. For the first set of analyses, the moderation by perceived normativeness was modeled in a multilevel regression, with families nested within countries. We modeled intercepts as randomly varying by countries, with other effects as fixed. Predictors were grand mean-centered. The family-level equation included main effects of the frequency of the mothers' use of physical discipline and either mothers' or children's reports of how frequently other parents used physical discipline along with the interaction between the two (centered) variables, with child age and gender as covariates. The clustering within country was modeled by the multilevel aspect, which had the effect of adjusting out the country effect on the mean to make it possible to interpret results within each country. Analyses were conducted separately to predict YSR aggression, YSR anxiety, CBC aggression, and CBC anxiety. Results of the multilevel regressions are summarized in Table 1. Of particular interest is the significance of the interaction terms because these provide a test of whether mothers' use of physical discipline relates to children's aggression and anxiety differently, depending on how normative mothers and children perceive the use of physical discipline to be. The multilevel regression coefficients reported are a composite of the within-country regressions, with the country effect on the mean adjusted out; thus, a significant interaction indicates that normativeness within a country moderates the association between mothers' use of physical discipline and children's aggression and anxiety.

As shown in Table 1, one of the four interaction terms involving mothers' reports of normativeness was significant, as were two of the four interaction terms involving children's reports of normativeness, and a third was nearly so. The significant interactions are depicted in Figure 5, which shows the expected values of the outcome variables at representative values (+1 and −1 SD from the mean) of the predictors. In all three cases of significant interactions, the interaction coefficients were negative, indicating that more frequent use of physical discipline is less strongly associated with adverse child outcomes in conditions of greater perceived normativeness of physical discipline. However, as shown in Figure 5, children who perceive the use of physical discipline to be highly normative have higher levels of YSR aggression, regardless of whether they personally experience high or low levels of physical discipline. In addition, although the slope of the line is attenuated if mothers and children perceive the use of physical discipline as being highly normative, more frequently experiencing physical discipline is associated with higher levels of CBC anxiety regardless of whether physical discipline is perceived as being normative.

The second set of analyses approached the same hypothesis using mother-reported use of physical discipline to derive the normative level of use. The mean mother-reported use was calculated for each site. This was entered into a multilevel regression as a country-level variable, with individual mothers' reports of use as a family-level predictor, and their interaction, with child age and gender as covariates. Power was extremely low, of course, for assessing the main effect of norms; however, the loss of power was less extreme for assessing the interaction effects of interest. This analysis was repeated for each of the four outcomes. The analysis predicting YSR aggression did not converge, perhaps because of the even smaller number of countries for which we obtained YSR data. Results for the other three outcomes are summarized in Table 2. As shown, the interaction of interest was significant and negative for the two mother-reported outcomes; the interactions are plotted in Figure 6. The countries with the lowest normative use of physical discipline show the strongest positive association between individual mothers' use of physical discipline and their children's behavior problems, although in all countries high physical discipline was associated with more negative outcomes.

Discussion

The results showed that countries differed in the reported use and normativeness of physical discipline and in the way that physical discipline was related to children's adjustment. Perceived normativeness of physical discipline, particularly children's perceptions, moderated the association between experiencing physical discipline and child aggression and anxiety. When significant moderation occurred, more frequent use

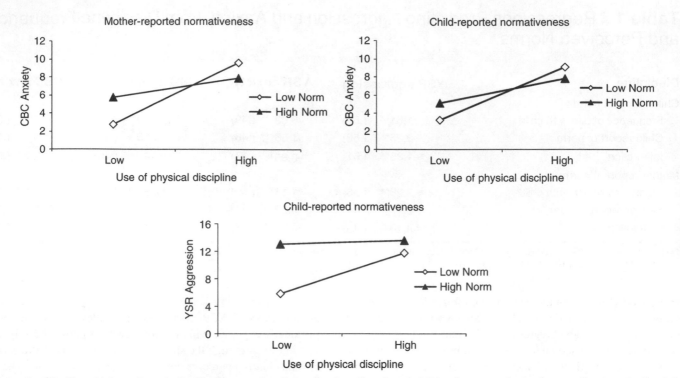

Figure 5 Significant interactions indicating the moderating role of mothers' and children's perceptions of normativeness in the link between mothers' use of physical discipline and children's adjustment. "High" and "low" reflect the use of physical discipline at values +1 and −1 *SD* from the mean, calculated across the entire sample.

of physical discipline was less strongly associated with adverse child outcomes in conditions of greater perceived normativeness. This effect was found within countries and therefore cannot be attributed to lack of comparability among countries. However, more frequently experiencing physical discipline was associated with higher levels of CBC anxiety regardless of whether physical discipline was perceived as being normative, and children who perceived the use of physical discipline as being highly normative had higher levels of YSR aggression, regardless of whether they personally experienced high or low levels of physical discipline. Furthermore, the countries with the lowest normative use of physical discipline showed the strongest positive association between individual mothers' use of physical discipline and their children's behavior problems, but high physical discipline was associated with more CBC aggression and anxiety in all countries. Thus, the findings supported the hypothesis that the association between mothers' use

of physical discipline and child adjustment is moderated by the normativeness of physical discipline, whether actual normativeness or children's and mothers' perceptions of normativeness were considered. The findings also suggested some negative effects of physical discipline, regardless of its normativeness.

In the anthropology literature, there are many examples of parental behaviors that appear to have no detrimental effects on children's adjustment, despite the perception in other cultural contexts that these behaviors would be harmful to children. For instance, folk remedies for a variety of medical symptoms sometimes involve parenting practices that leave burns or other marks but that are intended, within certain cultural contexts, to facilitate children's recovery from illness (e.g., Hansen, 1997; Risser & Mazur, 1995). It appears that such behaviors become problematic only when parents engage in them outside of their normative context, such as when they immigrate to the United States and their

Table 2 Regressions Predicting Aggression and Anxiety from Discipline Frequency and Sample-Based Norms

Discipline	YSR aggression	YSR anxiety	CBC aggression	CBC anxiety
Frequency of use with child		1.28** (0.44)	3.16*** (0.38)	2.12*** (0.38)
Calculated norm	Model did not converge	−1.97 (2.22)	−2.77 (4.49)	−1.14 (2.53)
Interaction		−2.21 (1.57)	−7.06*** (1.60)	−3.68* (1.46)

Note. Analyses control for child age and gender. Tabled values are unstandardized regression coefficients and standard errors (in parentheses).
*p < .05. **p < .01. ***p < .001.

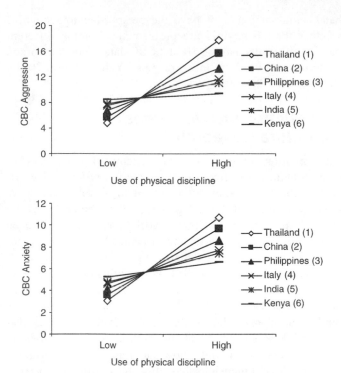

Figure 6 Significant interactions indicating the moderating role of actual normativeness in the link between mothers' use of physical discipline and children's adjustment. "High" and "low" reflect the use of physical discipline at values +1 and −1 SD from the mean, calculated across the entire sample. Numbers in parentheses after the country name indicate the rank order of the country in the normativeness of physical discipline as indicated by the average of mothers' reports within a country of how frequently they use physical discipline (with 1 being the least normative and 6 being the most normative).

practices conflict with American definitions of child abuse or neglect (see Levesque, 2000). Indeed, cultural evidence has been used to inform related legal cases (for a review see Coleman, 1996). For example, in one case that involved a mother who made small cuts on the cheeks of her two sons, the judge dismissed the case after hearing that the significance of the cuts in the mother's native tribe was to initiate the sons into the tribe of her ancestors (Fischer, 1998). To make the same point from a different perspective, ear piercing and male circumcision are examples of practices that physically hurt children in the short term and permanently alter their appearance, yet are normative within the United States (and thus not defined as abuse and, presumably, not detrimental to children's adjustment).

On the other hand, even if a practice is sanctioned by a cultural group, it does not mean that the practice is necessarily acceptable. Regardless of where they live, children have rights and parents have responsibilities toward children. In the global community, female circumcision is an example of a behavior that has been condemned as being abusive and having long-term negative effects on women, even though the cultures that practice it defend it as a culturally based practice with spiritual implications (see Coleman, 1998). Leaving parents within cultures to decide what is in the best interests of their children is likely to strike a balance between short-term harm and long-term good most of the time; however, there are times when it

may be necessary to apply a global standard to protect children from serious long-term harm. Thus, it is important not to take an extreme position on cultural relativism.

If cultural normativeness and acceptance of a discipline strategy contribute to children's perception of their parents' use of it as being indicative of "good" and caring parenting, there may be less of an association between that type of discipline and children's adjustment problems. However, if children do not perceive that type of discipline as being indicative of good parenting (perhaps because it is not culturally normative), they may associate being disciplined in that manner with being rejected by their parents, which could be related to higher levels of child adjustment problems. Thus, it makes sense that mothers' use of physical discipline was related less strongly to children's aggression and anxiety when the child perceived the discipline strategy as being culturally normative than when the child did not. Caution must be exercised in applying these findings, however, because despite the attenuated link, more frequent use of physical discipline was associated with more adjustment problems, even when it was perceived as being normative. The findings do not address the issue of whether physical discipline itself is appropriate in this day and age. In particular, there are a number of examples of practices that were condoned historically (e.g., child labor) and that are now condemned, at least in certain countries. A larger question is whether a practice is acceptable, regardless of whether it is normative within a cultural group.

The physical discipline moderation effects were similar to those that have been reported for African American and European American children in the United States (Deater-Deckard et al., 1996; Gunnoe & Mariner, 1997; Lansford et al., 2004). That is, in cultural groups that use physical discipline more frequently (e.g., Kenya in this study, African Americans in previous research), the link between experiencing more frequent physical discipline and adjustment problems is attenuated. We found that children's perceptions appeared to moderate more often the links between mothers' reports of their use of physical discipline and children's adjustment than do mothers' reports of normativeness, suggesting that children's cognitive interpretations of discipline events might be more important than parents' interpretations in determining how the event will relate to children's adjustment.

Results for the countries expected to be at the extremes in terms of parents' use of physical discipline largely supported our hypotheses. Like prior research (Awuor & Palmérus, 2001; Oburu & Palmérus, 2003), we found that physical discipline is frequently used and perceived as being normative in Kenya. In addition, as expected on the basis of Buddhist teachings and cultural values regarding peacefulness in Thailand (Weisz et al., 1987), physical discipline was used rarely and not perceived as being normative. Mothers and children in Italy and India generally perceived the use of physical discipline as being more frequent and normative, whereas mothers and children in China and, to a smaller extent, the Philippines generally perceived the use of physical discipline as being less frequent and normative.

Despite the differences between countries in normativeness of physical discipline, we acknowledge that there is within-country variability as well. That is, not everyone within a country similarly supports or condemns the use of physical discipline. For example, although the use of physical discipline was less normative in Thailand than in the other countries, there is also diversity of attitudes and behaviors within Thailand. Child protection laws have been enacted in Thailand recently because of concern regarding reports of child physical abuse, and there is a saying that "If you care about your cows, tie them up; if you love your children, beat them." Thus, a useful direction for future research would be to examine not just differences between countries but also variability within the countries and factors that may contribute to within-country variability.

Within the overarching framework of examining associations between parents' discipline strategies and children's adjustment, we chose to focus on three physical discipline strategies. Studies have varied in terms of which specific behaviors are included in the construct of physical discipline, although spanking, slapping, and grabbing are often included, and behaviors as severe as beating up the child generally are not (see Gershoff, 2002). Where to draw the line between physical discipline and physical abuse has been a question that has plagued this line of research (e.g., Whipple & Richey, 1997). In this study, we included spanking/slapping, grabbing/shaking, and beating up as the three physical discipline strategies. Although in the United States beating up would be considered physical abuse rather than physical discipline, its inclusion enabled us to test the limits of the theory that the effects of physical discipline on children's adjustment depend on the normativeness of the discipline. That is, at some point a discipline strategy may become so severe that it would have negative effects on all children, regardless of how normative it is within a cultural context. Because our preliminary analyses in which the three physical discipline strategies were examined separately supported the same conclusions regarding the importance of normativeness as a moderator of the link between parents' use of a discipline strategy and children's adjustment, our subsequent analyses focused on a composite physical discipline variable that included all three indicators.

We focused on four measures of child adjustment: aggression and anxiety as reported by the mother and by the child. The findings were somewhat different, depending on the outcome measure under consideration. In the analyses that used mother-reported use of physical discipline to derive the normative level of use (i.e., actual normativeness), we had more power to detect differences in the CBC outcomes than the YSR outcomes because the YSR was available in only five of the six countries, whereas the CBC was available in all six countries. This could explain the significant findings for the two CBC outcomes and the lack of significant findings and lack of model convergence for the YSR outcomes. On a more substantive note, mothers and children may differ in terms of which behaviors they believe are problematic and which behaviors they know about (Yeh & Weisz, 2001). For example, parents may not know about problem behaviors their child engages in at school or with peers; furthermore, parents may not have access to children's internal states and may have to rely on external manifestations of emotions, which may or may not accurately reflect what a child is really feeling. On the other

hand, children may not have the perspective to recognize whether their behaviors are problematic. Finding different patterns of results using YSR and CBC data is not uncommon in studies that use both measures (e.g., Yeh & Weisz, 2001). Both are useful perspectives.

Limitations and Directions for Future Research

One limitation of this study is that the sampled countries differ along a number of dimensions that are not reflected specifically in the analyses, even though country-level effects were modeled in the multilevel regressions. One dimension is the culture's predominant religious affiliation, which has been found to be importantly related to parents' discipline strategies even within the United States (e.g., Gershoff et al., 1999). A second dimension is notable laws involving family life (e.g., the one-child policy in China). A third dimension is socioeconomic resources available in a culture. A fourth dimension is other cultural norms that are distinct from, yet related to, physical discipline (e.g., views about children as property, beliefs about aggression generally, how parenting fits with religious beliefs). These dimensions may affect how normative parents within a country believe physical discipline to be. It is also possible that these dimensions are related to parents' use of physical discipline without being related to the links between parents' use of physical discipline and children's adjustment. Future research should attempt to unpack these elements to investigate what, in particular, are the important cultural features that are related to differences in discipline strategies and the effects of these strategies on children's adjustment. Future research should also examine different aspects of children's experience of discipline such as the duration of the discipline and its severity.

It would have been possible to select other cultural groups that would also have been informative, and we do not claim to have sampled all of the potentially relevant subgroups within a given country. Most of the cultural groups that were included in this study are underrepresented in the parenting literature specifically and in the psychological literature more generally. Within each country we would expect a great deal of variability depending on a family's socioeconomic status, rural or urban domesticity, and other circumstances; along with attending to cultural diversity one must also be conscious of the diversity that exists within cultures (Chaudhary, 2004). Nevertheless, we believe our selection process resulted in a diverse set of cultural groups that enabled us to test our hypotheses well. Our primary goal was to examine how perceived and actual normativeness moderate the association between mothers' use of physical discipline and children's adjustment rather than to present an exhaustive summary of which groups perceive physical discipline to be more or less normative.

An additional caveat in our study is the possibility that child adjustment causes parenting practices. That is, more difficult children may elicit more physical discipline from their parents (e.g., Campbell, 1990). A direction for future research will be to use longitudinal designs to control for initial child behavior problems when examining associations between parents' discipline strategies and children's subsequent behavior problems and whether culture moderates these associations.

Strengths and Conclusions

Despite its limitations, this study has many strengths, including the collection of data from mothers and children in six countries. The proposed mechanisms of perceived and actual normativeness to account for country differences go a step beyond much cross-cultural research that simply identifies differences between countries without understanding why those differences arise. Furthermore, children's perceptions of normativeness appear to be more important than mothers' perceptions of normativeness in moderating the link between mothers' use of physical discipline and children's aggression and anxiety.

Overall, our results support two main conclusions. First, there are differences across the six included countries in the reported use and normativeness of physical discipline. Second, experiencing high levels of physical discipline is related to more adjustment problems, but perceived normativeness and actual normativeness moderate the association between mothers' use of physical discipline and child aggression and anxiety. More frequent use of physical discipline is less strongly associated with adverse child outcomes in conditions of greater perceived normativeness; countries with the lowest normative use of physical discipline show the strongest positive association between individual mothers' use of physical discipline and their children's behavior problems. Overall, the findings suggest that cultural normativeness plays a role in the way that physical discipline is related to child adjustment, yet also suggest potential problems in using physical discipline even in contexts in which it is normative.

References

Achenbach, T. M. (1991). *Integrative guide for the 1991 CBCL 14–18, YSR, and TRF profiles.* Burlington: Department of Psychiatry, University of Vermont.

Artigas, J. (1999). Manifestaciones psicológicas de la epilepsia en la infancia. *Revista de Neurologia, 28,* S135–S141.

Awuor, R., & Palmérus, K. (2001, August). *Parental discipline in Western Kenya.* Paper presented in K. Palmérus symposium "Parental discipline in Kenya and Sweden. Cultural and individual differences." European Developmental Conference, Uppsala, Sweden.

Bitensky, S. H. (1998). Spare the rod, embrace our humanity: Toward a new legal regime prohibiting corporal punishment of children. *University of Michigan Journal of Law Reform, 31,* 353–474.

Campbell, S. B. (1990). *Behavior problems in preschool children.* New York: Guilford.

Chang, L., Lansford, J. E., Schwartz, D., & Farver, J. M. (2004). Marital quality, maternal depressed affect, harsh parenting and child externalizing in Hong Kong Chinese families. *International Journal of Behavioral Development, 28,* 311–318.

Chang, L., McBride-Chang, C., Stewart, S., & Au, E. (2003). Life satisfaction, self-concept, and family relations in Chinese adolescents and children. *International Journal of Behavioral Development, 27,* 182–190.

Chang, L., Schwartz, D., Dodge, K., & McBride-Chang, C. (2003). Harsh parenting in relation to child emotion regulation and aggression. *Journal of Family Psychology, 17,* 598–606.

Chaudhary, N. (2004). *Listening to culture: Constructing culture from everyday talk.* New Delhi: Sage.

Coleman, D. L. (1996). Individualizing justice through multiculturalism: The liberals' dilemma. *Columbia Law Review, 96,* 1093–1167.

Coleman, D. L. (1998). The Seattle compromise: Multicultural sensitivity and Americanization. *Duke Law Journal, 47,* 717–783.

Deater-Deckard, K., & Dodge, K. A. (1997). Externalizing behavior problems and discipline revisited: Nonlinear effects and variation by culture, context, and gender. *Psychological Inquiry, 8,* 161–175.

Deater-Deckard, K., Dodge, K. A., Bates, J. E., & Pettit, G. S. (1996). Physical discipline among African American and European American mothers: Links to children's externalizing behaviors. *Developmental Psychology, 32,* 1065–1072.

Deater-Deckard, K., Dodge, K. A., & Sorbring, E. (2005). Cultural differences in the effects of physical punishment. In M. Rutter & M. Tienda (Eds.), *Ethnicity and causal mechanisms* (pp. 204–226). New York: Cambridge University Press.

Dong, Q., Wang, Y., & Ollendick, T. H. (2002). Consequences of divorce on the adjustment of children in China. *Journal of Clinical Child and Adolescent Psychology, 31,* 101–110.

Eron, L. D., Huesmann, L. R., & Zelli, A. (1991). The role of parental variables in the learning of aggression. In D. Pepler & K. Rubin (Eds.), *The development and treatment of childhood aggression* (pp. 169–188). Hillsdale, NJ: Erlbaum.

Farrington, D. P., & Hawkins, J. D. (1991). Predicting participation, early onset and later persistence in officially recorded offending. *Criminal Behavior and Mental Health, 1,* 1–33.

Fischer, M. (1998). The human rights implications of a cultural defense. *Southern California Interdisciplinary Law Journal, 6,* 663–702.

Florencio, C. (1988). *Nutrition, health and other determinants of academic achievement and school-related behavior of grades one to six pupils.* Quezon City: University of the Philippines.

Florsheim, P., Tolan, P. H., & Gorman-Smith, D. (1996). Family processes and risk for externalizing behavior problems among African American and Hispanic boys. *Journal of Consulting and Clinical Psychology, 64,* 1222–1230.

Gershoff, E. T. (2002). Corporal punishment by parents and associated child behaviors and experiences: A meta-analytic and theoretical review. *Psychological Bulletin, 128,* 539–579.

Gershoff, E. T., Miller, P. C., & Holden, G. W. (1999). Parenting influences from the pulpit: Religious affiliation as a determinant of parental corporal punishment. *Journal of Family Psychology, 13,* 307–320.

Gill, R., & Kang, T. (1995). Relationship of home environment with behavioural problems of pre-school children. *Indian Journal of Psychometry and Education, 26,* 77–82.

Giovannoni, J. M., & Becerra, R. M. (1979). *Defining child abuse.* New York: Free Press.

Grusec, J. E., & Goodnow, J. J. (1994). Impact of parental discipline methods on the child's internalization of values: A reconceptualization of current points of view. *Developmental Psychology, 30,* 4–19.

Gunnoe, M. L., & Mariner, C. L. (1997). Toward a developmental-contextual model of the effects of parental spanking on children's aggression. *Archives of Pediatrics and Adolescent Medicine, 151,* 768–775.

Hansen, K. K. (1997). Folk remedies and child abuse: A review with emphasis on caida de mollera and its relationship to shaken baby syndrome. *Child Abuse and Neglect, 22,* 117–127.

Hesketh, T., Hong, Z. S., & Lynch, M. A. (2000). Child abuse in China: The views and experiences of child health professionals. *Child Abuse and Neglect, 24,* 867–872.

Ho, D. Y. F. (1986). Chinese patterns of socialization: A critical review. In M. H. Bond (Ed.), *The psychology of the Chinese people* (pp. 1–37). New York: Oxford University Press.

Kakar, S. (1978). *The inner world: A psychoanalytic study of childhood and society in India.* New Delhi: Oxford University Press.

Lansford, J. E., Deater-Deckard, K., Dodge, K. A., Bates, J. E., & Pettit, G. S. (2004). Ethnic differences in the link between physical discipline and later adolescent externalizing behaviors. *Journal of Child Psychology and Psychiatry, 45,* 801–812.

Levesque, R. J. R. (2000). Cultural evidence, child maltreatment, and the law. *Child Maltreatment, 5,* 146–160.

Maccoby, E. E., & Martin, J. A. (1983). Socialization in the context of the family: Parent–child interaction. In P. H. Mussen & E. M. Hetherington (Eds.), *Handbook of child psychology: Vol. IV. Socialization, personality, and social development* (4th ed., pp. 1–101). New York: Wiley.

Markus, H. R., & Kitayama, S. (1991). Culture and the self: Implications for cognition, emotion, and motivation. *Psychological Review, 98,* 224–253.

McCord, J. (1991). Questioning the value of punishment. *Social Problems, 38,* 167–179.

Monyooe, L. A. (1996). Teachers' views towards corporal punishment in Lesotho schools. *Psychological Reports, 79,* 121–122.

Mosby, L., Rawls, A. W., Meehan, A. J., Mays, E., & Pettinari, C. J. (1999). Troubles in interracial talk about discipline: An examination of African American child rearing narratives. *Journal of Comparative Family Studies, 30,* 489–521.

National Identity Board. (1995). *Thailand in the 90s.* Office of the Prime Minister, Thailand: Author.

Oburu, P. O., & Palmérus, K. (2003). Parenting stress and self-reported discipline strategies of Kenyan caregiving grandmothers. *International Journal of Behavioral Development, 27,* 505–512.

Pinderhughes, E. E., Dodge, K. A., Bates, J. E., Pettit, G. S., & Zelli, A. (2000). Discipline responses: Influences of parents' socioeconomic status, ethnicity, beliefs about parenting, stress, and cognitive–emotional processes. *Journal of Family Psychology, 14,* 380–400.

Polaha, J., Larzelere, R. E., Shapiro, S. K., & Pettit, G. S. (2004). Physical discipline and child behavior problems: A study of ethnic group differences. *Parenting: Science and Practice, 4,* 339–360.

Risser, A. L., & Mazur, L. J. (1995). Use of folk remedies in a Hispanic population. *Archives of Pediatric and Adolescent Medicine, 149,* 978–981.

Rohner, R. P. (1986). *The warmth dimension: Foundations of parental acceptance–rejection theory.* Thousand Oaks, CA: Sage.

Rohner, R. P., Kean, K. J., & Cournoyer, D. E. (1991). Effects of corporal punishment, perceived caretaker warmth, and cultural beliefs on the psychological adjustment of children in St. Kitts, West Indies. *Journal of Marriage and the Family, 53,* 681–693.

Segal, U. A. (1995). Child abuse by the middle class? A study of professionals in India. *Child Abuse and Neglect, 19,* 217–231.

Straus, M. A. (1979). Measuring intrafamily conflict and violence: The Conflict Tactics Scale. *Journal of Marriage and the Family, 41,* 75–88.

Straus, M. A. (1996). Spanking and the making of a violent society. *Pediatrics, 98,* 837–842.

Straus, M. A., & Stewart, J. H. (1999). Corporal punishment by American parents: National data on prevalence, chronicity, severity, and duration in relation to child, and family characteristics. *Clinical Child and Family Psychology Review, 2,* 55–70.

Tao, S., Wang, Y., Wang, Y.-P., & Dong, Q. (1998). Maternal parenting behavior of 3-6 year old children: Its structure and relation to children's characteristics. *Psychological Development and Education, 14,* 42–46.

Weisz, J. R., Sigman, M., Weiss, B., & Mosk, J. (1993). Parent reports of behavioral and emotional problems among children in Kenya, Thailand, and the United States. *Child Development, 64,* 98–109.

Weisz, J. R., Suwanlert, S., Chaiyasit, W., & Walter, B. R. (1987). Over- and undercontrolled referral problems among children and adolescents from Thailand and the United States: The wat and wai of cultural differences. *Journal of Consulting and Clinical Psychology, 55,* 719–726.

Weisz, J. R., Suwanlert, S., Chaiyasit, W., Weiss, B., Achenbach, T. M., & Eastman, K. L. (1993). Behavioral and emotional problems among Thai and American adolescents: Parent reports for ages 12–16. *Journal of Abnormal Psychology, 102,* 395–403.

Whipple, E. G., & Richey, C. A. (1997). Crossing the line from physical discipline to child abuse: How much is too much? *Child Abuse and Neglect, 21,* 431–444.

WorldSAFE. (2004). *World Studies of Abuse in Family Environments.* Retrieved July 29, 2004, from **http://www.inclen.org/research/ws.html#Pilot**

Yeh, M., & Weisz, J. R. (2001). Why are we here at the clinic? Parent–child (dis)agreement on referral problems at outpatient treatment entry. *Journal of Consulting and Clinical Psychology, 69*, 1018–1025.

This work was funded by the Josiah Charles Trent Memorial Foundation and the Duke University Center for Child and Family Policy. We are grateful to the children and parents who participated in this research and to Lina Ramos for her contributions to data collection.

Correspondence concerning this article should be addressed to Jennifer E. Lansford, Center for Child and Family Policy, Box 90545, Durham, NC 27708-0545. Electronic mail may be sent to lansford@duke.edu.

From *Child Development,* Vol. 76, no. 6, November/December 2005, pp. 1234-1246. Copyright © 2005 by Society for Research in Child Development. Reprinted by permission of Blackwell Publishing, Ltd.

A Nation of Wimps

Parents are going to ludicrous lengths to take the lumps and bumps out of life for their children. However well-intentioned, parental hyerconcern and microscrutiny have the net effect of making kids more fragile. That may be why the young are breaking down in record numbers.

Hara Estroff Marano

MAYBE IT'S THE CYCLIST IN THE PARK, TRIM under his sleek metallic blue helmet, cruising along the dirt path … at three miles an hour. On his tricycle.

Or perhaps it's today's playground, all-rubber-cushioned surface where kids used to skin their knees. And … wait a minute … those aren't little kids playing. Their mommies—and especially their daddies—are in there with them, coplaying or play-by-play coaching. Few take it half-easy on the perimeter benches, as parents used to do, letting the kids figure things out for themselves.

Then there are the sanitizing gels, with which over a third of parents now send their kids to school, according to a recent survey. Presumably, parents now worry that school bathrooms are not good enough for their children.

Consider the teacher new to an upscale suburban town. Shuffling through the sheaf of reports certifying the educational "accommodations" he was required to make for many of his history students, he was struck by the exhaustive, well-written—and obviously costly—one on behalf of a girl who was already proving among the most competent of his ninth-graders. "She's somewhat neurotic," he confides, "but she is bright, organized and conscientious—the type who'd get to school to turn in a paper on time, even if she were dying of stomach flu." He finally found the disability he was to make allowances for: difficulty with Gestalt thinking. The 13-year-old "couldn't see the big picture." That cleverly devised defect (what 13-year-old can construct the big picture?) would allow her to take all her tests untimed, especially the big one at the end of the rainbow, the collegeworthy SAT.

Behold the wholly sanitized childhood, without skinned knees or the occasional C in history. "Kids need to feel badly sometimes," says child psychologist David Elkind, professor at Tufts University. "We learn through experience and we learn through bad experiences. Through failure we learn how to cope."

Messing up, however, even in the playground, is wildly out of style. Although error and experimentation are the true mothers of success, parents are taking pains to remove failure from the equation.

"Life is planned out for us," says Elise Kramer, a Cornell University junior "But we don't know what to want." As Elkind puts it, "Parents and schools are no longer geared toward child development, they're geared to academic achievement."

No one doubts that there are significant economic forces pushing parents to invest so heavily in their children's outcome from an early age. But taking all the discomfort, disappointment and even the play out of development, especially while increasing pressure for success, turns out to be misguided by just about 180 degrees. With few challenges all their own, kids are unable to forge their creative adaptations to the normal vicissitudes of life. That not only makes them risk averse, it makes them psychologically fragile, riddled with anxiety. In the process they're robbed of identity, meaning and a sense of accomplishment, to say nothing of a shot at real happiness. Forget, too, about perseverance, not simply a moral virtue but a necessary life skill. These turn out to be the spreading psychic fault lines of 21st century youth. Whether we want to or not, we're on our way to creating a nation of wimps.

The Fragility Factor

College, it seems, is where the fragility factor is now making its greatest mark. It's where intellectual and developmental tracks converge as the emotional training wheels come off. By all accounts, psychological distress is rampant on college campuses. It takes a variety of forms, including anxiety and depression—which are increasingly regarded as two faces of the same coin—binge drinking and substance abuse, self-mutilation and other forms of disconnection. The mental state of students is now so precarious for so many that, says Steven Hyman, provost of Harvard University and former director of the National Institute of Mental Health, "it is interfering with the core mission of the university."

The severity of student mental health problems has been rising since 1988, according to an annual survey of counseling center directors. Through 1996, the most common problems raised by students were relationship issues. That is developmentally appropriate, reports Sherry Benton, assistant director of counseling at Kansas State University. But in 1996, anxiety overtook relationship concerns and has remained the major problem. The University of Michigan Depression Center, the nation's first, estimates that 15 percent of college students nationwide are suffering from that disorder alone.

Overparenting can create lifelong vulnerability to anxiety and depression.

Relationship problems haven't gone away; their nature has dramatically shifted and the severity escalated. Colleges report ever more cases of obsessive pursuit, otherwise known as stalking, leading to violence, even death. Anorexia or bulimia in florid or subclinical form now afflicts 40 percent of women at some time in their college career. Eleven weeks into a semester, reports psychologist Russ Federman, head of counseling at the University of Virginia, "all appointment slots are filled. But the students don't stop coming."

Drinking, too, has changed. Once a means of social lubrication, it has acquired a darker, more desperate nature. Campuses nationwide are reporting record increases in binge drinking over the past decade, with students often stuporous in class, if they get there at all. Psychologist Paul E. Joffe, chair of the suicide prevention team at the University of Illinois at Urbana-Champaign, contends that at bottom binge-drinking is a quest for authenticity and intensity of experience. It gives young people something all their own to talk about, and sharing stories about the path to passing out is a primary purpose. It's an inverted world in which drinking to oblivion is the way to feel connected and alive.

"There is a ritual every university administrator has come to fear," reports John Portmann, professor of religious studies at the University of Virginia. "Every fall, parents drop off their well-groomed freshmen and within two or three days many have consumed a dangerous amount of alcohol and placed themselves in harm's way. These kids have been controlled for so long, they just go crazy."

Heavy drinking has also become the quickest and easiest way to gain acceptance, says psychologist Bernardo J. Carducci, professor at Indiana University Southeast and founder of its Shyness Research Institute. "Much of collegiate social activity is centered on alcohol consumption because it's an anxiety reducer and demands no social skills," he says. "Plus it provides an instant identity; it lets people know that you are willing to belong."

Welcome to the Hothouse

Talk to a college president or administrator and you're almost certainly bound to hear tales of the parents who call at 2 a.m. to protest Branden's C in economics because it's going to damage his shot at grad school.

Shortly after psychologist Robert Epstein announced to his university students that he expected them to work hard and would hold them to high standards, he heard from a parent—on official judicial stationery—asking how he could dare mistreat the young. Epstein, former editor in chief of *Psychology Today*, eventually filed a complaint with the California commission on judicial misconduct, and the judge was censured for abusing his office—but not before he created havoc in the psychology department at the University of California San Diego.

Enter: grade inflation. When he took over as president of Harvard in July 2001, Lawrence Summers publicly ridiculed the value of honors after discovering that 94 percent of the college's seniors were graduating with them. Safer to lower the bar than raise the discomfort level. Grade inflation is the institutional response to parental anxiety about school demands on children, contends social historian Peter Stearns of George Mason University. As such, it is a pure index of emotional overinvestment in a child's success. And it rests on a notion of juvenile frailty—"the assumption that children are easily bruised and need explicit uplift," Stearns argues in his book, *Anxious Parenting: A History of Modern Childrearing in America.*

Parental protectionism may reach its most comic excesses in college, but it doesn't begin there. Primary schools and high schools are arguably just as guilty of grade inflation. But if you're searching for someone to blame, consider Dr. Seuss. "Parents have told their kids from day one that there's no end to what they are capable of doing," says Virginia's Portmann. "They read them the Dr. Seuss book *Oh, the Places You'll Go!* and create bumper stickers telling the world their child is an honor student. American parents today expect their children to be perfect—the smartest, fastest, most charming people in the universe. And if they can't get the children to prove it on their own, they'll turn to doctors to make their kids into the people that parents want to believe their kids are."

What they're really doing, he stresses, is "showing kids how to work the system for their own benefit."

And subjecting them to intense scrutiny. "I wish my parents had some hobby other than me," one young patient told David Anderegg, a child psychologist in Lenox, Massachusetts, and professor of psychology at Bennington College. Anderegg finds that anxious parents are hyperattentive to their kids, reactive to every blip of their child's day, eager to solve every problem for their child—and believe that's good parenting. "If you have an infant and the baby has gas, burping the baby is being a good parent. But when you have a 10-year-old who has metaphoric gas, you don't have to burp him. You have to let him sit with it, try to figure out what to do about it. He then learns to tolerate moderate amounts of difficulty, and it's not the end of the world."

Arrivederci, Playtime

In the hothouse that child raising has become, play is all but dead. Over 40,000 U.S. schools no longer have recess. And what play there is has been corrupted. The organized sports many kids participate in are managed by adults; difficulties that arise are not worked out by kids but adjudicated by adult referees.

"So many toys now are designed by and for adults," says Tufts' Elkind. When kids do engage in their own kind of play parents become alarmed. Anderegg points to kids exercising

A Dangerous New Remedy for Anxiety

Of all the disorders now afflicting young people, perhaps most puzzling is self-injury—deliberate cutting, cigarette-burning or other repetitive mutilation of body tissue. No one knows whether it's a sudden epidemic or has been rising gradually, but there appears to be an absolute increase in occurrence: "It has now reached critical mass and is on all our radar screens," says Russ Federman, director of counseling at the University of Virginia.

It's highly disturbing for a student to walk into a dorm room and find her roommate meticulously slicing her thighs with a shard of glass or a razor. But it may be the emblematic activity of the psychically shielded and overly fragile. People "do it to feel better. It's an impulsive act done to regulate mood," observes Armando Favazza, author of Bodies Under Siege: Self Mutilation in Psychiatry and Culture.

It's basically a very effective "home remedy" for anxiety, states Chicago psychiatrist Arthur Neilsen, who teaches at Northwestern University. People who deliberately hurt themselves—twice as many women as men—report "it's like popping a balloon." There's an immediate release of tension. It also serves an important defense—distraction—stresses Federman. "In the midst of emotional turmoil, physical pain helps people disconnect from the turmoil." But the effect is very short-lived.

Self-harm reflects young people's inability to find something that makes them feel fully alive. Earlier generations sought meaning in movements of social change or intellectual engagement inside and outside the classroom. "But young people are not speaking up or asking questions in the classroom," reports John Portmann, professor of religious studies at the University of Virginia and author of Bad for Us: The Lure of Self-Harm. It may be that cutting is their form of protest. So constrained and stressed by expectations, so invaded by parental control, they have no room to turn—except against themselves. —HEM

time-honored curiosity by playing doctor. "It's normal for children to have curiosity about other children's genitals," he says. "But when they do, most parents I know are totally freaked out. They wonder what's wrong."

Kids are having a hard time even playing neighborhood pickup games because they've never done it, observes Barbara Carlson, president and cofounder of Putting Families First. "They've been told by their coaches where on the field to stand, told by their parents what color socks to wear, told by the referees who's won and what's fair. Kids are losing leadership skills."

A lot has been written about the commercialization of children's play but not the side effects, says Elkind. "Children aren't getting any benefits out of play as they once did." From the beginning play helps children learn how to control themselves, how to interact with others. Contrary to the widely held belief that only intellectual activities build a sharp brain, it's in play that cognitive agility really develops. Studies of children and adults around the world demonstrate that social engagement actually improves intellectual skills. It fosters decision-making, memory and thinking, speed of mental processing. This shouldn't come as a surprise. After all, the human mind is believed to have evolved to deal with social problems.

The Eternal Umbilicus

It's bad enough that today's children are raised in a psychological hothouse where they are overmonitored and oversheltered. But that hothouse no longer has geographical or temporal boundaries. For that you can thank the cell phone. Even in college—or perhaps especially at college—students are typically in contact with their parents several times a day, reporting every flicker of experience. One long-distance call overheard on a recent cross-campus walk: "Hi, Mom. I just got an ice-cream cone; can you believe they put sprinkles on the bottom as well as on top?"

"Kids are constantly talking to parents," laments Cornell student Kramer, which makes them perpetually homesick. Of course, they're not telling the folks everything, notes Portmann. "They're not calling their parents to say, 'I really went wild last Friday at the frat house and now I might have chlamydia. Should I go to the student health center?'"

The perpetual access to parents infantilizes the young, keeping them in a permanent state of dependency. Whenever the slightest difficulty arises, "they're constantly referring to their parents for guidance," reports Kramer. They're not learning how to manage for themselves.

Think of the cell phone as the eternal umbilicus. One of the ways we grow up is by internalizing an image of Mom and Dad and the values and advice they imparted over the early years. Then, whenever we find ourselves faced with uncertainty or difficulty, we call on that internalized image. We become, in a way, all the wise adults we've had the privilege to know. "But cell phones keep kids from figuring out what to do," says Anderegg. "They've never internalized any images; all they've internalized is 'call Mom or Dad.'"

Some psychologists think we have yet to recognize the full impact of the cell phone on child development, because its use is so new. Although there are far too many variables to establish clear causes and effects, Indiana's Carducci believes that reliance on cell phones undermines the young by destroying the ability to plan ahead. "The first thing students do when they walk out the door of my classroom is flip open the cell phone. Ninety-five percent of the conversations go like this: 'I just got out of class; I'll see you in the library in five minutes.' Absent the phone, you'd have to make arrangements ahead of time; you'd have to think ahead."

Herein lies another possible pathway to depression. The ability to plan resides in the prefrontal cortex (PFC), the executive branch of the brain. The PFC is a critical part of the self-regulation system, and it's deeply implicated in depression, a disorder increasingly seen as caused or maintained by unregulated thought patterns—lack of intellectual rigor, if you will. Cognitive therapy owes its very effectiveness to the systematic application of critical thinking to emotional reactions. Further, it's in the setting of goals and progress in working toward them, however mundane they are, that positive feelings are generated. From such everyday activity, resistance to depression is born.

What's more, cell phones—along with the instant availability of cash and almost any consumer good your heart desires—promote fragility by weakening self-regulation. "You get used to things happening right away," says Carducci. You not only want the pizza now, you generalize that expectation to other domains, like friendship and intimate relationships. You become frustrated and impatient easily. You become unwilling to work out problems. And so relationships fail—perhaps the single most powerful experience leading to depression.

From Scrutiny to Anxiety … and Beyond

The 1990s witnessed a landmark reversal in the traditional patterns of psychopathology. While rates of depression rise with advancing age among people over 40, they're now increasing fastest among children, striking more children at younger and younger ages.

Parents need to give kids—and themselves—a break by loosening their invasive control: sooner or later, most kids will be forced to confront their own mediocrity.

In his now-famous studies of how children's temperaments play out, Harvard psychologist Jerome Kagan has shown unequivocally that what creates anxious children is parents hovering and protecting them from stressful experiences. About 20 percent of babies are born with a high-strung temperament. They can be spotted even in the womb; they have fast heartbeats. Their nervous systems are innately programmed to be overexcitable in response to stimulation, constantly sending out false alarms about what is dangerous.

As infants and children this group experiences stress in situations most kids find unthreatening, and they may go through childhood and even adulthood fearful of unfamiliar people and events, withdrawn and shy. At school age they become cautious, quiet and introverted. Left to their own devices they grow up shrinking from social encounters. They lack confidence around others. They're easily influenced by others. They are sitting ducks for bullies. And they are on the path to depression.

While their innate reactivity seems to destine all these children for later anxiety disorders, things didn't turn out that way. Between a touchy temperament in infancy and persistence of anxiety stand two highly significant things: parents. Kagan found to his surprise that the development of anxiety was scarcely inevitable despite apparent genetic programming. At age 2, none of the overexcitable infants wound up fearful if their parents backed off from hovering and allowed the children to find some comfortable level of accommodation to the world on their own. Those parents who overprotected their children—directly observed by conducting interviews in the home—brought out the worst in them.

A small percentage of children seem almost invulnerable to anxiety from the start. But the overwhelming majority of kids are somewhere in between. For them, overparenting can program the nervous system to create lifelong vulnerability to anxiety and depression.

Teens use irony and detachment to "hide in plain sight." They just don't want to be exposed to any more scrutiny.

There is in these studies a lesson for all parents. Those who allow their kids to find a way to deal with life's day-to-day stresses by themselves are helping them develop resilience and coping strategies. "Children need to be gently encouraged to take risks and learn that nothing terrible happens," says Michael Liebowitz, clinical professor of psychiatry at Columbia University and head of the Anxiety Disorders Clinic at New York State Psychiatric Institute. "They need gradual exposure to find that the world is not dangerous. Having overprotective parents is a risk factor for anxiety disorders because children do not have opportunities to master their innate shyness and become more comfortable in the world." They never learn to dampen the pathways from perception to alarm reaction.

Hothouse parenting undermines children in other ways, too, says Anderegg. Being examined all the time makes children extremely self-conscious. As a result they get less communicative; scrutiny teaches them to bury their real feelings deeply. And most of all, self-consciousness removes the safety to be experimental and playful. "If every drawing is going to end up on your parents' refrigerator, you're not free to fool around, to goof up or make mistakes," says Anderegg.

Parental hovering is why so many teenagers are so ironic, he notes. It's a kind of detachment, "a way of hiding in plain sight. They just don't want to be exposed to any more scrutiny."

Parents are always so concerned about children having high self-esteem, he adds. "But when you cheat on their behalf to get them ahead of other children"—by pursuing accommodations and recommendations—"you just completely corrode their sense of self. They feel 'I couldn't do this on my own.' It robs them of their own sense of efficacy." A child comes to think, "if I need every advantage I can get, then perhaps there is really something wrong with me." A slam dunk for depression.

Virginia's Portmann feels the effects are even more pernicious; they weaken the whole fabric of society. He sees young people becoming weaker right before his eyes, more responsive to the herd, too eager to fit in—less assertive in the classroom, unwilling to disagree with their peers, afraid to question authority, more willing to conform to the expectations of those on the next rung of power above them.

Un-Advice For Parents

CHILL OUT! If you're not having fun, you may be pushing your kids too hard.

- Never invest more in an outcome than your child does.
- Allow children of all ages time for free play. It's a natural way to learn regulation, social skills and cognitive skills.
- Be reasonable about what is dangerous and what is not. Some risk-taking is healthy,
- Don't overreact to every bad grade or negative encounter your child has. Sometimes discomfort is the appropriate response to a situation—and a stimulus to self-improvement,
- Don't be too willing to slap a disease label on your child at the first sign of a problem; instead, spend some time helping your child learn how to deal with the problem.
- Peers are important, but young people also need to spend time socializing with adults in order to know how to be adults.
- Modify your expectations about child-raising in light of your child's temperament; the same actions don't work with everyone.
- Recognize that there are many paths to success. Allow your children latitude—even to take a year off before starting college.
- Don't manipulate the academic system on behalf of your child; it makes kids guilty and doubtful of their own ability,
- Remember that the goal of child-rearing is to raise an independent adult. Encourage your children to think for themselves, to disagree (respectfully) with authority, even to incur the critical gaze of their peers.

Endless Adolescence

The end result of cheating childhood is to extend it forever. Despite all the parental pressure, and probably because of it, kids are pushing back—in their own way. They're taking longer to grow up.

Adulthood no longer begins when adolescence ends, according to a recent report by University of Pennsylvania sociologist Frank E. Furstenberg and colleagues. There is, instead, a growing no-man's-land of postadolescence from 20 to 30, which they dub "early adulthood." Those in it look like adults but "haven't become fully adult yet—traditionally defined as finishing school, landing a job with benefits, marrying and parenting—because they are not ready or perhaps not permitted to do so." Using the classic benchmarks of adulthood, 65 percent of males had reached adulthood by the age of 30 in 1960. By contrast, in 2000, only 31 percent had. Among women, 77 percent met the benchmarks of adulthood by age 30 in 1960. By 2000, the number had fallen to 46 percent.

Boom Boom Boomerang

Take away play from the front end of development and it finds a way onto the back end. A steady march of success through regimented childhood arranged and monitored by parents creates young adults who need time to explore themselves. "They often need a period in college or afterward to legitimately experiment—to be children," says historian Stearns. "There's decent historical evidence to suggest that societies that allow kids a few years of latitude and even moderate [rebellion] end up with healthier kids than societies that pretend such impulses don't exist."

Marriage is one benchmark of adulthood, but its antecedents extend well into childhood. "The precursor to marriage is dating, and the precursor to dating is playing," says Carducci. The less time children spend in free play, the less socially competent they'll be as adults. It's in play that we learn give and take, the fundamental rhythm of all relationships. We learn how to read the feelings of others and how to negotiate conflicts. Taking the play out of childhood, he says, is bound to create a developmental lag, and he sees it clearly in the social patterns of today's adolescents and young adults, who hang around in groups that are more typical of childhood. Not to be forgotten: The backdrop of continued high levels of divorce confuses kids already too fragile to take the huge risk of commitment.

Just Whose Shark Tank Is It Anyway?

The stressful world of cutthroat competition that parents see their kids facing may not even exist. Or it exists, but more in their mind than in reality—not quite a fiction, more like a distorting mirror. "Parents perceive the world as a terribly competitive place," observes Anderegg. "And many of them project that onto their children when they're the ones who live or work in a competitive environment. They then imagine that their children must be swimming in a big shark tank, too."

"It's hard to know what the world is going to look like 10 years from now," says Elkind. "How best do you prepare kids for that? Parents think that earlier is better. That's a natural intuition, but it happens to be wrong."

What if parents have micromanaged their kids' lives because they've hitched their measurement of success to a single event whose value to life and paycheck they have frantically overestimated? No one denies the Ivy League offers excellent learning experiences, but most educators know that some of the best programs exist at schools that don't top the *U.S. News and World Report* list, and that with the right attitude—a willingness to be engaged by new ideas—it's possible to get a meaningful education almost anywhere. Further, argues historian Stearns, there are ample openings for students at an array of colleges. "We have a competitive frenzy that frankly involves parents more than it involves kids themselves," he observes, both as a father of eight and teacher of many. "Kids are more ambivalent about the college race than are parents."

Yet the very process of application to select colleges undermines both the goal of education and the inherent strengths of young people. "It makes kids sneaky," says Anderegg. Bending rules and calling in favors to give one's kid a competitive edge is morally corrosive.

Like Stearns, he is alarmed that parents, pursuing disability diagnoses so that children can take untimed SATs, actually encourage kids to think of themselves as sickly and fragile. Colleges no longer know when SATs are untimed—but the kids know. "The kids know when you're cheating on their behalf," says Anderegg, "and it makes them feel terribly guilty. Sometimes they arrange to fail to right the scales. And when you cheat on their behalf, you completely undermine their sense of self-esteem. They feel they didn't earn it on their own."

In buying their children accommodations to assuage their own anxiety, parents are actually locking their kids into fragility. Says the suburban teacher: "Exams are a fact of life. They are anxiety-producing. The kids never learn how to cope with anxiety."

Putting Worry in Its Place

Children, however, are not the only ones who are harmed by hyperconcern. Vigilance is enormously taxing—and it's taken all the fun out of parenting. "Parenting has in some measurable ways become less enjoyable than it used to be," says Stearns. "I find parents less willing to indulge their children's sense of time. So they either force feed them or do things for them."

Parents need to abandon the idea of perfection and give up some of the invasive control they've maintained over their children. The goal of parenting, Portmann reminds, is to raise an independent human being. Sooner or later, he says, most kids will be forced to confront their own mediocrity. Parents may find it easier to give up some control if they recognize they have exaggerated many of the dangers of childhood—although they have steadfastly ignored others, namely the removal of recess from schools and the ubiquity of video games that encourage aggression.

The childhood we've introduced to our children is very different from that in past eras, Epstein stresses. Children no longer work at young ages. They stay in school for longer periods of time and spend more time exclusively in the company of peers. Children are far less integrated into adult society than they used to be at every step of the way. We've introduced laws that give children many rights and protections—although we have allowed media and marketers to have free access.

There are kids worth worrying about—kids in poverty.

In changing the nature of childhood, Stearns argues, we've introduced a tendency to assume that children can't handle difficult situations. "Middle-class parents especially assume that if kids start getting into difficulty they need to rush in and do it for them, rather than let them flounder a bit and learn from it. I don't mean we should abandon them," he says, "but give them more credit for figuring things out." And recognize that parents themselves have created many of the stresses and anxieties children are suffering from, without giving them tools to manage them.

While the adults are at it, they need to remember that one of the goals of higher education is to help young people develop the capacity to think for themselves.

Although we're well on our way to making kids more fragile, no one thinks that kids and young adults are fundamentally more flawed than in previous generations. Maybe many will "recover" from diagnoses too liberally slapped on to them. In his own studies of 14 skills he has identified as essential for adulthood in American culture, from love to leadership, Epstein has found that "although teens don't necessary behave in a competent way, they have the potential to be every bit as competent and as incompetent as adults."

Parental anxiety has its place. But the way things now stand, it's not being applied wisely. We're paying too much attention to too few kids—and in the end, the wrong kids. As with the girl whose parents bought her the Gestalt-defect diagnosis, resources are being expended for kids who don't need them.

There are kids who are worth worrying about—kids in poverty, stresses Anderegg. "We focus so much on our own children," says Elkind, "It's time to begin caring about all children."

From *Psychology Today*, November/December 2004, pp. 58-70, 103. Copyright © 2004 by Sussex Publishers, Inc. Reprinted by permission.

Why Our Kids Are Out of Control

Whiny, arrogant, rude, violent. America's children are showing their bad side. Child psychologist Jacob Azerrad, Ph.D., and Paul Chance, Ph.D., show us what we can do to save our children.

JACOB AZERRAD, PH.D., WITH PAUL CHANCE, PH.D.

MICHAEL IS OUT OF CONTROL. HE HAS SEVERAL TEMPER tantrums a day, throws food during meals, deliberately breaks toys and household items, hits and bites his younger brother and sister and refuses to comply with reasonable requests. Asked to put away his toys or go to bed, the 5-year-old replies, "No. And you can't make me." He is, in truth, a very unpleasant child. He is also very unhappy: No one can behave as he does and feel good about himself or be pleased with life.

We seem to be in the midst of an epidemic of Michaels. I have been a child psychologist for 35 years, and each year I see parents dealing with more and more severe problems. Their children are not just ill-mannered, they are whiny, selfish, arrogant, rude, defiant and violent. Most of them are also miserable, as are their parents.

Such disgraceful behavior in young children predicts serious problems later in life. As adolescents they are more likely to drop out of school, use drugs, engage in delinquency and be clinically depressed. And when I read newspaper articles about road rage, commuter rage and office rage it seems to me that many out-of-control children are growing up to be out-of-control adults.

Why are there so many out-of-control children today? Many explanations have been proposed: high-sugar diets, environmental toxins, allergies, television, psychiatric disorders. In considering these theories, it is useful to note that the rise in outrageous child behavior is largely an American phenomenon. Psychologist Tiffany Field, Ph.D., of the University of Miami School of Medicine, found that in France, for example, 3-year-olds behave admirably in restaurants. They sit quietly and talk and eat their meals like "little adults." They do not argue or throw food or refuse to eat as many American children do.

In a separate study, Field noted another major difference in the behavior of French and American preschoolers: On playgrounds, French youngsters were aggressive toward their playmates only 1 percent of the time; American preschoolers, by contrast, were aggressive 29 percent of the time. It is probably not a coincidence that France has the lowest murder rate in the industrialized world, and the United States has the highest.

Can such dramatic differences in behavior between advanced, industrialized nations be accounted for by differences in diet, toxins, allergies, television or psychiatric disorders? It seems extremely unlikely, and I have found no scientific evidence to support these theories. I suggest that the fundamental reason behind so many more American children running amuck is child-rearing practices.

Let me explain: Studies have consistently shown that the problem behavior of children is typically the result of misplaced adult attention. In a study done many years ago, psychologist Betty Hart, Ph.D., and her colleagues at the University of Washington, studied the effects of attention on Bill, a 4-year-old "crybaby" enrolled in a morning preschool. Each morning Bill had between five and 10 crying spells: He cried when he fell, bumped his head or if another child took away a toy. Each time Bill cried a teacher went to him to offer comfort. Hart and her colleagues reasoned that this adult attention, though intended to reassure and comfort Bill, might actually be the reason for all his crying.

To test their hypothesis, the researchers asked the teachers to try a new strategy. Now when Bill cried, the teachers glanced at him to be sure he was not injured but did not go to him, speak to him or look at him. If he happened to cry when a teacher was nearby, she turned her back or walked away. Teachers paid special attention to Bill only when he suffered a mishap without crying. If he fell, for example, and went about his business without a whimper, a teacher would go to him and compliment him on his grown-up behavior. The result of this new approach: In five days the frequency of Bill's crying spells fell from an average of about seven per morning to almost zero.

To be certain that Bill's change in behavior was because of the new strategy, Hart and colleagues asked the teachers to once again pay attention to Bill when he cried. Bill returned to crying several times a day. When the teachers again ignored the crying and attended to Bill only when he acted maturely, the crying spells dropped sharply (see figure). Hart and her coworkers repeated this experiment with another "crybaby," Alan, and got nearly identical results. Similarly, researchers have shown that the disruptive behavior of school children is often a result of

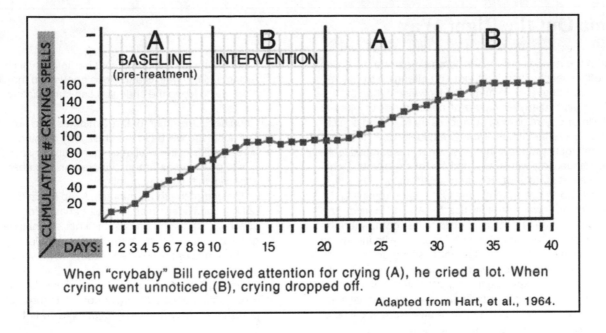

When "crybaby" Bill received attention for crying (A), he cried a lot. When crying went unnoticed (B), crying dropped off.

Adapted from Hart, et al., 1964.

adult attention. In studies of elementary school classrooms, for example, researchers found some students repeatedly left their seats without good reason. Typically the teacher interrupted the lesson to reprimand them. But these efforts often increased the frequency of wandering. When the teacher ignored children who wandered and paid attention to those who worked hard, the frequency of the problem behavior usually fell sharply. It may seem odd that reprimands, threats and criticism can actually reward bad behavior, but such is the tremendous power of adult attention. When children can get attention by behaving well, they do.

"It may seem odd that reprimands, threats and criticism can reward bad behavior, but such is the power of adult attention."

Unfortunately, many adults are far more likely to attend to annoying behavior than they are to desirable behavior. Glenn Latham, Ed.D., a family and educational consultant, has found that adults typically ignore 90 percent or more of the good things children do. Instead, they pay attention to children when they behave badly.

I believe that Americans attend more to bad behavior than to good behavior because they have come under the spell of self-described child-rearing authorities. These kiddie gurus—who include pediatrician Benjamin Spock, M.D., child psychiatrists T. Barry Brazelton, M.D., and Stanley Turecki, M.D., and child psychologist Ross W. Greene, Ph.D., among others—repeatedly urge parents to give special attention to children when they behave badly. Consider the following example.

In *Dr. Spock's Baby and Child Care* (Pocket Books, 1998), a book that has sold 40 million copies, Dr. Spock recommends this approach in dealing with aggressive behavior:

"If your child is hurting another or looks as if he were planning murder, pull him away in a matter-of-fact manner and get him interested in something else."

Given what research shows about the effects of adult attention, getting a child "interested in something else" whenever he is aggressive is a sure formula for producing a highly aggressive child.

If a child gets angry and throws or smashes things, Dr. Brazelton suggests the following:

"Sit down with her in your lap until she's available to you. Then, discuss why you think she needed to do it, why she can't do it and how badly you know she feels for this kind of destructive, out-of-control behavior."

If your child has a particularly intense tantrum, Dr. Turecki gives this advice:

"With these tantrums you should be physically present with your child, with your arms around him if he'll permit it or just be there with him as a comforting physical presence in the room. Be calm and say reassuring things: 'I know you're upset, but it will be okay.'"

If the child has a tantrum that is not so intense, Turecki recommends being "menacing and firm." In other words, having a mild tantrum doesn't pay off, but having a severe tantrum does. I can scarcely imagine a more effective way of teaching a child to have severe tantrums.

Many of the most popular child-rearing books are full of such nonsense. They repeatedly urge parents to hold, soothe, comfort and talk to a child who bites, hits, screams, throws or breaks things, ignores or refuses parental requests or otherwise behaves in obnoxious, infantile ways. Common sense and a truckload of research argue solidly against this practice. Yet these experts seem to be unaware of the well-established fact that children do what gets noticed, that adult attention usually makes behavior more likely to occur, not less.

Nevertheless, thousands of parents follow the bad advice of these and like-minded child-rearing gurus every day. And the more faithfully they follow the advice, the worse their children

Time Out the Right Way

Most of the annoying things children do can be dealt with very effectively by ignoring them and attending to children when they behave more maturely. However, when the behavior is particularly immature or poses a risk of injury to the child or others, it may be necessary to turn to punishment. In these instances, Time Out usually does the trick.

Time Out is probably the most widely researched technique for dealing with unwanted behavior in young children. Unfortunately, it is often used incorrectly. It is therefore worth noting that Time Out means removing the child from all rewarding activities for a short period. The common practice of sending a child to his room, where he can play computer games, watch TV or talk with friends on the telephone, is not Time Out, nor is sitting on the couch with the child and discussing the merits of his behavior. Time Out means exposing the child to a very boring, unrewarding environment. For the sake of illustration, let's assume that your child has bitten someone. Here is a simple, highly effective way of discouraging this behavior:

1. Say to her: "We do not bite." Say nothing more than this—give no further description of the behavior, no explanation of what you are doing. Say nothing except, "We do not bite."

2. Take her by the hand and seat her in a small chair facing a blank wall. Stand close enough so that if she attempts to leave the chair you can immediately return her to it.

3. Keep her in the chair for three minutes. (Do not tell her how long she will be in the chair. Say nothing.) If she screams, kicks the wall, asks questions or says she has to go to the bathroom, ignore her. It is absolutely essential that you say nothing.

4. At the end of the three minutes, keep her in the chair until she has been quiet and well-behaved for five more seconds. When she does so, tell her she has been good and may now leave the chair. Never let her leave until she has been well-behaved for at least a few seconds.

5. Following Time Out, say nothing about it. Do not discuss the punished behavior or the fairness of the punishment. Say nothing except, "We do not bite."

Once the child realizes that you mean business, that she cannot manipulate you into providing attention for bad behavior, Time Out will proceed more smoothly and quickly and there will be far fewer times when you need to use it.

---

become. Some of these parents eventually find their way to my office, desperate for help. I advise them to redirect their attention from infantile behavior to grown-up behavior. They are often amazed by the change in their children.

"It is a sad reality that many (perhaps most) forms of child psychotherapy are a consumer rip-off."

—R. Christopher Barden, Ph.D., J.D., president, National Association for Consumer Protection in Mental Health Practices

Take Dennis, for example. Ten-year-old Dennis was a "born liar," according to his mother, who added, "he wouldn't tell the truth if his life depended on it." Dennis had several siblings, but he was the only chronic liar. Why Dennis? With several children in the family, there was a good deal of competition for adult attention. Dennis wanted more than his share, and he got it by lying: His mother spent a lot of time with him trying to separate fact from fiction and trying to understand why he lied. Mom didn't realize it, but all this attention just encouraged dishonesty.

The solution was to give Dennis attention when it was clear he was telling the truth and to ignore him when he might be lying. When Mom knew that Dennis had given her the right amount of change after a purchase, or when a discrete call to his teacher proved that he really had been kept after school, he got time with Mom and approval for telling the truth. Instead of

"tell a lie, get attention," the rule became, "tell the truth, get attention." When the rule changed, so did Dennis.

Five-year-old Debbie offered a different sort of challenge, but the solution was essentially the same. She woke up every night screaming because of nightmares about "the big germ" and "the terrible lion." Every night her parents rushed to her side to comfort her and assure her there were no big germs or terrible lions in the house. During the day, Debbie talked about her nightmares with anyone who would listen. Her mother encouraged this behavior because she thought it would be therapeutic for Debbie to get her fears "out in the open." In fact, all this attention to her fears made them worse, not better. From Debbie's standpoint, the lesson was: "If Mom and Dad are so interested in what I say about the big germ and the terrible lion, these monsters must really exist."

"These kiddie gurus urge parents to give special attention to children when they behave badly."

The solution to Debbie's problem was to pay less attention to talk about nightmares and more attention to grown-up behavior. When Mom and Dad started saying things like, "I appreciated it when you helped me set the table today" and "I heard you taking the phone message from Mrs. Smith. You were very grown up," they provided Debbie with better ways of getting attention than screaming in the night and complaining about monsters.

Even Michael, the screaming, out-of-control boy who made life miserable for himself and everyone near him, soon became a happy, self-disciplined child. He was more challenging than most children, but once again the most important step to turning him around was giving him the attention he wanted when he gave his parents the behavior they wanted.

It sounds easier than it is. Parents who have fallen into the habit of offering attention for disagreeable behavior often have a hard time shifting their focus to agreeable behavior. Over the years I have devised a simple procedure to help parents do this. I call it the Nurture Response:

1. Be on the alert for behavior that indicates growing maturity: Taking disappointment calmly, performing spontaneous acts of kindness and demonstrating an interest in learning. When you see this kind of grown-up behavior, make a mental note of it. Perhaps Margaret, who usually responds to disappointments with a tantrum, is unperturbed when told her favorite breakfast cereal is unavailable. Maybe Sam, who is typically selfish with his belongings, shares his toys with the neighbor's child.

Seven to 25 percent of preschoolers meet the criterion for ODD—oppositional-defiant disorder.

---

2. Some time later (anywhere from five minutes to five hours after the event), remind the child of the behavior you observed. You might say, "Do you remember when Harry's bike fell over and he couldn't straighten it because it was too heavy for him? You went over and helped him. Do you remember doing that?"

3. When you're sure the child remembers the event in question, praise her for it. You might say, "It was very good of you to help Harry with his bike. I'm proud of you." Often the highest praise you can offer children is to tell them they acted like an adult. You might say, "I know you were disappointed that you couldn't go to the mall, but you were very grown up about it. I was impressed."

Don't mix the praise with criticism. Don't say, for example, "I was proud of the way you helped Harry; you're usually so mean to him," or even, "I'm glad you were finally nice to Harry."

"The fundamental reason behind so many more American children running amok is child-rearing practices."

---

4. Immediately after praising the child, spend some time with him in an activity he enjoys. Do this in a spontaneous way, without suggesting that it is payment for the grown-up behavior. You might play a favorite game, go for a walk, or read a story. Remember that nothing is more important to a child than the undivided attention of a parent, so give the child your full attention for these few minutes.

The nurture response is not a panacea, of course. Some dangerous or extremely annoying forms of behavior, such as knocking other children down or having screaming tantrums, may require additional measures, including punishment. But it is amazing how much can be accomplished by simply ignoring the behavior you don't want and noticing the behavior you do want.

For decades many child-rearing icons have urged parents to pay special attention to troublesome behavior, to offer sympathy, understanding and reassurance when children behave in outrageous ways. This view so pervades our society that scarcely anyone questions it. Both common sense and scientific evidence tell us, however, that this approach is bound to backfire, and it does.

Parents should think of themselves as gardeners. A good gardener encourages desirable plants and discourages undesirable ones. In the same way, a good parent encourages desirable acts and discourages undesirable ones.

Do you want your children to be well-behaved and happy? Then ignore experts who tell you to shower attention on children when they are badly behaved and miserable. Remember that gardeners must nurture the flowers, not the weeds.

JACOB AZERRAD, PH.D., has been a child psychologist for 35 years.

PAUL CHANCE, PH.D., is the book review editor of *Psychology Today*.

Reprinted with permission from *Psychology Today*, September/October 2001, pp. 42-48. Copyright © 2001 by Sussex Publishers, Inc.

Siblings' Direct and Indirect Contributions to Child Development

ABSTRACT—Since the early 1980s, a growing body of research has described the contributions of sibling relationships to child and adolescent development. Interactions with older siblings promote young children's language and cognitive development, their understanding of other people's emotions and perspectives, and, conversely, their development of antisocial behavior. Studies address the ways in which parents' experiences with older children contribute to their rearing of younger children, which in turn contributes to the younger children's development. Finally, by virtue of having a sibling, children may receive differential treatment from their parents. Under some conditions, differential treatment is associated with emotional and behavioral problems in children.

GENE H. BRODY

T he first studies of the contributions that older siblings make to their younger brothers' and sisters' development were conducted in Britain around the turn of the 20th century by Sir Francis Galton, a cousin of Charles Darwin. Sibling research, however, only recently has begun to address many of the issues that concern families. Parents, clinicians, and now researchers in developmental psychology recognize the significance of the sibling relationship as a contributor to family harmony or discord and to individual children's development. Since the early 1980s, a growing interest in the family has prompted research on those aspects of sibling relationships that contribute to children's cognitive, social, and emotional adjustment. These contributions can be direct, occuring as a result of siblings' encounters with one another, or indirect, occurring through a child's impact on parents that influences the care that other brothers and sisters receive. Differential treatment by parents is a third way in which having a sibling may contribute to child development. Children may be treated differently by their parents than their siblings are, or at least believe that they are treated differently. The development of this belief has implications for children's and adolescents' mental health. In this article, I present an overview of the ways in which siblings' direct and indirect influences and parental differential treatment contribute to child development.

Siblings' Direct Contributions to Development

Currently, research suggests that naturally occurring teaching and caregiving experiences benefit cognitive, language, and psychosocial development in both older and younger siblings. Studies conducted in children's homes and in laboratories show that older siblings in middle childhood can teach new cognitive concepts and language skills to their younger siblings in early childhood. Across the middle childhood years, older siblings become better teachers as they learn how to simplify tasks for their younger siblings. The ability to adjust their teaching behaviors to their younger siblings' capacities increases as older siblings develop the ability to take other people's perspectives (Maynard, 2002). Older siblings who assume teaching and caregiving roles earn higher reading and language achievement scores, gain a greater sense of competence in the caregiving role, and learn more quickly to balance their self-concerns with others' needs than do older siblings who do not assume these roles with their younger siblings (Zukow-Goldring, 1995). When caregiving demands on the older sibling become excessive, however, they may interfere with the older child's time spent on homework or involvement in school activities. Caregiving responsibilities during middle childhood and adolescence can compromise older siblings' school performance and behavioral adjustment (Marshall et al., 1997).

Children who are nurtured by their older siblings become sensitive to other people's feelings and beliefs (Dunn, 1988). As in all relationships, though, nurturance does not occur in isolation from conflict. Sibling relationships that are characterized by a balance of nurturance and conflict can provide a unique opportunity for children to develop the ability to understand other people's emotions and viewpoints, to learn to manage anger and resolve conflict, and to provide nurturance themselves. Indeed, younger siblings who experience a balance of nurturance and conflict in their sibling relationships have been found to be more socially skilled and have more positive peer relationships compared with children who lack this experience (Hetherington, 1988).

Sibling relationships also have the potential to affect children's development negatively. Younger siblings growing up with aggressive older siblings are at considerable risk for developing conduct problems, performing poorly in school, and having few positive experiences in their relationships with their peers (Bank, Patterson, & Reid, 1996). The links between older siblings' antisocial behavior and younger siblings' conduct problems are stronger for children living in disadvantaged neighborhoods characterized by high unemployment rates and pervasive poverty than for children living in more advantaged neighborhoods (Brody, Ge, et al., 2003). Younger siblings who live in disadvantaged neighborhoods have more opportunities than do children living in more affluent areas to practice the problematic conduct that they learn during sibling interactions as they interact with peers who encourage antisocial behavior.

The importance of the sibling relationship is probably best demonstrated by older siblings' ability to buffer younger siblings from the negative effects of family turmoil. Younger siblings whose older siblings provide them with emotional support (caring, acceptance, and bolstering of self-esteem) during bouts of intense, angry interparental conflict show fewer signs of behavioral or emotional problems than do children whose older siblings are less supportive (Jenkins, 1992).

Siblings' Indirect Contributions

Conventional wisdom suggests that parents' experiences with older children influence their expectations of subsequent children and the child-rearing strategies that parents consider effective. Similarly, the experiences that other adults, particularly teachers, have with older siblings may influence their expectations and treatment of younger siblings. Research has confirmed the operation of these indirect effects on younger siblings' development. Whiteman and Buchanan (2002) found that experiences with earlier-born children contributed to parents' expectations about their younger children's likelihood of experiencing conduct problems, using drugs, displaying rebellious behavior, or being helpful and showing concern for others. Teachers are not immune from the predisposing effects of experiences with older siblings. As a result of having an older sibling in class or hearing about his or her accomplishments or escapades, teachers develop expectations regarding the younger sibling's academic ability and conduct even before the younger child becomes their student (Bronfenbrenner, 1977). Some parents and teachers translate these expectations into parenting and teaching practices they subsequently use with younger siblings that influence the younger children's beliefs about their academic abilities, interests, and choice of friends; children often choose friends whom they perceive to be similar to themselves.

Rather than viewing behavioral influence as flowing in one direction, from parents to children, developmental psychologists now recognize that these influences are reciprocal. The behaviors that children use during everyday interactions with their parents partially determine the behaviors that the parents direct toward their children. Children with active or emotionally intense personalities receive different, usually more negative, parenting than do children with calm and easygoing personalities. Some studies suggest that older siblings' individual characteristics may contribute indirectly to the quality of parenting that younger siblings receive. For example, East (1998) discovered that negative experiences with an earlier-born child lead parents to question their ability to provide good care for their younger children and to lower their expectations for their younger children's behavior.

In our research, my colleagues and I explored the specific ways in which older siblings' characteristics contribute to the quality of parenting that younger siblings receive, which in turn contributes to younger siblings' development of conduct problems and depressive symptoms. The premise of the study was simple. Rearing older siblings who are doing well in school and are well liked by other children provides parents with opportunities for basking in their children's achievements. (Basking is a phenomenon in which one's psychological well-being increases because of the accomplishments of persons to whom one is close.) Using a longitudinal research design in which we collected data from families for 4 years, we found that academically and socially competent older siblings contributed to an increase in their mothers' self-esteem and a decrease in their mothers' depressive symptoms. Positive changes in mothers' psychological functioning forecast their use of adjustment-promoting parenting practices with younger siblings. Over time, these practices forecast high levels of self-control and low levels of behavior problems and depressive symptoms in the younger siblings (Brody, Kim, Murry, & Brown, 2003). We expect future research to clarify further the indirect pathways through which siblings influence one another's development, including the processes by which children's negative characteristics affect their parents' child-rearing practices. A difficult-to-rear older sibling, for example, may contribute over time to decreases in his or her parents' psychological well-being, resulting in increased tension in the family. Under these circumstances, the parents' negativity and distraction decrease the likelihood that a younger sibling will experience parenting that promotes self-worth, academic achievement, and social skills.

Parental Differential Treatment

Any discussion of siblings' contributions to development would be incomplete without acknowledging parental differential treatment. Having a sibling creates a context in which parental behavior assumes symbolic value, as children use it as a barometer indicating the extent to which they are loved, rejected, included, or excluded by their parents. Children's and adolescents' beliefs that they receive less warmth and more negative treatment from their parents than do their siblings is associated with poor emotional and behavioral functioning (Reiss, Neiderhiser, Hetherington, & Plomin, 2000).

Not all children who perceive differential treatment develop these problems, however. Differential parental treatment is associated with poor adjustment in a child only when the quality of the child's individual relationship with his or her parents is distant and negative. The association between differential treatment and adjustment is weak for children whose parents treat them well, even when their siblings receive even warmer and more positive treatment (Feinberg & Hetherington, 2001). Children's perceptions of the legitimacy of differential treatment also help determine its contribution to their adjustment. Children who perceive their parents' differential behavior to be justified report fewer behavior problems than do children who consider it to be unjust, even under conditions of relatively high levels of differential treatment. Children and adolescents who perceive differential treatment as unfair experience low levels of self-worth and have high levels of behavior problems (Kowal, Kramer, Krull, & Crick, 2002). Children justify differential treatment by citing ways in which they and their siblings differ in age, personality, and special needs. Sensitive parenting entails treating children as their individual temperaments and developmental needs require. Nevertheless, it is important that children understand why parents treat siblings differently from one another so that they will be protected from interpreting the differences as evidence that they are not valued or worthy of love.

Future Directions

Considerable work is needed to provide a comprehensive understanding of the processes through which siblings influence one another's cognitive development, language development, psychological adjustment, and social skills. Current studies can best be considered "first generation" research. They describe associations between older and younger siblings' behaviors and characteristics. Some studies have demonstrated that the prediction of younger siblings' outcomes is more accurate if it is based on older siblings' characteristics plus parenting, rather than parenting alone (Brody, Kim, et al., 2003). More research is needed to isolate influences other than parenting, such as shared genetics, shared environments, and social learning, before siblings' unique contributions to development can be specified. The next generation of research will address the ways in which sibling relationships contribute to children's self-images and personal identities, emotion regulation and coping skills, explanations of positive and negative events that occur in family and peer relationships, use of aggression, and involvement in high-risk behaviors.

Acknowledgments—I would like to thank Eileen Neubaum-Carlan for helpful comments. Preparation of this article was partly supported by grants from the National Institute of Child Health and Human Development, the National Institute of Mental Health, and the National Institute on Alcohol Abuse and Alcoholism.

References

Bank, L., Patterson, G.R., & Reid, J.B. (1996). Negative sibling interaction patterns as predictors of later adjustment problems in adolescent and young adult males. In G.H. Brody (Ed.), *Sibling relationships: Their causes and consequences* (pp. 197–229). Norwood, NJ: Ablex.

Brody, G.H., Ge, X., Kim, S.Y., Murry, Y.M., Simons, R.L., Gibbons, F.X., Gerrard, M., & Conger, R. (2003). Neighborhood disadvantage moderates associations of parenting and older sibling problem attitudes and behavior with conduct disorders in African American children. *Journal of Consulting and Clinical Psychology, 71*, 211–222.

Brody, G.H., Kim, S., Murry, V.M., & Brown, A.C. (2003). Longitudinal direct and indirect pathways linking older sibling competence to the development of younger sibling competence. *Developmental Psychology, 39*, 618–628.

Bronfenbrenner, U. (1977). Toward an experimental ecology of human development. *American Psychologist, 32*, 513–531.

Dunn, J. (1988). Connections between relationships: Implications of research on mothers and siblings. In R.A. Hinde & J. Stevenson-Hinde (Eds.), *Relationships within families: Mutual influences* (pp. 168–180). New York: Oxford University Press.

East, P.L. (1998). Impact of adolescent childbearing on families and younger siblings: Effects that increase younger siblings' risk for early pregnancy. *Applied Developmental Science, 2*, 62–74.

Feinberg, M., & Hetherington, E.M. (2001). Differential parenting as a within family variable. *Journal of Family Psychology, 15*, 22–37.

Hetherington, E.M. (1988). Parents, children, and siblings: Six years after divorce. In R.A. Hinde & J. Stevenson-Hinde (Eds.), *Relationships within families: Mutual influences* (pp. 311–331). New York: Oxford University Press.

Jenkins, J. (1992). Sibling relationships in disharmonious homes: Potential difficulties and protective effects. In F. Boer & J. Dunn (Eds.), *Children's sibling relationships: Developmental and clinical issues* (pp. 125–138). Hillsdale, NJ: Erlbaum.

Kowal, A., Kramer, L., Krull, J.L., & Crick, N.R. (2002). Children's perceptions of the fairness of parental preferential treatment and their socioemotional well-being. *Journal of Family Psychology, 16*, 297–306.

Marshall, N.L., Garcia-Coli, C., Marx, F., McCartney, K., Keefe, N., & Ruh, J. (1997). After-school time and children's behavioral adjustment. *Merrill-Palmer Quarterly, 43*, 497–514.

Maynard, A.E. (2002). Cultural teaching: The development of teaching skills in Maya sibling interactions. *Child Development, 73*, 969–982.

Reiss, D., Neiderhiser, J.M., Hetherington, E.M., & Plomin, R. (2000). *The relationship code: Deciphering genetic and social influences on adolescent development*. Cambridge, MA: Harvard University Press.

Whiteman, S.D., & Buchanan, C.M. (2002). Mothers' and children's expectations for adolescence: The impact of perceptions of an older sibling's experience. *Journal of Family Psychology, 16*, 157–171.

Zukow-Goldring, P.G. (1995). Sibling caregiving. In M.H. Bornstein (Ed.). *Handbook of parenting: Vol. 3. Status and social conditions of parenting* (pp. 177–208). Mahwah, NJ: Erlbaum.

Address correspondence to Gene H. Brody, University of Georgia, Center for Family Research, 1095 College Station Rd., Athens, GA 30602-4527.

From *Current Directions in Psychological Science,* Vol. 13, No. 4, pp.124-126. Copyright ©2004 by Blackwell Publishing, Ltd. Reprinted by permission. **www.blackwell-synergy.com**

The Environment of Childhood Poverty

GARY W. EVANS
Cornell University

Poor children confront widespread environmental inequities. Compared with their economically advantaged counterparts, they are exposed to more family turmoil, violence, separation from their families, instability, and chaotic households. Poor children experience less social support, and their parents are less responsive and more authoritarian. Low-income children are read to relatively infrequently, watch more TV, and have less access to books and computers. Low-income parents are less involved in their children's school activities. The air and water poor children consume are more polluted. Their homes are more crowded, noisier, and of lower quality. Low-income neighborhoods are more dangerous, offer poorer municipal services, and suffer greater physical deterioration. Predominantly low-income schools and day care are inferior. The accumulation of multiple environmental risks rather than singular risk exposure may be an especially pathogenic aspect of childhood poverty.

Researchers in public health, medicine, and more recently, psychology have come to appreciate the value of studying poverty in its own right. Initially this meant descriptive analyses demonstrating physical and psychological sequelae of poverty or low socioeconomic status (SES; Aber, Bennett, Conley, & Li, 1997; Adler, Boyce, Chesney, Folkman, & Syme, 1993; Bradley & Corwyn, 2002; Chen, Matthews, & Boyce, 2002; Duncan & Brooks-Gunn, 1997; Huston, McLoyd, & Garcia Coll, 1994; Luthar, 1999; McLoyd, 1998; Williams & Collins, 1995). But psychologists have begun to move beyond a social address perspective, turning their attention to underlying explanations for poverty's harmful impacts on children and their families. A limitation of psychological research on poverty is the absence of an ecological perspective—that is, recognizing that the answer to why poverty is harmful probably does not lie with anyone underlying agent or process (Bronfenbrenner & Morris, 1998). Psychologists are aware of the multiple disadvantages accompanying low income in America. Yet the search for explanatory processes of poverty's impacts on children has focused almost exclusively on psychosocial characteristics within the family, particularly negative parenting (Bornstein & Bradley, 2003; G. H. Brody et al., 1994; Conger & Elder, 1994; Luthar, 1999; McLoyd, 1998).

This focus on psychosocial processes is limited in two respects. First, psychological research on poverty has largely ignored the physical settings that low-income children and families inhabit. Families reside in both a social and a physical world (Bradley, 1999; Evans, Kliewer, & Martin, 1991; Parke, 1978; Wachs, 2000; Wohlwill & Heft, 1987), and each has well-documented impacts on human development. Second, poor children face a daunting array of suboptimal psychosocial and physical conditions. Many adverse physical and psychosocial conditions covary and do not occur in isolation. The quality of physical and social living conditions is not randomly distributed in the population (Schell, 1997). Cumulative rather than singular exposure to a confluence of psychosocial and physical environmental risk factors is a potentially critical aspect of the environment of childhood poverty.

Herein I document the wide array of suboptimal physical and psychosocial conditions that low-income children face. I focus on income and childhood environmental risk except in cases where useful social class data are available. These cases are clearly noted. I briefly summarize evidence for the pathogenic influence of each of these singular, income-related physical and psychosocial childhood risk factors and then argue that exposure to multiple stressors may be a unique, key feature of the environment of childhood poverty. I do not review evidence on the impacts of poverty on human development in this article. Both space limitations and recent reviews on the psychological (Bradley & Corwyn, 2002; Duncan & Brooks-Gunn, 1997; Huston et al., 1994; Luthar, 1999; McLoyd, 1998) and physical (Aber et al., 1997; Chen et al., 2002) health impacts of poverty and SES on children preclude the need for doing so.

The Psychosocial Environment of Childhood Poverty

Low-income children in comparison to middle-income children are exposed to greater levels of violence, family disruption, and separation from their family. Household income is inversely related to exposure to familial violence (Emery & Laumann-Billings, 1998) and the incidence of crime within one's neighborhood (Sampson, Raudenbush, & Earls, 1997). Contact with aggressive peers is related to social class (parental education and occupation) in a study of preschoolers in three U.S. metropolitan areas (Sinclair, Pettit, Harrist, Dodge, & Bates, 1994). For example, low-relative to middle-class two- to four-year-olds interact with aggressive peers 40% more often in their neighborhood, 25% more often in child-care settings, and have 70% more contacts with friends who are aggressive (Sinclair et al., 1994). Neighborhood disadvantage (multiple indicators including poverty), net of household income, is positively associated with affiliation with deviant peers among preadolescents (G. H. Brody et al., 2001).

Poor children are more likely to spend a week or more in foster or other institutional care (Rutter, 1981), and they are substantially more likely to live in a family where divorce has occurred (U.S. Census Bureau, 2000; see Table 1).[1] The divorce rate in a nationwide analysis of unskilled workers in British families is four-and-a-half times the rate for skilled and white collar workers (Reid, 1989). The latter two data sets are also noteworthy because they reflect representative, national data sets. Most data on poverty and environmental risk are from convenience samples and thus may not be representative. For several risk factors, however, results from multiple convenience samples converge.

Another limitation of the database on childhood poverty and risk is the absence of statistical analyses beyond descriptive data as presented herein (see Bradley, Corwyn, McAdoo, & Coll, 2001; Grant et al., 2003) for some notable exceptions. This occurs because income is typically incorporated as a statistical control (i.e., covariate), with the focus of inquiry on other variables. Although information on statistical significance or effect sizes is not typically presented, the magnitude of income-related differences in risk exposure as reported herein is frequently so great that further statistical analyses seem superfluous. Table 1 is a good example of this point.

A likely pathway linking poverty and family separation is marital quality. Numerous large-scale studies, including some with nationally representative samples, have demonstrated positive associations between family income and marital quality (e.g., Lewis & Spanier, 1979). More microanalyses have revealed that couples, particularly husbands, facing financial pressure suffer greater conflict and less warmth and support in their marital relationships (Conger & Elder, 1994).

Unresponsive and harsher, more punitive parenting occurs more often among low-income families, beginning as early as infancy (Conger & Elder, 1994; Magnusson & Duncan, 2002; McLoyd, 1998). In a nationwide study, 85% of American parents above the poverty line were responsive to their young children (from newborns to three-year-olds), compared with 74% of parents in low-income homes (Bradley et al., 2001). Similar income-related gaps in parental responsiveness to older children were uncovered. Furthermore, another national data set indicates that the longer the duration of poverty, the stronger the link between poverty and harsher, less unresponsive parenting (Miller & Davis, 1997). A recent meta-analysis has revealed a strong and consistent negative relation ($d \pm = .48, .55$, for cross-sectional and longitudinal studies, respectively) between socioeconomic disadvantage and harsh, less responsive parenting (Grant et al., 2003). Comparable class differences have been found in a large national study in Britain (Reid, 1989). Both lower job status and parental education levels are significantly related to elevated parental rejection of adolescents (Felner et al., 1995).

In a remarkable research program, John and Elizabeth Newson (1963, 1968, 1976, 1977) have chronicled developmental sequelae of social class among a large sample of preschool and primary school children growing up in a midsized British city. For example, parents in unskilled worker families were nearly twice as likely (40%) to frequently rely on corporal punishment for seven-year-olds than parents in professional families (21%). The latter were nearly six times more likely (57%) than the former (10%) to use responsive, child-centered parenting practices. Similar trends were noted among these families when the child was four years old. Two additional class differences in parenting quality noted by the Newsons are noteworthy. Newson and Newson (1968) recorded maternal responses to the following query: "What sort of things make you get on each other's [your four-year-old's] nerves?" Four percent of mothers in unskilled laborer families indicated awareness of the possibility that they could get on their four-year-old's nerves; comparable figures ranged from 10% to 18% for mothers in skilled laborer and professional families. Parental monitoring also varied significantly by social class. Nine percent of professional class families could not locate their child in the neighborhood when needed, this compared with 17% of the families of unskilled workers (Newson & Newson, 1976). In a national study, low-income American parents of eighth graders compared with middle-income parents knew significantly fewer of the parents of their children's friends (Lee & Croninger, 1994). Linkages between class and parenting may be influenced by parental working conditions. Fathers in jobs that are less complex and have lower decision latitude tend to encourage conformity and discourage self-directedness in their children (Kohn, 1977; Luster, Rhoades, & Haas, 1989).

Table 1 Percentage of Children Under 18 With Household Head Divorced, Separated by Household Income Quintiles

Household income quintiles				
First (<$21,844)	Second ($21,845-$39,000)	Third ($39,001-$58,026)	Fourth ($58,027-$86,320)	Fifth (>$86,321)
25.4	16.9	11.9	8.3	5.7
27.9	17.5	11.5	7.0	4.4

Note. Percentiles in row 1 are adjusted for household size (household income divided by the square root of the number of individuals in the household). Percentiles in row 2 are unadjusted by household size. Tabulation by Andrew Houtenville. Adapted from Table 3 in *Population Survey* (March Supplement), 162, U.S. Census Bureau, 2000, Washington, DC: U.S. Government Printing Office.

Numerous national studies have revealed that low-income American households have smaller social networks, fewer organizational involvements, and less frequent contact with social network members compared with families that are not poor (House, Umberson, & Landis, 1988). Parallel results have been reported when comparing white and blue collar workers in the United States and three Northern European countries (Cochran, Larner, Riley, Gunnarson, & Henderson, 1990).

In addition to income and class differences in social networks, perceived social support also relates to poverty. Unemployment is associated cross-sectionally and prospectively with lower social support within the family (Atkinson, Liem, & Liem, 1986), and familial social support is inversely related to income and parental education level in the general population (Conger & Elder, 1994; Wright, Treiber, Davis, Bunch, & Strong, 1998, respectively). Social support among clinically depressed adults is inversely related to education levels as well (Mitchell & Moos, 1984). Mothers of lower SES offered less emotional support to their young children. This same longitudinal survey of American families also uncovered greater instability in peer relationships from preschool through third grade in relation to lower SES (Dodge et al., 1994). Among the children of British unskilled laborers, 22% in the Newsons' study (Newson & Newson, 1976) never had friends come over to play in their home, compared with 4% of the children of professional families. Poor parents are also much less likely to receive social support than their more economically advantaged counterparts. Poor women two to four weeks postpartum received less emotional support than middle- and upper-income mothers of newborns (Turner & Noh, 1983). Low-income mothers of low birth weight, premature babies in a national sample received significantly less social support when their child was one year old compared with their counterparts who were not poor (Liaw & Brooks-Gunn, 1994).

Lower social class (parental education and occupation) adolescents have smaller social support networks and are more dependent upon their peers than upon adults for social support (Bo, 1994). As an illustration, among 16-year-old boys, social class was negatively associated with social network size ($r = -.30$) and time spent with parents ($r = -.25$) and positively related to time spent with peers ($r = .23$) (Bo, 1994). Adolescent boys whose families previously lost at least 35% of their income during the Great Depression were significantly more dependent upon their peer group compared with youths from families who had not suffered such economic losses (Elder, van Nguyen, & Caspi, 1995).

Social resources also vary by neighborhood quality. Disadvantaged neighborhoods have less social capital than wealthier neighborhoods. Across multiple urban sites with representative samples, residents of disadvantaged neighborhoods compared with their more advantaged counterparts (e.g., percent unemployed, percent in poverty, percent with inadequate housing, percent single head of household) have weaker social ties, experience less interpersonal trust and norms of reciprocity, and perceive lower levels of instrumental support and mutual aid (Kawachi, 1999; Leventhal & Brooks-Gunn, 2000; Sampson et al., 1997). Poor neighborhoods have fewer social resources and

diminished capacity for informal social controls. Neighborhood disadvantage accounts for more than 70% of the variance in informal social control across different urban neighborhoods in Chicago and about one third of the variance in social integration (Sampson et al., 1997). Adolescents in a representative sample of Los Angeles who live in poorer neighborhoods (median income, percent below poverty line, percent nonmanagerial occupations) experienced less social cohesion in their neighborhoods compared with those in more affluent neighborhoods (Aneshensal & Sucoff, 1996).

Low-income children experience substantially less cognitive stimulation and enrichment in comparison to wealthier children. Low-income compared with middle-income parents speak less often and in less sophisticated ways to their young children, and as the children grow older, low-income parents are less likely than middle-income parents to engage jointly with their children in literary activities such as reading aloud or visiting the library. Kagan and Tulkin (1971) observed mother-daughter interactions among 60 low- and middle-class 10-month-olds. Class was defined by parental occupation and education. Middle-class mothers spent twice as much time in face-to-face interaction with their infants, talked to their daughters for significantly longer intervals, and were substantially more likely to focus vocalizations to their child without providing competing sensory input. In an extraordinary study, Hart and Risley (1995) observed parent-child verbalizations once per month from 6 months to 3 years of age among 42 families. Observations in the home revealed highly significant and consistent class differences. Class was defined by occupational status (welfare, lower/middle, professional), which was highly correlated with income and parental education. The quantity, quality, and responsiveness of parental speech to children varied strongly by class. Hart and Risley's data shows a fourfold difference in the amount of parental verbalizations to children in families on welfare versus professional families. Similar class differences were also found for speech quality (e.g., nouns, modifiers per utterance) and for verbal responsiveness of parents to children's verbal and nonverbal behaviors.

Hart and Risley (1995) also found that social class is inversely related to the function of parental speech. The higher the social class of parents, the less likely they are to direct or order their children's behaviors and the more likely they are to speak to their children in order to initiate and sustain conversation. Similar SES trends (parental education and occupation) have been shown by Hoff, Laursen, and Tardiff (2002) in a larger sample studied at ages two and four-and-a-half, both at home and in the laboratory. Moreover, significant positive relations between SES and two-year-olds' growth in productive vocabulary over time were largely accounted for by shorter utterances of parental speech among lower class mothers (Hoff, 2003).

In a representative American sample, 38% of low-income parents read to their 3-5-year-old children daily, and 22% have taken their children at least once in the past month to the public library. Comparison figures for families above line are 58% and 40%, respectively (Federal Interagency Forum on Child and Family statistics, 2000). In a nationwide study of American kindergarten children, 36% of parents in the lowest-income quintile read to their children on a daily basis, compared with 62% of parents from the highest-income quintile (Coley, 2002). comparable class differences in reading and library activities were found by the Newsons in their studies of British primary school children (Newson & Newson, 1968, 1976, 1977). Children in low-income families also watch considerably more television than their more affluent counterparts (Larson & Verma, 1999). For example, 18% of low-income American 13-year-olds watch more than six hours of television daily, whereas 10% of 13-year-olds above the poverty line watch this much (U.S. Department of Health and Human Services, 2000).

Parental involvement in school activities is strongly linked to income. In a national survey, 59% of American parents above the poverty line were involved in three or more school activities on a regular basis; this contrasts with 36% of parents below the poverty line (U.S. Department of Health and Human Services, 1999). Better educated mothers of eighth graders monitor their children's school experiences more closely than their less educated counterparts. For example, they are more likely to know their child's teachers by name, can more accurately identify their child's best and worst subject, and more often know how well their child is performing in classes (Baker & Stevenson, 1986). Ethnographic research in 16 elementary and middle schools in California revealed parallel trends (Benveniste, Carnoy, & Rothstein, 2003). Parents in low-income communities volunteered less, attended school functions relatively infrequently, and were typically inattentive to homework and other assignments compared with the parents of children from middle- and upper-income communities.

Adolescents in lower SES (education and occupation) families feel less of a sense of belonging to their school vis-á-vis adolescents in middle and upper SES families (Felner et al., 1995). Multilevel analyses of national data from American middle and high school students reveal evidence that disadvantages at both the individual household level and at the school level are associated with feeling less connected to school (McNeely, Nonnemaker, & Blum, 2002). For example, adolescents from single-parent families and those attending schools with a higher proportion of single-parent families felt less connected to their school.

Children in low-income schools are also less likely to have well-qualified teachers. For example, 27% of high school math teachers in low-income school districts major in mathematics in college. This contrasts with the 43% of high school mathematics teachers in more affluent school districts (Ingersoll, 1999). Student absenteeism and teacher turnover are greater in low-income schools (Lee & Croninger, 1994; Rutter et al., 1974), and as noted earlier, there is much less parental involvement in low-income schools (Lee & Croninger, 1994; U.S. Department of Health and Human Services, 1999). The incidence of violence is greater in low-income American schools as well. A nationwide study has shown that low-income adolescents are twice as likely as middle-income adolescents to report the presence of weapons (12%) or the incidence of physical assaults (32%) in their schools (Gallup, 1993). Access to school itself in much of the Third World is tied to family economic resources. Many poor children are forced to work (Bartlett, Hart, Satterthwaite, de la Barra, & Missiar, 1999).

In terms of day-care facilities, two different national data sets have indicated that the ratio of children to caregivers is lower in predominantly high-income centers (National Institute of Child Health and Human Development Early Child Care Research Network, 1997; Phillips, Voran, Kisker, Howes, & Whitbook, 1994). Although early childhood day-care subsidies have partially offset low-income deficiencies in day-care offerings, inequities remain. For example, in low-income centers, caregivers show less warmth, responsiveness, and sensitivity to children's needs (Phillips et al., 1994). In-depth qualitative work has revealed that staff in low-income centers speak to children in more authoritarian and less cognitively complex ways than do staff in middle-income centers (Ferris Miller, 1989). For example, staff in predominantly low-income centers use verbal commands more often and are less likely to direct questions to toddlers that encourage answers.

A prerequisite for security in young children's lives is constancy and predictability in the immediate environment. Several national data sets have shown that children who live at or below the poverty line in America change residences more than twice as often and are five times more likely to be evicted in a given year than children who do not live in poverty (Federman et al., 1996). A representative sample of Canadian households with children showed that household income is inversely associated with changes in day-care arrangements, changes in schools, and residential relocations (Kohen, Hertzman, & Wiens, 1998). Insecurity of housing tenure is unfortunately normative for millions of the poorest children in economically underdeveloped countries (Bartlett et al., 1999). Daily life within the immediate households of low-income American families (G. H. Brody & Flor, 1997; Jensen, James, Boyce, & Hartnett, 1983) and lower class (occupation) families (Matheny, Wachs, Ludwig, & Phillips, 1995) is more chaotic relative to nonpoor or higher occupational status households, respectively, with fewer routines and less structure.

The Physical Environment of Childhood Poverty

Although the term *environment* within psychology typically means the psychosocial milieu, there is stark evidence of physical, environmental injustice among the poor in America. Low-income families live closer to toxic waste dumps (Bullard & Wright, 1993), and their children carry a heavier body burden of toxins. As an illustration, the prevalence of unsafe lead levels in American children from a national survey was four times higher in low-income families (16.3%) than in high-income families (4%) (D. J. Brody et al., 1994). Statewide screening in Massachusetts of children nine months to four years of age uncovered similarly strong links between childhood poverty and lead exposure. This study also documented that lead exposure was largely coming from residence in older homes where lead-based paint was prevalent (Sargent, Brown, Freedman, & Bailey, 1995). Similar data have been uncovered in other studies (Mielke et al., 1997; Nordin et al., 1998). Pesticide exposure has also been strongly tied to income in the United States

(Moses et al., 1993). Ambient air pollution (e.g., sulfur oxides, particulates) in St. Louis has been linearly related to household income (Freeman, 1972). In Britain the distribution of major industrial pollution is strongly skewed by income. For example, the lowest income postal zones (equivalent households per zone having less than £10,000) have 54% more pollution sources than expected if pollution were randomly distributed across postal zones. This contrasts markedly with affluent postal zones (having more than £30,000), which have 81% fewer pollution sources than expected (Friends of the Earth, United Kingdom, 1999). Families living in the lowest income deciles are exposed to 80% of the total carcinogenic emissions from factories in England (Friends of the Earth, United Kingdom, 2001).

The picture for indoor air quality is comparable. National statistics show that 65% of low-income American preschool children are exposed to parental smoking at home relative to 47% of those not in poverty (National Center for Health Statistics, 1991). Low-income homes have higher levels of nitrogen dioxide, carbon monoxide, and radon (Chi & Laquatra, 1990; Goldstein, Andrews, & Hartel, 1988, Laquatra, Maxwell, & Pierce, in press) and allergen exposures associated with asthma (Sarpong, Hamilton, Eggleston, & Adkinson, 1996). Access to safe drinking water in both the Third World (Bartlett, 1999; Clauson-Kaas et al., 1997) and America is inversely related to income (Calderon et al., 1993). In addition to the direct impacts that inadequate water supplies and poor sanitation have on physical health, there are additional costs. A disproportionate expenditure of time and effort often accompanies access to drinking water, latrines, and waste facilities among the poor in Third World countries (Bartlett et al., 1999).

Poorer children from a large, representative sample of London schools were more likely to be exposed to noise where they attend school (Haines, Stansfeld, Head, & Job, 2002). Leq is a 24-hour average in decibels. Decibels is a logarithmic scale, with a 10-decibel increase experienced as twice as loud. In a national survey of major American metropolitan areas, the correlation between household income and Leq was –.61 (U.S. Environmental Protection Agency, 1977).

In addition to examining ambient environmental quality such as toxins, air, water, and noise pollution, it is important also to investigate the more immediate living conditions of poor children. U.S. Census data reveal that the percentage of people living in homes with more than one person per room is linearly related to household income levels (Myers, Baer, & Choi, 1996) and that poor families with one or more children under 18 years of age are more than three times likely (29.4%) to live in crowded homes (more than one person/room) than families who are not poor (8.7%) (Children's Defense Fund, 1995). Premature babies were more than twice as likely to live in crowded housing compared with infants in families that were not poor (Liaw & Brooks-Gunn, 1994). A nationwide British study showed that 78% of unskilled laborer families with children under 18 years of age lived in homes with more than one person per room, compared with 14% of professional families (Davie, Butler, & Goldstein, 1972). The availability of open space and nature to families is tied to income levels as well. In New York City, low-income neighborhoods average 17 square yards of park space per child, compared with 40 square yards for the rest of the city (Sherman, 1994). Manual laborers in Britain are four times more likely (14%) to have a garden or yard too small to sit outside in compared with managers or professionals (3%) (Townsend, 1979).

Other aspects of housing quality are linked with income, as shown in census data from the American Housing Survey (Mayer, 1997). Additional data from this nationally representative survey of housing stock show that children living at or below the poverty line are 3.4 times more likely to live in houses with structural defects (22.3%), 3.6 times more likely to live in houses infested with rodents (14.4%), and 2.7 time more likely to have inadequate heat in the winter (17.9%), compared with children living above the poverty line (Children's Defense Fund, 1995). Furthermore, several nationwide public health screenings have revealed that poverty in America is strongly tied to childhood injuries related to risks in the home. Low-income families live in homes with fewer smoke detectors and fire extinguishers, more ungated stairs, more unlocked storage closets, and are more likely to have scalding tap water (Gielen, Wilson, Faden, Wissow, & Harvilchuck, 1995; Sanger & Stocking 1991; Sharp & Carter, 1992). The provision of designated play spaces for young children in the home is also inversely related to social class (Newson & Newson, 1976). National data also show that American low-income families are less likely to have amenities such as washing machines, clothes dryers, or air-conditioning (Federman et al., 1996). Even greater income-related housing inequities have been uncovered in the Third World (Satterthwaite et al., 1996; Stephens et al., 1997). Moreover, low-income housing in many of these economically deprived countries is more likely to be situated in hazardous locations where flooding and other disasters occur (Bartlett, 1999).

In addition to substandard housing quality, low-income families face a housing affordability crisis in America. The federal standard for affordable housing in America is less than 30% of income. More than 75% of American households below the poverty line exceed this standard, and nearly half of them pay more than 70% of their income for housing (Timmer, Eitzen, & Talley, 1994).

One of the reasons low-income children engage in fewer literary activities may be the home environment. Several large national studies covering children from birth through elementary school found that the longer the child lived below the poverty line, the more impoverished the home learning resources (e.g., age-appropriate toys, books) and the fewer the supportive parental behaviors (e.g., encouragement to learn the alphabet), as assessed by independent ratings of the home (Duncan, Brooks-Gunn, & Klebanov, 1994; Smith, Brooks-Gunn, & Klebanov, 1997). Fifty-nine percent of American children between three and five years of age have 10 or more children's books at home. Eighty-one percent of the nonpoor have 10 or more children's books in their home (Sherman, 1994). In their study of social class and human development in the United Kingdom, Newson and Newson (1977) demonstrated that 40% of the homes of unskilled laborers contained fewer than 3 books; in comparison, none of the homes of professionals lacked books. Moreover, as noted earlier, low-income children watch much more television than their wealthier counterparts (Larson & Verma, 1999; U.S. Department of Health and Human Services, 2000).

Low-income children in America are much less likely to have access to a home computer or the Internet. U.S. Census data reveal more than a fourfold increase in home computer access in households with incomes greater than $75,000 in comparison to households with incomes below $20,000 (Becker, 2000). Ninety-four percent of inner-city children in the United States have no Internet access compared with 57% of more affluent, urban children (Annie Casey Foundation, 2000). In addition to having less access to computers, low-income children who have computers have poorer quality hardware (e.g., CD ROM, mouse, on-line-access) and tend to use them in less sophisticated ways (e.g., games vs. word processing) than more affluent children (Becker, 2000). Low-income schools also lag far behind schools serving more affluent populations in terms of the availability and quality of computer technology (Becker, 2000).

Not only are the immediate home settings of poor children fraught with physical inequities, but the neighborhoods they live in are frequently characterized by multiple risks. Low-income neighborhoods have significantly more crime (Federman et al., 1996; Sampson et al., 1997). A meta-analysis of poverty and crime showed a mean correlation of .44 between the percentage of households below the poverty line and violent crime rates in American standard metropolitan statistical areas (Hsieh & Pugh, 1993). The basic infrastructure of low-income neighborhoods is often lacking, with substandard housing stock, more abandoned lots and boarded-up buildings, inadequate municipal services (e.g., garbage collection, police and fire protection), and fewer retail facilities (Joint Center for Housing Studies at Harvard University, 1999; Wallace & Wallace, 1998; Wandersman & Nation, 1998). Low-income neighborhoods often lack amenities such as retail and service merchants (Macintyre, Maciver, & Sooman, 1993). Although the well-documented link between household income levels and insufficient nutrition in children (Alaimo, Olson, & Frongillo, 2001; Miller & Korenman, 1994) is a complex subject, one likely contributor to this relationship is inaccessibility to healthy food. Using the median income of homes per census tract as an index of wealth in a study across multiple metropolitan areas, Moreland, Wing, Diez-Rioux, and Poole (2002) found that low-income neighborhoods had three times fewer supermarkets, comparable numbers of small grocers and convenience stores, and three times more bars and taverns as middle- and upper-income neighborhoods. Higher prices and less readily accessible healthy food for the poor have been uncovered in several other countries as well (Mackerras, 1997; Sooman, Macintrye, & Anderson, 1993). There are direct links between access to supermarkets and healthier dietary intake (Glanz, Basil, Maibach, Goldberg, & Snyder, 1998; Moreland, Wing, & Diez-Rioux, 2002).

The neighborhoods in which poor children live are also more physically hazardous. American elementary school aged children from low-income families are exposed to more street traffic (50% more street crossings per day relative to the nonpoor), which largely accounts for the sixfold greater risk of pedestrian accidents among poor children (Macpherson, Roberts, & Pless,

1998). British children of unskilled laborers are five times more likely to suffer a pedestrian accident than the children of professionals (Roberts & Power, 1996). Poor children's play spaces are more hazardous as well. For example, Suecoff, Avner, Chou, and Drain (1999) found 50% more hazards in playgrounds located in low- relative to middle- and upper-income neighborhoods in New York City.

Per-pupil school expenditure in America is strongly tied to financial advantage. As an illustration, in 1991 the expenditure in the 47 largest urban school districts in the United States averaged $875 less per pupil than in surrounding suburban districts (National Research Council, 1993). For a class of 25 children, this calculates to more than $20,000 annually per classroom. Not surprisingly, the physical infrastructure of school facilities in poor communities suffers accordingly. As shown in Figure 1, the quality of school building facilities in a representative sample of American public schools is tied to the income profile of the student body (National Center for Education Statistics, 2000). Predominantly low-income schools are more likely to have leaky roofs, inadequate plumbing and heating, problems with lighting, inadequate ventilation, and acoustical deficiencies (National Center for Education Statistics, 2000). Children in predominantly low-income schools are also more likely to be overcrowded. Twelve percent of low-income schools are above 125% of building capacity; this compares with 6% of relatively affluent schools (National Center For Education Statistics, 2000).

Environmental Risk and Developmental Outcomes

Many of the specific social and physical environmental characteristics associated with poverty are established risk factors for children's healthy development. Family turmoil and discord as well as nonresponsive and harsh parenting affect socioemotional and cognitive development (Emery & Laumann-Billings, 1998; Grant et al., 2003; Repetti, Taylor, & Seeman, 2002; Taylor, Repetti, & Seeman, 1997) as well as physical health (Chen et al., 2002; Repetti et al., 2002). Cognitive enrichment activities such as quantity and quality of parent-to-child speech (Hart & Risley, 1995; Hoff et al., 2002) and exposure to print media (Neuman & Roskos, 1993) enhance cognitive development. Unpredictable, chaotic households are inimical to healthy socioemotional development (Bronfenbrenner & Evans, 2000; Fiese & Kline, 1993; Repetti et al., 2002; Wachs, 2000), and instability both at home (Ackerman, Kogos, Youngstrom, Schoff, & Izard, 1999; Humke & Schaefer, 1995; Kohen et al., 1998) and at school (Lee & Croninger, 1994; Rutter et al., 1974) is associated with adverse socioemotional and cognitive outcomes. Exposure to violence is clearly harmful to children (Osofsky, 1995). Diminished social support, smaller social networks, and lower neighborhood social capital are all associated with adverse child outcomes (Leventhal & Brooks-Gunn, 2000; McNeeley et al., 2002; Repetti et al., 2002; Taylor et al., 1997; Wandersman & Nation, 1998). Less immersion in literacy ac-

Figure 1
Percentage of Poor Children and Schools With Inadequate Physical Quality

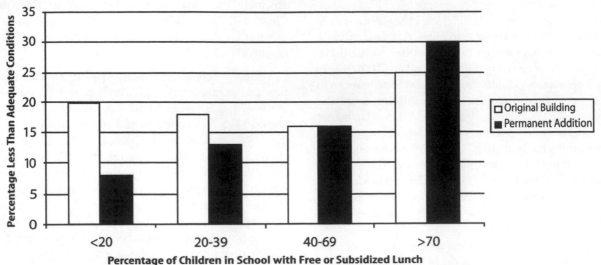

Note. The association between school income levels and structural inadequacy is marginal (p<.10) for original buildings and significant (p<.05) for permanent additions. Adapted from *Condition of America's Public School Facilities: 1999* (NCES 2000-032) (Table 4), by the National Center for Education Statistics, 2000, Washington, DC: U.S. Department of Education.

tivities and more time watching television adversely affect cognitive development and possibly behavioral conduct disorders as well (Coley, 2002; Larson & Verma, 1999).

Exposure to toxins such as lead and pesticides, along with residence in areas with poorer air and water quality, causes physical health problems and cognitive deficits in children (Holgate, Samet, Koren, & Maynard, 1999; National Research Council, 1991; Riley & Vorhees, 1991). Residential crowding and noise have both been associated with socioemotional distress and elevated psychophysiological stress among children (Evans, 2001). High noise levels (e.g., airport operations) reliably interfere with reading acquisition (Evans, 2001). Substandard housing quality causes respiratory morbidity and childhood injuries (Lawrence, 2002; Matte & Jacobs, 2000; Satterthwaite et al., 1996) and may elevate psychological distress in children (Evans, Wells, & Moch, 2003; Gifford, in press). Low-quality school facilities are associated with poor learning outcomes (Moore & Lackney, 1993; Schneider, 2002). Living close to streets with high traffic volume increases childhood injuries (MacPherson et al., 1998; Mueller, Rivara, Lii, & Weiss, 1990).

Although the surroundings of low-income children contain more singular psychosocial and physical environmental risk factors with known adverse developmental outcomes, the confluence of multiple psychosocial and physical risk factors may be a key, unique feature of childhood poverty. Adverse socioemotional and cognitive developmental outcomes are accelerated by exposure to multiple risks relative to singular risk exposure (Ackerman, Izard, Schoff, Youngstrom, & Kogos, 1999; Barocas, Seifer, & Sameroff, 1985; Evans, 2003; Lengua, 2002; Liaw & Brooks-Gunn, 1994; Rutter, 1983; Sameroff, 1998; Werner & Smith, 1982). Parallel trends have been shown

for the development of physical health problems from cumulative risk exposure (Evans, 2003, McEwen, 1998; 2000; McEwen & Seeman, 1999).

There are limited data suggesting that cumulative risk exposure may account for some of the developmental disarray accompanying poverty. Both the frequency and intensity of stressful life events and daily hassles are greater among low-income children (Attar, Guerra, & Tolan, 1994; Brown, Cowen, Hightower, & Lotyczewski, 1986; Dubow, Tisak, Causey, Hryshko, & Reid, 1991; Liaw & Brooks-Gunn, 1994; Rutter, 1981) and lower social class families (Felner et al., 1995). As an illustration, low-income fourth graders had 35% more life events and hassles in one year than their middle-income counterparts in the Chicago metropolitan region (Attar et al., 1994). Lower social class (parental occupation), inner-city children in London compared with working class children lived more often with a single parent, experienced greater marital discord, were more likely to have been in foster care for a week or more, experienced higher rates of paternal incarceration, lived in more crowded homes, lived more often in public housing, and attended schools with higher turnover rates (in terms of teachers as well as students; Rutter et al., 1974). In a national study of low birth weight, premature infants and low-income toddlers experienced two-and-a-half times more risk factors than premature infants and toddlers from middle-income families (Liaw & Brooks-Gunn, 1994). Thirty-five percent of the low-income toddlers in the Liaw and Brooks-Gunn study had been exposed to six or more risk factors, as opposed to 5% of the middle-income toddlers. Low-income households face a significantly greater array of material hardships (housing, food, medical costs) than middle- and upper-income households (Mayer & Jencks, 1989). Family adjustments to multiple material depriva-

Figure 2

Percentage of Poor and Nonpoor Children Exposed to Cumulative Physical and Psychosocial Environmental Risks

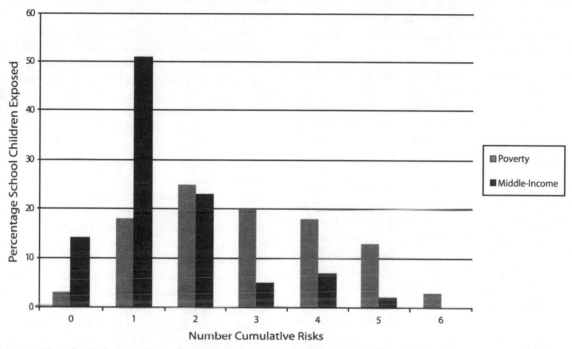

Cumulative Risk Exposure in Relation to Poverty/Not Poverty

Note. The mean number of multiple stressors is significantly higher (p<.001) for the poverty sample compared with middle income sample. Data adapted from a corrected version of Table 2 in *Child Development*, 74(5), p. 1388, which originally appeared in "The Environment of Poverty: Multiple Stressor Exposure, Psychophysiological Stress, and Socioemotional Adjustment," by G. W. Evans and K. English, 2002, *Child Development*, 73, p. 1242. Copyright 2002/2003 by the Society for Research in Child Development.

tion can indirectly exacerbate environmental risks as well. For example, elevated utility bills in the winter months in the Northeast are inversely related to nutritional intake in low-income infants and toddlers (Frank et al., 1996).

Although these various studies uncovered associations between poverty, cumulative risk exposure, and developmental problems, none examined whether multiple risk exposure could account for the adverse consequences of poverty on children. We recently tested this hypothesis directly among a sample of rural low- and middle-income children in grades three through five (Evans & English, 2002). Multimethodological assessments of developmental outcomes included a behavioral index of emotion regulation (delay of gratification), standardized maternal and self-report measures of psychological distress, and neuroendocrinological and cardiovascular indexes of chronic physiological stress. With the exception of norepinephrine, all measures indicated greater adversity among the low-income children (Evans & English, 2002).

Compared with their middle-income counterparts, low-income children experienced greater multiple risks (see Figure 2). Family turmoil, child separation, and exposure to violence were assessed by maternal reports on a standardized index of life events for children (Work, Cowen, Parker, & Wyman, 1990; Wyman, Cowen, Work, & Parker, 1991). Crowding was in-

dexed in terms of people per room, and noise exposure in the home was indexed in multiple measures of decibel levels. Housing quality was measured with a reliable and valid rater-based instrument (Evans, Wells, Chan, & Saltzman, 2000). Each psychosocial and physical factor was defined as risk/no risk by dichotomizing exposure. Thus, the multiple stressor exposure metric varied from zero to six.

The confluence of psychosocial and physical environmental risks may play a particularly important role in precipitating the developmental disarray associated with poverty. In order to examine this hypothesis more closely, we then tested whether the significant adverse relations between poverty and children's development were mediated by multiple stressor exposure (Evans & English, 2002). For chronic physiological stress, the data consistently showed that a primary pathway through which poverty influences physiological stress in children is exposure to multiple stressors. Low-income children experienced significantly more multiple stressors (zero to six), and this in turn elevated chronic physiological stress vis-à-vis middle-income children. For maternal and self-ratings of psychological distress, partial mediation occurred. Emotion regulation was fully mediated by multiple stressor exposure (Evans & English, 2002). Consistent with our findings, positive relations between parental educational attainment and middle school adolescents' psychological adjustment and grades, respectively, were mediated by stressor exposure, family social climate, and sense of belonging at school (Felner et al., 1995). Multiple measures of developmental disarray associated with poverty are conveyed, at least in part, by cumulative exposure to multiple psychosocial and physical stressors in the immediate environment. Because our study is the only one to directly test this mediational pathway and involves cross-sectional data, caution is warranted in drawing causal conclusions.

Any attempt to attribute the negative developmental consequences of poverty to the high-risk environments that these children inhabit must also grapple with the potential role of genetics. Family income effects on cognitive and socioemotional development after partialing out essential child (e.g., birth weight) and parental (e.g., maternal verbal ability) characteristics (Linver, Brooks-Gunn, & Kohen, 2002), twin studies incorporating direct measures of environment and genetic variance (Caspi, Taylor, Moffitt, & Plomin, 2000), sibling variability in income within families over time (Duncan, Yeung, Brooks-Gunn, & Smith, 1998), intrafamily income variability over time (Dearing, McCartney, & Taylor, 2001), adoption studies placing at-risk children into families of varying SES (parental occupation; Duyme, Dumaret, & Tomkiewicz, 1999), housing improvement programs that relocate public housing families to neighborhoods varying in income levels (Johnson, Ladd, & Ludwig, 2002; Katz, Kling, & Liebman, 2001; Leventhal & Brooks-Gunn, 2003; Rosenbaum & Harris, 2001), and income intervention experiments that randomly alter household income for indigent families (Gennetian & Miller, 2002; Salkind & Haskins, 1982) all converge on poverty adversely impacting children independent of genetic inheritance. I am not arguing that genes play no role in the relation between poverty and children's development, but I am asserting that they alone cannot account for the effects of poverty on children's well-being.

Conclusions

Poverty is harmful to the physical, socioemotional, and cognitive well-being of children, youths, and their families. A potent explanation for this relation is cumulative, environmental risk exposure. Compared with middle- and high-income children, low-income children are disproportionately exposed to more adverse social and physical environmental conditions. They suffer greater family turmoil, violence, and separation from their parents. Their parents are more nonresponsive and harsh, and they live in more chaotic households, with fewer routines, less structure, and greater instability. Poor children have fewer and less socially supportive networks than their more affluent counterparts, live in neighborhoods that are lower in social capital, and as adolescents are more likely to rely on peers than adults. Low-income children have fewer cognitive enrichment opportunities both at home and in their neighborhoods. They read less, have fewer books at home, are infrequent library patrons, and spend considerably more time watching TV than their middle-income counterparts.

Poor children reside in more polluted, unhealthy environments. They breathe air and drink water that are more polluted. Their households are more crowded, noisier, and more physically deteriorated, and they contain more safety hazards. Low-income neighborhoods are more dangerous, have poorer services, and are more physically deteriorated. The neighborhoods where poor children live are more hazardous (e.g., greater traffic volume, more crime, less playground safety) and less likely to contain elements of nature. Poor children are more likely to attend schools and day-care facilities that are inadequate. Although low-income children face a bewildering array of psychosocial and physical risk factors, there is emerging evidence of accelerating levels of chaos among American children across the socioeconomic spectrum (Bronfenbrenner, McClelland, Wethington, Moen, & Ceci, 1996).

Although each of these singular psychosocial and physical risk factors has adverse developmental consequences, exposure to cumulative risks accompanying poverty may be a key, unique aspect of the environment of poverty. The confluence of multiple demands from the psychosocial and physical environment appears to be a powerful force leading to physical and psychological morbidity among low-income children. Duration of exposure to poverty is also important to consider from an ecological perspective. Persistent, early childhood poverty has more adverse impacts relative to intermittent poverty exposure (Bolger, Patterson, Thompson, & Kupersmidt, 1995; Duncan & Brooks-Gunn, 1997; Duncan et al., 1994). Chronic poverty leads to a greater accumulation of social and environmental risk exposure. Psychologists need to come to grips with the ecological reality of poverty and desist relegating income and SES to unexplained, confounding variables in their models of human behavior and well-being.

Editor's note. Edison J. Trickett served as action editor for this article.

Author's note. I have benefited from the sage counsel of Urie Bronfenbrenner throughout our work on poverty and human development. I am grateful to Elyse Kantrowitz for background research and thank Sherry Bartlett, Rachel Dunifon, Lorraine Maxwell, and Ted Wachs for critical feedback on earlier versions of the manuscript.

Preparation of this article was partially supported by the W. T. Grant Foundation, the John D. and Catherine T. MacArthur Foundation Network on Socioeconomic Status and Health, the National Institute of Child Health and Human Development (Grant I F33 HD08473-01), and the Cornell University Agricultural Experiment Station (Project Nos. NYC 327404, NYC 327407).

Correspondence concerning this article should be addressed to Gary W. Evans, Departments of Design and Environmental Analysis and of Human Development, Cornell University, Ithaca, NY 14853-4401. Email: gwel@cornell.edu

Note

1. Statistical significance data are reported in the tables and figures when available.

References

Aber, L., Bennett, N., Conley, D., & Li, J. (1997). The effects of poverty on child health and development. *Annual Review of Public Health, 18,* 463–483.

Ackerman, B. P., Izard, C. E., Schoff, K., Youngstrom, E., & Kogos, J. (1999). Contextual risk, caregiver emotionality, and the problem behaviors of six- and seven-year-old children from economically disadvantaged families. *Child Development, 70,* 1415–1427.

Ackerman, B. P., Kogos, J., Youngstrom, E., Schoff, K., & Izard, C. E. (1999). Family instability and the problem behaviors of children from economically disadvantaged families. *Developmental Psychology, 35,* 258–268.

Adler, N. E., Boyce, T., Chesney, M., Folkman, S., & Syme, L. (1993). Socioeconomic inequalities in health: No easy solution. *Journal of the American Medical Association, 269,* 140–145.

Alaimo, K., Olson, C. M., & Frongillo, E. A. (2001). Food insufficiency, family income, and health in U.S. preschool and school-aged children. *American Journal of Public Health, 91,* 781–786.

Aneshensal, C., & Sucoff, C. (1996). The neighborhood context of adolescent mental health. *Journal of Health and Social Behavior, 37,* 293–310.

Annie Casey Foundation. (2000). *Kid's count data book.* Seattle, WA: Author.

Atkinson, T., Liem, R., & Liem, J. (1986). Social costs of unemployment: Implications for social support. *Journal of Health and Social Behavior, 27,* 317–331.

Attar, B., Guerra, N., & Tolan, P. (1994). Neighborhood disadvantage, stressful life events, and adjustment in urban elementary school children. *Journal of Clinical Child Psychology, 23,* 391–400.

Baker, D. P., & Stevenson, D. (1986). Mothers' strategies for children's school achievement: Managing the transition to high school. *Sociology of Education, 59,* 156–166.

Barocas, R., Seifer, R., & Sameroff, A. (1985). Defining environmental risk: Multiple dimensions of psychological vulnerability. *American Journal of Community Psychology, 13,* 433–447.

Bartlett, S. (1999). Children's experience of the physical environment in poor urban settlements and the implications for policy, planning, and practice. *Environment and Urbanization, 11,* 63–73.

Bartlett, S., Hart, R., Satterthwaite, D., de la Barra, X., & Missair, A. (1999). *Cities for children: Children's rights, poverty and urban managment.* London: Earthscan.

Becker, H. J. (2000). Who's wired and who's not: Children's access to and use of computer technology. *The Future of Children, 10,* 44–75.

Benveniste, L., Carnoy, M., & Rothstein, R (2003). *All else equal.* New York: Routledge-Farmer.

Bo, I. (1994). The sociocultural environment as a source of support. In F. Nestmann & K. Hurrelmann (Eds.), *Social networks and social support in childhood and adolescence* (pp. 363–384). New York: Walter de Gruyter.

Bolger, K. E., Patterson, D. J., Thompson, W., & Kupersmidt, J. B. (1995). Psychosocial adjustment among children experiencing persistent and intermittent family economic hardship. *Child Development, 66,* 1107–1129.

Bornstein, M. H., & Bradley, R. H. (Eds.). (2003). *Socioeconomic status, parenting, and child development.* Mahwah, NJ: Erlbaum.

Bradley, R. H. (1999). The home environment. In S. L. Friedman & T. D. Wachs (Eds.), *Measuring environment across the lifespan* (pp. 31–58). Washington, DC: American Psychological Association.

Bradley, R. H., & Corwyn, R. F. (2002). Socioeconomic status and child development. *Annual Review of Psychology, 53,* 371–399.

Bradley, R. H., Corwyn, R. F., McAdoo, H., & Coll, C. (2001). The home environments of children in the United States: Part I. Variations by age, ethnicity, and poverty status. *Child Development, 72,* 1844–1867.

Brody, D. J., Pirkle, J., Kramer, R., Flegal, K., Matte, T. D., Gunter, E., & Pascal, D. (1994). Blood lead levels in the U.S. population: Phase I of the Third National Health and Nutrition Examination Survey (NHANES III, 1988–1991). *Journal of the American Medical Association, 272,* 277–283.

Brody, G. H., & Flor, D. (1997). Maternal psychological functioning, family processes, and child adjustment in rural, single-parent, African-American families. *Developmental Psychology, 33,* 1000–1011.

Brody, G. H., Ge, X., Conger, R. D., Gibbons, F., Murry, V., Gerrard, M., & Simons, R. (2001). The influence of neighborhood disadvantage, collective socialization, and parenting on African American children's affiliation with deviant peers. *Child Development, 72,* 1231–1246.

Brody, G. H., Stoneman, Z., Flor, D., McCrary, C., Hastings, L., & Conyers, O. (1994). Financial resources, parental psychological functioning, parent co-care giving, and early adolescent competence in rural two-parent African-American families. *Child Development, 65,* 590–605.

Bronfenbrenner, U., & Evans, G. W. (2000). Developmental science in the 21st century: Emerging theoretical models, research designs, and empirical findings. *Social Development, 9,* 115–125.

Bronfenbrenner, U., McClelland, P., Wethington, E., Moen, P., & Ceci, S. (1996). *The state of Americans: This generation and the next.* New York: Free Press.

Bronfenbrenner, U., & Morris, P. (1998). The ecology of developmental process; In W. Damon (Series Ed.) & R. Lerner (Vol. Ed.), *Handbook of child psychology: Vol. 1: Theoretical models of human development* (5th ed., pp. 992–1028). New York: Wiley.

Brown, I., Cowen, E., Hightower, A., & Lotyczewski, S. (1986). Demographic differences among children in judging and experiencing specific stressful life events. *Journal of Special Education, 20,* 339–346.

Bullard, R. D., & Wright, B. (1993). Environmental justice for all: Current perspectives on health and research needs. *Toxicology and Industrial Health, 9,* 821–841.

Calderon, R., Johnson, C., Craun, G., Dufour, A, Karlin, R., Sinks, T., & Valentine, J. (1993). Health risks from contaminated water: Do class and race matter? *Toxicology and Industrial Health, 9,* 879–900.

Caspi, A., Taylor, A., Moffitt, T., & Plomin, R. (2000). Neighborhood deprivation affects children's mental health: Environmental risks identified in a genetic design. *Psychological Science, 11,* 338–342.

Chen, E., Matthews, K. A., & Boyce, T. (2002). Socioeconomic status differences in health: What are the implications for children? *Psychological Bulletin, 128,* 295–329.

Chi, P., & Laquatra, J. (1990). Energy efficiency and radon risks in residential housing. *Energy, 15,* 81–89.

Children's Defense Fund. (1995). *The state of America's children year book 1995.* Washington, DC: Author.

Clauson-Kass, J., Surjadi, C., Hojlyng, N., Baare, A., Dzikus, A., Jensen, H., et al. (1997). *Crowding and health in low-income communities.* Aldershot, England: Avebury.

Cochran, M., Larner, M., Riley, D., Gunnarson, L., & Henderson, C. (1990). *Extending families: The social networks of parents and their children.* New York: Cambridge University Press.

Coley, R. J. (2002). *An uneven start: Indicators of inequality in school readiness.* Princeton, NJ: Educational Testing Service.

Conger, R. D., & Elder, G. H., Jr. (1994). *Families in troubled times.* New York: Aldine de Gruyter.

Davie, R., Butler, N., & Goldstein, H. (1972). *From birth to seven.* London: Conger.

Dearing, E., McCartney, K., & Taylor, B. (2001). Change in family income-to-needs matters more for children with less. *Child Development, 72,* 1779–1793.

Dodge, K. A., Pettit, G., & Bates, J. (1994). Socialization mediators of the relation between socioeconomic status and child conduct problems. *Child Development, 65,* 649–665.

Dubow, E., Tisak, J., Causey, D., Hryshko, A., & Reid, G. (1991). A two-year longitudinal study of stressful life events, social support, and social problem-solving skills: Contributions to children's behavioral and academic adjustment. *Child Development, 62,* 583–599.

Duncan, G. J., & Brooks-Gunn, J. (1997). Income effects across the life span: Integration and interpretation. In G. J. Duncan & J. Brooks-Gunn (Eds.), *Consequences of growing up poor* (pp. 596–610). New York: Russell Sage Foundation.

Duncan, G. J., Brooks-Gunn, J., & Klebanov, P. (1994). Economic deprivation and early childhood development. *Child Development, 65,* 296–318.

Duncan, G. J., Yeung, W., Brooks-Gunn, J., & Smith, J. (1998). How much does poverty affect the life chances of children? *American Sociological Review, 63,* 406–423.

Duyme, M., Dumaret, A., & Tomkiewicz, S. (1999). How can we boost IQs of dull children?: A late adoption study. *Proceedings of the National Academy of Sciences, 96,* 8790–8794.

Elder, G. H., Jr., van Nguyen, T., & Caspi, A. (1995). Linking family hardship to children's lives. *Child Development, 56,* 361–375.

Emery, R. E., & Laumann-Billings, L. (1998). An overview of the nature, causes, and consequences of abusive family relationships. *American Psychologist, 53,* 121–135.

Evans, G. W. (2001). Environmental stress and health. In A. Baum, T. Revenson, & J. E. Singer (Eds.), *Handbook of health psychology* (pp. 365–385). Mahwah, NJ: Erlbaum.

Evans, G. W. (2003). A multimethodological analysis of cumulative risk and allostatic load among rural children. *Developmental Psychology, 39,* 924–933.

Evans, G. W., & English, K. (2002). The environment of poverty: Multiple stressor exposure, psychophysiological stress, and socioemotional adjustment. *Child Development, 73,* 1238–1248.

Evans, G. W., Kliewer, W., & Martin, J. (1991). The role of the physical environment in the health and well being of children. In H. E. Schroeder (Ed.), *New directions in health psychology assessment* (pp. 127–157). New York: Hemisphere.

Evans, G. W., Wells, N. M., Chan, E., & Saltzman, H. (2000). Housing and mental health. *Journal of Consulting and Clinical Psychology, 68,* 526–530.

Evans, G. W., Wells, N. M., & Moch, A. (2003). Housing and mental health: A review of the evidence and a methodological and conceptual critique. *Journal of Social Issues, 59,* 475–500.

Federal Interagency Forum on Child and Family Statistics. (2000). *America's children: Key national indicators.* Washington, DC: Author.

Federman, M., Garner, T., Short, K., Cutter, W., Levine, D., McGough, D., & McMillen, M. (1996, May). What does it mean to be poor in America? *Monthly Labor Review,* 3–17.

Felner, R. D., Brand, S., DuBois, D. L., Adan, A., Mulhall, P., & Evans, E. (1995). Socioeconomic disadvantage, proximal environmental experiences, and socioemotional and academic adjustment in early adolescence: Investigation of a mediated effects model. *Child Development, 66,* 774–792.

Ferris Miller, D. (1989). *First steps toward cultural difference: Socialization in infant toddler day care.* Washington, DC: Child Welfare League of America.

Fiese, B. H., & Kline, C. (1993). Development of the Family Ritual Questionnaire: Initial reliability and validation studies. *Journal of Family Psychology, 6,* 290–299.

Frank, D. A., Roos, N., Meyers, A., Napoleone, M., Peterson, K., Cather, A., & Cupples, L. (1996). Seasonal variation in weight-for-age in a pediatric emergency room. *Public Health Reports, 111,* 366–371.

Freeman, A. (1972). The distribution of environmental quality. In A. Kneess & B. Bower (Eds.), *Environmental quality analysis* (pp. 243–280). Baltimore: Johns Hopkins University Press.

Friends of the Earth, United Kingdom. (1999). *The geographic relation between household income and polluting factories.* London: Author.

Friends of the Earth, United Kingdom. (2001). *Pollution and poverty: Breaking the link.* London: Author.

Gallup, G. (1993). *America's youth in the 1990's.* Princeton, NJ: Gallup Institute.

Gennetian, L. A., & Miller, C. (2002). Children and welfare reform: A view from an experimental welfare program in Minnesota. *Child Development, 73,* 601–620.

Gielen, A. C., Wilson, M., Faden, R., Wissow, L., & Harvilchuck, J. (1995). In-home injury prevention practices for infants and toddlers: The role of parental beliefs, barriers, and housing quality. *Health Education Quarterly, 22,* 85–95.

Gifford, R. (in press). Satisfaction, health, security, and social relations in high rise buildings. In A. Seidel & T. Heath (Eds.), *Social effects of the building environment.* London: E & FN Spon.

Glanz, K., Basil, M., Maibach, E., Goldberg, J., & Snyder, D. (1998). Why Americans eat what they do: Taste, nutrition, cost, convenience, and weight control concerns as influences on food consumption. *Journal of the American Dietetic Association, 98,* 1118–1126.

Goldstein, I., Andrews, L., & Hartel, D. (1988). Assessment of human exposure to nitrogen dioxide, carbon monoxide, and respirable particulates in New York inner city residents. *Atmospheric Environment, 22,* 2127–2139.

Grant, K. E., Compas, B. E., Stuhlmacher, A., Thurm, A., McMahon, S., & Halpert, J. (2003). Stressors and child and adolescent psychopathology: Moving from markers to mechanisms of risk. *Psychological Bulletin, 129,* 447–466.

Haines, M. M., Stansfeld, S. A., Head, J., & Job, R. F. S. (2002). Multilevel modelling of aircraft noise on performance tests in schools around Heathrow Airport London. *International Journal of Epidemiology and Community Health, 56,* 139–144.

Hart, B., & Risley, T. R. (1995). *Meaningful differences in the everyday experiences of young American children.* Baltimore: Brookes.

Hoff, E. (2003). The specificity of environmental influence: Socioeconomic status affects early vocabulary development via maternal speech. *Child Development, 74,* 1368–1378.

Hoff, E., Laursen, B., & Tardiff, T. (2002). Socioeconomic status and parenting. In M. H. Bornstein (Ed.), *Handbook of parenting* (2nd ed., pp. 231–252). Mahwah, NJ: Erlbaum.

Holgate, S., Samet, J., Koren, H., & Maynard, R. (1999). *Air pollution and health.* New York: Academic Press.

House, J. S., Umberson, D., & Landis, K. (1988). Structures and processes of social support. *Annual Review of Sociology, 14,* 293–318.

Hsieh, C. C., & Pugh, M. D. (1993). Poverty, income inequality, and violent crime: A meta-analysis of recent aggregate data studies. *Criminal Justice Review, 18,* 182–202.

Humke, C., & Schaefer, C. (1995). Relocation: A review of the effects of residential mobility on children and adolescents. *Psychology: A Journal of Human Behavior, 32,* 16–24.

Huston, A. C., McLoyd, V. C., & Garcia Coll, C. (Eds.). (1994). Children in poverty [Special issue]. *Child Development, 65*(2).

Ingersoll, R. (1999). The problem of under qualified teachers in American secondary schools. *Educational Researcher, 28,* 26–37.

Jensen, E., James, S., Boyce, T., & Hartnett, S. (1983). The Family Routine Inventory: Development and validation. *Social Science and Medicine, 17,* 201–211.

Johnson, M. P., Ladd, H., & Ludwig, J. (2002). The benefits and costs of residential mobility programmes for the poor. *Housing Studies, 17,* 125–138.

Joint Center for Housing Studies at Harvard University. (1999). *The state of the nation's housing.* Cambridge, MA: Harvard University.

Kagan, J., & Tulkin, S. R. (1971). Social class differences in child rearing during the first year. In H. R. Schaffer (Ed.), *The origins of human social relations* (pp. 165–185). New York: Academic Press.

Katz, L. F., Kling, J., & Liebman, J. (2001). Moving to opportunity in Boston: Early results of a randomized mobility experiment. *Quarterly Journal of Economics, 116,* 607–654.

Kawachi, I. (1999). Social capital and community effects on population and individual health. In N. E. Adler, M. Marmot, B. S. McEwen, & J. Stewart (Eds.), *Annals of the New York Academy of Sciences; Vol. 896. Socioeconomic status and health in industrial nations* (pp. 120–130). New York: New York Academy of Sciences.

Kohen, D. E., Hertzman, C., & Wiens, M. (1998). *Environmental changes and children's competencies* (W-98-25E). Hull, Quebec, Canada: Applied Research Branch, Strategic Policy, Human Resources Development.

Kohn, M. L. (1977). *Social class and conformity.* Chicago: University of Chicago.

Laquatra, J., Maxwell, L. E., & Pierce, M. (in press). Indoor air pollutants, limited resource households and childcare facilities. *Journal of Environmental Health.*

Larson, R. W., & Verma, S. (1999). How children and adolescents spend time around the world: Work, play, and developmental opportunities. *Psychological Bulletin, 125,* 701–736.

Lawrence, R. J. (2002). Healthy residential environments. In R. B. Bechtel & A. Churchman (Eds.), *The handbook of environmental psychology* (2nd ed., pp. 394–412). New York: Wiley.

Lee, V. E., & Croninger, R. (1994). The relative importance of home and school in the development of literacy skills for middle-grade-students. *American Journal of Education, 102,* 286–329.

Lengua, L. J. (2002). The contribution of emotionality and self-regulation to the understanding of children's response to multiple risk. *Child Development, 73,* 144–161.

Leventhal, T., & Brooks-Gunn, J. (2000). The neighborhoods they live in: The effects of neighborhood residence on child and adolescent outcomes. *Psychological Bulletin, 126,* 309–337.

Leventhal, T., & Brooks-Gunn, J. (2003). Moving to opportunity: An experimental study of neighborhood effects on mental health. *American Journal of Public Health, 93,* 1576–1582.

Lewis, R. A., & Spanier, G. (1979). Theorizing about the quality and stability of marriage. In W. R. Burr (Ed.), *Contemporary theories about the family* (pp. 268–294). New York: Free Press.

Liaw, F., & Brooks-Gunn, J. (1994). Cumulative familial risks and low birth weight children's cognitive and behavioral development. *Journal of Clinical Child Psychology, 23,* 360–372.

Linver, M. R., Brooks-Gunn, J., & Kohen, D. (2002). Family processes in pathways from income to young children's development. *Developmental Psychology, 38,* 719–734.

Luster, T., Rhoades, K., & Haas, B. (1989). The relations between parental values and parenting behavior: A test of the Kohn hypothesis. *Journal of Marriage and the Family, 51,* 139–147.

Luthar, S. (1999). *Poverty and children's adjustment.* Los Angeles: Sage.

Macintyre, S., Maciver, S., & Sooman, A. (1993). Area, class, and health: Should we be focusing on places or people? *International Journal of Social Policy, 22,* 213–234.

Mackerras, D. (1997). Disadvantaged and the cost of food. *New Zealand Journal of Public Health, 21,* 218.

Macpherson, A., Roberts, I., & Pless, I. (1998). Children's exposure to traffic and pedestrian injuries. *American Journal of Public Health, 88,* 1840–1845.

Magnusson, K. A., & Duncan, G. J. (2002). Parents in poverty. In M. H. Bornstein (Ed.), *Handbook of parenting* (2nd ed., pp. 95–121). Mahwah, NJ: Erlbaum.

Matheny, A., Wachs, T. D., Ludwig, J., & Phillips, K. (1995). Bringing order out of chaos: Psychometric characteristics of the Confusion, Hubbub, and Order Scale. *Journal of Applied Developmental Psychology, 16,* 429–444.

Matte, T., & Jacobs, D. (2000). Housing and health: Current issues and implications for research and progress. *Journal of Urban Health Bulletin of the New York Academy of Medicine, 77,* 7–25.

Mayer, S. E. (1997). Trends in the economic well being and life chances of America's children. In G. J. Duncan & J. Brooks-Gunn (Eds.), *Consequences of growing up poor* (pp. 49–69). New York: Russell Sage Foundation.

Mayer, S. E., & Jencks, C. (1989). Poverty and the distribution of material hardship. *Journal of Human Resources, 24,* 88–114.

McEwen, B. S. (1998). Protective and damaging effects of stress mediators. *New England Journal of Medicine, 338,* 171–179.

McEwen, B. S. (2000). The neurobiology of stress: From serendipity to clinical relevance. *Brain Research, 886,* 172–189.

McEwen, B. S., & Seeman, T. E. (1999). Protective and damaging effects of mediators of stress: Elaborating and testing the concept of allostasis and allostatic load. In N. E. Adler, M. Marmot, B. S. McEwen, & J. Stewart (Eds.), *Annals of the New York Academy of Sciences: Vol. 896. Socioeconomic status and health in industrial nations* (pp. 30–47). New York: New York Academy of Sciences.

McLoyd, V. C. (1998). Socioeconomic disadvantage and child development. *American Psychologist, 53,* 185–204.

McNeely, C. A., Nonnemaker, J., & Blum, R. W. (2002). Promoting school connectedness: Evidence from the National

Longitudinal Study of Adolescent Health. *Journal of School Health, 72,* 138–146.

Mielke, H. W., Dugas, D., Mielke, P., Smith, K., Smith, S., & Gonzales, C. (1997). Associations between soil lead and childhood blood lead in urban New Orleans and rural Lafourche Parish of Louisiana. *Environmental Health Perspectives, 9,* 950–954.

Miller, J., & Davis, D. (1997). Poverty history, marital history, and quality of children's home environments. *Journal of Marriage and Family, 59,* 996–1007.

Miller, J. E., & Korenman, S. (1994). Poverty and children's nutritional status in the United States. *American Journal of Epidemiology, 140,* 233–243.

Mitchell, R., & Moos, R. H. (1984). Deficiencies in social support among depressed patients. *Journal of Health and Social Behavior, 25,* 438–452.

Moore, G. T., & Lackney, J. (1993). School design. *Children's Environments, 10,* 99–112.

Moreland, K., Wing, S., & Diez-Rioux, A. (2002). The contextual effect of the local environment on residents' diets: The arteriosclerosis risk in communities study. *American Journal of Public Health. 92,* 1761–1767.

Moreland, K., Wing, S., Diez-Rioux, A., & Poole, C. (2002). Neighborhood characteristics associated with the location of food stores and food service places. *American Journal of Preventative Medicine, 22,* 23–29.

Moses, M., Johnson, E., Anger, W., Burse, V., Horstman, S., Jackson, R., et al. (1993). Environmental equity and pesticide exposure. *Toxicology and Industrial Health, 9,* 913–959.

Mueller, B. A., Rivara, F., Lii, S., & Weiss, N. (1990). Environmental factors and the risk for childhood pedestrian-motor vehicle collision occurrence. *American Journal of Epidemiology, 132,* 550–560.

Myers, D., Baer, W., & Choi, S. (1996). The changing problem of overcrowded housing. *Journal of the American Planning Association, 62,* 66–84.

National Center for Education Statistics. (2000). *Condition of America's public school facilities: 1999* (NCES 2000-032). Washington, DC: U.S. Department of Education.

National Center for Health Statistics. (1991). *Children's exposure to environmental cigarette smoke* (Advance data from vital and health statistics, No. 202). Hyattsville, MD: Author.

National Institute of Child Health and Human Development Early Child Care Research Network. (1997). Poverty and patterns of child care. In G. J. Duncan & J. Brooks-Gunn (Eds.), *Consequences of growing up poor* (pp. 100–131). New York: Russell Sage Foundation.

National Research Council. (1991). *Environmental epidemiology* (Vol. 1). Washington, DC: National Academy Press.

National Research Council. (1993). *Losing generations.* Washington, DC: National Academy Press.

Neuman, S. B., & Roskos, K. (1993). Access to print for children of poverty. *American Educational Research Journal, 30,* 95–122.

Newson, J., & Newson, E. (1963). *Patterns of infant care in an urban community.* Baltimore: Pergamon Press.

Newson, J., & Newson, E. (1968). *Four-year-olds in an urban community.* Chicago: Aldine.

Newson, J., & Newson, E. (1976). *Seven-year-olds in the home environment.* New York: Wiley.

Newson, J., & Newson, E. (1977). *Perspectives on school at seven years old.* London: Allen & Unwin.

Nordin, J., Rolnick, S., Ehlinger, E., Nelson, A., Ameson, T., Cherney-Stafford, L., & Griffin, J. (1998). Lead levels in high-risk and low-risk children in the Minneapolis-St. Paul metropolitan area. *Pediatrics, 101,* 72–76.

Osofsky, J. (1995). The effects of exposure to violence on young children. *American Psychologist, 50,* 782–788.

Parke, R. D. (1978). Children's home environments: Social and cognitive effects. In J. F. Wohlwill & I. Altman (Eds.), *Children and the environment* (pp. 33–81). New York: Plenum Press.

Phillips, D., Voran, M., Kisker, E., Howes, C., & Whitbook, M. (1994). Childcare for children in poverty: Opportunity or inequity? *Child Development, 65,* 472–492.

Reid, J. (1989). *Social class differences in Britain.* London: Fontana.

Repetti, R., Taylor, S. E., & Seeman, T. E. (2002). Risky families: Family social environments and the mental and physical health of offspring. *Psychological Bulletin, 128,* 330–366.

Riley, E., & Vorhees, C. (Eds.). (1991). *Handbook of behavioral teratology.* New York: Plenum Press.

Roberts, I., & Power, C. (1996). Does the decline in injury mortality vary by social class? *British Medical Journal, 313,* 784–786.

Rosenbaum, E., & Harris, L. (2001). Low-income families in their new neighborhoods. *Journal of Family Issues, 22,* 183–210.

Rutter, M. (1981). Protective factors in children's responses to stress and disadvantage. In M. Kent & J. Rolf (Eds.), *Prevention of psychopathology* (Vol. 3, pp. 49–74). Hanover, NH: University Press.

Rutter, M. (1983). Stress, coping, and development. In N. Garmezy & M. Rutter (Eds.), *Stress, coping, and development in children.* (pp. 1–41). New York: McGraw-Hill.

Rutter, M., Yule, B., Quinton, D., Rowland, O., Yule, W., & Berger, M. (1974). Attainment and adjustment in two geographic areas: III. Some factors accounting for area differences. *British Journal of Psychiatry, 125,* 520–533.

Salkind, N. J., & Haskins, R. (1982). Negative income tax: The impact on children from low-income families. *Journal of Family Issues, 3,* 165–180.

Sameroff, A. (1998). Environmental risk factors in infancy. *Pediatrics, 102,* 1287–1292.

Sampson, R., Raudenbush, S., & Earls, F. (1997). Neighborhoods and violent crime: A multilevel study of collective efficacy. *Science, 277,* 918–924.

Sanger, L. J., & Stocking, C. (1991). Safety practices and living conditions of low income urban families. *Pediatrics, 88,* 1112–1118.

Sargent, J. D., Brown, M., Freedman, J., & Bailey, A. (1995). Childhood lead poisoning in Massachusetts communities: Its association with sociodemographic and housing characteristics. *American Journal of Public Health, 85,* 528–534.

Sarpong, S., Hamilton, R., Eggleston, P., & Adkinson, N. (1996). Socioeconomic status and race as risk factors for cockroach allergen exposure and sensitization in children with asthma. *Journal of Allergy and Clinical Immunology, 97,* 1393–1401.

Satterthwaite, D., Hart, R., Levy, C., Mitlin, D., Ross, D., Smit, J., & Stephens, C. (1996). *The environment for children.* London: Earthscan.

Schell, L. M. (1997). Culture as a stressor: A revised model of bicultural interaction. *American Journal of Physical Anthropology, 102,* 67–77.

Schneider, M. (2002). *Do school facilities affect academic outcomes?* Washington, DC: National Clearing House for Educational Facilities.

Sharp, G. B., & Carter, M. (1992). Prevalence of smoke detectors and safe tap-water temperatures among welfare recipients in Memphis, Tennessee. *Journal of Community Health, 17,* 351–365.

Sherman, A. (1994). *Wasting America's future.* Boston: Beacon Press.

Sinclair, J., Pettit, G., Harrist, A., Dodge, K., & Bates, J. (1994). Encounters with aggressive peers in early childhood: Frequency, age differences, and correlates of risk for behavior problems. *International Journal of Behavioral Development, 17,* 675–696.

Smith, J. R, Brooks-Gunn, J., & Klebanov, P. (1997). Consequences of living in poverty for young children's cognitive and verbal ability and early school achievement. In G. J. Duncan & J. Brooks-Gunn (Eds.), *Consequences of growing up poor* (pp. 132–189). New York: Russell Sage Foundation.

Sooman, A., Macintyre, S., & Anderson, A. (1993). Scotland's health: A more difficult challenge for some? The price and availability of healthy foods in socially contrasting localities in the west of Scotland. *Health Bulletin, 51,* 276–284.

Stephens, C., Akerman, M., Avle, S., Maia, P., Companario, P., Doe, B., & Tetteh, D. (1997). Urban equity and urban health: Using existing data to understand inequalities in health and environment in Accra, Ghana and Sao Paulo, Brazil. *Environment and Urbanization, 9,* 181–202.

Suecoff, S., Avner, J., Chou, K., & Drain, E. (1999). A comparison of New York City playground hazards in high and low income areas. *Archives of Pediatrics and Adolescent Medicine, 153,* 363–366.

Taylor, S. E., Repetti, R., & Seeman, T. E. (1997). Health psychology: What is an unhealthy environment and how does it get under the skin? *Annual Review of Psychology, 48,* 411–447.

Timmer, D. A., Eitzen, D. S., & Talley, K. D. (1994). *Paths to homelessness: Extreme poverty and the urban housing crisis.* Boulder, CO: Westview Press.

Townsend, P. (1979). *Poverty in the United Kingdom.* Berkeley: University of California Press.

Turner, R. J., & Noh, S. (1983). Class and psychological vulnerability among women: The significance of social support and personal control. *Journal of Health and Social Behavior, 24,* 2–15.

U.S. Census Bureau. (2000). *Population survey* (March Suppl. 2000). Washington, DC: U.S. Government Printing Office.

U.S. Department of Health and Human Services. (1999). *Trends in the well being of America's children and youth 1999.* Washington, DC: U.S. Government Printing Office.

U.S. Department of Health and Human Services. (2000). *Trends in the well being of America's children and youth 2000.* Washington, DC: U.S. Government Printing Office.

U.S. Environmental Protection Agency. (1977). *The urban noise survey* (EPA 550/9–77–100). Washington, DC: Author.

Wachs, T. D. (2000). *Necessary but not sufficient; The respective roles of single and multiple influences on individual development.* Washington, DC: American Psychological Association.

Wallace, D., & Wallace, R. (1998). *A plague on your houses.* London: Verso Press.

Wandersman, A., & Nation, M. (1998). Urban neighborhoods and mental health. *American Psychologist, 53,* 647–656.

Werner, E., & Smith, R. (1982). *Vulnerable but invincible: A longitudinal study of resilient children and youth.* New York: McGraw-Hill.

Williams, D. R., & Collins, C. (1995). U.S. socioeconomic and racial differences in health. *Annual Review of Sociology, 21,* 349–386.

Wohlwill, J. F., & Heft, H. (1987). The physical environment and the development of the child. In D. Stokols & I. Altman (Eds.), *Handbook of environmental psychology* (pp. 281–328). New York: Wiley.

Work, W., Cowen, E., Parker, G., & Wyman, P. (1990). Stress resilient children in an urban setting. *Journal of Primary Prevention, 11,* 3–19.

Wright, L. B., Treiber, F., Davis, H., Bunch, C., & Strong, W. B. (1998). The role of maternal hostility and family environment upon cardiovascular functioning among youth two years later: Socioeconomic and ethnic differences. *Ethnicity and Disease, 8,* 367–376.

Wyman, P., Cowen, E., Work, W., & Parker, G. (1991). Developmental and family milieu correlates of resilience in urban children who have experienced major life stress. *American Journal of Community Psychology, 19,* 405–426.

From *American Psychologist,* Vol. 59, No. 2, February/March 2004, pp. 77-92. Copyright © 2004 by the American Psychological Association. Reprinted with permission.

UNIT 5
Cultural and Societal Influences

Unit Selections

Key Points to Consider

- Our culture is saturated with powerful marketing and advertising of products and images. There are now products, even food items, directed solely at the child and young adult market. Have you noticed this increasing trend and how do you feel about this new, niche marketing? Will you, or how can you, help educate children about being critical consumers of this powerful media force?

- The well-publicized McMartin child abuse case was one of the first cases to receive widespread public attention regarding the potential problems with young children's testimony of suspected child abuse. According to the research, what are some of the myths and realities surrounding child testimony in cases of suspected child abuse? How might you guard against faulty testimony?

- We take so much of our quality of life for granted in America. For example, in many other poor countries, millions of children die early in childhood due to causes such as hunger, malnutrition, unsafe air and water, diseases, inadequate medical care, even wartime violence. Children in other countries such as Uganda and Iraq are witness to the horrors of wartime death and violence. What can be done to help safeguard children, even those far from our own shores?

Student Website
www.mhcls.com/online

Internet References
Further information regarding these websites may be found in this book's preface or online.

Association to Benefit Children (ABC)
http://www.a-b-c.org
Children Now
http://www.childrennow.org
Council for Exceptional Children
http://www.cec.sped.org
Prevent Child Abuse America
http://www.preventchildabuse.org

Social scientists and developmental psychologists have come to realize that children are influenced by a multitude of social forces that surround them. In this unit we present articles to illuminate how American children and adolescents are influenced by broad factors such as economics, culture, politics, and the media. These influences also affect the family, which is a major context of child development, and many children are now faced with more family challenges than ever. In addition, analysis of exceptional or atypical children gives the reader a more comprehensive account of child development. Thus, articles are presented on special challenges of development, such as the effects of sexual abuse, autism, ADHD, bereavement, wartime violence, and other circumstances. Other external societal factors that influence children's development include the powerful influence of the media and advertising. Several articles in this section show how the media can shape children's young minds.

For many children today, it's hard for them to imagine a world before television and computers. In "Watch and Learn" the author chronicles the power of educational television to promote cognitive learning in children by watching shows such as *Sesame Street, The Electric Company,* and now *Blue's Clues* as well as encouraging children to choose healthier food options. But television and other forms of advertising have a darker side

when it comes to aggressive consumerist marketing to child audiences. "Childhood For Sale" includes information showing how manufacturers are spending billions of dollars to capture children's preferences and fostering potentially harmful consumerist attitudes in young and older children. The author of this article advocates for a series of recommendations that would make advertisers more responsible in marketing to children.

While another article in this edition points to the potentially devastating effects of poverty on children's development, researcher Suniya Luthar in "The Culture of Affluence: Psychological Costs of Material Wealth" offers counterpoint data showing that children from wealthy families may also exhibit problems in a number of areas such as substance use, anxiety, and depression due primarily to unrelenting pressures to achieve and social and emotional disconnection from their parents.

Some children must cope with special psychological, emotional, and cognitive challenges such as ADHD, autism, emotional or psychological disorders. Such children are often misunderstood and mistreated and pose special challenges. These issues are discussed in "Attention Deficit Hyperactivity Disorder in Very Young Children: Early Signs and Interventions," "When Does Autism Start?," "The Pedatric Gap," "Three Reasons Not to Believe in an Autism Epidemic" and "Savior Parents."

Still other children both here and abroad face terrible conditions related to physical abuse, international poverty, and malnutrition, and even coping with situations such as the horrors related to wartime violence. "Forensic Developmental Psychology: Unveiling Four Common Misconceptions," "Childhood's End," and "Children of the Fallen" address these additional challenges. Although these articles are sometimes difficult to read, as future parents, teachers, and professionals it is important for us to learn more about these difficult and challenging situations in order to find ways to improve and ameliorate future problems.

Childhood for Sale

Consumer culture is pervasive and invasive. It is targeting kids in surprising and troubling ways—with harmful consequences. Here's what to do about it.

MICHELE STOCKWELL

For today's children, the world is a parade of brand names. They wake up in the morning to breakfasts of Kellogg's *Star Wars* cereal, and go to sleep at night in Hello Kitty or *Spiderman* pajamas. In between, snack-food companies vie for vending positions in the hallways of their schools; pop stars and celebrities beckon them in designer-label clothes; and popular TV shows, movies, books, and music pelt them with subliminal product placements—from soft drinks to computers. McDonald's has even hired an entertainment marketing firm to help it buy mentions of Big Mac sandwiches in hip-hop songs.

Advertising and marketing campaigns aimed at children are nothing new, of course. Baseball cards go back more than a century, and TV ads during Saturday morning cartoons have been a staple for decades. America is, after all, a capitalist society; marketing is a central part of our economic system. But the scale and sophistication of today's campaigns far exceeds anything that has come before. The consumer culture has turned pervasive and invasive, and it is targeting kids in increasingly surprising and troubling ways to entice them to spend their pocket money—more than $200 billion per year—and then become lifelong customers.

Indeed, analysts say children are the new darlings of Madison Avenue. Marketers hire psychologists and child development experts to help them devise strategies that take advantage of children's deeply impressionable nature. The modern marketing repertoire now includes word-of-mouth campaigns in which companies identify the "alpha kids" on playgrounds and in malls and hire them to generate enthusiasm about new products among their friends—without ever telling those friends they've been recruited to do so.

Another technique takes advantage of young people's enthusiasm for video and computer games: Marketers develop hybrid "advergames" that are specifically designed CO promote certain products and brands. While children play these games, brand logos and product images flash at them repeatedly. After a few rounds of an online advergame associated with candy or junk food, for example, a child is likely to remember a brand well enough to ask for it at the grocery store.

At the same time, marketers survey kids' interests by prompting them to participate in online contests, chat rooms, and the like, culling their personal information and preferences in order to design more tailored, personalized marketing strategies.

And then there is the next frontier: cell phones. Nearly one-half of all 10 to 18 year olds have them, and they are evolving into mini-personal entertainment centers for playing games, listening to music, and watching videos. Cell phones have the dual virtue for marketers of offering (a) direct communication with children, either by voice or touch-key interactive programs, and (b) a clear path around the protective eyes of gatekeeper parents. Maybelline and Timex have both announced plans for cell phone-based marketing campaigns aimed at teenagers.

Some of the techniques for marketing to children may not seem particularly odious. But the cumulative effect is to commercialize childhood to an unprecedented degree—with unhealthy consequences.

In fact, a growing body of research indicates that the consumer culture's harmful effects on children can run the gamut from physical and emotional problems to increased parent-child conflicts over spending decisions, distorted value systems, and strained family budgets. One study found a strong correlation between children's immersion in the consumer culture their feelings of depression, anxiety, and low self-esteem. Meanwhile ads for alcohol and tobacco have, not surprisingly, been linked to underage alcohol and tobacco use. Studies have also found correlations between child obesity rates and the prevalence of TV ads for junk food; research has specifically shown that children's exposure to food advertising and marketing may be influencing their food choices.

Equally troubling is children's frequent exposure to ads for violent entertainment—adult-rated movies, TV shows, video games, and music—because watching violent media has been linked to childhood displays of violent and aggressive behavior. Sexual imagery in marketing campaigns and consumer products geared for kids (like padded push-up bras and high-heeled shoes for young girls) is also hyper-charging children's sexuality before they may be cognitively or emotionally ready.

Parents may not be aware of every last marketing practice, but they see enough to know basically what is happening, and they don't like it. As Sen. Hillary Clinton (D-N.Y.) said in a speech last March, "Parents worry that their children will not grow up with the same values that they did or that they believe in because of the overwhelming presence of the media telling them to buy this and that, or conveying negative messages filled with explicit sex content and violence."

There is no doubt that the primary responsibility for shielding America's children from the damaging effects of a rampant commercial culture lies with parents. But they can't—and shouldn't—do it alone. Helping parents do their job better represents both a policy challenge and a political opportunity. Democrats, in particular, would do well to become champions for children's and parents' interests, because, as Progressive Policy Institute senior fellow Barbara Dafoe Whitehead explained in the April 2005 issue of BLUEPRINT, parents doubt Democrats' commitment on these cultural issues. That's one big reason they have been voting Republican in recent presidential elections. {See a longer report, "Closing the Parent Gap," at **ppionline.org**.)

So what is there to do? Here are some ideas:

Ensure that marketing practices aimed at children are fair. Experts argue that a well-established principle in communications law holds that for an ad to be considered fair, an audience must be able to recognize that it is an ad and must be able to identify the seller. But psychological research concludes that children—particularly children younger than 8—may be able to associate Ronald McDonald with McDonald's restaurants, but they lack the cognitive maturity to understand the persuasive intent of marketing, or to view ads with skepticism. They are likely to see advertising as truthful and entertaining, not as a come-on. Because children are developmentally vulnerable to advertising, child health experts, including the American Academy of Pediatrics, argue that ads aimed at them are inherently unfair, particularly for children under 8.

The Federal Trade Commission (FTC) has traditionally had the regulatory authority to uphold U.S. laws that prohibit "unfair or deceptive" commercial practices. But Congress In 1980 explicitly stripped the commission of the power to regulate unfair advertising to children. That was after it proposed banning TV ads for children on the grounds that children were not discerning enough to keep the ads in perspective. The commission was particularly concerned that most ads aimed at children were for sugary foods, and children did not understand the health risks of excessive sugar consumption. Congress balked after industry and marketers reacted strongly. It passed a blanket restriction, prohibiting the FTC from issuing any sort of rule in the area of children's advertising on the grounds of unfairness.

But since then, a growing body of scientific evidence has more conclusively shown how children in certain stages of cognitive development react to advertising, and what its harmful effects may be. Equally important, marketers have found more surreptitious means than traditional print ads for reaching children. They are capitalizing in particular on children's comfort with technology and their immersion in the new interactive environment of the Web. More research is needed on the effects of all this marketing and consumerism, but enough is known to conclude that Congress should lift its restriction on the FTC's authority, and direct it to investigate all forms of marketing

aimed at children. Once started, the FTC should issue a report on its findings within a year, and then issue rules to guide marketing practices directed at children.

Ensure that advertising is appropriate for the media in which it appears. General-audience entertainment should include only general-audience advertising. Ads for beer and R-rated movies, for example, shouldn't be aired during primetime sitcoms, when children are watching. To stop that practice, Congress should direct the Department of Health and Human Services (HHS) to monitor the advertising that appears in media that are popular among young people. The HHS should then begin systematically naming and shaming companies that advertise adult-rated entertainment or adult products like alcohol or tobacco on TV shows, in magazines, and in other popular media that have large youth audiences. And if a pattern emerges in which some companies continue to advertise adult-restricted products to large youth audiences, Congress should give the FTC the authority to impose fines on repeat offenders.

For more on these policy proposals, look for the forthcoming report "Childhood for Sale: Consumer Culture's Bid for Our Kids" at *ppionline.org*.

Require toys and other products based on movies and TV shows to carry consistent age ratings. Consider the slew of *Star Wars: Episode III* toys now being marketed to children ages 4 and up, despite the fact that the movie is rated PG-13, and its director has discouraged parents from taking young children to see it because of its violent content. Or, consider the line of toys based the on R-rated Arnold Schwarzenegger movie *Terminator 3—Rise of the Machines*. One toy, recommended for kids 12 and up, is an action figure that depicts Schwarzenegger's character with a bloody face. Other toys based on the movie are designed for children as young as 5. Why not ensure that the age recommendations displayed on packaging match the age ratings of the original movies, and let parents decide if the toys are appropriate for their children?

Protect children's privacy. Providing consumers information to help them make purchasing decisions is always a sound policy principle. But when information flows in the other direction—from consumers to marketers—there should be appropriate safeguards to ensure the consumers' privacy. That is particularly true when the information in question is about children: their names and addresses, personal preferences, and more. In the burgeoning interactive marketplace of websites, cell phones, digital TV, and other communication devices, marketers have many opportunities to collect personal data from children. Congress established protections for children under 13 in the Children's Online Privacy Protection Act of 1998. That law dictates the circumstances under which companies may collect information from children. Congress should now extend the same protections to everyone under 16. It should also ban corporations from selling or purchasing the personal information of children under 16 for commercial marketing purposes, unless parents give express consent.

Curtail marketing activities inside public schools. The consumerism that children encounter daily is by no means confined to TV, the Internet, and pocket-sized gadgetry. The parade also marches straight through schools. Cash-strapped school districts open their doors to marketers to generate much-needed revenues—sometimes millions of dollars. Beverage contracts alone may generate up to $1.5 million per year for a large school district. The National Soft Drink Association estimates that 62 percent of U.S. principals have signed "pouring rights" contracts, giving soda companies exclusive access to their schools. Advertising also shows up on billboards, yearbooks, newsletters, textbook covers, screen savers, team uniforms, vending machines, and school buses. (San Francisco students have in past years ridden to and from school in buses sponsored by Old Navy, for example.)

Companies even create educational materials. Oil companies, for example, sponsor lessons about energy. Consumer products companies donate packets of deodorant sticks and feminine hygiene products to kids in 5th grade sex education classes, a time when many are struggling with adolescent insecurities. Some packets include testimonials like this one from an adolescent boy: "I used to be really worried about sweating a lot, but since I started using an antiperspirant every morning, I'm dry all day."

A Government Accountability Office report found that few states have laws or comprehensive regulations governing in-school marketing. Schools and school districts have widely varying policies. So Congress should direct the secretary of education to investigate all forms of marketing in schools and then develop a set of voluntary recommendations for states to use in establishing comprehensive policies on marketing. Why not set a goal of completely eliminating marketing in elementary schools, where many children don't yet understand what advertising is?

End the practice of using children's friendships for marketing purposes. Of course, it is doubly hard for children to understand that they are being marketed to when the pitch is coming from their peers who have been recruited to spread enthusiasm for products by word-of-mouth on playgrounds and in malls, either for pay or for freebies. That technique is a new variation on the concept that experts call "viral" marketing, which spreads information from person to person, like a virus. (A more innocuous type of viral marketing is common on websites: links that say, "email this article to a friend.") But taking commercial advantage of children's friendships crosses a line into ethically murky territory.

Congress should require companies to disclose what they are doing when they use adolescents in these viral marketing campaigns. And the FTC should require marketers to ensure that the "alpha kids" they enlist to promote products tell their peers up front that they are working for a sponsor.

Protect children involved in product research. Many of the products marketed to children today are based on focus groups, demonstrations, and other trials with children. We should demand that the marketing industry protect children by following the same standards that federally funded researchers must follow. Those standards include oversight by diverse and credible professional review boards, which approve and monitor research projects, and protect the rights and welfare of child participants.

Ask more from broadcasters. We are way beyond old-fashioned TV ads now. But TV is still a very important conduit for the consumer culture. Congress should strike a new bargain with broadcasters: In exchange for free use of the public spectrum, they should provide more—and better—children's programming. Broadcasters are now required to air three hours of children's programming per week. That should double to six hours. Broadcasters should also make it commercial-free programming, target it to 6 to 12 year olds, and schedule it to air after school, when children are most likely to be watching.

Ask more from cable and satellite TV providers, too. Striking a new bargain with broadcasters is a good start, but 85 percent of American households subscribe to cable or satellite TV. Regardless of how they get it, polls show that parents are deeply concerned about sex and violence on TV. Furthermore, most are unaware of, or confused by, parental control technologies like the V-chip. Therefore, Congress should give cable and satellite TV companies a choice: Start offering parents the option of subscribing to family-friendly channel packages, or face the same indecency regulations that apply to over-the-air broadcasters, as some powerful lawmakers are proposing. Family-friendly channel packages could include channels like Nickelodeon, The Learning Channel, Animal Planet, and news channels, but not MTV and other channels that tend to be inappropriate for younger children.

There is no way to totally eliminate marketing from the culture—nor should that be the goal. A highly developed market economy needs advertising. But policymakers can help parents shield their children from some of the culture's corrosive influences by demanding more responsible and age-appropriate marketing that does not exploit children's psychological and cognitive weak spots or push them too quickly into adulthood.

Michele Stockwell is director of social and family policy at the Progressive Policy Institute.

The Culture of Affluence: Psychological Costs of Material Wealth

Children of affluence are generally presumed to be at low risk. However, recent studies have suggested problems in several domains—notably, substance use, anxiety, and depression—and 2 sets of potential causes: pressures to achieve and isolation from parents. Recognizing the limited awareness of these issues, the objectives in this paper are to collate evidence on the nature of problems among the wealthy and their likely causes. The first half of the paper is focused on disturbances among affluent children and the second half is focused on characteristics of their families and neighborhoods. Widespread negative sentiments toward the rich are then discussed, and the paper concludes with suggestions for future work with families at the upper end of the socioeconomic spectrum.

SUNIYA S. LUTHAR

In the contemporary child development literature, the phrase *at-risk children* usually implies those from low-income families. For the early part of the 20th century, children in poverty were largely ignored by scientists, and theories of child development were based on work with middle-class youth (Graham, 1992). Beginning in the 1950s, however, there was a growing recognition of the unique risks facing low-income children and a parallel growth in empirical studies of their development (Huston, McLoyd, & Garcia Coll, 1994). In contrast to this enhanced attention to disadvantaged youngsters, there has been almost no research concerning those at the other end of the socioeconomic spectrum—those living in affluent families.

The near total neglect of affluent youngsters probably reflects two interrelated assumptions among developmental scientists. The first is that they are no different from the middle-class majority (who have been amply studied); the second is that given their "privileged" circumstances, the lives of these youth must be utterly benign (and ostensibly, therefore, not worthy of scarce research resources). Neither of these assumptions has been subjected to careful empirical testing, however, and as is demonstrated in discussions that follow, both seem to be tenuous at best.

In this paper the objective is to highlight various adjustment disturbances that can be prominent among children in wealthy families and to appraise the potential causes of these disturbances. Toward this end, discussions begin with an overview of existing evidence on problems among suburban youth. The second section focuses on aspects of the contextual surrounds of these affluent children, with attention on the functioning of parents and families in upper-class suburbia. Consistent with the developmental psychopathology perspective (Cicchetti & Cohen, 1995; Sroufe & Rutter, 1984), evidence in both of these

sections is drawn from different disciplines including sociology, economics, education, and psychiatry, as well as from social, clinical, and evolutionary psychology. Concluding arguments present some caveats and qualifications to major inferences that might be drawn from this paper, along with directions for future work with upper-class children across the domains of research, practice, and policy.

Evidence of Adjustment Problems Among Affluent Youth

One of the first empirical studies to provide a glimpse into problems of affluent youth was a comparative investigation of low-income, urban 10th graders and their upper socioeconomic status (SES), suburban counterparts (Luthar & D' Avanzo, 1999). Central aims were to explore potential differences, by sociodemographic context, in links between adolescents' internalizing problems (depression and anxiety) and their substance use, as well as ramifications of substance use for their behavioral competence at school (i.e., peer relationships and academic functioning). The sample included 264 suburban students who were mostly from Caucasian, white-collar families, and 224 inner-city youth who were predominantly minority and of low SES. Descriptive analyses in this study revealed that on several indexes of maladjustment, mean scores of suburban youth were substantially higher than those of their inner-city counterparts (Luthar & D' Avanzo, 1999). Specifically, affluent youth reported significantly higher levels of anxiety across several domains, and greater depression. They also reported significantly higher substance use than inner-city students, consistently indicating more frequent use of cigarettes, alcohol, marijuana, and other illicit drugs.

Appraisal of psychopathology among youth in this sample in relation to national norms yielded more startling findings. Among suburban girls in the 10th grade, one in five reported clinically significant levels of depressive symptoms, reflecting rates 3 times as high as those among normative samples. Incidence of clinically significant anxiety among both girls and boys in the suburban high school was also higher than normative values (22% and 26% vs. 17%). Similar patterns were seen for substance use. Of suburban girls, 72% reported ever having used alcohol, for example; as compared with 61 % in normative samples, and parallel values for boys' use of illicit drugs were 59% versus 38%.

This study also revealed two sets of disturbing patterns concerning correlates of substance use. Among affluent (but not inner-city) youth, substance use was significantly linked with depressive and anxiety symptoms, suggesting efforts at self-medication (Luthar & D' Avanzo, 1999). These findings are of particular concern as substance use of this negative affect subtype shows relatively high continuity over time (e.g., Zucker, Fitzgerald, & Moses, 1995). Second, findings suggested that the teenage peer group might actively endorse substance use among suburban boys. High substance use was linked to their popularity with peers, and this association remained significant despite statistical controls in regression equations for various possible confounds, including both internalizing and externalizing problems (Luthar & D' Avanzo, 1999).

In an effort to follow up on these preliminary signs of disturbance among affluent teens, Luthar and Becker (2002) conducted a study of suburban middle school students with two major goals: to determine whether the problems previously detected might generalize to preadolescents as well, and to explore causes of high distress in the context of material affluence. These issues were examined in a cross-sectional study involving sixth and seventh graders in another high-SES community, similar to that studied by Luthar and D'Avanzo (1999). Again, the group was predominantly Caucasian; median annual family income in the town sampled was more than $125,000.

Results of this study showed that suburban sixth graders reported low levels of depression, anxiety, and substance use, but seventh grade students showed some elevations in these domains. Rates of clinically depressive symptoms, for example, were twice as high among suburban seventh-grade girls as compared with rates in normative samples, that is, 14% versus 7% (Luthar & Becker, 2002). Similarly, 7% of seventh-grade boys reported drinking until intoxicated or using marijuana approximately once a month, whereas no sixth-grade boys had. Finally, analyses of data from this middle school cohort replicated earlier findings on correlates of substance use: There were significant links with various internalizing symptoms among both boys and girls, and with high levels of peer popularity among the older (seventh-grade) boys (Luthar & Becker, 2002).

In exploring causes of suburban students' distress, Luthar and Becker (2002) examined two constructs likely to be salient in affluent milieus: achievement pressures and isolation from adults. In upwardly mobile communities, children are often pressed to excel at multiple academic and extracurricular pursuits to maximize their long-term academic prospects—a phe-

nomenon that may well engender high stress. With regard to isolation, sociological research has shown that junior high students from upper-income families are often alone at home for several hours a week, as parents believe that this promotes self-sufficiency (Hochschild, 1997). At an emotional level, similarly, isolation may often derive from the erosion of family time together because of the demands of affluent parents' career obligations and the children's many after-school activities (Luthar & D'Avanzo, 1999; Rosenfeld & Wise, 2000; Shafran, 1992).

To operationalize major constructs, Luthar and Becker (2002) considered two facets each of achievement pressures and isolation from parents. Students were asked about their own perfectionistic strivings as well as perceptions of their parents' emphasis on children's personal accomplishments, relative to their character and well-being. Isolation was considered both literally and emotionally, that is, in terms of the absence of adult supervision in the hours after school and the degree of emotional closeness to mothers and fathers.

Findings of this study showed patterns largely consistent with expectations. Links between hypothesized predictors and adjustment outcomes were examined using hierarchical regression analyses, with statistical partialing of variance due to shared measurement in self-reports. Results showed significant associations for all predictors with one or more maladjustment domains—internalizing symptoms, delinquency, and substance use—corroborating the likely role of overemphasis on achievement and isolation from parents in the adjustment disturbances of affluent youth (Luthar & Becker, 2002).

Obviously, no inferences about generalizability can be made based on the two previously described studies; at the same time, there are other findings in the literature that resonate with the major themes highlighted. In a study involving more than 800 American teens, for example, Csikszentmihalyi and Schneider (2000) found a low inverse link between SES and emotional well-being. The most affluent youth in this sample reported the least happiness, and those in the lowest SES reported the most.

There is also consistent evidence on findings on substance use. Data from the Monitoring the Future study (Johnston, O'Malley, & Bachman, 1998) showed that during preadolescence, family SES had low associations with drug use. By the 12th grade, on the other hand, high-SES youth reported the highest rate of several drugs, including marijuana, inhalants, and tranquilizers. Regarding correlates of drug use, Way, Stauber, Nakkula, and London (1994) found, as did Luthar and D'Avanzo (1999), that high-SES youth (but not their inner-city counterparts) often used substances in efforts to alleviate emotional distress. Similarly, Cooper (1994) noted that among adolescent boys in general, more so than girls, alcohol use is often tied to social conformity motives such as drinking to fit in with a crowd, and Feldman, Rosenthal, Brown, and Canning (1995) showed that popular preadolescent boys were among those most prone to partying and heavy drinking later as high school students.

Various case study and clinical reports lend support to suggestions on causes of children's distress in the context of upper-class suburbia. With regard to the role of achievement pressures, for example, family social scientist William Doherty has cautioned, "We're losing our kids to overscheduled hyperactivity. Dance and karate, these are all good things... but we want parents to say, 'Am I overdoing the providing of activity opportunities and underdoing the providing of family time?'" (cited in Belluck, 2000, p. A18). In the words of developmental psychologist William Damon (cited in Kantrowitz & Wingert, 2001, pp. 51-52), "These are supposed to be the years that kids wander around and pal around, without being faced with the pressures of the real world...Instead, the parenting experience is being ruined and parents' effectiveness is being diminished."

Also resonant are views of psychotherapists working with wealthy families. Describing the "intensely competitive society of the rich," Pittman (1985, p. 464) noted that in such milieus, successes are expected and failures are both highly visible and apparently inexplicable. Faced with unrelenting pressures to excel (to be average is tantamount to having failed), many children develop stress-related symptoms such as insomnia, stomachaches, headaches, anxiety, and depression (Gilbert, 1999); some youngsters come to exaggerate the slightest of health problems to attain "acceptable" routes out of competing with others, (Pittman, 1985).

Regarding the issue of parents' presence in their children's lives, survey findings (Capizzano, Tout, & Adams, 2002) indicate that 10- to 12-year-olds are more likely to be unsupervised by adults after school if they are Caucasian and if their families are of higher SES (possibly reflecting wealthy parents' beliefs in the relative safety of their neighborhoods). An investigative report following the outbreak of syphilis among teens in a prosperous Georgia town involved interviews with a cross-section of the town's youth (PBS Online, 1999). Repeatedly mentioned in these interviews were themes of sexual promiscuity, yearning to fit in and have friends, and desire for attention and even discipline from parents. Comments by developmental scientists, in reaction to this show, were as follows: "What is (particularly) disturbing... is the tremendous disconnect that exists between the children of Rockdale County and their families" (Blum, 1999). "We heard a lot about emptiness. Houses that were empty and devoid of supervision, adult presence, oversight. There was for far too many of the adolescents a fundamental emptiness of purpose; a sense that they were not needed, not connected to adults, to tasks, to anything meaningful other than the raw and relentless pursuit of pleasure" (Resnick, 1999). (For a full report on this show and transcripts, see **http://www.pbs.org/wgbh/pages/frontline/shows/georgia/etc/synopsis.html**)

On the issue of low psychological closeness, child psychotherapist Shafran (1992) has underscored the costs of unpredictability regarding caregivers. Noting that children in wealthy families are often cared for by housekeepers or nannies, he argued, "Fluctuations in the presence and attentiveness of the primary caregiver... whether that person is the biological mother or father or is an employed nanny, will interfere with the development of a secure sense of self, with the confidence that one's needs will be respected and met and that the world is populated with people who can be counted upon" (Shafran, 1992, p. 270). Pittman (1985) similarly indicated that parents who have strong drives toward competitive success are also highly invested in the "star qualities" of their offspring. The children therefore fail to develop secure attachments based on the knowledge that they are valued for the individuals they are and not just for the splendor of their accomplishments. Finally, national survey data (U.S. Department of Health and Human Services, 1999) showed that among 12- to 17-year-olds, closeness to parents was inversely linked with household income. Feelings of high closeness to resident biological mothers, for example, were reported by approximately 75% of adolescents whose family incomes were below $15,000, but by only 65% of those with family incomes more than $75,000. Comparable statistics for closeness to resident biological fathers were 66% and 54%, respectively.

The Ecological Context: Suburban Parents and Communities

Although there has been comparatively little empirical research conducted with wealthy children, more has been done with their adult counterparts, and relevant evidence is presented here. Consideration of these findings is important even for those interested primarily in child development, inasmuch as the processes that affect rich adults will affect their children too, both indirectly (through their parents) and directly through exposure to the same subculture. Discussions in this section begin, accordingly, with a brief summary of scientific evidence on adjustment problems associated with material wealth. This is followed by more detailed descriptions of conceptual arguments offered to explain such problems, which collectively implicate processes that operate at the level of the individual, of the community, and of the broader culture of affluence.

Affluence and Well-Being: Research With Adults

In a special issue of the *American Psychologist* published at the turn of the 21st century, several scholars argued that high material wealth can be associated with low psychological well-being. Reviewing cross-national epidemiological data, Buss (2000) noted that rates of depression are higher in more economically developed countries than in less developed countries. Considering the United States, historical trends show that Americans have far more luxuries than they had in the 1950s, with twice as many cars per person, plus microwave ovens, VCRs, air conditioners, and color TVs. Despite this, they are no more satisfied with their lives (Diener, 2000). In the words of Myers (2000b, p. 61), "[Americans] are twice as rich and no happier. Meanwhile, the divorce rate doubled. Teen suicide tripled... Depression rates have soared, especially among teens and young adults... I call this conjunction of material prosperity and social recession *the American paradox*. The more people strive for extrinsic goals such as money, the more numerous their problems and the less robust their well being."

Wealth-unhappiness associations: Individual-level processes. Links between wealth and unhappiness have been explained, by some, in terms of high stress levels and dearth of intrinsic rewards. Deiner (2000), for example, has argued that to the extent that the high productivity associated with affluence involves little leisure time, people become increasingly prone to distress, as economist Schor (1999) has described how the pressures to work, acquire, and consume tend to deplete personal energies. Csikszentmihalyi (1999, p. 823) has reasoned that "to the extent that most of one's psychic energy becomes invested in material goals, it is typical for sensitivity to other rewards to atrophy. Friendships, art, literature, natural beauty, religion and philosophy become less and less interesting."

Other scholars have specifically implicated individuals' lack of intimacy in personal relationships. Pittman (1985), for instance, has argued that people who accumulate high wealth often have a special talent and are single-mindedly dedicated to its development and marketing, resulting in scant time for personal relationships. Warner (1991) has noted that the very attributes that make for success in the world's marketplace, such as self-protectiveness and opportunism, can inhibit the development of intimacy, as these attributes represent a generalized lack of trust of others. In a series of studies, Kasser, Ryan, and their colleagues (Kasser & Ryan, 1993, 1996; Ryan et al., 1999; Sheldon & Kasser, 1995) established poorer mental health and lower well-being among individuals who disproportionately valued extrinsic rewards such as fame and wealth over intrinsic rewards such as interpersonal relatedness, personal growth, and community service. Perkins (1991) similarly showed that adults with Yuppie values—preferring affluence, professional success, and prestige over intimacy in marriage and with friends—reported being fairly or very unhappy twice as often as did others.

Although inordinately high desires for wealth can impoverish relationships, causal links can also operate in the opposite direction. Kasser, Ryan, Zax, and Sameroff (1995) found that teens exposed to cold, controlling maternal care came to develop relatively materialistic orientations, whereas better nurtured teens came to more strongly value intrinsic goals such as personal growth and relationships. Adults who are unhappy also tend to seek solace in the acquisition of material goods (Diener & Biswas-Diener, 2002). Experiments by Chang and Arkin (2002) indicated that people tend to turn to materialism when they experience uncertainty either in relation to the self (feelings of self-doubt) or in relation to society (e.g., questioning the meaning of their existence in society).

Individual-level explanations of affluence-unhappiness links have also implicated discontent following habituation to new wealth, in a process similar to any unfolding addiction. Following Brickman and Campbell's (1971) suggestion that people tend to labor on a "hedonic treadmill," psychologists have argued that when individuals strive for a certain level of affluence and reach it, they become quickly habituated and then start hankering for the next level up, becoming frustrated when this is not achieved (Meyers, 2000b; Schor, 1999). Csikszentmihalyi (1999) has noted that wealth, like many good things, is beneficial in small quantities, but it becomes increasingly desired and ultimately becomes harmful in large doses. Resonant is Pittman's (1985, p. 470) characterization: "Wealth is addictive. It enticingly offers happiness, but it cannot provide satisfaction, so those who attain some of it keep thinking more of it will provide satisfaction... [Those] who have become addicted to it... can experience severe withdrawal when they can't get it. Withdrawal from wealth, and the hope of wealth, can be terrifying."

Community-level forces. Competitive structures of market economies can promote distress by inhibiting the formation of supportive relationship networks. Political scientist Putnam (1993, 2000) has argued that when there is high use of market-based services, there is, correspondingly, limited engagement of individuals outside the marketplace, low levels of cooperation for shared goals, and growing use of the market to acquire child care and other services historically provided by family and neighbors. Collectively, such trends erode social capital, as exemplified by diminished attendance at PTA meetings, churches and temples, or community development groups, all groups that are vital for the well-being of communities.

Evolutionary psychologists have suggested, furthermore, that wealthy communities can, paradoxically, be among those most likely to engender feelings of friendlessness and isolation in their inhabitants. As Tooby and Cosmides (1996) argued, the most reliable evidence of genuine friendship is that of help offered during times of dire need: People tend never to forget the sacrifices of those who provide help during their darkest hours. Modern living conditions, however, present relatively few threats to physical well-being. Medical science has reduced several sources of disease, many hostile forces of nature have been controlled, and laws and police forces deter assault and murder. Ironically, therefore, the greater the availability of amenities of modern living in a community, the fewer are the occurrences of critical events that indicate to people which of their friends are truly engaged in their welfare and which are only fair-weather companions. This lack of critical assessment events, in turn, engenders lingering mistrustfulness despite the presence of apparently warm interactions (Tooby & Cosmides, 1996).

These contentions are relevant to processes among the affluent inasmuch as material wealth reduces the need to depend solely on friends. Affluent individuals are amply able to purchase various services such as psychotherapy for depression, medical care for physical illness, and professional caregivers for children, and in not having to rely on friends for such assistance, they rarely obtain direct "proof" of others' authentic concern. In essence, therefore, the rich are the least likely to experience the security of deep social connectedness that is routinely enjoyed by people in communities where mutual dependence is often unavoidable (Myers, 2000a).

Physical characteristics of wealthy suburban communities may also contribute to feelings of isolation. Houses in these communities are often set far apart with privacy of all ensured by long driveways, high hedges, and sprawling lawns (Weitzman, 2000; Wilson-Doenges, 2000). Neighbors are unlikely to casually bump into each other as they come and go in their communities, and children are unlikely to play on street corners. Paradoxically, once again, it is possible that the wealthiest neighborhoods are among the most vulnerable to low levels of cohesiveness and efficacy (Sampson, Raudenbush, & Earls, 1997). When encountering an errant, disruptive child of the millionaire acquaintance next door, neighbors tend to be reluctant to intervene not only because of respect for others' privacy but also, more pragmatically, because of fears of litigation (e.g., Warner, 1991).

The culture of affluence. At the wider systemic level, the individualism of cultures of affluence can exacerbate people's unhappiness because of the relatively transient nature of social groups. Cross-cultural researcher Triandis (1994) noted that in complex, individualistic settings, people can belong to many groups without being strongly committed to any. They can choose their churches or clubs from among many choices, for example, and they tend to remain with these or leave them as suits their needs. In simpler, collectivist societies, by contrast, choices are fewer and groups (such as village or tribe) are often assigned. As allegiances shift less often, there are concomitantly more opportunities for the development of strong group-based relationship networks.

Arguments offered by Schwartz (2000) are also based on cultural emphases on individualism, except in this case the mechanisms involve high choice and control on the one hand, and vulnerability to depression on the other. The reasoning in this case is as follows. Extraordinary material wealth usually implies high levels of autonomy and choice, so that many affluent people can live exactly the kind of lives they want. They are able to purchase an endless variety of goods and services, and given high professional skills, they are able to move from one job to another with relative ease. Whereas all these options might be assumed to engender happiness, they often lead to depression instead. Why? Because increases in experienced control are accompanied by increases in expectations about control. "The more we are allowed to be the masters of our fates in one domain of life after another, the more we expect to be. ... In short, life is supposed to be perfect". (Schwartz, 2000, p. 85). Continuing this argument, Schwartz noted that when perfection is not achieved, the ethos of individualism biases people toward attributing failures to personal rather than to external causes. As Seligman's (1975) seminal works established, this sort of causal attribution is just the type that fosters depression.

Finally, cultures of materialism carry the strong message that affluence brings happiness—with the implicit corollary, of course, that wealthy people who are unhappy must be ungrateful, self-indulgent, or both. Psychotherapists report, in fact, that affluent individuals commonly struggle with confusion and guilt about their distress (e.g., Wolfe & Fodor, 1996), as captured in the following report: "I cannot begin to count the number of times that an expensively dressed, immaculately groomed woman drove her luxury car into my parking area, walked gracefully into my office, sat down, and announced, 'My life is perfect. I have everything I could ask for,' and then, bursting into tears, 'Why am I so unhappy? This makes no sense at all—I must get over this!'" (R. Tower, personal communication, April 7, 2002). Our own work with suburban teens has revealed similar themes. Over the years, several troubled youth have reported that disclosure of their depression has elicited negative reactions ranging from incredulity (that they could have anything to be unhappy about) to dismissal or even scorn of what are seen as self-centered and entirely unwarranted complaints. The cultural trivialization of their depression—via the ubiquitous message that the rich have no right to feel emotionally deprived—only exacerbates existing feelings of isolation and alienation.

Gender-specific stressors. Aside from intrapersonal, community-based, and cultural factors that contribute to wealth-un-happiness links, there are also some challenges relatively specific to women in upper-class communities and other challenges more salient for men. To consider women first: Many affluent mothers do not work outside the home. Despite excellent qualifications and, frequently, stellar early career trajectories, several of these women leave the work force once they have children. As a result, they are deprived of various work-related gratifications, including the self-efficacy and positive identity that derive from jobs well done (Csikszentmihalyi, 1997) and the vital networks of supportive relationships and sense of community that can be accessed in the workplace (Myers & Diener, 1995). As sociologist Hochschild (1997) has demonstrated, American parents in general—from diverse backgrounds and socioeconomic strata—tend to prefer being in the office to staying at home to care for young children, perceiving the former as generally more gratifying and the latter as comparatively more stressful.

Mothers who do remain employed, conversely, often experience the dual pressures of having to excel not only at fast-paced, demanding jobs such as investment banking or corporate law but equally in their roles as mothers (e.g., Berger, 2000). The professional culture demands that they put as much time and effort into their jobs as do their male colleagues (although women are particularly uneasy about outperforming others in traditionally male domains, such as income or occupational prestige, see Exline & Lobel, 1999). At the same time, many of these women set very high standards for themselves as parents. Thus, the disdainful moniker "soccer mom" often refers to women who find themselves, frequently, "on their mobile phones taking care of business while they're cheering their kids on the football field, [and]… working late at the office, correcting their kids' homework by e-mail and fax" (Kantrowitz & Wingert, 2001, p. 51).

The pressures faced by upper-class women, along with a strong subcultural emphasis on privacy, lead many of them to self-medicate through alcohol or prescription drugs (Wolfe & Fodor, 1996). Describing this phenomenon, Dr. David Brizer, Chair of Norwalk Hospital's Department of Psychiatry, has said, "The drug problem is endemic to wealthy suburban areas, due in part to social isolation… Women who live in parts of the country such as ours may have gone from a very culturally and intellectually rich atmosphere of being in college to being stuck at home—and it can be maddening, not to mention the very real challenge of raising children" (quoted in Duff, 2002, p. 102).

Also believed to be highly prevalent are eating disorders such as anorexia, bulimia, and crash dieting, all of which derive from the strong emphasis on physical appearance in the upper classes (Wolfe & Fodor, 1996). Although this concern with appearance may be disparaged by some as a shallow preoccupation unique to the rich, evolutionary psychology experiments suggest otherwise. As Gutierres, Kenrick, and Partch (1999) and others have argued (e.g., Buss, 1989), the ability to attract mates is linked with characteristics strongly valued in the opposite sex, and these among women are signs of fertility (i.e., healthy and youthful physical attractiveness). Thus, women in general can come to doubt their own appeal as mates when surrounded by others who are highly physically attractive. Consistent with this reasoning, results of experiments established that female participants, when shown pictures of other physically attractive women, subsequently reported lower feelings of personal adequacy and decreased ratings of their own attractiveness as marriage partners (Gutierres et al., 1999; see also Brown, Novick, Lord, & Richards, 1992; Richins, 1991).

Juxtaposed with women's adverse reactions to pictures of physically attractive others, Gutierres et al.'s (1999) research showed, in parallel, that men's reports of their desirability as marriage partners suffered when they were exposed to socially dominant men (see also Kenrick & Keefe, 1992; Kenrick, Neuberg, Zierk, & Krones, 1994; Sadalla, Kendrick, and Vershure, 1987). Given that dominant and influential men are likely to be ubiquitous in the most high-paying professions, there is again considerable potential for the festering of self-doubt and insecurity among men working in such settings.

Furthermore, failures can be particularly painful for those most accustomed to power and success. In their studies of vervet monkeys, Raleigh, McGuire, Brammer, Pollack, and Yuwiler (1991) found that the highest ranking (alpha) males had levels of the neurotransmitter serotonin that were twice as high as those of other males in the group. When these alpha males lost their position, however, their serotonin levels fell and their behaviors resembled those of depressed humans: They huddled, rocked, and refused food. These behaviors were then reduced with the administrations of drugs that raise serotonin levels, such as Prozac. As Buss (2000, p. 20) concluded, "Perhaps the most difficult challenge posed by our evolved psychological mechanisms is managing competition and hierarchy negotiation, given that selection has fashioned powerful mechanisms that drive rivalry and status striving."

A final problem stemming from men's career patterns pertains to their fluctuating levels of integration with family life. Based on her ethnographic research with families of fishermen, Mederer (1999) has provided a vivid view into stresses experienced as a result of the fathers' frequent trips away. Frequently, spouses and children find it difficult to readjust their role boundaries and everyday routines to accommodate to the men's reentry after prolonged absences. Mederer correctly noted that such struggles are not unique to fisherman's families but generalize to any situation where a parent is frequently away for work (e.g., in military or corporate careers).

Judgments About Choices and Control

Undoubtedly, the preceding arguments will evoke, in some, the equivalent of the sardonic colloquialism, "I should only have their problems!" Many have scant sympathy for the rich, believing that they can and should walk away from their frenetic lifestyles. High-income professionals are commonly seen as excessively ambitious, volitionally choosing their fast-paced careers given lopsided priorities concerning the importance of money or fame versus the welfare of their families.

Although there may be some validity to such views, there are at least three factors that bear consideration before making sweeping judgments in this regard. One is that it is a universal human phenomenon to want more—more than one currently has, and more than what others in one's life space have. As

cryptically noted by Myers (2000b, p. 60), "Thanks to our capacity to adapt to ever greater fame and fortune, yesterday's luxuries can soon become today's necessities and tomorrow's relics." A cardinal premise of Festinger's (1954) social comparison theory, similarly, is that people evaluate themselves not so much by objective standards as by comparison with people around them (see also Exline & Lobel, 1999; Tesser, Millar, & Moore, 2000). Illustrating this, Myers (2000a) pointed out that most people are happier making $50,000 when those around them make 40,000 than they are making $60,000 when those around them make $70,000.

The second consideration is that many parents in upper-class communities can be reluctant to give up their high-paying careers not out of shallow greed or insatiable consumerism but because it could imply reductions in opportunities for their children (cf. Wolfe & Fodor, 1996). In this regard, again, rich parents are not unique: All parents want to do the best they can for their young. Whereas fencing lessons or designer clothes might be viewed as frivolous indulgences, the desire for high-quality educational experiences is less easily dismissed. There could, therefore, be at least two interpretations of economist Linder's (1970) assertion that as income and therefore the value of one's time increases, it becomes less and less rational to spend it on things other than making money. To be sure, this could reflect parents' selfish acquisitiveness. Equally, however, it could given the materialistic culture of contemporary America—reflect their guilt at voluntarily choosing not to work hard at acquiring all they possibly could, for the next generation.

Finally, parents' resolute commitment to fast-paced careers does not necessarily stem from egotistical, narcissistic self-absorption but may often derive from deep-seated personal unhappiness. As previously noted, research has shown that many people become highly invested in acquiring wealth and prestige in reaction to, or as compensation for, lack of emotional gratifications (Kasser et al., 1995). Consistent with this view is Miller's (1995) vivid description of *The Drama of the Gifted Child*, where the lack of early parental acceptance of the whole child—with all of his or her imperfections—leads some highly intelligent children to become excessively invested in their achievements as a source of their self-worth. As they move through life, the driving sentiment increasingly becomes, "I am what I achieve," with the chilling corollary, of course, "Without my achievements, I will become a failure."

Negative Judgments: The Rich and the Poor

Interestingly, some negative views of the very rich are similar to those applied to their counterparts at the other extreme of the economic continuum. In her literature review, Lott (2002) noted that the poor are often characterized as being dishonest, indolent, promiscuous, uninterested in education, and personally responsible for their plight. There is a parallel set of adjectives commonly applied to the rich: unethical, entitled, arrogant, superficial, and narcissistic, and entirely responsible for their own unhappiness (Pittman, 1985; Pollak & Schaffer, 1985; Shafran, 1992; Warner, 1991; Weitzman, 2000).

The wealthy may actually evoke more widespread dislike than the poor given their status as the keepers of the power rather than those excluded from it (much as the schoolyard bully is usually more disliked than is the victim). Social psychologists have suggested, in fact, that misfortunes of the wealthy can evoke a malicious pleasure in others, for people in general feel some satisfaction in the downfall of those far more successful than they themselves are (a phenomenon labeled *schadenfreude;* see Brigham, Kelso, Jackson, & Smith, 1997; Feather & Sherman, 2002; Smith, 2000; Smith et al., 1996).

It should be noted, too, that affluent, powerful people are likely to be well aware of others' resentment of them and to be troubled by this. Based on their extensive literature review, Exline and Lobel (1999) concluded that outperforming others can be privately satisfying, by engendering, for example, feelings of pride and efficacy. At the same time, it can be a source of much stress—and most so among those highly successful—because of feelings of guilt or embarrassment; empathic sadness for those outperformed; worries about conflicted relationships with them; and fears of provoking their envy, exclusion, or retaliation. Exline and Lobel noted, furthermore, that wealth and possessions are among the domains in which people tend to experience high stress about having outperformed others, an assertion that implies, in turn, that wealthy folk are probably well aware that societal attitudes toward their difficulties will be unsympathetic at best. To summarize, then, families in poverty are obviously greatly handicapped from the standpoint of basic necessities such as food, shelter, and education, but in terms of being disliked or distanced by society in general, the affluent may be at least as disadvantaged if not more so.

Parallels in negative attitudes toward the poor and the rich are also apparent in service providers' countertransferential reactions. Clinicians working with poor heroin-abusing abusing mothers are often cautioned about reactions such as judgments of their moral depravity or neglect of children (e.g., Luthar, D' Avanzo, & Hites, 2003; Luthar & Suchman, 2000). In parallel, therapists working with the very rich are warned of reactions ranging from dismissiveness at the one end to envy and active contempt at the other. Weitzman (2000), for example, reported that many service providers trivialize complaints of spousal abuse from affluent women, assuming that they have all the resources needed to leave their abusive partners; consequently, assistance is often denied and referrals not made. Several authors have written of envy among psychotherapists (Pollak & Schaffer, 1985; Shafran, 1992; Warner, 1991), which stems from their typically lower access to material possessions and life opportunities than their very wealthy clients. As envy is an emotion that is particularly socially disapproved (Exline & Lobel, 1999), furthermore, many therapists (and no doubt, many in society more generally) then defend it by converting it into other less repugnant emotions. These usually include pejorative or contemptuous attitudes such as scorn about their self-indulgent, querulous complaining or covert pleasure in seeing the rich get "knocked down to size" (Pollak & Schaffer, 1985, p. 351; see also Shafran, 1992).

Counterarguments, Caveats, and Future Directions

While discussions presented thus far highlight the psychological costs of affluence, several counter-arguments warrant consideration in weighing the overall magnitude of the problems suggested. The first of these concerns the authenticity of disturbance reported by affluent youth. Although a few samples of high-SES teenagers have shown elevated levels of depression, anxiety, and substance use, it is possible that these problems reflect normative complaints in the culture of upper-class suburbia rather than serious psychopathology. In other words, for some if not many youth, reports of adolescent angst might reflect conformity to what is expected (or even approved of) in the subculture of affluence (Luthar & Becker, 2002). In the years ahead, longitudinal research will be critical in illuminating this issue, identifying the degree to which high self-reported distress among suburban teens does in fact presage subsequent deterioration in critical domains, by affecting their school grades, for example, or leading to diagnosable mental illness.

A second issue concerns the geographic generalizability of problems among affluent youth. Extant evidence of modest inverse links between family wealth and positive adolescent outcomes (i.e., subjective happiness and closeness to parents) has derived from cross-national samples (Csikszentmihalyi & Schneider, 2000; U.S. Department of Health and Human Services, 1999). On the other hand, the studies showing elevations in negative outcomes—greater psychopathology as compared with normative samples—were conducted in Northeastern suburbs (e.g., Luthar & Becker, 2002; Luthar & D'Avanzo, 1999). It is plausible that regions of the country vary in the degree to which affluence implies highly stressful, competitive lifestyles and, thus, increased vulnerability to symptoms. In a similar vein, it is not clear whether the problems suggested represent a largely suburban phenomenon or might generalize to high-SES children in large cities.

The third issue constitutes a critical caveat to the substantive take-home messages that might be gleaned from this paper: that it is not the surfeit of riches in itself but rather an overemphasis on status and wealth that is likely to compromise well-being. All things considered, it is better to be rich than to be poor; cross-national data clearly show that money enhances subjective well-being when it implies the difference between being able versus unable to meet basic life needs (Diener & Biswas-Diener, 2002). It is only when individuals become disproportionately invested in extrinsic rewards, concomitantly neglecting intrinsic rewards such as closeness in relationships, that there are likely to be ill effects on their mental health outcomes (Kasser, 2002; Tooby & Cosmides, 1996; Triandis, 1994).

In the years ahead, it is vital that developmental scientists critically examine the conditions under which parents' affluence spells high risk for children. To be sure, epidemiological evidence will be required to ascertain the degree to which child psychopathology rates are truly elevated among the wealthy. Even as we await such evidence, however, it would be wise to recognize that (a) no child is immune to stressors from the environment, (b) extreme environments of all kinds are likely to have their own sets of problems, and (c) there is almost no developmental research on the ecological context of affluence. In the decade since Graham's (1992) admonishment that developmental research until then had involved mostly middle-class children, there has been, appropriately, growing attention to youth in poverty. It is critical that we now begin to consider the other extreme that has remained ignored thus far, making a concerted effort to illuminate the challenges particularly salient for children of affluence, along with the severity and continuity of problems they might develop.

As researchers begin to clarify these issues, it would also be prudent for applied professionals—educators, pediatricians, and other clinicians—to remain vigilant to the mental health vulnerabilities of high-SES youth. Research on child psychopathology has shown that, in general, most parents tend to be aware when their children are emotionally troubled but, at the same time, tend not to seek help for these problems (Puura et al., 1998). Affluent parents are less likely than most to seek professional help, partly to protect the veneer of perfection they feel compelled to maintain (Wolfe & Fodor, 1996) and partly for fear that this may constitute a significant impediment for the child's academic and professional future (Pollak & Schaffer, 1985). By the same token, if school personnel are concerned about children's adjustment, they are cautious in exhorting professional care for fear of parental displeasure (or even litigation). Paradoxically, therefore, children of the wealthy can be deprived of the school-based mental health services that are routinely accessed by those from more modest backgrounds (Pollak & Schaffer, 1985).

In considering the need for any external interventions, some might protest that the scant policy resources available for children's mental health should be reserved only for the truly needy—those in poverty—but this position would be questionable from an ethical and pragmatic perspective. Classism is unconscionable whomever the target; a child who is suicidal or dependant on drugs deserves help regardless of how much money his or her parents earn. From a practical standpoint, furthermore, it is useful to consider that the external resources needed to foster children's mental health will be exponentially lower for the rich than the poor. In most low-income communities, the creation of quality mental health services would necessitate considerable financial support. In communities where such services are already in place, an expedient first step, as Doherty (2000) has argued, would simply be to raise adults' awareness of the psychological costs of overscheduled, competitive lifestyles. Such awareness promotion can be effectively accomplished through books comprehensible to the lay public (for excellent examples, see Kasser, 2002; Myers, 2000a; Rosenfeld. & Wise, 2000), interviews with journalists (e.g., Belluck, 2000; Julien, 2002; Smith, 2002; Wen, 2002), and workshops with parent, school, and community groups (see Kantrowitz, 2000, p. 49). Although obviously not panaceas for extant ills, such efforts could begin to sensitize caregivers to potentially insidious stressors in the context of affluence, stressors that they (like we, in developmental science) may have been only faintly aware of in prior years.

Conclusions

Although children of the very affluent are typically seen as low risk, there are some suggestions that they manifest more disturbance than others, particularly in relation to substance use, anxiety, and depression. Exploration of causes suggests two factors as being implicated: excessive pressures to achieve and isolation from parents (both literal and emotional).

Extant studies with adults have also suggested psychological costs of material wealth. At the individual level, inordinate emphasis on material success can limit attainment of other rewards critical for well-being, such as close relationships. At the community level, material affluence can inhibit the formation of supportive networks, as services tend to be bought and not shared. At the systemic level, the subculture of affluence emphasizes personal autonomy and control, with the associated dangers of blaming oneself when control is not achieved.

Some adults' stressors are gender specific. Many upper-class mothers give up professional careers and are thus deprived of work-related gratifications; those who remain employed can face exacting demands both in their jobs and at home. Fathers, in turn, can contend with the substantial ramifications (or fears) of losing positions of power—the higher the status, the greater the fall—and with frequent absences from home due to professional obligations.

Many might believe that rich people should simply walk away from their pressured lifestyles, but to relinquish a lucrative career can be hard for anyone. Although not all possess wealth, the desire for more of it is universal. Moreover, many rich parents may stay with their high-pressure jobs not out of personal greed but to provide their children with the best they can (in many cases; a stellar education).

Classism is directed to some degree at the rich, as it unambiguously has been directed at the poor. Without question, for those concerned about the next meal, the misery borne of ennui can seem ludicrous. On the other hand, the desire to be liked and accepted by others is universal, and the rich are not only often the focus of envy and dislike—from society in general and sometimes from clinicians—but are also aware that their misfortunes tend to evoke malicious pleasure in others.

Additional developmental research is clearly needed to illuminate the nature, magnitude, and continuity of problems particularly salient in subcultures of affluence. Also critical is the need to consider the mental health needs of high-SES children, who unlike adults cannot obtain therapy for themselves, and many of whom may be discouraged from using services available in their schools or communities. As a beginning step in this direction, much can be accomplished by promoting parents' awareness of the emotional damage incurred by the unrelenting pursuit of "more."

Although in no way detracting from the myriad and formidable challenges faced by the poor, it is vital that psychologists correct their long-standing lack of concern with the isolation unique to affluence. No child should want for either food or affection; at the same time, it is worth remembering Harlow's (1958) findings that forced to choose, baby monkeys preferred the latter, just as Mother Teresa noted that the hunger for love is much more difficult to remove than the hunger for bread. In our approach to the affairs of the wealthy, the time is nigh to heed Csikszentmihalyi's (1999, p. 827) exhortation: "The job description for psychologists should encompass discovering what promotes happiness, and the calling of psychologists should include bringing this knowledge to public awareness."

Suniya S. Luthar, Developmental and Clinical Psychology Programs, Columbia University Teachers College.

Preparation of the manuscript was supported in part by grants from the National Institutes of Health (RO1-DA10726, R01-DA11498, and RO1-DA14385) and from the William T. Grant Foundation.

Correspondence concerning this article should be sent to Suniya S. Luthar, Developmental and Clinical Psychology Programs, Teachers College Box 133, Columbia University, 525 West 120th Street, New York, NY 10027-6696. Electronic mail may be sent to Suniya.Luthar@columbia.edu.

References

Belluck, P. (2000, June 13). Parents try to reclaim their children's time. *New York Times* p. A18.

Berger, B. (2000). Prisoners of liberation: A psychoanalytic perspective on disenchantment and burnout among career women lawyers. *Journal of Clinical Psychology, 56,* 665–673.

Blum, R. W. (1999). Cited in PBS Online, *The lost children of Rockdale Country. Is it isolated, or is it everywhere? Experts who work with teens and families offer their perspectives on this FRONTLINE report.* Retrieved December 22, 2002, from **http://www.pbs.org/wgbh/pages/frontline/shows/georgia/isolated/.**

Brickman, P. D., & Campbell, D. T. (1971). Hedonic relativism and planning the good society. In M. H. Appley (Ed.), *Adaptation level theory: A symposium* (pp. 287–304). New York: Academic Press.

Brigham, N. L., Kelso, K. A, Jackson, M. A, & Smith, R. H. (1997). The roles of invidious comparisons and deservingness in sympathy and Schadenfreude. *Basic & Applied Social Psychology, 19,* 363–380.

Brown, J. D., Novick, N. J., Lord, K. A., & Richards, J. M. (1992). When Gulliver travels: Social context, psychological closeness, and self-appraisals. *Journal of Personality & Social Psychology, 62,* 717–727.

Buss, D. M. (1989). Sex differences in human mate preferences: Evolutionary hypotheses tested in 37 cultures. *Behavioral & Brain Sciences, 12,* 1–49.

Buss, D. M. (2000). The evolution of happiness. *American Psychologist, 55,* 15–23.

Capizzano, J., Tout, K., & Adams, G. (2002). Child care patterns of school-age children with employed mothers: A report from the Urban Institute. Retrieved December 20, 2002, from **http://www.urban.org/template.cfm? Template= /TaggedContent/ViewPublication.cfm&PublicationID=7259&NavMenuID=95).**

Chang, L. C., & Arkin, R. M. (2002). Materialism as an attempt to cope with uncertainty. *Psychology & Marketing, 19,* 389–406.

Cicchetti, D., & Cohen, D. (Eds.). (1995). *Developmental psychopathology.* New York: Wiley.

Cooper, M. L. (1994). Motivations for alcohol use among adolescents: Development and validation of a four-factor model. *Psychological Assessment, 6,* 117–128.

Csikszentmihalyi, M. (1997). *Finding flow: The psychology of engagement with everyday life.* New York: Basic Books.

Csikszentmihalyi, M. (1999). If we are so rich, why aren't we happy? *American Psychologist, 54,* 821–827.

Csikszentmihalyi, M., & Schneider, B. (2000). *Becoming adult: How teenagers prepare for the world of work.* New York: Basic Books.

Diener, E. (2000). Subjective well-being: The science of happiness, and a proposal for a national index. *American Psychologist, 55,* 34–43.

Diener, E., & Biswas-Diener, R. (2002). Will money increase subjective well-being? *Social Indicators Research, 57,* 119–169.

Doherty, W. J. (2000). Family science and family citizenship: Toward a model of community partnership with families. *Family Relations: Journal of Applied Family & Child Studies, 49,* 319–325.

Duff, B. L. (2002). Women who abuse prescription drugs can find help: Rx for addiction. *New Canaan, Darien, & Rowayton, 4,* 102–106.

Exline, J. J., & Lobel, M. (1999). The perils of outperformance: Sensitivity about being the target of a threatening upward comparison. *Psychological Bulletin, 125,* 307–337.

Feather, N. T., & Sherman, R. (2002). Envy, resentment, Schadenfreude, and sympathy: Reactions to deserved and underserved achievement and subsequent failure. *Personality & Social Psychology Bulletin, 28,* 953–961.

Feldman, S. S., Rosenthal, D. R., Brown, N. L., & Canning, R. D. (1995). Predicting sexual experience in adolescent boys from peer rejection and acceptance during childhood. *Journal of Research on Adolescence, 5,* 387–411.

Festinger, L. (1954). A theory of social comparison processes. *Human Relations, 7,* 117–140.

Gilbert, S. (1999, August 3). For some children, it's an afterschool pressure cooker. *New York Times,* p. F7.

Graham, S. (1992)."Most of the subjects were White and middle class": Trends in published research on African Americans in selected APA journals, 1970–1989. *American Psychologist, 47,* 629–639.

Gutierres, S. E., Kenrick, D. T., & Partch, J. J. (1999). Beauty, dominance, and the mating game: Contrast effects in self-assessment reflect gender differences in mate selection. *Personality & Social Psychology Bulletin, 25,* 1126–1134.

Harlow, H. E. (1958). The nature of love. *American Psychologist, 13,* 673–685.

Hochschild, A. R. (1997). *The time bind: When work becomes home and home becomes work.* New York: Metropolitan Books.

Huston, A. C., McLoyd, V. C., & Garcia Coll, C. (1994). Children and poverty: Issues in contemporary research. *Child Development, 65,* 275–282.

Johnston, L. D., O'Malley, P. M., & Bachman, J. G. (1998). *National survey results on drug use from The Monitoring the Future Study, (1975–1997): Volume 1: Secondary school students.* Rockville, MD: National Institute on Drug Abuse.

Julien, A. (2002, December 16). Parents turn up the heat. *Hartford Courant,* Retrieved December 22, 2002, from **http://www.ctnow.com/news/health/hcgenstressday2dec16.story.**

Kantrowitz, B. (2000, July 17). Busy around the clock. *Newsweek, 136,* pp. 49–50.

Kantrowitz, B., & Wingert, P. (2001, January 29). The parent trap. *Newsweek, 137,* pp. 48–53.

Kasser, T. (2002). *The high price of materialism.* Cambridge, MA: MIT Press.

Kasser, T., & Ryan, R. M. (1993). A dark side of the American dream: Correlates of financial success as a central life aspiration. *Journal of Personality & Social Psychology, 65,* 410–422.

Kasser, T., & Ryan, R. M. (1996). Further examining the American dream: Differential correlates of intrinsic and extrinsic goals. *Personality & Social Psychology Bulletin, 22,* 280–287. .

Kasser, T., Ryan, R M., Zax, M., & Sameroff, A. J. (1995). The relations of maternal and social environments to late adolescents' materialistic and prosocial values. *Developmental Psychology, 31,* 907–914.

Kenrick, D. T., & Keefe, R. C. (1992). Age preferences in mates reflect sex differences in human reproductive strategies. *Behavioral & Brain Sciences, 15,* 75–133.

Kenrick, D. T., Neuberg, S. L., Zierk, K. L., & Krones, J. M. (1994). Evolution and social cognition: Contrast effects as a function of sex, dominance, and physical attractiveness. *Personality & Social Psychology Bulletin, 20,* 210–217.

Linder, S. (1970). *The harried leisure class.* New York: Columbia University Press.

Lott, B. (2002). Cognitive and behavioral distancing from the poor. *American Psychologist, 57,* 100–110.

Luthar, S. S., & Becker, B. E. (2002). Privileged but pressured: A study of affluent youth. *Child Development, 73,* 1593–1610.

Luthar, S. S., & D'Avanzo, K. (1999). Contextual factors in substance use: A study of suburban and inner-city adolescents. *Development and Psychopathology, 11,* 845–867.

Luthar, S. S., D'Avanzo, K., & Hites, S. (2003). Parental substance abuse: Risks and resilience. In S. S. Luthar (Ed.), *Resilience and vulnerability. Adaptation in the context of childhood adversities* (pp. 104–129). New York: Cambridge University Press.

Luthar, S. S., & Suchman, N. E. (2000). Relational psychotherapy mothers' group: A developmentally informed intervention for at-risk mothers. *Development and Psychopathology, 12,* 235–253.

Mederer, H. J. (1999). Surviving the demise of a way of life: Stress and resilience in Northeastern commercial fishing families. In H. I. McCubbin & E. A. Thompson (Eds.), *The dynamics of resilient families. Resiliency in families* (pp. 203–235). Thousand Oaks, CA: Sage.

Miller, A. (1995). *The drama of the gifted child: The search for the true self.* New York: Basic Books.

Myers, D. G. (2000a). *The American paradox: Spiritual hunger in an age of plenty.* New Haven, CT: Yale University Press.

Myers, D. G. (2000b). The funds, friends, and faith of happy people. *American Psychologist, 55,* 56–67.

Myers, D. G., & Diener, E. (1995). Who is happy? *Psychological Science, 6,* 10–19.

PBS Online (1999). *The lost children of Rockdale Country. Is it isolated, or is it everywhere? Experts who work with teens and families offer their perspectives on this FRONTUNE report.* Retrieved December 22, 2002, from **http://www.pbs.org/wgbh/pages/frontline/shows/georgia/isolated/** .

Perkins, H. W. (1991). Religious commitment, Yuppie values, and well-being in post-collegiate life. *Review of Religious Research, 32,* 244–251.

Pittman, F. S. (1985). Children of the rich. *Family Process, 24,* 461–472.

Pollak, J. M., & Schaffer, S. (1985). The mental health clinician in the affluent public school setting. *Clinical Social Work Journal, 13,* 341–355.

Putnam, R. D. (1993). The prosperous community. *The American Prospect, 4,*(13).

Putnam, R. D. (2000). *Bowling alone: The collapse and revival of American community.* New York: Simon & Schuster.

Puura, K., Almqvist, F., Tamminen, T., Piha, J., Kumpulainen, K., & Raesaenen, E., et al. (1998). Children with symptoms of depression—What do adults see? *Journal of Child Psychology & Psychiatry & Allied Disciplines, 39,* 577–585.

Raleigh, M. J., McGuire, M. T., Brammer, G. L., Pollack, D. B., & Yuwiler, A. (1991). Serotonergic mechanisms promote dominance acquisition in adult male vervet monkeys. *Brain Research, 559,* 181–190.

Resnick, M. D. (1999). Cited in PBS Online, *The lost children of Rockdale Country. Is it isolated, or is it everywhere? Experts who work with teens and families offer their perspectives on this FRONTLINE report.* Retrieved December 22, 2002, from **http://www.pbs.org/wgbh/pages/frontline/shows/georgia/isolated/.**

Richins, M. L. (1991). Social comparison and the idealized images of advertising. *Journal of Consumer Research, 18,* 71–83. .

Rosenfeld, A., & Wise, N. (2000). *The overscheduled child: Avoiding the hyper-parenting trap.* New York: St. Martin's Griffin.

Ryan, R. M., Chirkov, V. I., Little, T. D., Sheldon, K. M., Timoshina, E., & Deci, E. L. (1999). The American dream in Russia: Extrinsic aspirations and well-being in two cultures. *Personality & Social Psychology Bulletin, 25,* 1509–1524.

Sadalla, E. K., Kenrick, D. T., & Vershure, B. (1987). Dominance and heterosexual attraction. *Journal of Personality & Social Psychology, 52,* 730–738.

Sampson, R. J., Raudenbush, S. W., & Earls, F. (1997). Neighborhoods and violent crime: A multilevel study of collective efficacy. *Science, 277,* 918–924.

Schor, J. (1999). *The overspent American: Why we want what we don't need.* New York: Harper Collins.

Schwartz, B. (2000). Self-determination: The tyranny of freedom. *American Psychologist, 55,* 79–88.

Seligman, M. E. P. (1975). *Helplessness: On depression, development, and death.* San Francisco: Freeman.

Shafran, R. B. (1992). Children of affluent parents. In J. D. O'Brien & D. J. Pilowsky (Eds.), *Psychotherapies with children and adolescents: Adapting the psychodynamic process* (pp. 269–288). Washington, DC: American Psychiatric Association.

Sheldon, K. M., & Kasser, T. (1995). Coherence and congruence: Two aspects of personality integration. *Journal of Personality & Social Psychology, 68,* 531–543.

Smith, M. (2002, November 17). Are kids from affluent families more likely to drink? *Mobile Register,* p. A1.

Smith, R. H. (2000). Assimilative and contrastive emotional reactions to upward and downward social comparisons. In J. Suls & L. Wheeler (Eds.), *The Plenum series in social/clinical psychology. Handbook of social comparison: Theory and research* (pp. 173–200). New York, London: Kluwer Academic/Plenum.

Smith, R. H., Turner, T. J., Garonzik, R., Leach, C. W., UrchDruskat, V., & Weston, C. M. (1996). Envy and Schadenfreude. *Personality & Social Psychology Bulletin, 22,* 158–168.

Sroufe, L. A., & Rutter, M. (1984). The domain of developmental psychopathology. *Child Development, 55,* 17–29.

Tesser, A., Millar, M., & Moore, J. (2000). Some affective consequences of social comparison and reflection processes: The pain and pleasure of being close. In E. T. Higgins & A. W. Kruglanski (Eds.), *Motivational science: Social and personality perspectives. Key reading in social psychology* (pp. 60–75). New York: Psychology Press.

Tooby, J., & Cosmides, L. (1996). Friendship and the banker's paradox: Other pathways to the evolution of adaptations for altruism. In W. G. Runciman, J. M. Smith, & R. I. M. Dunbar (Eds.), *Evolution of social behaviour patterns in primates and* man: *A joint discussion meeting of the Royal Society and the British Academy. Proceedings of The British Academy, Vol.* 88 (pp. 119–143). New York: Oxford University Press.

Triandis, H. C. (1994). *Culture and social behavior.* New York: McGraw Hill.

U.S. Department of Health and Human Services. (1999). *America's children* Retrieved November 12, 2002, from **http://www.childstats.gov/ac1999.asp.**

Warner, S. L. (1991). Psychoanalytic understanding and treatment of the very rich. *Journal of the American Academy of Psychoanalysis, 19,* 578–594.

Way, N., Stauber, H. Y., Nakkula, M. J., & London, P. (1994). Depression and substance use in two divergent high school cultures: A quantitative and qualitative analysis. *Journal of Youth & Adolescence, 23,* 331–357.

Weitzman, S. (2000). *Not to people like us: Hidden abuse in upscale marriages.* New York: Basic Books.

Wen, P. (2002, October 7). Early pressures tied to drug abuse. *Boston Globe,* p. A1.

Wentzel, K. R., & Caldwell, K. (1997). Friendships, peer acceptance, and group membership: Relations to academic achievement in middle school. *Child Development, 68,* 1198–1209.

Wolfe, J. L., & Fodor, I. G. (1996). The poverty of privilege: Therapy with women of the "upper classes". *Women & Therapy, 18,* 73–89.

Wilson-Doenges, G. (2000). An exploration of sense of community and fear of crime in gated communities. *Environment & Behavior, 32,* 597–611.

Zucker, R. A., Fitzgerald, H. E., & Moses, H. D. (1995). Emergence of alcohol problems and the several alcoholisms: A developmental perspective on etiologic theory and life course trajectory. In D. Cicchetti & D. Cohen (Eds.), *Developmental psychopathology, Vol. 2: Risk, disorder, and adaptation* (pp. 677–711). New York: Wiley.

Watch and Learn

Children's educational television has had a successful beginning and middle, but as it extends its lessons through the Internet and classroom activities, will it help kids live happily ever after?

ERIC JAFFE

In the early 1970s, graduate student Barbara Flagg, who studied children's attention patterns and beginning reading, made the realization that outgoing graduate students make every year, right around May: she was broke. But like most in the field she had heard about a new educational television show teaching kids all kinds of basic skills. The show was *Sesame Street*, and it was doing something completely new to children's educational television. It was paying behavioral researchers like her to make it better.

A few years earlier, the Department of Education had granted Children's Television Workshop $8 million to create educational television programs that would prepare young kids for school. The workshop was given a two-year lead time to develop a show curriculum and test the show's effectiveness before it was broadcast. The opportunity for trial, error, and retrial was an industry rarity. Traditionally, producers had created shows based on sellable ideas that could be ready to air quickly. Consultation with educators, if it happened at all, occurred after much of the groundwork had already been done. The workshop, however, had gathered a mixture of scientists and television people. Working in close collaboration on all aspects of production—from story ideas to scripts to the color of Big Bird's plumage—the team figured out how to get kids to *Sesame Street*, and how to keep them there.

"In the early days of *Sesame Street*, in 1969, no one was thinking this way—that you could try out material with kids before you developed curriculum," said Flagg, who got a job with the workshop's math show, *The Electric Company*, during this era. "It seems so logical now. When you think about it—why not?"

This preliminary testing, called formative research, helped *Sesame Street* balance entertainment and teaching. Often, formative researchers simply watched kids watch television. They set two screens side by side—one with *Sesame Street* or *The Electric Company*, the other with colorful slides—and noted when kids looked away from the show. Sometimes they hooked up kids to eye movement recorders. "In the '70s, this meant kids sitting with their heads in a harness," said Shalom Fisch, who left the workshop a few years ago as vice president (by that time it was called Sesame Workshop). The equipment couldn't be transported, so parents brought their kids to the laboratory. The children sat in barbershop-style chairs and only watched short spurts of video, because movement disrupted the recorders. Without the head fixtures, said Flagg, the 4- and 5-year-olds would look around for their mothers.

Discomfort aside, the research made a difference. By knowing what part of the screen kids watched, producers could make their educational messages more effective. For example, *The Electric Company*, a show that taught basic grammar and reading skills, often ran a skit about forming words. During the skit, two faces looked at one another. Letters came out of the mouths and met up in the middle to make a word. This seemed like a logical presentation until the researchers looked at the eye movement results and found that children weren't looking at the words at all—they were looking at the faces. In the new version, producers changed the faces to silhouettes, directing the focus back onto the letters, and children made the connection.

"As we developed new methodologies for testing the appeal, comprehensibility, and attention-attracting potential of *Sesame Street* and *The Electric Company*, research staffs were pilot testing these methods and procedures, and providing almost instant feedback as to what worked and what did not," said Jennings Bryant, University of Alabama, who helped develop some of the workshop's early research.

Thirty-six years later, *Sesame Street* has been shown empirically to benefit children's learning up to 10 years after they watch the program, said Fisch, who specializes in both formative research and evaluating shows after they air, a process called summative research. Another crucial development was the realization that licensed children's products could lead to big business, as typified by the *Sesame*-based toy Tickle Me Elmo sending parents into a Christmas craze in 1996. Thanks to licensing revenue, the workshop no longer relies primarily on government funding. This confluence of research value, potential marketing capital, and more television channels set the stage for other children's shows to build on *Sesame's* success, said APS Charter Member Daniel Anderson, University of Massachusetts. It also set the stage for what Anderson calls the "golden age of television for young children."

Blue's Clues

Also in the 1970s, not far from where Flagg ran tests for *The Electric Company*, Anderson was lecturing to an undergraduate child development class. The lesson focused on the development of attention in children. After class, one student approached Anderson with a question. If younger children are more distractible than older children and have a hard time maintaining attention, the student asked, why can my 4-year-old brother sit and stare at *Sesame Street*? The question, Anderson concluded, was a good one.

At the time, said Anderson, the dominant theory was set by Jean Piaget. According to Piaget followers, children couldn't comprehend a video montage. For example, they argued, shown a building's exterior followed by a character sitting in a room, adults assume the room is in the building, but children don't make that connection. If Piaget's theory was accurate, thought Anderson, children might have a difficult time following *Sesame Street*, which uses a similar sequencing technique, known as a magazine format.

To test his theory, Anderson rearranged segments of *Sesame Street* and had children watch the altered show. Before long, he found that changing the events did affect children's comprehension. Some kids, in fact, were so upset at the muddled sequence that they approached the screen and tried to make the change themselves. "We found that kids don't just sit and stare," Anderson said. "For kids as young as 24-months, it was important to the kids that the show makes sense." It turned out kids could make the connection—they just had to work harder than adults to do it.

In 1993, Nickelodeon asked Anderson to design a block of preschool programs based on what his years of child research had taught him: When children watch television, they are active, intellectually and behaviorally. One of these shows was called *Blue's Clues*. Each episode of *Blue's Clues* presents a puzzle that viewers solve by answering clues peppered throughout. To keep kids focused on the content, Anderson minimized editing and video montage. As a result, the show is lively but not rapidly paced. Repetition is a crucial element. "Kids have to work to understand transition, even though they can," Anderson said. "You want them to spend the work on the content."

In an episode called "Blue's Predictions," the show's human host, Joe, says some variation of the word "predict" around 15 times. At one point, Joe and an animated bookmark (named Bookmark) read a story. "Once upon a time, there was a penguin," says Bookmark. "His name was Penguin Pierre." Bookmark stops and points to the penguin. "That's Penguin Pierre," it says. Another pause. "I think that's Penguin Pierre," Joe says. The children watching probably don't realize that the voice of Bookmark is none other than The Fonz, Henry Winkler, but they are able to focus on the penguin's story, which helps them solve the episode's puzzle.

Simple as it seems, *Blue's Clues* became a smash hit, thanks largely to Anderson's research, as well as the producers' practice of testing each episode three times before it airs. "What was different about *Blue's Clues* was that it took the philosophical position that the audience wanted to play a role in the show, that the audience is not passive," Anderson said. "It took a position that kids watch television to learn. If you challenge them, they'll rise to the challenge."

ADHDTV

Elizabeth Lorch remembers the first time she saw *Blue's Clues*. About eight years ago, she and her 4-year-old daughter were lying on the couch at home, ill with a stomach bug. Lorch turned on the television and flipped the channels in search of something to pass the time. When she got to Nickelodeon, which was running a *Blue's Clues* marathon, her daughter perked up immediately. "Wow," Lorch remembers thinking. "This is how you get a preschooler to pay attention."

Lorch studied under Anderson as a graduate student, has co-authored chapters with him, and still keeps a close eye on his research. From what she sees, children's research in this area is focusing more on younger and younger viewers. The popularity of *Barney*, said Lorch, showed researchers that very young children—under four years old—could be pulled into television. Its success brought on *Teletubbies*, *Baby Einstein*, and other toddler shows. It also aroused controversy over whether children this young should be spending so much time in front of the screen. "Kids have become more sophisticated. They're watching TV much earlier," Flagg said. "The things we learned in the '70s about television apply at an earlier age than they used to, because there's so much exposure."

In 1999, the American Academy of Pediatrics decided that "so much exposure" had become too much exposure. The Academy released a statement that children ages 2 to 16 should spend no more than two hours a day in front of *any* screen—television, computer, or video game—and that kids under age 2 should watch no television at all. "Our concern is, we know in the first couple years of life that children's brains are physically developing, and that development is dependent on interaction with people," said Daniel Broughton, a pediatrician at the Mayo Clinic in Minnesota, and a member of the Academy's Committee on Communication that prepared the statement. "There's no value in watching TV at this age, and it's potentially harmful."

As an example of this potential harm, Broughton points to a 2004 study published in the academy's journal *Pediatrics*. In the study, researchers found a correlation between television viewing in children ages 1 and 3 and decreased attention spans in these same children around age 7. "Limiting young children's exposure to television as a medium during formative years of brain development—consistent with the American Academy of Pediatrics' recommendations—may reduce children's subsequent risk of developing ADHD," the authors write.

The authors acknowledge that their results, while highly suggestive, call for scrutiny and replication. But the implications are explosive. According to the Centers for Disease Control and Prevention, four million children aged 3 to 17 had been diagnosed with attention deficit hyperactivity disorder, or ADHD, as of 2003. Lorch has taken many of these kids, from age 4 to 12, and placed them back in front of the television to see just what their attention difficulties mean for learning. Instead of using children to inform what works in television, Lorch is using television to inform what works—or doesn't work—in children. What she found harkens back to the Piaget period: they have difficulty making connections.

Lorch studied how kids with ADHD watch television by placing them in a room with toys. In the early days of *Sesame Street*, such "distracters" were used to see which parts of a show children liked, and which parts they didn't. Lorch told children they would be tested on what happened during the show after the experiment. To no surprise, the attention of children with ADHD dropped when toys were present. But Lorch found that these same children did not score lower on remembering the show's discrete, individual events. Where they scored lower was connecting the events into a flowing narrative. "There's something about understanding a structure of a story that kids with ADHD are missing," Lorch said. "Stories are seen as individual events."

Lorch is running some pilot experiments on how to help kids acquire the needed links. She's showing students the episodes and having them map out the story on paper before they talk about it. "It's a way of getting them to zero in on what's this character trying to accomplish," she said. It's exactly this integration of different formats—television, as well as the Internet and after-school teaching guides—that has Fisch, Flagg, and the producers of a show called *Cyberchase* excited for the future of children's educational media.

Interactive Media

Cyberchase is a PBS show in which three curious kids solve math-related problems to save the universe. In formative research sessions, Flagg, the show's director of multimedia research, wanted to see how kids understand problem solving—for example, getting from Point A to Point B. Flagg gave third graders a game board and a Monopoly piece, and provided them the same directions the *Cyberchase* characters would have. As the kids worked their way through the directions, Flagg videotaped their misconceptions, their "aha!" moments, and the language they used to describe their thoughts, which then helped writers improve the script.

"If you want to communicate education, you need to know who your audience is and how you can communicate with them," Flagg said. "We focus on letting our audience have a voice in all areas of what we do." With *Cyberchase*, this means taking its role as an educational tool beyond the screen. The very title indicates a new direction in children's attention—from the living room to the Web. The villain's name is Hacker. A quick glance at the show's Web site shows not a few but dozens of educational, interactive games that Flagg says are closely tied to the show's content.

Two years ago, in his role as summative evaluator, Fisch began to document the significant educational impact of the *Cyberchase* television series. Since then, he has turned his eye toward multiple media. "The trend now is not to produce a TV show, and then follow it with other materials. Instead producers approach each project through multiple media, like a TV show, Web site, and after school outreach materials'," said Fisch, who has become president of MediaKidz Research & Consulting

since leaving Sesame Workshop. "Nobody has looked at the cumulative impact when you put all these pieces together." Since the research is so novel, Fisch had to reassess its value at many points along the way. The National Science Foundation gave money to Fisch and the producers of *Cyberchase* to examine the literature in several disciplines—developmental psychology, education, communication, and media effects—and figure out the directions that such research might take. Now, they plan to to pursue the next step: pilot testing methods and measure to assess impact.

Indeed, formative research suggests that interactive media may go a long way in reinforcing the educational tools television has honed over the past decades. "I've been very struck by the high degree of consistency that I've seen in kids' responses over time and across different media," Fisch said. "Each medium presents its own unique issues, but in many ways, the things that make content work in one medium overlap greatly with the things that make it work in another."

Among these findings is the effectiveness of after-school educational materials. The show provides many schools with hands-on *Cyberchase*-related activities for children to work on while waiting for parents to pick them up. "As opposed to TV or the Web, where every kid is seeing the same stuff, [after-school materials] will have a different style based on the teacher," Fisch said. "The experiences will vary a lot, because teachers can tailor their approaches to the needs and abilities of individual kids."

APS Fellow Ed Palmer, Davidson College, believes interactive media will provide the next wave of children's educational material. "We can educate kids about TV viewing through computer software," said Palmer (no relation to the psychologist Ed Palmer who played a major role in *Sesame Street's* early days). But with the potential benefits of interactive media, said Palmer, come the caveats. As children's programs move from cable television to digital television and the Internet, the already-limited commercial aspect will disappear entirely, forcing advertisers to invade children's media in other, subtler ways. "When a kid buys a game now, the advertising company outfits it with their ads, and kids don't have a clue this is happening," Palmer said. "Kids give the same credibility to commercials as programming. We need education to get on top of sophistication in the Internet—what the advertising industry is already on top of. If we get there with educational messages, I think we'd have a major stride forward."

It Isn't Easy Eating Green

Recently, Sesame Workshop launched a program intended to do exactly what Palmer believes it should: use educational message to make a positive social impact. The program, called Healthy Habits for Life, addresses the growing problem of child obesity. The problem is so bad that Cookie Monster now calls cookies a "sometimes food," said Jennifer Kotler, the workshop's director of research. "We're trying to promote nutrition and healthy segments of shows," Kotler said. "We realized there's not much research out there on how to get preschool kids to like healthier foods."

To tackle the problem, the workshop called in one of the experts: Elmo. The ticklish red Muppet with the high-pitched voice is the face of the Elmo-Broccoli study, which has helped researchers find out what 3-, 4-, and 5-year-olds think of when they hear the word "healthy." It doesn't take a trained researcher to know that given the option of broccoli or chocolate, children will choose chocolate. But what researchers did find interesting was that as children get older they seem to have a better sense of what's healthy, even though their preference for the unhealthier option stays the same. "A 3-year-old thinks what he likes is healthy, but a 5-year-old knows it's not," Kotler said. "That's a two-year window where we might be able to intervene with education."

Taking advantage of that window meant finding out exactly why children choose one food over another. So researchers went into schools and showed children two cards: one with a picture of broccoli, the other with a snapshot of chocolate. At this stage, 78 percent of the kids preferred the chocolate card. When research-ers put Elmo in the chocolate card and a generic red puppet in the broccoli card, the preference for chocolate shot up to 89 percent. But when Elmo was placed next to the broccoli and the generic character next to the chocolate, children's preferences split right down the middle. It wasn't just a need for green; the same thing happened with grapes and bananas.

The workshop recently received funding from the Atkins company to move forward with the study, which means giving children the actual food instead of a picture. "Maybe something as small as a sticker on healthy foods can influence what a child wants to eat," Kotler said. But more importantly for the future of children's education, the results indicate to Kotler just how influential children's programming has become. "We're here to educate," Kotler said. "Children spend more time with TV than anything besides sleeping, so we should focus on it like we focus on helping them in the classroom."

Eric Jaffe is a freelance writer in New York.

Forensic Developmental Psychology

Unveiling Four Common Misconceptions

ABSTRACT—We summarize recent developments in the field of forensic developmental psychology that challenge traditional conceptions about the reliability of children's reports. The areas covered involve the disclosure patterns of sexually abused children, the nature of suggestive interviews, developmental differences in suggestibility, and the amount of suggestion required to produce false reports and beliefs.

MAGGIE BRUCK[1] AND STEPHEN CECI[2]

[1]*Johns Hopkins University and* [2]*Cornell University*

A rapidly growing area in developmental psychology concerns the reliability of children's reports of autobiographical events and the mechanisms that promote accurate and inaccurate reports. Because this work was primarily motivated by and is applicable to the legal arena (namely, children's reports that they were victims or witnesses of a crime), we have labeled this field of inquiry "forensic developmental psychology."

When children report being a victim or a witness of a crime, two primary sets of issues arise. One concerns disclosure patterns of children who have experienced traumatic events. Topics that have been studied in this area include the cognitive, motivational, and emotional factors that influence the nature of children's reports of the trauma. The research in this field of study is based on the assumption that the children have actually experienced traumatic events. The second set of issues concerns whether suggestive interviews can result in children falsely reporting nonexperienced (traumatic) events. The major topics in this field of research include the conditions that precipitate false reports, the psychological status of false reports (false beliefs vs. lies), and developmental trends in false reports. In this review, we focus on four major misconceptions about children's disclosures and their suggestibility. Each of these misconceptions has not only made its way into courtroom testimony, but also provided foundational assumptions for subsequent research.

Misconception #1: Sexually Abused Children Do Not Disclose Their Abuse

A highly influential assumption is that sexually abused children do not readily disclose their abuse because of shame, guilt, and fear; consequently, there may never be a disclosure or else there is a long delay between the abuse and disclosure. In the latter case, it is asserted that children will initially deny their abuse when questioned, but will slowly divulge its details with repeated questioning. It is further claimed that these disclosures are frequently recanted, but will be reinstated with supportive questioning. The most popular embodiment of this idea is Summit's (1983) term *child sexual abuse accommodation syndrome* (CSAAS).

A corollary of CSAAS is that, in order to overcome emotional and motivational barriers that inhibit spontaneous disclosure of their abuse, children must be asked specific questions about it over a period of time. In part, this assumption is supported by the findings that children will provide more detailed answers to specific or cued questions than to open-ended questions. With age, children acquire cognitive structures that assist the organization of events into coherent narratives, and the need for specific questions declines. But when specific questions must be asked, such questioning comes with a cost; answers to specific questions are more error prone than those to open-ended questions (see Ceci & Bruck, 1995). The clinical practice of asking leading questions to children suspected of abuse is nonetheless defended by claiming that children will not falsely report abuse when asked specific questions (e.g., Rudy & Goodman, 1991).

Because the CSAAS model was based not on empirical data but on clinical intuitions, we recently reviewed the literature to determine its empirical support (London, Bruck, Ceci, & Shuman, in press). We identified 10 studies in which adults with histories of childhood abuse were asked to recall their disclosures in childhood. Across studies, an average of only 33% of the adults remembered disclosing the abuse in a timely fashion. These data support the view that sexually abused children are silent about their victimization and delay disclosure for long periods of time.

Although these studies are informative on the issue of delay of reporting, because the participants were never asked, "As a child, did anyone ever ask you or question you about abuse?" the data are silent on the phenomena of denial and recantation. Another set of studies provides some data relevant to this point. We identified 17 studies that examined rates of denial and recantation by sexually abused children who were asked directly about abuse when they were assessed or treated at clinics. The rates of denial at assessment interviews were highly variable (4% to 76%), as were the rates of recantation (4% to 27%). We found that the methodological adequacy of each study (sampling procedures, validation of sexual abuse) was directly related to the denial and recantation rates observed; the weakest studies produced the highest rates. For the 6 methodologically superior studies, the average rate of denial was only 14%, and the average rate of recantation was 7%. Thus, although the retrospective studies of adults show that children do not disclose abuse, the studies of children's response patterns indicate that if they are directly asked, they do not deny, but tell.

In part, the myth about children's patterns of disclosure has persisted because documentation of the first stage of the CSAAS model (children are silent and delay disclosures) has been interpreted as evidence for the full model, according to which denial and recantation are common. Also, as shown by our recent review and analysis, the most commonly cited studies in the literature are those that support the model—but sadly, these are the methodologically weakest of the studies.

Even if it is conceded that children will not deny their abuse when asked, the question of how to elicit disclosures remains. Even though there are known risks of using leading or specific questions, perhaps these are necessary to elicit reports or details from sexually abused children who feel frightened, ashamed, or guilty. This claim has recently been challenged by Lamb, Sternberg, and their colleagues, who constructed a structured interview protocol and then trained interviewers in its use. The protocol requires trained interviewers to encourage suspected child abuse victims to provide detailed life-event narratives through the guidance of open-ended questions (e.g., "Tell me what happened"; "You said there was a man; tell me about the man"). The use of specific questions is allowed only after exhaustive free recall. Suggestive questions are highly discouraged. In their latest study, Lamb et al. (2003) examined the interviews of police officers trained on the protocol with 4- to 8-year-old children who had made allegations of sexual abuse. Lamb et al. found that 83% of all allegations and disclosures were elicited through free-recall questions (78% for preschoolers), and 66% of all children identified the suspect through open-ended questions (60% for preschoolers). These data dispel the belief that interviewers need to bombard children with suggestive techniques in order to elicit details of trauma; rather, children can provide detailed information through open-ended prompts, and if a child denies abuse when asked directly, there is no scientifically compelling evidence that the child is "in denial." Abused children usually disclose the abuse when directly asked.

Misconception #2: Suggestive Interviews Can Be Indexed By The Number of Leading Questions

According to our model of the factors that influence suggestibility (Bruck, Ceci, & Hembrooke, 2002), the suggestiveness (and thus the risk of eliciting false information) of an interview is not directly reflected by the number of leading questions, but rather is indexed by how *interviewer bias* plays out in the target interview, as well as in all previous interviews. Interviewer bias characterizes interviewers who hold a priori beliefs about the occurrence of certain events and, as a result, conduct their interviews so as to obtain confirmatory evidence for these beliefs without considering plausible alternative hypotheses. When children provide such interviewers with inconsistent or bizarre evidence, it is either ignored or interpreted within the framework of the biased interviewer's initial hypothesis. According to our model, interviewer bias influences the entire architecture of interviews and is revealed through a variety of suggestive interviewing techniques, including the use of repeated specific questions (some of which may be leading) within and across interviews; implicit or explicit threats, bribes, and rewards for the desired answer; stereotype induction (e.g., telling children the suspected perpetrator "does bad things"); and guided imagery (asking children to create a mental picture of a specific event and to think about its details; see Ceci & Bruck, 1995). Although each suggestive technique is associated with error, the risk for false statements is greatly augmented when interviews contain a combination of suggestive techniques, which increase the salience of the interviewer's bias.

There is considerable empirical support for this model. When children are questioned about events they did not experience (e.g., seeing a thief steal food from the day-care center; Bruck et al., 2002) or about nonoccurring details within experienced events (e.g., "the man put something yucky in your mouth"; Poole & Lindsay, 2001), their reports are more error prone if these techniques are used than if the questioning takes place in a neutral, nonsuggestive manner.

Sometimes suggestive interviews can be void of leading questions; and sometimes leading questions may not pose a risk to the reliability of children's reports in the absence of interviewer bias. For example, Garven, Wood, and Malpass (2000) asked kindergarten children to recall details about a visitor named Paco who came to their classroom and read a story, gave out treats, and wore a funny hat. The children were asked misleading questions about plausible events (e.g., Did Paco break a toy?) and about bizarre events (e.g., Did Paco take you to a farm?). Some of the children were given selective feedback after their answers to the misleading questions. "No" responses were negatively evaluated, as in the following exchange:

Interviewer: Did Paco take you somewhere in a helicopter?

Child: No.

Interviewer: You're not doing good.

"Yes" responses were positively evaluated, as the following example illustrates:

Interviewer: Did Paco break a toy?

Child: Yes.

Interviewer: Great; you're doing excellent now.

This group of children provided the desired but false answer to 35% of the plausible questions and to 52% of the bizarre questions. In contrast, a second group of children who did not receive this selective feedback falsely agreed with 13% of the plausible and 5% of the bizarre questions. Thus, a simple count of misleading and leading questions would not reflect the suggestiveness of the interviews in this study; the children frequently agreed with the false suggestions only when the selective reinforcement provided sufficient information concerning the bias of the interviewer. Two weeks later, when the children were asked nonleading questions with no selective feedback, the same level of between-groups differences was obtained. Thus, interviewer bias in a prior interview has long-lasting negative effects on accuracy in a later unbiased interview.

Misconception #3: Suggestibility Is Primarily a Problem for Preschoolers

Although much of the literature pays lip service to the concept that suggestibility exists at all ages, including in adults, the primary view is that preschool children are disproportionately suggestible, and that there should be less concern about the tainting effects of suggestive interviews with older school-aged children. The focus on younger children reflects the disproportionate number of studies of preschool children at the end of the 20th century. This practice was directly motivated by forensic concerns of the day; in a number of high-profile criminal cases, preschool children made horrific claims about sexual abuse. Although the case facts showed that these children had been subjected to highly suggestive interviews, at that time there was no relevant body of scientific literature to indicate the risk of such interviews in producing false allegations about a range of salient events. When researchers began to fill in this empirical void, most of the studies focused on preschoolers, and few examined age-related differences. Those that did include age comparisons usually found that the older children rarely fell sway to suggestion, leading to the conclusion that only preschoolers are suggestible (e.g., Ceci, Ross, & Toglia, 1987). However, this conclusion is discrepant with the findings of another body of literature showing that many of the suggestive techniques used in the child studies also produce tainted reports or false memories in adults (e.g., see Loftus, 2003). By inference, one might assume that children in middle childhood must also be quite suggestible, given that both younger and older groups are.

Recent evidence supports this view: Susceptibility to suggestion is highly common in middle childhood, and under some conditions there are small to no developmental differences in suggestibility. For example, Finnilä, Mahlberga, Santtilaa, and

Niemib (2003) staged an event (a version of the Paco visit we described earlier) for 4- to 5-year-olds and 7- to 8-year-olds. One week later, half the children were given a low-pressure interview that contained some misleading questions with abuse themes (e.g., "He took your clothes off, didn't he?"). The other children received a high-pressure interview; they were told that their friends had answered the leading questions affirmatively, they were praised for assenting to the misleading questions, and when they did not assent, the question was repeated. In both conditions, there were no significant age differences in the percentage of misleading questions answered affirmatively, although a significant number (68%) were assented to in the high-pressure condition (see also Bruck & London, 2003; Zaragoza, Payment, Kichler, Stines, & Drivdahl, 2001). It has also been found that under some conditions, older children are more suggestible than younger children (e.g., Finniluä et al., 2003; Zaragoza et al., 2001).

Misconception #4: Multiple Suggestive Interviews Are Needed to Taint a Report

The final misconception is that it is very difficult to implant memories or to taint reports, and that false reports occur only when multiple suggestions are repeated over time (e.g., Ceci & Bruck, 1995). However, many studies have reported that children can incorporate suggestions about salient events after a single interview. In the study by Garven et al. (2000), for example, children's reports were significantly tainted after a single suggestive interview. Moreover, one interview had lasting effects: Children's initial inaccurate responses to the suggestions may have reflected social pressure; however, their continued false reports when queried by different (neutral) interviewers at later sessions reflected their false belief that the events planted by suggestion had actually occurred.

Recent evidence also suggests that, contrary to common psychological principles, there are a number of circumstances in which one suggestive interview produces the same amount of taint as two or more suggestive interviews. The risks that a second interview will increase suggestibility depend on the spacing of the interviews and also on the memory strength of the original event (Melnyk & Bruck, in press).

Finally, there can be significant tainting of reports and production of false beliefs when interviews are only very mildly suggestive. For example, Poole and Lindsay (2001) had parents read their children short narratives that outlined the children's previous encounters with a character known as Mr. Science at the researchers' laboratory. Unknown to the parents, some of the details in the stories were inaccurate, and thus were not experienced by the children when they met Mr. Science. Nonetheless, even under these mildly suggestive conditions, significant numbers of children (4- to 8-year-olds) later told an interviewer that they had experienced the suggested events (e.g., "The man put something yucky in my mouth").

Conclusion

We have reviewed some recent advances in the field of forensic developmental psychology that challenge four common misconceptions, some of which have acquired the status of urban legends in the field of clinical practice and forensic psychology. The data indicate that there should be greater concern that interviews with possible victims of child abuse are conducted using scientifically validated methods and less concern that true victims will deny that they were abused.

Theoretically, these new findings challenge current views of the developmental trends in suggestibility, and thus of the developmental mechanisms underlying children's suggestibility. Traditionally, researchers studied candidate mechanisms (e.g., theory of mind—knowledge that other people may have feelings, intentions, and beliefs different from one's own; social compliance) that were known to develop by the end of the preschool years (because it was thought that suggestibility was greatly reduced by that time). However, if suggestibility levels remain relatively high throughout childhood, a new perspective is required. For example, the relationship of suggestibility to skills that develop throughout childhood (e.g., resolution of conflicting information, insight into a questioner's motives) should become the focus of future study. It may also be useful to examine whether there are developmental changes in the mechanisms underlying suggestibility, with different mechanisms playing a causal role at different developmental levels.

Recommended Reading

Ceci, S.J., & Bruck, M. (1995). (See References)
Rabinowitz, D. (2003). *No crueler tyrannies.* New York: Simon & Schuster.
Summit, R. (1983). (See References)

References

Bruck, M., Ceci, S.J., & Hembrooke, H. (2002). The nature of children's true and false narratives. *Developmental Review, 22,* 520–554.
Bruck, M., & London, K. (2003, April). *Memory and suggestibility during middle childhood.* Paper presented at the biennial meeting of the Society for Research in Child Development, Tampa, FL.

Ceci, S.J., & Bruck, M. (1995). *Jeopardy in the courtroom.* Washington, DC: American Psychological Association.
Ceci, S.J., Ross, D., & Toglia, M. (1987). Suggestibility of children's memory. *Journal of Experimental Psychology: General, 116,* 38–49.
Finnilä, K., Mahlberga, N., Santtilaa, P., & Niemib, P. (2003). Validity of a test of children's suggestibility for predicting responses to two interview situations differing in degree of suggestiveness. *Journal of Experimental Child Psychology, 85,* 32–49.
Garven, S., Wood, J.M., & Malpass, R.S. (2000). Allegations of wrongdoing: The effects of reinforcement on children's mundane and fantastic claims. *Journal of Applied Psychology, 85,* 38–49.
Lamb, M.E., Sternberg, K., Orbach, Y., Esplin, P., Stewart, H., & Mitchell, S. (2003). Age differences in children's responses to openended invitations in the course of forensic interviews. *Journal of Consulting and Clinical Psychology, 71,* 926–934.
Loftus, E.F. (2003). False memory. In L. Nadel (Ed.), *Encyclopedia of cognitive science* (Vol. 2, pp. 120–125). London: Nature Publishing Group.
London, K., Bruck, M., Ceci, S., & Shuman, D. (in press). Disclosure of child sexual abuse: What does the research tell us about the ways that children tell? *Psychology, Public Policy, and the Law.*
Melnyk, L., & Bruck, M. (in press). Timing moderates the effects of repeated suggestive interviewing on children's memory. *Applied Cognitive Psychology.*
Poole, D.A., & Lindsay, D.S. (2001). Children's eyewitness reports after exposure to misinformation from parents. *Journal of Experimental Psychology: Applied, 7,* 27–50.
Rudy, L., & Goodman, G.S. (1991). Effects of participation on children's reports. *Developmental Psychology, 27,* 527–538.
Summit, R. (1983). The child sexual abuse accommodation syndrome. *Child Abuse and Neglect, 7,* 177–193.
Zaragoza, M., Payment, K., Kichler, J., Stines, L., & Drivdahl, S. (2001, April). *Forced confabulation and false memory in child witnesses.* Paper presented at the biennial meeting of the Society for Research in Child Development, Minneapolis, MN.

Address correspondence to Maggie Bruck, Johns Hopkins Medical Institutions, Department of Psychiatry and Behavioral Science, Division of Child and Adolescent Psychiatry, 600 N. Wolfe St., Baltimore, MD 21287-3325; e-mail: mbruck1@jhmi.edu.

From *Current Directions in Psychological Science,* Vol. 13, 2004. Copyright ©2004 by Blackwell Publishing, Ltd. Reprinted by permission. www.blackwell-synergy.com

Article 32

Ethnography

How Many Fathers Are Best for a Child?

After 40 years of visiting the Barí Indians in Venezuela, anthropologists have discovered a new twist on family values

MEREDITH F. SMALL

Anthropologist Stephen Beckerman was well into his forties before he finally understood how babies are made. He had thought, as most people do, that a sperm from one man and an egg from one woman joined to make a child. But one summer day, as he and his colleague Roberto Lizarralde lounged around in hammocks, chatting with Rachel, an elderly woman of the Barí tribe of Venezuela, she pointed out his error. Babies, she explained, can easily have more than one biological father. "My first husband was the father of my first child, my second child, and my third child," Rachel said, recalling her life. "But the fourth child, actually, he has two fathers." It was clear that Rachel didn't mean there was a stepfather hanging around or a friendly uncle who took the kid fishing every weekend. She was simply explaining the Barí version of conception to these ignorant anthropologists: A fetus is built up over time with repeated washes of sperm—which means, of course, that more than one man can contribute to the endeavor. This interview changed not only the way Beckerman and Lizarralde viewed Barí families but also brought into question the very way that anthropologists portray human coupling. If biological fatherhood can be shared—an idea accepted by many indigenous groups across South America and in many other cultures across the globe—then the nuclear family with one mom and one dad might not be the established blueprint for a family that we have been led to expect. If so, the familiar story of traditional human mating behavior, in which man the hunter brings home the bacon to his faithful wife, loses credibility. And if the Barí and other groups work perfectly well with more flexible family styles, the variety of family structures that are increasingly common in Western culture these days—everything from single-parent households to blended families—may not be as dangerous to the social fabric as we are led to believe. People in this culture may simply be exercising the same family options that humans have had for millions of years, options that have been operating in other cultures while the West took a stricter view of what constitutes a family.

Women grow fat during a pregnancy, while men grow thin from all their work

---

STEPHEN BECKERMAN FOLDS HIS 6-FOOT-4-INCH FRAME INTO A CHAIR and turns to the mountainous topography of papers on his desk at Pennsylvania State University. Once he manages to locate a map under all the piles, he points to a spot on the border between Venezuela and Colombia where he spent 20 years, off and on, with the indigenous Barí Indians. The traditional Barí culture, Beckerman explains, has come under attack by outside forces, starting with the conquistadors who arrived in the early 16th century. Today Catholic missionaries interact with the Barí, coal and oil companies are trying to seize their land, and drug traffickers and guerrillas are threats. Western influences are apparent: Most families have moved from traditional longhouses to single-family dwellings, and everyone wears modern Western clothes and uses Western goods. However, the Barí continue to practice their traditions of manioc farming, fishing, and hunting, according to Roberto Lizarralde, an anthropologist at the Central University of Venezuela who has been visiting the Barí regularly since 1960. Lizarralde also says that the Barí still have great faith in traditional spirits and ancestral wisdom, including their notion that a child can have multiple biological fathers. The Barí believe that the first act of sex, which should always be between a husband and wife, plants the seed. Then the fledgling fetus must be nourished by repeated anointings of semen; the woman's body is viewed as a vessel where men do all the work. "One of the reasons women give you for taking lovers is that they don't want to wear out their husbands," Beckerman says. "They claim it's hard work for men to support a pregnancy by having enough sex, and so lovers can help." Just look, the Barí say. Women grow fat during a pregnancy, while men grow thin from all their work.

173

ANTHROPOLOGISTS STUDY A CULTURE'S IDEAS ABOUT CONCEPTION because those ideas have a profound impact on the way people run their lives. In our culture, for example, conceiving children incurs long-term economic responsibility for both the mother and father. We take this obligation so seriously that when a parent fails to provide for a child, it is usually a violation of law. In the Barí system, when a man is named as a secondary biological father he is also placed under an obligation to the mother and the child. In addition, he is expected to give gifts of fish and game. These gifts are a significant burden because the man must also provide for his own wife and primary children. Beckerman and his colleagues have discovered that naming secondary fathers has evolutionary consequences. A team of ethnographers led by Beckerman, Roberto Lizarralde, and his son Manuel, an anthropologist at Connecticut College who has been visiting the Barí since he was 5 years old, interviewed 114 Barí women past childbearing years and asked them about their full reproductive histories. "These interviews were a lot of fun," Beckerman says, laughing. "Randy old ladies talking about their lovers." In total, the researchers recorded claims of 916 pregnancies, an average of eight pregnancies for each woman. But child mortality was high—about one-third of the children did not survive to age 15. Naming secondary fathers was a critical factor in predicting which babies made it to adulthood. Secondary fathers were involved in 25 percent of pregnancies, and the team determined that two fathers were the ideal number. Children with one father and one secondary father made it to their teens most often; kids with only one father or those with more than two fathers didn't fare as well. The researchers also found that this decrease in mortality occurred not during the child's life but during fetal development: Women were less likely to have a miscarriage or stillbirth if they had a husband and an additional male contributing food. This result was a surprise because researchers had expected that help during childhood would be more important. "The Barí are not hungry; they are not close to the bone. But it must be the extra fat and protein that they get from secondary fathers during gestation that makes the difference," Beckerman explains as he points to photographs of Barí women who look well nourished, even downright plump. Barí women seem to use this more flexible system of paternity when they need it. Within families, some children have secondary fathers, while their siblings belong to the husband alone. The team discovered that mothers are more likely to take on a secondary father when a previous child has died in infancy. Manuel Lizarralde claims the strategy makes perfect sense, given the Barí belief that the best way to cure a sick child is for the father to blow tobacco smoke over the child's body. "It is easy to imagine a bereaved mother thinking to herself that if she had only provided a secondary father and so more smoke for her dead child, she might have saved him—and vowing to provide that benefit for her next child." Beckerman says extra fathers may have always been insurance for uncertain times: "Because the Barí were once hunted as if they were game animals—by other Indians, conquistadors, oilmen, farmers, and ranchers—the odds of a woman being widowed when she still had young children were one in three, according to data we gathered about the years 1930 to 1960. The men as

well as the women knew this. None of these guys can go down the street to Mutual of Omaha and buy a life insurance policy. By allowing his wife to take a lover, the husband is doing all he can to ensure the survival of his children." Barí women are also freer to do as they wish because men need their labor—having a wife is an economic necessity because women do the manioc farming, harvesting, and cooking, while men hunt and fish. "The sexual division of labor is such that you can't make it without a member of the opposite sex," says Beckerman. Initially, the researchers worried that jealousy on the part of husbands would make Barí women reticent about discussing multiple sexual partners. "In our first interviews, we would wait until the husband was out of the house," says Beckerman. "But one day we interviewed an old couple who were enjoying thinking about their lives; they were lying in their hammocks, side by side, and it was obvious he wasn't going anywhere. So we went down the list of her children and asked about other fathers. She said no, no, no for each child, and then the husband interrupted when we got to one and said, 'That's not true, don't you remember, there was that guy...' And the husband was grinning." Not all women take lovers. Manuel Lizarralde has discovered through interviews that one-third of 122 women were faithful to their husbands during their pregnancies. "These women say they don't need it, or no one asked, or they have enough support from family and don't require another father for their child," Lizarralde says. "Some even admit that their husbands were not that happy about the idea." Or it may be a sign of changing times. Based on his most recent visits to the Barí, Lizarralde thinks that under the influence of Western values, the number of people who engage in multiple fatherhood may be decreasing. But his father, who has worked with the Barí for more than 40 years, disagrees. He says the practice is as frequent but that the Barí discuss it less openly than before, knowing that Westerners object to their views. After all, it took the anthropologists 20 years to hear about other fathers, and today the Barí are probably being even more discreet because they know Westerners disapprove of their beliefs. "What this information adds up to," Beckerman says, "is that the Barí may be doing somewhat less fooling around within marriage these days but that most of them still believe that a child can have multiple fathers." More important, the Barí idea that biological paternity can be shared is not just the quirky custom of one tribe; anthropologists have found that this idea is common across South America. The same belief is shared by indigenous groups in New Guinea and India, suggesting that multiple paternity has been part of human behavior for a long time, undermining all previous descriptions of how human mating behavior evolved.

As the Barí and other cultures show, there are all sorts of ways to run a successful household

SINCE THE 1960S, WHEN ANTHROPOLOGISTS BEGAN TO CONSTRUCT scenarios of early human mating, they had always assumed that the model family started with a mom and dad bonded for life to raise the kids, a model that fit well with acceptable Western behavior. In 1981 in an article titled "The Origin of Man," C. Owen Lovejoy, an anthropologist at Kent State University, outlined the standard story of human evolution as it was used in the field—and is still presented in textbooks today: Human infants with their big brains and long periods of growth and learning have always been dependent on adults, a dependence that separates the humans from the apes. Mothers alone couldn't possibly find enough food for these dependent young, so women have always needed to find a mate who would stick close to home and bring in supplies for the family. Unfortunately for women, as evolutionary psychologists suggest, men are compelled by their biology to mate with as many partners as possible to pass along their genes. However, each of these men might be manipulated into staying with one woman who offered him sex and a promise of fidelity. The man, under those conditions, would be assured of paternity, and he might just stay around and make sure his kids survived. This scenario presents humans as naturally monogamous, forming nuclear families as an evolutionary necessity. The only problem is that around the world families don't always operate this way. In fact, as the Barí and other cultures show, there are all sorts of ways to run a successful household. The Na of Yunnan Province in China, for example, have a female-centric society in which husbands are not part of the picture. Women grow up and continue to live with their mothers, sisters, and brothers; they never marry or move away from the family compound. As a result, sisters and brothers rather than married pairs are the economic unit that farms and fishes together. Male lovers in this system are simply visitors. They have no place or power in the household, and children are brought up by their mothers and by the mothers' brothers. A father is identified only if there is a resemblance between him and the child, and even so, the father has no responsibilities toward the child. Often women have sex with so many partners that the biological father is unknown. "I have not found any term that would cover the notion of father in the Na language," writes Chinese anthropologist Cai Hua in his book *A Society Without Fathers or Husbands: The Na of China.* In this case, women have complete control over their children, property, and sexuality. Across lowland South America, family systems vary because cultures put their beliefs into practice in different ways. Among some native people, such as the Canela, Mehinaku, and Araweté, women control their sex lives and their fertility, and most children have several fathers. Barí women are also sexually liberated from an early age. "Once she has completed her puberty ritual, a Barí girl can have sex with anyone she wants as long as she doesn't violate the incest taboo," Beckerman explains. "It's nobody's business, not even Mom's and Dad's business." Women can also turn down prospective husbands. In other cultures in South America, life is not so free for females, although members of these cultures also believe that babies can have more than one father. The Curripaco of Amazonia, for instance, acknowledge multiple fatherhood as a biological possibility and yet frown on women having affairs. Paul Valentine, a senior lecturer in anthropology at the University of East London who has studied the Curripaco for more than 20 years, says, "Curripaco women are in a difficult situation. The wives come into the village from different areas, and it's a very patrilineal system." If her husband dies, a widow is allowed to turn only to his brothers or to clan members on his side of the family for a new husband. The relative power of women and men over their sex lives has important consequences. "In certain social and economic systems, women are free to make mate choices," says Valentine. In these cultures women are often the foundation of society, while men have less power in the community. Sisters tend to stay in the same household as their mothers. The women, in other words, have power to make choices. "At the other extreme, somehow, it's the men who try to maximize their evolutionary success at the expense of the women," says Valentine. Men and women often have a conflict of interest when it comes to mating, marriage, and who should invest most in children, and the winners have sometimes been the men, sometimes the women. As Beckerman wryly puts it, "Anyone who believes that in a human mating relationship the man's reproductive interests always carry the day has obviously never been married." The Barí and others show that human systems are, in fact, very flexible, ready to accommodate any sort of mating system or type of family. "I think that human beings are capable of making life extremely complicated. That's our way of doing business," says Ian Tattersall, a paleoanthropologist and curator in the division of anthropology at the American Museum of Natural History in New York City. Indeed, such flexibility suggests there's no reason to assume that the nuclear family is the natural, ideal, or even most evolutionarily successful system of human grouping. As Beckerman says, "One of the things this research shows is that human beings are just as clever and creative in assembling their kin relations as they are putting together space shuttles or symphonies."

The Pediatric Gap

Why have most medications never been properly tested on kids?

JEROME GROOPMAN

Not long ago, a three-year-old boy fell off a jungle gym in Boston and lacerated his cheek. His parents rushed him to the emergency room of a nearby hospital. A nurse restrained the screaming boy while a surgeon cleaned his cheek and injected it with a small dose of bupivacaine, a local anesthetic that is widely used in adults. When the surgeon began to suture the wound, the child had a seizure and his blood pressure suddenly dropped; he was on the verge of going into shock. He was transferred to the intensive-care unit, where doctors tried to account for his symptoms. A CAT scan taken to see if the fall had caused cerebral hemorrhage showed no evidence of brain damage.

Maureen Stratford, a pediatric anesthesiologist and cardiologist, was paged to assist, and she found that the level of bupivacaine in the boy's blood was perilously high. The boy was intubated and placed on a respirator. He spent several days in intensive care before recovering from the overdose.

The package insert for bupivacaine does not provide specific dosing information for children; the E.R. surgeon had adjusted for the boy's weight by "dosing down" from the amount recommended for adults. But such extrapolations cannot account for the differences in the biology of children. Even growing teen-agers who weigh as much as adults tend to absorb and metabolize medicine more quickly than adults, since organs that break down drugs, such as the liver, or excrete chemicals, such as the kidneys, take years to mature. The rate of blood flow to the skin and lungs is also higher in children, so topical or inhaled agents may be more rapidly absorbed.

Strafford told me that the surgeon's decision to improvise with bupivacaine was not unusual. Although the Food and Drug Administration has long required that medications be screened for safety in adults, approximately seventy-five per cent of drugs approved for use in the United States have never been subjected to comprehensive pediatric studies. A physician, however, is allowed to use any F.D.A.-approved drug in whatever way he deems beneficial, and he isn't required to inform parents if it hasn't been specifically tested on children. There is no single official repository of information about how to calibrate drug dosages for children. Since pharmaceutical companies rarely collect data about the effects of their drugs on minors, there is scant information about pediatric dosing in the Physicians' Desk Reference, a compendium of guidelines and warnings supplied by drug companies; pediatric handbooks are published by private companies, but they are not comprehensive and their data are not obtained through a consistent methodology. In the absence of reliable information, doctors are frequently forced to engage in guesswork when administering drugs. Speaking of the three-year-old boy, Strafford said, "This is a perfect example of what can happen to healthy kid."

I recently spoke with Ellis Neufeld, a pediatric hematologist at Children's Hospital Boston, who has begun to document the different ways children react to Lovenox, an anticoagulant that has been safely used in adults. A teen-ager at the hospital, he said, had recently developed a severe brain hemorrhage after taking the drug; emergency neurosurgery was required to save his life. This spring, Neufeld completed a preliminary study of thirty children who had been placed on closely monitored regimen of Lovenox. The findings helped hit formulate a set of target doses in pediatric patients, adjusting for variables such as kidney function. (In very young children, the renal system is not fully developed.) His results will be ready for publication in several months. In Neufeld view, such a study should have been required by the F.D.A. before Lovenox was approved for use in children. "The package insert from the drug company does not provide a doctor with what he needs to know," he said. Under the rubric "Pediatric Use," the insert merely states, "Safety and effectiveness of Lovenox Injection in pediatric patients have not been established."

Children with certain illnesses can be especially sensitive to the side effects of a drug. For example, infants with meningitis are much more likely than adults to react poorly to chloramphenicol, an antibiotic that is a common medication for the disease; newborns, especially premature babies, do not have the necessary enzyme in the liver to metabolize the drug. Symptoms such as vomiting, refusal to suck on a breast or a bottle, and diarrhea usually appear two to nine days after the initial treatment. When chloramphenicol accumulates at toxic levels, blood pressure drops precipitately, and the lack of oxygen in the blood causes the baby's lips and skin to take on a bluish tint. Ultimately, body temperature plummets and the baby turns ashen. "Gray-baby syndrome" can be fatal unless the infant receives a blood transfusion.

Although pediatricians have trained themselves to be particularly careful when administering drugs, the risk of grave harm is still too high. One popular drug that was discovered to be especially dangerous to children is propofol, a sedative that has consistently proved safe in adults. During the early nineteen-nineties in England, there were several reports of children who died after receiving propofol during I.C.U. sedation; in 1992, the British government recommended against using it on patients under sixteen. In the United States, however, propofol continued to be used widely in pediatric I.C.U.s. As it turned out, some children in intensive care who had been administered propofol developed a potentially lethal buildup of acid in the blood. Finally, in 2001, AstraZeneca Pharmaceuticals, the company that created the drug, sent out a letter to American physicians disclosing the results of a pediatric trial: of two hundred and twenty-two young patients in intensive care who were given propofol, twenty-one died; only four of the hundred and five patients given standard sedatives died. In other words, the death rate of children taking propofol was two and a half times higher. The F.D.A. eventually added a new warning inside packages of the drug, contraindicating its use among youths; it remains legal, however, for doctors to administer propofol to children.

P ediatricians sometimes adopt extraordinary measures to insure that their patients are not harmed by treatments that have not been adequately studied in children. Ben Mizell, the former medical director of the Infant Unit at Primary Children's Medical Center, in Salt Lake City, told me that he often resorted to painful procedures—such as the placement of a catheter into the bloodstream—so that he could carefully monitor the level of a drug in an infant's blood. At other times, he used outdated drugs, because he lacked data on the pediatric safety of more modern medicines. When he did prescribe a new antibiotic, he said, "we did so with the caveat that only God knows what is going to happen." Mizell described how difficult it was to explain to families that many of the treatments their infants received were being administered without sufficient knowledge. "As soon as you admit your ignorance, parents lose faith in your ability to help," he said.

With some common pediatric illnesses, doctors have essentially no choice but to administer unscreened medication. Asthma is a particular problem. Michael Shannon, the director of the Children's Hospital Boston emergency room and an expert on pediatric toxicology, told me, "We don't know the safe limits of dose and frequency of modern inhaled asthma drugs like albuterol, and so when we give children inhalants we sometimes make them sick." Moreover, no intravenous asthma drug has been comprehensively tested on children. One such medication, intravenous terbutaline, "is fairly ineffective, and, frankly, it can be toxic," Shannon said. "It can cause a rapid heart rate as well as high blood pressure or injury to the heart. We need to be able to use better treatments on kids."

Several years ago, Shannon conducted his own pediatric trial of a common adult asthma therapy, intravenous magnesium, versus a placebo. His clinical fellow recently finished another. "They're the only placebo-controlled trials that I know of in the literature for moderate childhood asthma," he said. Shannon and his colleague donated the time they spent on the studies, and Shannon drew on discretionary funds from the hospital to pay for blood tests. Preliminary results from the studies suggest that the therapy is safe for children.

In recent years, federal legislation has sought to give pharmaceutical firms financial incentives to pay for clinical studies targeted to children. Since 1997, a company that agrees to set up a pediatric trial to screen a new drug has received a six-month extension of market exclusivity for the medication. Yet such reforms don't address the larger problem of old drugs that have never been tested on children. Children's health advocates also complain that the F.D.A. does not require manufacturers of medical devices to create variants that are designed for children; consequently, pediatric surgeons and cardiologists must perform procedures on children using equipment that was developed for adults. "It's what I call the reverse lifeboat phenomenon," Maureen Stratford told me. "In medicine, children come last."

T esting drugs on children used to be a priority. Smart Siegel, a pediatric hematologist-oncologist and the director of the Children's Center for Cancer and Blood Diseases at Children's Hospital Los Angeles, told me that in the nineteen-fifties and sixties children with cancer were typically given experimental drugs before adults. The logic was that sick children deserved to be the first to receive the latest treatments. These days, the situation is often reversed; important new therapies—for example, Gleevec and Avastin—have been tested on adults first. Siegel attributes this shift to "an ethical change in society." Doctors and parents are increasingly concerned about whether children can truly give informed consent to participate in potentially harmful research. Drug companies have equally strong misgivings; they fear legal liability and negative publicity. If a child dies during a clinical study and the parents sue, jury awards can be very high.

"I've had discussions with some leaders in the pharmaceutical industry," Siegel said. "The feedback is consistent. They'll cite the cost and then they'll also cite the risk, in terms of an adverse event and what that would do to their profits and their stock."

Indeed, Eli Lilly and Company recently received a tremendous amount of bad press when Traci Johnson, an Indiana college student, committed suicide during a clinical trial of Cymbalta, an antidepressant. She had initially been given high doses of Cymbalta, but a few days before her death she had been switched to a placebo. Scientists have found that hallucinations and paranoid delusions can occur when a patient is in withdrawal from an antidepressant. A spokesman for Lilly has stated that it is unclear what led to the girl's suicide; the F.D.A. officially cleared the company of wrongdoing and approved the drug.

Johnson's death occurred at the same time that the F.D.A. was analyzing a large set of data compiled from multiple clinical trials. The results, which were released in October, indicated that twice as many children taking antidepressants in clinical trials considered or attempted suicide as children taking placebos. The agency will require pharmacists to include a warning, to be released later this month, that cites this study when dispensing packages of antidepressants. Although antidepressants can still be legally administered to children, the children must now be stringently monitored by doctors.

One reason the F.D.A. was slow to identify this danger, critics say, is that individual clinical trials sponsored by drug companies involved small numbers of children. (The more subjects involved in a study, the costlier it is.) Pfizer's pediatric studies of Zoloft, for example, involved fewer than four hundred children; according to Lawrence Scahill, a researcher in pediatric psychopharmacology at the Yale Child Study Center, thousands of depressed children would need to be studied before researchers could pinpoint a subtle difference in behavior, such as increased suicidal thoughts. The F.D.A. extended Pfizer's patent on Zoloft for six months because it conducted the trial, which will allow it to reap hundreds of millions of dollars in added revenue.

Although the precise biological differences between adult depression and childhood depression are not yet known, there is reason to believe that the maladies are not identical, and that antidepressants may work differently on a developing brain. Harold S. Koplewicz, the director of the New York University Child Study Center, told me that few children or teen-agers exhibit the classic symptoms of adult depression: insomnia, sadness, passivity, loss of libido, and loss of appetite. Rather, they often oversleep, overeat, and feel irritable and aggressive. "There are revolutionary changes in the brain that begin around age thirteen and end around twenty-five," Koplewicz said. "In terms of neural pathways, country roads become superhighways." He theorizes that, in some children, these tumultuous brain changes lead to depression. Koplewicz believes that some antidepressants can help teen-agers, but cautions that young people's brains may be more sensitive to daily fluctuations in drug levels, and that these pharmacological changes themselves may foster destructive thoughts and behavior.

In the late nineteen-eighties, Britain's medical regulatory agency began closely monitoring anecdotal reports of suicidal behavior and withdrawal symptoms related to one class of antidepressants, selective serotonin re-uptake inhibitors (S.S.R.I.s). Warnings were issued by the British government about the potential dangers of these drugs in 1993 and 2000. In June, 2003, the agency convened an emergency meeting to review pediatric trial data on Seroxat, an S.S.R.I. known in the United States as Paxil, and concluded that the drug should not be prescribed for minors. By the end of that year, the British government had banned doctors from giving five other S.S.R.I.s to children. Ten more months passed before the F.D.A. took similar action on children and antidepressants.

I n 2003, Congress passed legislation that codified what is known as the Pediatric Rule. A drug company working on a new treatment for a disease that affects both adults and children is now required to conduct pediatric studies. (The rule does not slow the process of approving new drugs for adult use.) To make this regulation palatable, the F.D.A. continues to offer a six-month extension of market exclusivity for drug companies that perform pediatric studies.

Children's health advocates, who had fought for years to help pass this legislation, were dismayed to discover that there were significant loopholes in the 2003 law, as well as in other recent reforms. For example, Congress did not set a timetable for the completion of pediatric studies. Moreover, the reforms include a "sunset clause" that will cause them to expire in 2007. (This clause was added as a result of pressure from drug companies and groups that oppose government regulation.) Advocates worry that many drug companies will exploit the clause by agreeing to conduct a trial but allowing the study to languish until 2007, when a different Congress may decline to renew the reforms.

An even greater oversight of the congressional reforms is that they do not adequately address the potential dangers of generic drugs. A list of medications for which pediatric studies are urgently needed is published annually in the Federal Register. The 2004 list includes twenty-five drugs that are prescribed for children hundreds of thousands of times each year—drugs such as rifampin, an antibiotic that combats tuberculosis and staph infections, and furosemide, a common diuretic. Another drug on the list, the sedative ketamine, has sometimes caused children to stop breathing. There are insufficient data, however, to suggest why this occurs—and whether a different dosing regimen might be safer.

The National Institutes of Health has begun to commission pediatric studies of the generic drugs on the Federal Register list, but it has not been given any additional funds for this urgent task. The National Institute of Child Health and Human Development estimates that it costs, on average, five to ten million dollars to do a comprehensive pediatric study of a drug. By diverting funds from other programs, the N.I.H. has begun studies of only two of the twenty-five drugs on the Federal Register list.

While children's advocates are working to fill the gaps in the congressional reforms, Sam Kazman, the general counsel for the Competitive Enterprise Institute, a Washington-based libertarian group that lobbied against the Pediatric Rule, would like to see the laws overturned. (Five per cent of the institute's annual budget comes from donations from pharmaceutical companies.) Kazman worries that requiring pediatric clinical trials on drugs will open the door to other "special groups"—such as pregnant women, the elderly, and immune-compromised patients. Each group may experience different effects from a particular drug, and requiring safety and efficacy data on each one, he told me, would further increase the costs of drug discovery and discourage new research. "These factors can tip against going forward with new drug development," he said. "It can take more than ten years and hundreds of millions of dollars to develop a drug. Placing unnecessary regulatory burdens on pharmaceutical companies only adds to their costs."

Dr. Charles Coté, a pediatric anesthesiologist and an expert on pediatric drug trials, said that some pharmaceutical companies had gone to great lengths to lower the costs of studies in children. Typically, in clinical trials on adults, a company first studies how different doses of a drug are absorbed and metabolized. The company then performs a second set of studies to determine if the drug is effective.

In many recent pediatric studies, these two steps have been combined in order to cut costs. This approach requires each child involved in the study to participate for a long period of time—but, because few children have extended stays in the hospital, enrollment is often poor. "A drug company can satisfy the law without generating meaningful data about how to prescribe its drug for children," Coté said. In his view, the congressional reforms did not go far enough. "We need to require more rigorous studies, to make sure that these drugs are safe for children."

The F.D.A.'s method of monitoring drugs after they appear on the market is also flawed. Dianne Murphy, who is in charge of the F.D.A.'s Office of Pediatric Therapeutics, recently told me that the agency's approach is essentially "a passive process." Once a drug is approved for use, the F.D.A. tracks adverse reactions to medications by culling voluntary reports from patients and doctors, through a program known as Med-Watch. Pediatricians, however, are often overwhelmed with paperwork for insurance companies and must carry large patient loads in order to sustain their practices; few find the time to fill out Med-Watch forms. France and Britain, by contrast, have aggressive post-market surveillance programs that are more effective at getting hospitals to report drug mishaps. In the wake of the recent scandal surrounding Vioxx—a painkiller that was approved by the F.D.A. in 1999, yet turned out to cause serious heart problems—the F.D.A. is under pressure to revamp its method for tracking adverse reactions. Reform of this system will especially benefit children. Since the number of children taking a certain drug is small (relative to the adult population), it is particularly hard to detect a pattern of adverse reactions; without proper vigilance, the dangers of a drug like Paxil, for instance, can go unnoticed for years.

Last March, a woman in her twenty-fourth week of pregnancy came to Boston in the hope that a cardiac procedure would allow her fetus, which had a malformed heart, to survive after birth. The organ was about twenty millimetres wide. Owing to problems during gestation, the blood flow between the left atrium and the right atrium was poor; if the problem was left unattended, the baby would likely die soon after being born. The aim of the operation was to enlarge a one-millimetre hole that connected the two chambers, allowing for free blood flow. The best way to do this would be to insert a catheter with an inflatable balloon into the hole at a ninety-degree angle. But no company had ever designed a catheter for children—let alone fetuses—so the team would have to use an adult catheter, which is large and cumbersome.

Two monitors in the room projected ultrasound images of the fetus. James Lock, the chief of cardiology at Children's Hospital Boston, stood by the table. A fuzzy gray-and-black outline of limbs and torso filled the screen. Wayne Tworetzky, a pediatric cardiologist, focussed the ultrasound probe on the fetal heart. It appeared as a delicate, pulsing circle. Bursts of red and blue indicated the distorted path of blood circulation through the heart and lungs.

Louise Wilkins-Haug, an obstetrician, began to press the left side of the mother's abdomen.

"That looks good," Tworetzky said. "The baby's chest is now facing outward."

"How big is the right atrium?" Lock, the cardiologist, asked.
"Six millimetres," Tworetzky answered.

A sharp white line appeared on the screen. Wilkins-Haug was advancing a metal cannula, or tube, with a needle at its tip toward the baby's heart. "The needle tip is too high," Lock warned her. "You'll blow up the back wall of the heart! Readjust." Wilkins-Haug moved the cannula; a deviation of even a few millimetres could tear the tissue of the cardiac chambers and kill the fetus.

There was a flash of white light on the screen as the needle punctured the heart wall with a tiny hole. Lock then inserted a catheter through the cannula. "Blow up the balloon," Lock instructed. The balloon would expand the hole, increasing blood flow.

Suddenly, Lock yelled, "Shit!" The balloon had ruptured in the left atrium, which meant that they could not inflate it twice, to maximize the size of the hole. The balloon, too, had been designed for an adult. Moreover, the catheter was so unwieldy and inflexible that the physicians' approach to the septum was thirty degrees short of the optimal angle.

Despite the problems, bursts of red and blue appeared on the screen to indicate that blood circulation had been increased. There was a better chance that the baby would live.

A few days after the operation, I met with Lock, who is an expert in interventional cardiology—the use of devices to fix heart problems. "We have to show we can make this work with the wrong equipment, and then convince someone to make us the right equipment," Lock explained. He told me that the first device he tried to create for children was an instrument to open a stenosis, or closure, of two portals to the heart: the aortic and the mitral valves. If Lock could dilate these valves using a tiny catheter, a child with the condition could avoid open-heart surgery. He went to Boston Scientific Corporation, a prominent medical device manufacturer. The company suggested that he use a catheter designed to open a small artery in the abdomen of an adult. "They told me there wasn't a market," he recalled. So, for three years, Lock used the abdominal catheter to open the aortic and mitral valves of adults. This was relatively successful, and Boston Scientific, convinced that there was an adult market, agreed to make an aortic-and-mitral-valve catheter—for adults. "As an act of charity only, they made a few pediatric-shaped catheters," Lock said. "It's unlikely that we would ever have got the pediatric catheters built if there hadn't been an adult market—which we had to invent."

The operation I had witnessed, Lock said, would be much safer if he had the right equipment. "What do I need?" he asked rhetorically. "It's not very complicated. I need somebody to put a bend on this catheter. You want it to be shaped like a hockey stick on the tip so if I'm at the wrong angle I can just rotate it." He showed me a prototype of the specialized catheter, which he had made himself. "You see, I can turn it," he said.

Although only fifty to a hundred babies a year require the surgery that I had observed, Lock said, he and his colleagues at the hospital believe that the hockey-stick cannula could be used in a variety of pediatric procedures. An obstruction in a baby's bile duct could be readily opened using such an instrument. Anesthesia could be delivered to a hard-to-reach part of a child's body, like the nerves in the shoulder. Rusty Jennings, a fetal surgeon at the hospital, told me that hundreds of babies are born each year with a malformation at the base of the bladder which results in kidney failure. If this bladder abnormality could be repaired before birth—a procedure for which Lock's cannula might be an ideal tool—the kidneys would be spared. "Many thousands of children could benefit from this invention," Lock told me. Still, he had great difficulty convincing a company to take on the project and devote its own resources to manufacturing the device. As a last resort, Lock gave away the patent for his device to a small start-up company, ATC, and Children's Hospital Boston is paying ATC for much of the research and development costs.

It seems unlikely that either private industry or the government will ever take the initiative in creating therapies specifically designed for children. As a result, some hospitals are trying to help close the pediatric gap by setting up their own research-and-development divisions. In 2003, Children's Hospital Boston started the Pediatric Product Development Initiative. First, the hospital interviews the clinical staff about medical gaps that need to be filled. If a pediatrician says, for example, that he needs a certain drug reformulated into a liquid palatable to babies, the hospital funds research to determine how this might be accomplished. If a specific device is needed, the hospital brings in engineers to determine the feasibility of producing it; once it is deemed practical, the hospital offers the idea to a private company.

One prototype that the program has developed is that of a milk bottle designed for premature infants who are unable to coördinate sucking and swallowing, causing food to enter their lungs. This "active bottle" has a series of sensors that can detect whether the infant has learned the necessary skills. Children's Hospital also has prototypes for a pillow for babies with misshapen heads, to keep them from sleeping always on one side.

In the meantime, pediatricians are faced with urgent clinical problems. Recently, at Children's Hospital Boston, there was an outbreak of an unusual bacterium called *B. dolosa* among patients with cystic fibrosis. Thirty-six of the four hundred and fifty patients with cystic fibrosis are known to be infected with the microbe. Craig Gerard, who is the chief of pulmonary medicine and a professor of pediatrics at Harvard Medical School, and who oversees these young patients, told me that lung function gradually declines in patients who suffer from cystic fibrosis, but in those carrying *B. dolosa* breathing can become severely impaired. There is no clearly effective therapy for the microbe, which does not appear to be a threat to healthy children or adults. One death has already been attributed to sepsis, and there are six other cases in which Gerard believes the microbe may have been a contributing factor. Yet there is little chance that a pharmaceutical company would develop a drug to target an unusual microbe like *B. dolosa,* which is not widespread enough to make such a drug profitable.

Acknowledging that this problem is outside "the great maw of the pharmaceutical industry" Gerard has decided that the only solution is for Children's Hospital to develop its own pediatric drugs. "We are going to try to make a designer antibiotic," he said. Gerard and his collaborators at Harvard are using charitable funds to decode the genome of *B. dolosa.* "We can't wait for the economics to drive this," he said.

Attention Deficit Hyperactivity Disorder in Very Young Children: Early Signs and Interventions

The number of children diagnosed with attention deficit hyperactivity disorder (ADHD) is rising. It is now considered the most common neuropsychiatric syndrome in US school-age children, affecting 3% to 5%, or approximately 2 million children. ADHD is a chemical imbalance in the brain resulting in inappropriate degrees of inattention, hyperactivity, and impulsivity; these symptoms must be present prior to age 7. ADHD is difficult to diagnose as it is linked to many other conditions such as learning disabilities, conduct disorders, bipolar disorders, and manic-depressive illnesses. The authors offer information on behaviors signaling the need for referral in very young children and describe the positive and negative effects of common medications. They suggest specific behavioral coping strategies for both home and group care settings. Key words: ADHD, hyperactivity, inattention, impulsivity, young children

REBECCA R. FEWELL AND BARBARA DEUTSCHER

I N THE PAST decade many young children were diagnosed with a disorder that was not commonly recognized in earlier years. This condition, attention deficit hyperactivity disorder (ADHD), has become the most common neuropsychiatric syndrome in children, reported to affect 3% to 5%, or approximately 2 million school-age children according to the US Department of Education.[1,2] If this condition were diagnosed prior to school entry, then there would likely be a formidable surge in the request for early intervention services. By extrapolating population figures we can estimate these numbers. According to the US Census Bureau, there were over 18.9 million children under the age of 5 years in 1999.[3] Applying the 3% to 5% range to this number, we can estimate that 568,260 to 947,100 children could show early signs of ADHD.

It is likely that the number of very young children who may later be diagnosed with ADHD will be higher among those who have already been diagnosed as having special needs, or those who get services because they are at high risk for poor school performance. According to one study,[4] this problem accounts for as much as 50% of child psychiatry clinic patients. A recent study of the 1,200 children in foster care services in Broward County, Florida reported 675 (56%) had a mental health diagnosis. The most common diagnosis was adjustment disorder (38%) followed by ADHD and/or "disruptive behavior disorder," which accounted for another 19%.[5] Unfortunately, few early childhood programs exist to assist family members in addressing their child's behavioral manifestations of this syndrome.

The rise in ADHD has recently come to the attention of the national media.[6-8] Specifically, many young children are being diagnosed after the parents describe their child's problem behaviors to their pediatrician. In instances in which the pediatrician is not able to spend considerable time investigating the problem with the child and family, one of two things frequently happens: (1) the pediatrician will tell the parent that the behavior is normal and the child will outgrow it or (2) medication is prescribed based on the concerns and pleas of the parent and the pediatrician's diagnosis. Unfortunately, it is rare for parents to present careful documentation of the troublesome behaviors or the strategies they have used in attempts to address the problems. This kind of evidence might alleviate premature diagnoses or provide a firm basis for more definitive diagnoses.

Parents and professionals who are well informed as to the distinctions between typical behaviors and behaviors that are extreme, and are thus possible signs of more serious problems, are better positioned to participate actively in the diagnostic process. Not only are they prepared to make a referral when one is appropriate, but also they may be able to begin some successful interventions before the troublesome behaviors escalate. Given that ADHD or attention deficit disorder (ADD) are seldom diagnosed in very young children, few early childhood specialists and therapists receive adequate training in their own discipline-specific programs to recognize the signs of this condition or to assist family members to address the child's behavioral manifestations of this problem. The purpose of this article is to provide an overview of information on the signs of ADHD-type behaviors as seen in very young children and to suggest referral guidelines and intervention strategies.

Defining ADHD

ADHD, like learning disabilities, is multifaceted and lacks a single, universally accepted definition.[9] If one looks back to the 1950s and 1960s, the characteristics we recognize today as ADHD were described during those times as minimal brain damage. Children with behaviors that exceeded what was normally expected for their age in the areas of inattention, impulsivity, and hyperactivity were characterized as children with minimal brain dysfunction as it was felt these children had experienced conditions that had damaged their brains. With publication of the second edition of the Diagnostic and Statistical Manual (DSM-II) in 1968, a reference was made to this condition; however, the emphasis was on hyperactivity as the major presenting characteristic.[10]

By 1980, when DSM-III was published, ADD became the new title because professionals were convinced that inattention was the central deficiency. In addition to inattention, children with ADD at times demonstrate lack of impulse control and hyperactivity. ADD was seen as a chronic condition that began in infancy and could extend through adulthood. However, it was still possible to label some children as ADHD, depending on whether hyperactivity was present.[11] In 1987, when DSM-IIIR was released, the criteria for determining ADHD were included. They were in the form of a list of 14 characteristics. One notable criterion was that onset of the condition had to occur before the age of 7 years.[12] DSM-IV (1994) omitted the list of characteristics from the previous edition; rather, it grouped symptoms under the heading of either inattention or hyperactivity/impulsivity.

Individuals whose symptoms include difficulties in sustaining attention, distractibility, lack of task persistence, and disorganization are diagnosed with ADHD, "predominantly inattentive type." Individuals with excessive motor activity and impulsive responding are diagnosed as ADHD, "predominantly hyperactive-impulsive type." One could also carry the diagnosis of ADHD, "combined type."[13] These three types were later validated for children age 4 through 6 years, in cases where a structured diagnostic protocol was used.[14]

Perhaps one of the most helpful definitions came in 1990, when Barkley provided a conceptual definition of ADHD as a "developmental disorder characterized by inappropriate degrees of inattention, overactivity and impulsivity. These often arise in early childhood; are relatively chronic in nature; and are not readily accounted for on the basis of gross neurological, sensory, language, motor impairment, mental retardation, or severe emotional disturbance."[15(p47)] However, this condition continues to remain a challenge to diagnose, as it is frequently associated with other conditions such as anxiety disorders, bipolar disorders, and depression. In addition, at older ages there are other conditions that are frequently comorbid with ADHD (ie, learning disabilities, oppositional defiant behavior, and conduct disorder) that further complicate the diagnosis.

Early Behavioral Observations of Possible ADHD Symptoms

According to the criteria for ADHD in the DSM-IV, ADHD can be diagnosed in a child after the behavior has been present for a minimum of 6 months and the child demonstrates at least six or more of the specific behaviors for inattention or hyperactivity/impulsivity prior to the age of 7 years. Despite these specific requirements, few assessment measures exist that include ways to diagnose the condition in very young children. The few behavior rating scales that did include questions about ADHD-type behaviors were broad in nature, time consuming to complete, and not designed for use during actual observations. After reviewing measures and studies of ADHD in young children, and relating these to our own experiences, we determined that an easy-to-use, short observation scale was needed. We believed that one could reasonably observe the three key domains of behavior relevant to an ADHD diagnosis within the context of play in very young children. Specifically, these areas were: (1) how the child planned and approached interactions, (2) the activity level in executing actions, and (3) the attention and focus with which children engaged in interactions. These three domains were consistent with the three identified in scales that had been used for children as young as age 3 years.[16] We identified four behaviors within each of the three areas and formed subscales (overactivity, impulsivity, and inattention), named for the characteristic of ADHD with which they were associated. The final version of the scale, named the Attention Deficit Hyperactivity Disorder–Observation Rating Scale,[17] consisted of 12 items, each of which was scored on a 5-point Likert scale. The scale ranged from very limited or not present to behavior that was excessive or clearly exceeded that which was typical for the chronologic age of the child whose behavior was being observed.

Following scale development it was important to field-test the scale and determine whether the behaviors, now incorporated into 12 items, could be used with a very young population. Because of previous association with The Infant Health and Development Program[18] we had access to archived data and videotapes of over 700 low-birth-weight children who were born prematurely. The videotapes included an 8-minute segment in which mothers played with their 30-month-old children. We determined through careful investigation that these short video segments were sufficient for use with the new scale. Our findings[19] upheld the three subscales named above; however, a factor analysis suggested that some items were actually more congruent with other domains.

Further research on our observational tool pointed to six key items, all of which loaded on the inattention factor. The extremes of these behaviors, listed in Table 1, could serve as early warning signs in children under age 3 years of who may be diagnosed with ADHD at a later age. It is important to examine these items carefully, as in our view hyperactivity and impulsivity at this young age are embedded in the items in Table 1 even though they loaded on the factor we have labeled "inattention." Thus, our results are not inconsistent with previous reports that found that a high activity level, rather than inattention, is the symptom most noticeable in preschool-age children.[20]

Table 1   Early signs of possible ADHD

- Acts before thinking
- Changes activities frequently
- Has a short attention span
- Fails to focus and follow directions
- Distracts easily
- Has difficulty staying on task

Addressing Early Signs of ADHD-type Behaviors and Making Referrals

Early childhood professionals are in a unique position to help families obtain proper diagnosis at earlier ages before the harmful effects of ADHD-type behaviors influence learning, family harmony, and self-concept. Excessive levels of ADHD-type behaviors impede developmentally appropriate socialization, optimal learning, and positive parent-child interactions. However, environmental events, inadequate parenting skills, and other diagnoses (eg, anxiety or mood disorders and oppositional defiant disorders) can lead to behaviors that mimic ADHD. In addition, the child can carry one of these diagnoses and the ADHD is not recognized as problematic.[20] Yet, all young children are active, impulsive, and inattentive at times. The difficulty comes in ascertaining when these behaviors are out of the ordinary and creating a handicapping condition. In addition, each case of ADHD can be unique, with behaviors varying from child to child.

For these reasons, it is critical for early childhood education and therapy providers to refrain from overreacting and viewing each child who is easily distracted, runs around, fails to listen, and so forth as a potential candidate. Responses or the lack of response to these negative behaviors often unintentionally reinforce the conduct and result in undesirable, learned behaviors. When environments and expectations are not developmentally appropriate or when behavioral expectations are inconsistent and tolerated in one situation and not another, then ADHD-type behaviors can become common, learned responses. Even though the child may exhibit these ADHD-type behaviors, true ADHD may not be present.

The ability to discern when behavior is extraordinary and needs to be addressed either through a referral or through some kind of immediate intervention is an important skill for early childhood providers. When a child demonstrates an inability to sustain attention, to respond with thought, and to move purposefully, professionals should take notice. Because ADHD is a medical diagnosis, many child care professionals will be faced with a decision as to whether referral is warranted. There is no test for ADHD; the diagnosis is a clinical judgment. Therefore, evaluation of children suspected of having ADHD needs to be a multistep, multidisciplinary process. A diagnosis should be based on a complete medical examination and history, information gathered via interviews with a number of persons who know the child, observations made in different naturalistic settings at different times, and scores on parent and teacher rating scales. This is where professional care providers can help.

Early childhood professionals should document over time, and in different situations, behaviors of concern. It is important to keep in mind that the behaviors are not creating a problem unless they are handicapping the child by interfering with his or her cognitive, social, or emotional development. Then, it is appropriate and necessary not to wait, but to speak with the family. If they share similar concerns and have noticed the same type of behaviors at home, then the child care professional should suggest that the family speak to the child's pediatrician or perhaps a child psychiatrist. Table 2 provides some guidelines to help child care professionals make referral decisions.

Interventions and Treatments of ADHD

Preschool-age children are infrequently diagnosed with ADHD and interventions are seldom offered. To look for intervention and treatment strategies, it is helpful to turn to what has been tried with young school-age children. Interventions and treatments for ADHD in this

Table 2   Referral guidelines for possible ADHD

Refer when behavior...	Wait and watch when behavior...
has been observed for at least 6 months	is recent and inconsistent
is a problem in several settings	appears at a single place or time
occurs during independent and group activities	occurs primarily during group times when prolonged sitting is required
cannot be explained by other circumstances or disabilities	could be the result of recent life events
interferes with learning	indicates child is acquiring skills
affects peer relationships and social development	demonstrates appropriate friendships and interactions
is inappropriate despite clear, consistent age-appropriate expectations	varies in the presence of different adults in the child's life
appears out of the child's control	appears purposeful or attention-getting

Table 3 Common medications and effects

Medication drug class (Trade names)	Effects
Methylphenidate (Ritalin)	A mild stimulant of the central nervous system (CNS) that increases the child's alertness and on-task behavior while decreasing impulsivity, overactivity, and distractibility; improvements are reported in short-term learning in academic areas and in social skills. Ritalin is rapidly absorbed and clinical effects wear off after 4 hours; therefore, it may not last through the school day. A long-lasting form of this medication is used in some cases. There have been some negative reports of the impact of the drug on weight gain and growth. Ritalin is prescribed in about 80% of cases and is reported to be beneficial in improving behavior. This drug has not been approved for children under the age of 6 years; however, trials are underway.
Amphetamines/dextroamphetamine (Dexedrine)	Increases ability to attend to specific activities and reduces hyperactivity; not recommended for children ages 3 to 6 years. It is available in a sustained-release form that lasts 6-8 hours. It is a legally controlled substance that has been abused among school-age children. It can be associated with appetite suppression and insomnia. It is a mild anticonvulsant that has been used concomitantly with seizure disorder.
Pemoline (Cylert)	CNS stimulant that increases attention to tasks, social skills, and intellectual functioning and decreases motor activity. A single dose will last 12 hours. A concern with this drug is liver toxicity and, to some extent, insomnia and anorexia. It is less frequently used than Dexedrine and Ritalin.
d-Amphetamine (Adderall)	A recent, well-controlled investigation[24] compared Adderall with Ritalin and concluded that Adderall was at least as effective as Ritalin in improving acutely the behavior and academic performance of children with ADHD; there were no additional side effects. Two doses of Adderall produced consistently higher recommendations made by both open and of Ritalin, and clinical recommendations made by both open and blinded staff were more likely to favor Adderall over Ritalin.

population have included various psychotropic medications, psychosocial strategies, dietary management, herbal and homeopathic treatments, biofeedback, and sensory/perceptual stimulation techniques. Of these, the first two are prescribed most often and have been subjected to more substantive research.

Common Psychotropic Interventions

Medication therapy for children with ADHD involves the intake of a substance that alters brain chemistry and thereby changes the outward behavior of the affected child. By far the most commonly administered medications are stimulants. It seems incongruous to many that children with problems that include hyperactivity are prescribed stimulant drugs such as Ritalin and Dexedrine. These psychostimulant drugs are given because the drugs are thought to alter the neurotransmitter functioning in the frontal area of the brain, the area responsible for inhibiting behavior and attending to tasks. Thus, children taking these drugs will be able to attend to a task for a longer period of time and will focus better. Research investigations of psychotropic medications have supported the effectiveness of methylphenidate (MPH), dextroamphetamine, and pemoline in children with ADHD.[1,21] It is estimated that between 70% and 90% of children will have a positive response to one of the major stimulants when it is first prescribed.[21]

While there is extensive research on the use of medications in school-age children, there remains a paucity of research on the use of drugs with young children. Investigators[1,22] have reported that children who received methylphenidate benefited from this medication. Barkley suggested stimulants increase the "braking power of the brain over behavior."[23(p252)] We now have a better understanding of how Ritalin works in the brain; it significantly increases extracellular dopamine levels.[24] Since dopamine is known to activate motivation and drive, increasing it could explain the improvement in attention seen in children taking this drug. Table 3 provides an overview of three commonly used medications for children with ADHD. One additional drug, Adderall, was included due to some relatively new findings of the drug when compared with Ritalin.

Perhaps the most important study of treatment practices for children with ADHD was conducted over a 14-month period at six sites in the United States, with children age 7 to 9.9 years.[25] This randomized clinical trial examined the effects of four treatment groups: medication management followed by monthly visits, intensive behavioral treatment, a combined medication/behavioral treatment group, and a standard care offered by community providers. Assessments across multiple domains occurred throughout phases of the investigation. Investigators reported reductions in the symptoms of ADHD over time in all four groups, with significant differences across the groups in degrees of change. The children in the medication management and the combined medication/behavioral treatment groups showed significantly greater improvement than those given behavioral treatment and community care. The combined treatment group did not differ significantly from the medication management group on core ADHD symptoms; however, for non-ADHD symptoms of oppositional/aggressive behavior, internalizing behavior, teacher-rated social skills, parent-child relations, and reading achievement, the combined treatment group offered greater benefits.

Psychosocial Strategies for Children with Early Signs of ADHD

A major responsibility of early childhood professionals is to recognize child behavior that is possibly delayed or abnormal. Parents and professionals will then meet to discuss the problem and determine whether or not it is a mutual concern. This could confirm or question whether the behavior should be brought to the attention of the child's pediatrician. However, regardless of whether the parent takes the child for an evaluation, it is likely that the parents and professional will want to implement some strategies to address the behaviors. Researchers in the large Multimodal Treatment Study of Children with ADHD (MTA) concluded that "behavioral treatments may help families actively cope with their child's disorder and make the necessary life accommodations to optimize family functioning, even when such treatments are not as effective as medication in reducing children's ADHD symptoms."[25(p1084)] Further support for parent-based therapies for preschool children with ADHD was reported in an investigation of two different models for such services. A parent training model and a parent counseling and support model plus a wait-list control group were compared. ADHD symptoms were reduced; moreover, parent training, when compared with the other two groups, increased mothers' sense of well-being. In addition, 53% of the children whose parents received the training also displayed clinically significant improvement.[26]

The earlier behaviors are identified and interventions are implemented, the more likely the behavior can be modified before it becomes a more serious barrier to learning. The aim is to redirect children on the preferred developmental trajectory. A common plan is for professionals and families to agree on some strategies. Some will be structural and address environmental arrangements; others will offer suggestions for adults in interactions with the child. Environments that can individualize and adapt routines and practices to make experiences more positive for the child's development are highly desired. When environments provide developmentally appropriate and meaningful activities, they invite the child's active involvement. Adults have numerous opportunities each day to influence the child's behavior in positive and constructive ways through their responses to the child's initiations. Among the strategies that facilitate the acquisition of appropriate behavior are clear and consistent expectations, directions, and follow-through. The adult can shape interaction by modifying his or her pace and intensity to encourage a calmer, more attentive atmosphere. Timely implementation of principles of behavior management, such as time-out to regain thoughts and composure, is sometimes helpful. These kinds of environments and interactions will help foster the development of a more positive self-concept in the child. Table 4 includes a more complete list of suggested strategies.

Table 4 Coping with ADHD: Strategies for home and school

- View the child as a good child with a special need.
- Remember that the child's misbehavior is organic in nature.
- Capitalize on the child's strengths and emphasize the positive.
- Provide a special time for the child each day.
- Plan ahead when introducing new concepts and for challenging situations.
- Reduce environmental distractions and be an alert listener.
- Establish clear rules and apply them consistently.
- Ensure that adults support the rules.
- Secure eye contact before giving directions.
- Give clear, simple, straightforward directions.
- Check child's understanding of directions and the consequences of failing to follow them.
- Be patient and low key, but firm.
- Act, don't over talk.
- Refrain from being drawn into debates or arguments.
- Use good and consistent behavior management techniques.
- Understand and use time-outs if the results are effective.
- Give positive feedback and praise frequently and quickly after appropriate behavior.
- Help the child recognize his or her own strengths and accomplishments.

Conclusion

In summary, it is critical to pay more attention to preschoolers in order to identify those externalizing behaviors, distinguishing features, and interactions that are reliable predictors for a future ADHD diagnosis. The needs are present when children are very young, but professionals have been reluctant to refer at young ages. By delaying this process, problems exacerbate and undesirable behaviors become learned. The earlier the recognition of a problem, the sooner appropriate interventions, treatments, and counseling can begin to counter the negative effects of family stress, lowered self-esteem, and ensuing learning and social difficulties. Regardless of a clear diagnosis, professionals can provide support to the families as they address the behaviors that are causing concerns. It is quite possible that some environmental changes can be made that can impact and redirect behavior in more productive ways. Continued research certainly needs to be conducted to further understanding of this handicapping disorder. Hopefully, more support for such research will be forthcoming, and more collaboration between academicians, the medical profession, and professionals in the field of early childhood development will result.

References

1. National Institutes of Health. Diagnosis and treatment of attention deficit hyperactivity disorder. Consensus development conference statement. 1998;16(2):1–37.

2. Aleman SR. Congressional Research Service Report for Congress: Special Education for Children with Attention Deficit Disorder: Current Issues. Washington, DC: Congressional Research Service; 1991.

3. US Census Bureau. No. 13. Resident population by sex and age: 1999. In: Statistical Abstract of the United States. Washington, DC: U.S. Government Printing Office; 2000.

4. Cantwell DP. Attention deficit disorder: a review of the past 10 years. J Am Acad Child Adolesc Psychiatry. 1996;35(8):978–984.

5. Report pointed to drugs used on state-care kids. The Miami Herald, May 11, 2001, 22A.

6. Pear R. Proposal to curb the use of drugs to calm the young. The New York Times, March 20, 2000, 1, A16.

7. Smith I. Ritalin for toddlers. Time, March 6, 2000, 84.

8. Zito J. Trends in the prescribing of psychotropic medications to preschoolers. JAMA. 2000;283:1025–1060.

9. Wodrich DL. Attention Deficit Hyperactivity Disorder. Baltimore: Paul H. Brookes; 1994.

10. American Psychological Association. Diagnostic and Statistical Manual of Mental Disorders. 2nd ed. Washington, DC: Author; 1968.

11. American Psychiatric Association. Diagnostic and Statistical Manual of Mental Disorders. 3rd ed. Washington, DC: Author; 1980.

12. American Psychiatric Association. Diagnostic and Statistical Manual of Mental Disorders. 3rd rev ed. Washington, DC: Author; 1987.

13. American Psychiatric Association. Diagnostic and Statistical Manual of Mental Disorders. 4th ed. Washington, DC: Author; 1994.

14. Lahey BB, Pelham WE, Stein MA, et al. Validity of DSM-IV attention-deficit/hyperactivity disorder for younger children. J Am Acad Child Adolesc Psychiatry. 1998;37:695–702.

15. Barkley RA. Attention-Deficit/Hyperactivity Disorder: A Handbook for Diagnosis and Treatment. New York: Guilford; 1990.

16. Gilliam JA. Attention-Deficit/Hyperactivity Disorder Test. Austin, TX: Pro-Ed; 1995.

17. Deutscher B, Fewell RR. Attention Deficit Hyperactivity Disorder-Observation Rating Scale. Miami, FL: University of Miami School of Medicine; unpublished document.

18. The Infant Health and Development Program. The Infant Health and Development Program: enhancing the outcomes of low-birth-weight, premature infants. JAMA. 1990;263:3035–3042.

19. Deutscher B, Fewell RR. The development and use of the Attention Deficit Hyperactivity Disorder-Observational Rating Scale: factor analysis and a preliminary investigation of predictive validity. J Psychoeduc Assess. In press.

20. Blackman JA. Attention-deficit/hyperactivity disorder in preschoolers. Does it exist and should we treat it? Pediatr Clin North Am. 1999;46:1011–1025.

21. Goldman LS, Genel M, Bezman RJ, Slanetz PJ. Diagnosis and treatment of attention-deficit/hyperactivity disorder in children and adolescents. JAMA. 1998;279:1100–1107.

22. Volkow ND, Wang GJ, Fowler JS, et al. Therapeutic doses of oral methylphenidate significantly increase extracellular dopamine in the human brain. J Neurosci. 2001;21(RC121):1–5.

23. Barkley RA. Taking Charge of ADHD: The Complete, Authoritative Guide for Parents. New York: Guilford; 1995.

24. Pelham WE, Aronoff HR, Midlam MA, et al. A comparison of Ritalin and Adderall: efficacy and time-course in children with attention-deficit/hyperactivity disorder. Pediatrics. 1999;103:1–14.

25. The MTA Cooperative Group. A 14-month randomized clinical trial of treatment strategies for attention-deficit/hyperactivity disorder. Arch Gen Psychiatry. 1999;56:1073–1086.

26. Edmund JSS-B, Daley D, Thompson M, Laver-Bradbury C, Weeks A. Parent-based therapies for preschool attention-deficit/hyperactivity disorder: a randomized, controlled trial with a community sample. J Am Acad Child Adolesc Psychiatry. 2001;40:402–408.

Rebecca R. Fewell, PhD
Professor of Pediatrics

Barbara Deutscher, BA
Senior Research Associate
The Debbie Institute
Department of Pediatrics
University of Miami School of Medicine
Miami, Florida

Childhood's End

For 19 years, Joseph Kony has been enslaving, torturing, raping, and murdering Ugandan children, many of whom have become soldiers for his "Lord's Resistance Army," going on to torture, rape, and kill other children. The author exposes the vicious insanity—and cynical politics—behind one of Africa's greatest nightmares

CHRISTOPHER HITCHENS

In William Faulkner's story "Raid," set in Alabama and Mississippi in the closing years of the Civil War, a white family becomes aware of a sudden, vast, nighttime migration through the scorched countryside. They can hear it and even smell it before they can see it; it's the black population voting with its feet and heading, so it fervently believes, for the river Jordan: "We couldn't see them and they did not see us; maybe they didn't even look, just walking fast in the dark with that panting, hurrying murmuring, going on ..."

Northern Uganda is centered on the headstreams of the Nile rather than the Jordan, and is a strange place for me to find myself put in mind of Faulkner, but every evening at dusk the main town of Gulu starts to be inundated by a mass of frightened humanity, panting, hurrying, and murmuring as it moves urgently through the crepuscular hours. Most of the "night commuters," as they are known locally, are children. They leave their outlying villages and walk as many as eight kilometers to huddle for safety in the towns. And then, in the morning, often without breakfast and often without shoes, they walk all the way back again to get to their schools and their families. That's if the former have not been burned and the latter have not been butchered. These children are not running toward Jordan and the Lord; they are running for their lives from the "Lord's Resistance Army" (L.R.A.). This grotesque, zombie-like militia, which has abducted, enslaved, and brainwashed more than 20,000 children, is a kind of Christian Khmer Rouge and has for the past 19 years set a standard of cruelty and ruthlessness that—even in a region with a living memory of Idi Amin—has the power to strike the most vivid terror right into the heart and the other viscera.

Here's what happens to the children who can't run fast enough, or who take the risk of sleeping in their huts in the bush. I am sitting in a rehab center, talking to young James, who is 11 and looks about 9. When he actually was nine and sleeping at home with his four brothers, the L.R.A. stormed his village and took the boys away. They were roped at the waist and menaced with bayonets to persuade them to confess what they could not know—the whereabouts of the Ugandan Army's soldiers. On the subsequent forced march, James underwent the twin forms of initiation practiced by the L.R.A. He was first savagely flogged with a wire lash and then made to take part in the murder of those children who had become too exhausted to walk any farther. "First we had to watch," he says. "Then we had to join in the beatings until they died." He was spared from having to do this to a member of his family, which is the L.R.A.'s preferred method of what it calls "registration." And he was spared from being made into a concubine or a sex slave, because the L.R.A. doesn't tolerate that kind of thing for boys. It is, after all, "faith-based." Excuse me, but it does have its standards.

"Children who have known pain know how to inflict it."

Talking to James about the unimaginable ruin of his childhood, I notice that when I am speaking he stays stock-still, with something a bit dead behind his eyes. But when it comes his turn to tell his story, he immediately starts twisting about in his chair, rubbing his eyes and making waving gestures with his arms. The leader of the L.R.A., a former Catholic acolyte in his 40s named Joseph Kony, who now claims to be a spirit medium with a special mission to impose the Ten Commandments, knows what old Fagin knew: that little boys are nimble and malleable if you catch them young enough, and that they make good thieves and runners. Little James was marched all the way to Sudan, whose Muslim-extremist government offers shelter and aid—such an ecumenical spirit!—to the Christian fanatics. There he was put to work stealing food from neighboring villages, and digging and grinding cassava roots. Soon enough, he was given a submachine gun almost as big as himself. Had he not escaped during an ambush, he would have gotten big enough to be given a girl as well, to do with what he liked.

I drove out of Gulu—whose approach roads can be used only in the daytime—to a refugee camp nearer the Sudanese border. A few Ugandan shillings and a few packets of cigarettes procured me a Ugandan Army escort, who sat heavily armed in the back of the pickup truck. As I buckled my seat belt, the driver told me to unbuckle it in spite of the parlous condition of the road. "If you have to jump out," he said, "you will have to jump out very fast." That didn't make me feel much safer, but only days after I left, two Ugandan aid workers were murdered in daylight on these pitted, dusty highways. We bounced along until we hit Pabbo, where a collection of huts and shanties huddle together as if for protection. In this place are packed about 59,000 of the estimated 1.5 million "internally displaced persons" (I.D.P.'s) who have sought protection from the savagery of the L.R.A. Here, I had the slightly more awkward task of interviewing the female survivors of Joseph Kony's rolling Jonestown: a campaign of horror and superstition and indoctrination.

Kony appointed himself the Lord's anointed prophet in 1987.

The women of Uganda are naturally modest and reserved, and it obviously involved an effort for them to tell their stories to a male European stranger. But they stood up as straight as spears and looked me right in the eye. Forced to carry heavy loads through the bush and viciously caned—up to 250 strokes—if they dropped anything. Given as gifts or prizes to men two or three times their age and compelled to bear children. Made to watch, and to join in, sessions of hideous punishment for those who tried to escape. Rose Atim, a young woman of bronze Nubian Nefertiti beauty, politely started her story by specifying her primary-school grade (grade five) at the time of her abduction. Her nostrils still flared with indignation when she spoke, whereas one of her fellow refugees, Jane Akello, a young lady with almost anthracite skin, was dull and dead-eyed and monotonous in her delivery. I was beginning to be able to distinguish symptoms. I felt a strong sense of indecency during these interviews, but this was mere squeamish self-indulgence on my part, since the women were anxious to relate the stories of their stolen and maimed childhoods. It was as if they had emerged from some harrowing voyage on the Underground Railroad.

Very few people, apart from his victims, have ever met or even seen the enslaving and child-stealing Joseph Kony, and the few pictures and films of him are amateur and indistinct. This very imprecision probably helps him to maintain his version of charisma. Here is what we know and (with the help of former captives and a Scotland Yard criminal

profiler) what we speculate. Kony grew up in a Gulu Province village called Odek. He appointed himself the Lord's anointed prophet for the Acholi people of northern Uganda in 1987, and by the mid-90s was receiving arms and cash from Sudan. He probably suffers from multiple-personality disorder, and he takes his dreams for prophecies. He goes into trances in which he speaks into a tape recorder and plays back the resulting words as commands. He has helped himself to about 50 captives as "wives," claiming Old Testament authority for this (King Solomon had 700 spouses), often insisting—partly for biblical reasons and partly for the more banal reason of AIDS dread—that they be virgins. He used to anoint his followers with a holy oil mashed from indigenous shea-butter nuts, and now uses "holy water," which he tells his little disciples will make them invulnerable to bullets. He has claimed to be able to turn stones into hand grenades, and many of his devotees say that they have seen him do it. He warns any child tempted to run away that the baptismal fluids are visible to him forever and thus they can always be found again. (He can also identify many of his "children" by the pattern of lashes that they earned while under his tender care.) Signs of his disapproval include the cutting off of lips, noses, and breasts in the villages he raids and, to deter informers, a padlock driven through the upper and lower lips. This is the sort of deranged gang—flagellant, hysterical, fanatical, lethal, underage—that an unfortunate traveler might have encountered on the roads of Europe during the Thirty Years' War or the last Crusade. "Yes," says Michael Oruni, director of the Gulu Children of War Rehabilitation Center, who works on deprogramming these feral kids, "children who have known pain know how to inflict it." We were sitting in a yard that contained, as well as some unreformed youngsters, four random babies crawling about in the dust. These had been found lying next to their panga-slashed mothers or else left behind when their ·mothers were marched away.

In October, the Lord of the Flies was hit, in his medieval redoubt, by a message from the 21st century. Joseph Kony and four other leaders of the L.R.A. were named in the first arrest warrants ever issued by the new International Criminal Court (I.C.C.). If that sounds like progress to you, then consider this. The whereabouts of Kony are already known: he openly uses a satellite phone from a base across the Ugandan border in southern Sudan. Like the United States, Sudan is not a signatory to the treaty that set up the I.C.C. And it has sponsored the L.R.A. because the Ugandan government—which *is* an I.C.C. signatory—has helped the people of southern Sudan fight against the theocracy in Khartoum, the same theocracy that has been sponsoring the genocide against Muslim black Africans in Darfur. Arrest warrants look pretty flimsy when set against ruthless cynicism of this depth and intensity. Kony has evidently made some kind of peace with his Sudanese Islamist patrons: in addition to his proclamation of the Ten Commandments, he once banned alcohol and announced that all pigs were unclean and that those who farm them, let alone eat them, were subject to death. So, unless he has undergone a conversion to Judaism in the wilderness, we can probably assume that he is repaying his murderous armorers and protectors.

I had a faintly nerve-racking drink with Francis Ongom, one of Kony's ex-officers, who defected only recently and who would not agree to be questioned about his own past crimes. "Kony has refused Sudan's request that he allow his soldiers to convert to Islam," said this hardened-looking man as he imbibed a Red Bull through a straw, "but he has found Bible justifications for killing witches, for killing pigs because of the story of the Gadarene swine, and for killing people because god did the same with Noah's flood and Sodom and Gomorrah." Nice to know that he is immersed in the Good Book.

The terrifying thing about such violence and cruelty is that only a few dedicated practitioners are required in order to paralyze everyone else with fear. I had a long meeting with Betty Bigombe, one of those staunch and beautiful women—it is so often the women—who have helped restore Uganda's pulse after decades of war and famine and tyranny and Ebola and West Nile fever and AIDS. She has been yelled at by Joseph Kony, humiliated by corrupt and hypocritical Sudanese "intermediaries," dissed by the Ugandan political elite, and shamefully ignored by the international "human rights" community. She still believes that an amnesty for Kony's unindicted commanders is possible, which will bring the L.R.A. children back from the bush, but she and thousands like her can always be outvoted by one brutalized schoolboy with a machete. We are being forced to watch yet another Darfur, in which the time supposedly set aside for negotiations is used by the killers and cleansers to complete their work.

The Acholi people are the chief sufferers in all this.

The Acholi people of northern Uganda, who are the chief sufferers in all this, have to suffer everything twice. Their children are murdered or abducted and enslaved and then come back to murder and abduct and enslave even more children. Yet if the Ugandan Army were allowed to use extreme measures to destroy the L.R.A., the victims would be … Acholi children again. It must be nightmarish to know that any feral-child terrorist who is shot could be one of your own. "I and the public know," wrote W. H. Auden in perhaps his greatest poem, "September 1, 1939":

What all schoolchildren learn,
Those to whom evil is done
Do evil in return.

And that's what makes it so affecting and so upsetting to watch the "night commuter" children when they come scuttling and scampering into town as the sun departs from the sky. These schoolchildren have not yet had evil done to them, nor are they ready to inflict any evil. It's not too late for them, in other words.

I sat in the deepening gloom for a while with one small boy, Jimmy Opioh, whose age was 14. He spoke with an appalling gravity and realism about his mother's inability to pay school fees for himself and his brother both, about the fatigue and time-wasting of being constantly afraid and famished and continually on the run. In that absurd way that one does, I asked him what he wanted to be when he grew up. His unhesitating answer was that he wanted to be a politician—he had his party, the Forum for Democratic Change, all picked out as well. I shamefacedly arranged, along with the admirable John Prendergast of the International Crisis Group, to get him the meager sum that would pay for his schooling, tried not to notice the hundreds of other eyes that were hungrily turned toward me in the darkness, wondered what the hell the actual politicians, here or there, were doing about his plight, and managed to get out of the night encampment just before the equatorial rains hit and washed most of the tents and groundsheets away.

Children Of the Fallen

Over 1,000 American kids have lost a parent in the Iraq war. Who they are, and how they're coping

JERRY ADLER

THEY WERE PREPARED TO DIE, even the truck drivers and supply clerks; any American who sets foot in Iraq must be. They made out wills, as the military requires, and left behind letters and videos for their families. The families in turn prepared for the day when they might open the door to find a chaplain on the other side. In military families the notion of duty is not confined to the battlefield. On the morning that 14-year-old Rohan Osbourne learned that his mother, Pamela, had been killed in a mortar attack on her Army base, his father dropped him off as usual at Robert M. Shoemaker High School, where three quarters of the students are the children of soldiers from nearby Fort Hood, Texas. "I might not get a lot of work done today, ma'am," Rohan politely explained to his teacher. "My mommy died yesterday in Iraq."

War notoriously robs parents of their sons, but it also steals husbands and fathers, and increasingly wives and mothers. The Pentagon doesn't keep these statistics, but using figures compiled by the Scripps-Howard News Service and other sources, NEWSWEEK has calculated that as of last week 1,043 American children had lost a parent in Iraq. To put it another way, nearly two years after the invasion on March 19, 2003, among the 1,508 American troops who have died as of March 11 were an estimated 450 fathers, and 7 mothers. A wartime death presents unique hardships for children. It occurs in a far-off country, often to a parent who left home months earlier; young children may find it hard to grasp the finality of the event. Offsetting that is the impressive panoply and ritual of a military funeral, and the consoling knowledge that the sacrifice was in a worthy cause. The death of a parent often leaves a family not just sadder, but poorer, and surviving spouses are agitating for improvements in their benefits. But there are needs no government program can fill.

The fathers were big strong men, like Nino Livaudais, a 23-year-old Army Ranger with two tours in Afghanistan behind him before the invasion. His son Destre, now 7, is still struggling to understand how such a hero could have been killed by a mere bomb. "I can kind of picture it," he says hesitantly. "But it's hard to picture it. I don't really think explosions hurt that much. My dad's usually a tough man. He went through about five wars." Livaudais left, besides Destre (then 5) and his wife, Jackie, a 2-year-old son, Carson, and Grant, who was born after

his death. As relatives gathered on the family porch after Nino's funeral, Carson grew excited by all the unexpected company and started calling for his daddy to join the party. He then turned around, puzzled, as the grown-ups all burst into tears.

'I might not get a lot of work done today, ma'am,' said Rohan, 14. 'My mommy died yesterday in Iraq.'

And their mothers were loving and devoted, like Spc. Jessica Cawvey, 21. Before she left for Iraq last February with her Illinois National Guard unit, her daughter, Sierra, made her pinkie-swear she wouldn't die. So when Cawvey was killed by a roadside bomb in Fallujah last October, it was not merely a tragedy for Sierra, it was a kind of betrayal. "We had to explain that even though she died, it wasn't her mommy's fault," said Kevin Cawvey, Sierra's grandfather. Vanessa Arroyave, who was 6 when her father, Marine S/Sgt. Jimmy Javier Arroyave, was deployed, was certain he would die in Iraq. "She was very adamant about that," says her mother, Rachelle. The little girl was right. Last April, when Arroyave was killed in a truck accident, Vanessa told her mother: "I told you so." So Rachelle faced the mirror image of the Cawvey family's problem. She had to reassure her daughter that by predicting her father's death, she hadn't brought it about.

The sudden onslaughts of grief are sometimes almost more than Nelda Howton, the principal of Osbourne's school near Fort Hood, can bear. She has picked up the phone to find a mother sobbing on the other end, begging Howton to drive her son home. One girl's aunt walked straight to the classroom and appeared in the doorway, tears streaming down her face. The students do characteristically thoughtless things, like asking Jessica Blankenbecler for her autograph because they had seen her on television. Blankenbecler, a pretty sophomore, was the first student at Shoemaker to lose a parent in Iraq. That wasn't the worst of it; one girl told her, "I wish something would happen to my dad because then we'd get rich"—a remark that carried a particular sting because Blankenbecler's mother, Linnie, thinks they're actually going to be poor.

Compensation for the families of soldiers killed in action is a politically and emotionally charged issue, particularly in light of the changing makeup of the military. The saying used to be that "if the Army wanted you to have a wife, they would have issued you one," but the proportion of married soldiers is higher today than in any previous war, says Charlie Moskos, a Northwestern University sociologist. The military today is a better-paid career than most high-school graduates could aspire to otherwise, which may explain why the average male soldier now gets married at 24—three years younger than the rest of the population. The heavy reliance on Reserves and National Guard troops also puts family men and women on the front lines in unprecedented numbers. Of the Americans killed in Iraq through the end of November 2004, more than two in five were married.

Characteristically, the military and Congress have responded to the urgent needs of the survivors by adding new layers of bureaucracy to a system that dates back to the Civil War (and, in fact, is still paying benefits to five offspring of Civil War veterans). Spouses receive a lump-sum "death gratuity" of $12,420, plus life insurance of as much as $250,000. This payment would be effectively doubled by a bill that is expected to pass in the next month. Families are eligible for Social Security payments and for two different kinds of government annuities, although the fine print requires an offsetting reduction in one if you also collect the other. Survivors are eligible for generous college-tuition grants and lifetime subsidized health care. As an illustration, the National Military Families Association calculated the benefits for the family (a wife and children ages 1 and 3) of an enlisted man with a salary of $38,064 a year, including a housing allowance and combat pay. Apart from the lump-sum payments, his wife would receive the equivalent of an annual income of $57,624, falling to $45,804 after two years, then declining in steps as the children reach adulthood. By the time the younger child turns 23, the wife's check would amount to only about a quarter of her husband's active-duty salary.

Last year the Department of Veterans Affairs added bereavement counseling to the package of benefits. This supplements the work of a voluntary organization called TAPS—Tragedy Assistance Program for Survivors—which organizes "emotional peer-to-peer" counseling among kids. There are also freelance outreach efforts by the adult children of servicemen killed in Vietnam, who are now approaching middle age themselves. Tony Cordero, who was 4 when his father, William, was killed in 1965, founded a survivors' group called Sons and Daughters in Touch, which has begun inviting the children of Iraqi casualties to its Father's Day memorials. Ever since the publication of her family memoir ("Hero Mama"), the writer Karen Spears Zacharias, whose father was killed in Vietnam, has become a magnet for bereaved kids, who write and call her at all hours. In quiet visits, she tells them she understands how they feel: "It's difficult to lose a father in an unpopular war."

Psychologists have learned a lot about how to help children through the grief process. Unfortunately one of the most important recommendations—to avoid unnecessary changes to the child's daily routine—is impossible for many military families, who generally have to move off base within six months. Previous advice that a healthy adjustment required a clean break with the deceased parent is now inoperative; current thinking is that children "want and need a continuing bond to their dead parent," according to J. William Worden, co-director of Harvard's Child Bereavement Study. "They talk to them, they keep things that belong to them, they dream about them and think about them," he says. Tony Bertolino Jr., 15, appears to have memorized the entire career and duties of his father, an Army sergeant who was killed in an ambush in late 2003. "He was a highly respected soldier and man," he says. David Kirchhoff Jr., whose father, an Iowa guardsman, died of heat stroke in Iraq in 2003, has turned his bedroom into a virtual shrine to his father, including a wall of photographs. Like many sons of soldiers, he imagines enlisting himself someday. His plan, though, is to "go over there and tell everybody it's not worth it." Compared with the 20,000 American children who lost a father in Vietnam, the families of Iraqi war casualties have the advantage that almost all of them are getting a body back. Many men back then were lost in the jungle or the air and were—or still are—listed as "missing," leaving their families to wonder, "Is he going to be coming around the corner one day?" says Cordero. It was with that in mind that Tina Cline, whose husband, Marine Lance Cpl. Donald Cline, was killed in an explosion on the fourth day of the invasion, decided to let 2-year-old Dakota look inside the flag-draped coffin at the uniformed body inside. The body had no head.

'God needed Daddy in Heaven,' Jordan said to her 6-year-old. 'Well,' he replied, 'I needed him, too.'

"Daddy's not coming home," she whispered to her son, who was dressed in a tiny dark suit and tie. "He's got a bigger job to do, helping God in heaven."

Parents have always said that, to little boys who stood at attention and promised their moms they would be brave. They wore their father's dog tags to school, and, in the way of things, eventually went off to fight in their own wars. On the same day that Cline's vehicle was hit by a shell, Marine Sgt. Phillip Jordan was killed in Nasiriya, leaving behind a 6-year-old son, Tyler, whom he called "Lavabug." For a week after, Tyler sulked around the house in his 6-foot-3-inch father's camouflage shirt, refusing to eat or to talk to his mother, Amanda.

"God needed Daddy in heaven," she explained recently.

"Well," he replied, "I needed him, too."

This story was written by JERRY ADLER *with reporting from* DEBRA ROSENBERG, T. TRENT GEGAX, PAT WINGERT, DAREN BRISCOE, HILARY SHENFELD, KIYOSHI MARTINEZ, DIRK JOHNSON, JAMIE RENO *and* Andrew Horesh

When Does Autism Start?

Scientists are now looking for the earliest signs of the mysterious disorder as desperate parents hunt for treatments that may improve their children's lives.

CLAUDIA KALB

It's a winter night in Northbrook, Ill., and brothers David and Jason Craven are on the move. They're watching a "Baby Beethoven" video. They're bouncing on a mattress in their basement playroom. They're climbing up their dad's legs. David, 7, and Jason, 5, with their mops of brown hair, look physically healthy. But both boys are suffering from a devastating developmental disorder: autism. David speaks only about 10 words, still wears diapers at night and sucks on a pacifier. Jason drinks from a baby bottle. Neither one can vocalize his glee as he plays. Neither one can communicate pain or joy in words. Neither one can say "I love you."

Since their sons were diagnosed, both at the age of 2, Barry and Dana Craven have tried a dizzying array of therapies: neurofeedback, music therapy, swimming with dolphins, social-skills therapy, gluten-free diets, vitamins, anti-anxiety pills and steroids. To reduce the boys' exposure to environmental chemicals, which the Cravens believe might aggravate their conditions, the couple replaced their carpeting with toxin-free wood floors and bought a special water-purifying system. They even installed a $3,500 in-home sauna, which they think will help remove metals like mercury and arsenic from the boys' bodies. Warm and loving parents, the Cravens spent $75,000 on treatments last year alone. "I'm willing to try just about anything if it makes sense," says Dana.

> **"I haven't been this excited about research in a very long time."**
> —**Wendy Stone,** Vanderbilt University

In the six decades since autism was identified, modern medicine has exploded: antibiotics cure infections, statins ward off heart disease, artificial joints combat osteoarthritis. And yet autism, a vexing brain disorder, remains largely a mystery. Researchers still don't know what causes it, nor do they know how best to treat a condition that prompts one child to stop speaking and another to memorize movie scripts. With a tenfold spike in numbers over the past 20 years—one in every 166 children is now diagnosed with an Autism Spectrum Disorder (ASD)—re-

searchers, advocacy groups and the government are racing to improve the lives of children and their families, many of them emotionally and financially drained. This year the National Institutes of Health will spend $99 million on autism research, up from $22 million in 1997.

Some of the most exciting new work involves efforts to spot clues of the disorder in infants as young as 6 months. In the complicated world of autism, where controversies reign and frustration festers, a two-word rallying cry is growing louder by the day: early diagnosis. This week the Centers for Disease Control and Prevention launches a $2.5 million autism-awareness campaign, "Learn the Signs. Act Early." The goal: to educate health-care providers and parents about red flags, to intervene as quickly as possible—and to give kids with autism a shot at productive, satisfying and emotionally connected lives. "This is an urgent public-health concern," says the CDC's Catherine Rice.

Today, most children aren't even seen by specialists until they've passed their 2nd birthdays, and many aren't diagnosed until at least the age of 3. Kids with Asperger's, on the higher-functioning end of ASD, may be overlooked until well into elementary school. "If we had a way of screening for autism at birth and then could begin very early to retrain the brain, that would really be the ticket," says Dr. Thomas Insel, head of the National Institute of Mental Health. Scientists are now attempting to do just that. In a joint effort by the National Alliance for Autism Research and the National Institute of Child Health and Human Development, researchers at 14 sites, from Harvard to the University of Washington, are studying the baby siblings of children with autism, who have a genetic liability for the disorder. By measuring the infants' visual and verbal skills and their social interactions, scientists hope to identify early markers of autism before children turn 1. "I haven't been this excited about research in a very long time," says consortium member Wendy Stone of Vanderbilt University. "Not only are we getting clues about the earliest features of autism, but we're helping these families along the way."

Canadian researchers Dr. Lonnie Zwaigenbaum and Susan Bryson have enrolled 200 siblings, half of whom have been observed to the age of 2. Roughly 10 percent have been diagnosed with autism. Zwaigenbaum, of McMaster University in Ontario, says that signs of the disorder, though at first subtle, are often there from the very beginning. Preliminary data show that 6-month-olds who are later diagnosed with autism generally have good eye contact, but they're often quieter and more passive than their peers. And they may lag behind in motor developments, like sitting up or reaching for objects.

The signs often become more obvious as children reach their 1st birthdays. By then, some show patterns of extreme reactivity, either getting very upset when a new toy or activity is presented or barely noticing at all. Others already exhibit repetitive behaviors characteristic of autism—rocking back and forth or becoming fixated on an object, like a piece of string dangling in front of their eyes. And they're less responsive to playful interactions with others. When a typically developing child plays peekaboo, her face lights up, she looks at the person she's playing with, she makes sounds, she reaches for the peekaboo blanket. Children with autism, by contrast, show little facial expression. They may not look at their playmate, and it can take enormous energy to elicit a reaction. "What's been striking," says Zwaigenbaum, "is the lack of response or the distress that these activities can elicit."

The Baby Sibs consortium is also looking for early physical markers of the disorder, starting with the size of children's heads. A landmark study published in 2003 found that kids with autism experienced unusually rapid head growth between 6 and 14 months. Consortium members want to see if their young siblings do, too. Scientists aren't sure what accounts for the increase, but one theory is that it has to do with an overgrowth of neuronal connections. Normally, the brain clears out biological debris as it forms new circuits. "Little twigs fall off to leave the really strong branches," says University of Michigan researcher Catherine Lord. In kids with autism, however, that pruning process may go awry.

In their hunt for neurological clues, scientists are unveiling the inner workings of the autistic mind. Using eye-tracking technology, Ami Klin, of the Yale Child Study Center, is uncovering fascinating differences in the early socialization skills of children with autism. Klin has found that when affected toddlers view videos of caregivers or babies in a nursery, they focus more on people's mouths—or on objects behind them—than on their eyes. Klin's toddler study echoes findings in adults and adolescents with autism when they watched clips of "Who's Afraid of Virginia Woolf?" "Richard Burton and Elizabeth Taylor were engaged in a passionate kiss, and they're focusing on the light switch," says Klin. "Our goal is to identify these vulnerabilities as early as possible."

Might it be that the autistic brain's operating platform is different, as if it's a Mac in a world of PCs? Functional MRI scans show that the brain's "fusiform face area," the control tower for face recognition, is underactive in people with autism. The more severe the disorder, the more disabled the fusiform. But is it actually dysfunctional? Or is it just not interested in people? In an intriguing early study, Yale's Robert Schultz took brain scans of a child with autism who had trouble distinguishing human faces but loved the cartoon character Digimon. "Lo and behold," says Schultz, "his fusiform showed strong activity." Schultz and James Tanaka at the University of Victoria in Canada are hoping computer games can help kids with autism learn how to engage with human faces and identify emotions. The children follow directions to shoot at smiley faces or click on the guy who looks sad. In "Emotion Maker," they choose features—angry eyes, a scowling mouth—to create their own faces. And in "Who's Looking at Me?" they scan an array of faces to sensitize them to eye contact. So far, says Schultz, the kids appear to be improving. But will it help change the course of their lives? "That's the million-dollar question," he says.

An intellectual thief, autism infiltrates children's brains, stalling or stealing cognitive and social development. In classic autism, babies fail to coo or babble by their 1st birthdays. Or words that do develop ("dada," "up," "toy") inexplicably disappear. One-year-olds don't respond to their names. A child once bursting with potential finds spinning tops more captivating than her mother's smile. Kids with Asperger's may not be as closed off, but they suffer severe social deficits. Many are verbal fanatics, immersing themselves in long-winded monologues about obscure topics, like fat fryers or snakes. Klin recalls a child who bowed and spoke in Shakespearean English, "almost as if I had plucked him from 14th-century Verona." Such oddities can make these children social pariahs. Baffled by human interactions and frustrated by their inability to make friends, some kids spiral into debilitating fits of anxiety and depression. Many children on the autism spectrum will never live independent lives. "We're talking about children who need lifelong care," says NIMH's Insel. "This is an astonishingly devastating disease."

"I am willing to try just about anything if it makes sense."

—**Dana Craven,** mother of two boys with autism

And its current treatment is all over the map. Every day, it seems, there's a new "cure." With no known cause and no clear guidance, parents must navigate a maze of costly therapies, most of which have little hard-core science to prove their effectiveness. Many children now take medications, ranging from anticonvulsants (about one third suffer from seizures) to stimulants like Ritalin to calm hyperactivity. Low doses of antidepressants such as Prozac may help reduce the severity of repetitive behaviors. And risperidone, an anti-psychotic drug, can quell aggression and tantrums, says Dr. Christopher McDougle, of the Indiana University School of Medicine. The drug, whose side effects include weight gain and sedation, is now before the FDA and could become the first medication approved specifically for autism.

Drugs, however, won't help a child learn to speak. One of the few treatments that just about everyone agrees is critical is behavioral intervention, which uses word repetition, game-playing and specialized exercises to develop a child's language and social skills. At the Lovaas Institute in Los Angeles, senior instructor Sona Gulyan engages Adam Ellis, who turns 4 next month, in language drills known as discrete trials. "Say 'hi'," says Gulyan. Adam, a chubby-cheeked little boy in jeans and a white T shirt, responds with a "k" sound. "No, 'hi'," says Gulyan. After several failed attempts, Gulyan switches the focus. "Do this," she says, pointing to her nose. Adam imitates the gesture and is congratulated. And then it's back to the original task: "Say 'hi'." Finally, success—and an orange balloon as a reward. In 1987, founder Ivar Lovaas reported that children who received an average of 40 hours a week of his intensive one-on-one therapy called Applied Behavior Analysis increased their IQs by 30 points, compared with a control group. Other studies, however, have been mixed, and critics believe the program is too militaristic. But for Adam's mother, Megan, it's progress that matters. "He has mastered so many skills," she says. "It's just amazing."

Things are more relaxed at Cleveland's Achievement Centers for Children, where Lisa and Tim Brogan play with their son, Alex. Alex is learning to communicate through an intervention called Floortime, which focuses on a child's individual strengths and his relationships with others. Kids learn to engage with their parents through "circles of communication." If Alex wants to line up toy cars in a row, his dad will join him, then nudge one out of place. The move prompts Alex to interact with his father—a circle of communication—rather than isolate himself with the toys. "We have come such a very long way," says Lisa.

Children with autism have as many styles and personalities as any group of toddlers. A behavioral intervention that suits one child (or his parent) won't necessarily work for another. Many treatment centers now mix techniques from different approaches, including one of the newest on the block: Relationship Development Intervention, or RDI. Here, parents learn how to use everyday events as teachable moments. A trip to the grocery store, for example, becomes an opportunity for kids to learn to adapt to sensory overload—the chatter of shoppers, 100 different kinds of cereal. In the past, Pam Carroll's son, Morgan, now 9, was fixated on instant oatmeal with blueberries, and he melted down if it wasn't available. Now he roams the aisles in Gainesville, Fla., and helps his mom shop. Linda Andron-Ostrow, a clinical social worker in Los Angeles, likes the way RDI empowers parents and allows for creative thinking. "Life isn't structured," she says.

With autism's medley of symptoms—which can include a heightened sensitivity to sound and picky eating habits—many families search for alternative treatments. Kacy Dolce and her husband, Christopher, recently took their son, Hank, 4, to see Mary Ann Block, an osteopath in Hurst, Texas, for a $2,500 assessment. Block prescribes vitamins and minerals, diets free of wheat and dairy, and a controversial treatment, chelation, which strips the body of metals like mercury. Block believes these toxins could come from vaccines and are at the core of autism. Mainstream doctors, pointing to scientific studies showing no connection, worry that chelation puts children at serious risk. Despite the possibility of dangerous side effects, like liver and kidney problems, the Dolces say they'd consider it. "We don't know enough yet to say no," says Kacy. "I'll do anything to help our child."

What parents really need is a road map. Earlier this month six U.S. medical centers joined forces to launch the Autism Treatment Network, which will evaluate therapies, pool data and, ultimately, create guidelines. "We can't have parents chasing down the latest treatment," says Peter Bell of Cure Autism Now, a research and advocacy group allied with the effort. "We need to understand what works." At the forefront of ATN is Massachusetts General's Ladders program, where Dr. Margaret Bauman is using a multidisciplinary approach. In addition to offering standard regimens like physical therapy and behavioral intervention, Bauman assesses overall health. When she saw a teenager crying and twisting her body, symptoms other doctors attributed to autism, Bauman sent her to a gastroenterologist, who found ulcers in her esophagus. The writhing was caused by pain. A boy's head-banging went away after he was treated for colitis. "We really have to start thinking out of the box," says Bauman.

And thinking early. Today many kids aren't getting treatment until well after their 3rd birthdays. Diagnosing an infant with autism at 6 months or a year—maybe even one day in the delivery room—could mean the difference between baby steps and giant leaps. At the Kennedy Krieger Institute in Baltimore, a handful of 2-year-olds toddle at the next frontier in autism treatment. The children are part of an NIH-funded study run by Rebecca Landa to see if early intervention, before the age of 3, can improve the trajectory of cognitive and social development. As Landa looks on, David Townsend fusses and stamps his feet. Then, he notices his twin sister, Isabel, turning the pages of "Ten Little Ladybugs." David looks at Isabel, watches her hands, then flips a page himself, accomplishing what autism experts call "joint engagement." "That was beautiful," says Landa. A fleeting moment, a developmental milestone—and, if all goes well, a new world of possibilities for a sweet little boy with dimples.

**With Karen Springen, Ellise Pierce,
Joan Raymond and Jenny Hontz**

Three Reasons Not to Believe in an Autism Epidemic

ABSTRACT—According to some lay groups, the nation is experiencing an autism epidemic—a rapid escalation in the prevalence of autism for unknown reasons. However, no sound scientific evidence indicates that the increasing number of diagnosed cases of autism arises from anything other than purposely broadened diagnostic criteria, coupled with deliberately greater public awareness and intentionally improved case finding. Why is the public perception so disconnected from the scientific evidence? In this article we review three primary sources of misunderstanding: lack of awareness about the changing diagnostic criteria, uncritical acceptance of a conclusion illogically drawn in a California-based study, and inattention to a crucial feature of the "child count" data reported annually by the U.S. Department of Education.

KEYWORDS—autism; epidemiology; epidemic

MORTON ANN GERNSBACHER,[1] MICHELLE DAWSON,[2] AND H. HILL GOLDSMITH[1]
[1]*University of Wisconsin-Madison* and [2]*University of Montreal, Montreal, Quebec, Canada*

If you have learned anything about autism lately from the popular media, you most likely have learned—erroneously—that there is "a mysterious upsurge" in the prevalence of autism (*New York Times*, October 20, 2002, Section 4, p. 10), creating a "baffling … outbreak" (CBSnews.com, October 18, 2002), in which new cases are "exploding in number" (*Time*, May 6, 2002, p. 48), and "no one knows why" (*USA Today*, May 17, 2004, p. 8D). At least a handful of U.S. Congress members decree on their .gov Web sites that the nation is facing an autism epidemic. Several national media have erroneously concluded that a set of data from California "confirms the autism epidemic," and the largest autism-advocacy organization in the world has expressed alarm over astronomical percentage increases in the number of autistic children served in the public schools since 1992. However, no sound scientific evidence indicates that the increase in the number of diagnosed cases of autism arises from anything other than intentionally broadened diagnostic criteria, coupled with deliberately greater public awareness and conscientiously improved case finding. How did public perception become so misaligned from scientific evidence? In this article, we review three major sources of misunderstanding.

The Changing Diagnosis of Autism

The phenomenon of autism has existed most likely since the origins of human society. In retrospect, numerous historical figures—for instance, the 18th-century "wild boy of Aveyron"—fit autism diagnostic criteria but were not so diagnosed in their day (Frith, 1989). Only in the 1940s did a constellation of differences in social interaction, communication, and focused interests come to be categorized by Leo Kanner as "autism." However, another 40 years would elapse before American psychiatric practice incorporated criteria for autism into what was by then the third edition of its *Diagnostic and Statistical Manual of Mental Disorders* (*DSM-III*; American Psychiatric Association, APA, 1980). Thus, estimates of the prevalence of autism prior to 1980 were based on individual clinicians' (e.g., Kanner & Eisenberg, 1956) or specific researchers' (e.g., Rutter, 1978) conceptions—and fluctuated because of factors that continue to introduce variation into current-day estimates (e.g., variation in the size of the population sampled and the manner of identification).

Autism has remained in the *DSM* (under the title, Pervasive Developmental Disorders), but not without modification through subsequent editions. Whereas the 1980 *DSM-III* entry required satisfying six mandatory criteria, the more recent 1994 *DSM-IV* (APA, 1994) offers 16 optional criteria—only half of which need to be met. Moreover, the severe phrasing of the 1980 mandatory criteria contrasts with the more inclusive phrasing of the 1994 optional criteria. For instance, to qualify for a diagnosis according to the 1980 criteria an individual needed to exhibit "*a pervasive lack of responsiveness* to other people" (emphasis added; APA, 1980, p. 89); in contrast, according to 1994 criteria an individual must demonstrate only "a lack of spontaneous seeking to share … achievements with other people" (APA, 1994, p. 70) and peer relationships less sophisticated than would be predicted by the individual's developmental level. The 1980 mandatory criteria of "*gross deficits* in language development" (emphasis added; APA, 1980, p. 89)

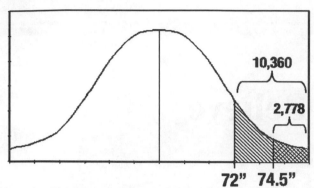

Figure 1 Distribution of male height in McClennan county, Texas. Shaded areas represent segments of the population defined as "tall" according to two standards: men over 74.5 in. (2,778) versus men over 72 in. (10,360).

and "if speech is present, peculiar speech patterns such as immediate and delayed echolalia, metaphorical language, pronominal reversal" (APA, 1980, p. 89) were replaced by the 1994 options of difficulty "sustain[ing] a conversation" (APA, 1994, p. 70) or "lack of varied … social imitative play" (p. 70). "*Bizarre responses* to various aspects of the environment" (emphasis added; APA, 1980, p. 90) became "persistent preoccupation with parts of objects" (APA, 1994, p. 71).

Furthermore, whereas the earlier 1980 (*DSM-III*) entry comprised only two diagnostic categories (infantile autism and childhood onset pervasive developmental disorder), the more recent 1994 (*DSM-IV*) entry comprises five. Three of those five categories connote what is commonly called autism: Autistic Disorder, Pervasive Developmental Disorder Not Otherwise Specified (PDDNOS), and Asperger's Disorder. Autistic Disorder requires meeting half of the 16 criteria, but Asperger's Disorder, which did not enter the *DSM* until 1994, involves only two thirds of that half, and PDDNOS, which entered the *DSM* in 1987, is defined by subthreshold symptoms. Therefore, Asperger's Disorder and PDDNOS are often considered "milder variants." These milder variants can account for nearly three fourths of current autism diagnoses (Chakrabarti & Fombonne, 2001). Consider also the recent practice of codiagnosing autism alongside known medical and genetic conditions (e.g., Down syndrome, Tourette's syndrome, and cerebral palsy; Gillberg & Coleman, 2000); the contemporary recognition that autism can exist among people at every level of measured intelligence (Baird et al., 2000), the deliberate efforts to identify autism in younger and younger children (Filipek et al., 2000), and the speculation that many individuals who would meet present-day criteria were previously mis- or undiagnosed (Wing & Potter, 2002), including some of the most accomplished, albeit idiosyncratic, historical figures such as Isaac Newton, Lewis Carroll, W.B. Yeats, Thomas Jefferson, and Bill Gates (Fitzgerald, 2004).

The California Data

In California, persons diagnosed with autism (and other developmental disabilities) qualify for services administered by the statewide Department of Developmental Services (DDS). In 1999, the California DDS reported that from 1987 to 1998 the number of individuals served under the category of "autism" had increased by 273% (California DDS, 1999). Alarmed by this 273% increase, the California legislature commissioned the University of California Medical Investigation of Neurodevelopmental Disorders (M.I.N.D.) Institute to determine whether the increase could be explained by changes in diagnostic criteria. The M.I.N.D. Institute (2002) concluded, on the basis of data we describe next, that there was "no evidence that a loosening in the diagnostic criteria has contributed to the increased number of autism clients served by the [California DDS] Regional Centers" (p. 5). Although this unrefereed conclusion made national headlines and continues to be articulated on innumerable Web sites, it is unwarranted.

The study involved two samples of children who had been served under the California DDS category of "autism": One sample was born between 1983 and 1985 (the earlier cohort); the other sample was born between 1993 and 1995 (the more recent cohort). Both cohorts were assessed with the same autism diagnostic instrument (an interview conducted with care providers). However, the autism diagnostic instrument was based on *DSM-IV* criteria—criteria that were not even published until 1994. When the same percentage of children in the earlier and the more recent cohort met the more recent *DSM-IV* criteria, the researchers imprudently concluded that the "observed increase in autism cases cannot be explained by a loosening in the criteria used to make the diagnosis" (M.I.N.D. Institute, 2002, p. 7).

To understand the fallacy of the conclusion, consider the following analogy, based on male height and graphically illustrated in Figure 1. Suppose the criterion for "tall" was 74.5 in. and taller in the mid-1980s, but the criterion was loosened to 72 in. and taller in the mid-1990s. A diagnostic instrument based on the looser, more recent criterion of 72 in. would identify males who met the 74.5-in. criterion as well as those who met the 72-in. criterion.[1] Although a perfectly reliable diagnostic instrument based on a looser criterion would identify 100% of the individuals who meet the looser criterion along with 100% of the individuals who meet the more restricted criterion, a highly reliable instrument might identify about 90% of each group; this is the percentage of each cohort in the California study who met the more recent autism criteria.

Most crucially, broadening the criterion will result in a dramatic increase in diagnosed cases. For instance, census data allow us to estimate that 2,778 males in McClennan County, Texas would be called tall by the more restricted 74.5-in. criterion, and 10,360 males would be called tall by the broader 72-in. criterion; if those two criteria had been applied a decade apart, a 273% increase in the number of males called tall would have emerged—without any real increase in Texans' height. In the same way, the 273% increase from 2,778 versus 10,360 California children who received services for "autism" in 1987 versus 1998 could well be a function of broadened criteria.

As we have already detailed, the commonly applied diagnostic criteria for autism broadened nationally from the 1980s to the 1990s; thus, it would be unusual if the criteria used for eligibility in California had not also broadened during this time. Two further aspects of the California data suggest that the criteria must have broadened. First, children in the more recent cohort were dramatically less likely to have intellectual impairment: Whereas 61% of the children in the earlier cohort were identified as having intellectual impairments, only 27% of the children in the more recent cohort were so identified. The lower rate of intellectual impairment in the more recent cohort matches recent epidemiological data, and the difference between the two rates suggests a major difference between the two cohorts (e.g., that the more recent cohort was drawn from a less cognitively impaired population).

Second, on two of the three dimensions measured by the autism diagnostic instrument, the children in the more recent cohort were, on average, less symptomatic than the children from the earlier cohort. The researchers stated that although these differences were statistically significant (i.e., they exceeded the criterion of a statistical test), they were likely not clinically significant (i.e., they were likely not of significance to the clinical presentation); therefore, the researchers suggested that these differences should not be taken as evidence that the diagnostic criteria had broadened. However, refer again to the tallness analogy: Comparing two cohorts of males in McClennan County diagnosed according to our more restricted (74.5-in.) versus our broader (72-in.) criterion would probably result in a statistically significant difference between the two cohorts' average height—but the difference would be just about an inch (i.e., most likely not a clinically significant difference).

The "Child Count" Data

The purpose of the federal Individuals With Disabilities Education Act (IDEA), passed in 1991, is to ensure that all children with disabilities are provided a free, appropriate, public education including an individually designed program. Schools comply with the IDEA by reporting to the federal Department of Education an annual "child count" of the number of children with disabilities served. It is the data from these annual child counts that have been the most egregiously misused in arguments for an autism epidemic.

For example, in October 2003, the Autism Society of America sent its 20,000 members the following electronic message: "Figures from the most recent U. S. Department of Education's 2002 Report to Congress on IDEA reveal that the number of students with autism [ages 6 to 21] in America's schools *jumped an alarming 1,354% in the eight-year period from the school year 1991-92 to 2000-01*" (emphasis added). What the Autism Society failed to note is the following fact (available in the *Report to Congress*, immediately under the autism data entries): Prior to the 1991–1992 school year, there was no child count of students with autism; autism did not even exist as an IDEA reporting category. Moreover, in 1991–1992, use of the autism reporting category was optional (it was required only in subsequent years).

Whenever a new category is introduced, if it is viable, increases in its usage will ensue. Consider another IDEA reporting category introduced along with autism in 1991–1992: "traumatic brain injury." From 1991–1992 to 2000–2001, this category soared an astronomical 5,059%. Likewise, the reporting category "developmental delay," which was introduced only in 1997–1998, grew 663% in only 3 years.

After the initial year, the number of children reported under the IDEA category of autism has increased by approximately 23% annually. Why the continuing annual increase? As is the case with new options in the marketplace, like cellular phones and high-speed Internet, new reporting categories in the annual child count are not capitalized upon instantaneously; they require incrementally magnified awareness and augmentation or reallocation of resources. Currently no state reports the number of children with autism that would be expected based on the results of three recent, large-scale epidemiological studies, which identified 5.8 to 6.7 children per 1,000 for the broader autism spectrum (Baird et al., 2000; Bertrand et al., 2001; Chakrabarti & Fombonne, 2001). In 2002–2003, front-runners Oregon and Minnesota reported 4.3 and 3.5 children with autism per 1,000, respectively, while Colorado, Mississippi, and New Mexico reported only 0.8, 0.7, and 0.7 children with autism per 1,000. Thus, most likely IDEA child counts will continue to increase until the number reported by each state approaches the number of children identified in the epidemiological studies.

Why do states vary so widely in the number of children reported (or served)? Each state's department of education specifies its own diagnostic criteria, and states differ (as do school districts within states, and individual schools within school districts) in the value given to a diagnosis in terms of services received. States also vary from year to year in the number of children served and reported. For instance, Massachusetts historically reported the lowest percentage of children with autism: only 0.4 or 0.5 per 1,000 from 1992 through 2001. Then, in 2002, Massachusetts reported a 400% increase in one year, Fig. 1. Distribution of male height in McClennan County, Texas. Shaded areas represent segments of the population defined as "tall" according to two standards: men over 74.5 in. (2,778) versus men over 72 in. (10,360) when it began using student-level data (i.e., actually counting the students) rather than applying a ratio, which was calculated in 1992, based on the proportion of students in each disability classification as reported in 1992. In their 2002 IDEA report to Congress, Massachusetts state officials warned that the increase will continue for several years as "districts better understand how to submit their data at the student level" (IDEA, 2002, p. 4) and "all districts comply completely with the new reporting methods" (IDEA, 2002, p. 4).

Other Reasons Not to Believe in an Autism Epidemic

In this article we have detailed three reasons why some laypersons mistakenly believe that there is an autism epidemic. They are unaware of the purposeful broadening of diagnostic criteria, coupled with deliberately greater public awareness; they accept the unwarranted conclusions of the M.I.N.D. Institute study; and they fail to realize that autism was not even an IDEA reporting category until the early 1990s and incremental increases will most likely continue until the schools are identifying and serving the number of children identified in epidemiological studies.

Apart from a desire to be aligned with scientific reasoning, there are other reasons not to believe in an autism epidemic.

Epidemics solicit causes; false epidemics solicit false causes. Google *autism* and *epidemic* to witness the range of suspected causes of the mythical autism epidemic. Epidemics also connote danger. What message do we send autistic children and adults when we call their increasing number an epidemic? A pandemic? A scourge? Realizing that the increasing prevalence rates are most likely due to noncatastrophic mechanisms, such as purposely broader diagnostic criteria and greater public awareness, should not, however, diminish societal responsibility to support the increasing numbers of individuals being diagnosed with autism. Neither should enthusiasm for scientific inquiry into the variety and extent of human behavioral, neuroanatomical, and genotypic diversity in our population be dampened.

Recommended Reading

Fombonne, E. (2003). Epidemiological surveys of autism and other pervasive developmental disorders: An update. *Journal of Autism and Developmental Disorders, 33*, 365–382.

Institute of Medicine. (2004). *Immunization safety review: Vaccines and autism.* Washington, DC: National Academies Press.

Wing, L., & Potter, D. (2002). (See References)

Note

1. Wing and Potter (2002) provide a similar illustration. The same percentage of children who met Kanner's earlier, more restricted criteria met *DSM-IV*'s more recent, broadened criteria; if the child was autistic according to Kanner's restricted criteria, the child was autistic according to *DSM-IV*'s broadened criteria. Of course, the reverse was not true. Only 33 to 45% of the children who met more recent *DSM-IV* criteria met earlier Kanner criteria.

References

American Psychiatric Association. (1980). *Diagnostic and statistical manual of mental disorders* (3rd ed.). Washington, DC: Author.

American Psychiatric Association. (1994). *Diagnostic and statistical manual of mental disorders* (4th ed.). Washington, DC: Author.

Baird, G., Charman, T., Baron-Cohen, S., Cox, A., Swettenham, J., Wheelwright, S., & Drew, A. (2000). A screening instrument for autism at 18 months of age: A 6 year follow-up study. *Journal of the American Academy of Child and Adolescent Psychiatry, 39,* 694–702.

Bertrand, J., Mars, A., Boyle, C., Bove, F., Yeargin-Allsopp, M., & Decoufle, P. (2001). Prevalence of autism in a United States population: The Brick Township, New Jersey, investigation. *Pediatrics, 108*, 1155–1161.

California Department of Developmental Services. (1999). *Changes in the population with autism and pervasive developmental disorders in California's developmental services system: 1987–1998.* A report to the legislature. Sacramento, CA: California Health and Human Services Agency.

Chakrabarti, S., & Fombonne, E. (2001). Pervasive developmental disorders in preschool children. *Journal of the American Medical Association, 285*, 3093–3099.

Filipek, P.A., Accardo, P.J., Ashwal, S., Baranek, G.T., Cook, E.H. Jr., Dawson, G., Gordon, B., Gravel, J.S., Johnson, C.P., Kallen, R.J., Levy, S.E., Minshew, N.J., Ozonoff, S., Prizant, B.M., Rapin, I., Rogers, S.J., Stone, W.L., Teplin, S.W., Tuchman, R.F., & Volkmar, F.R. (2000). Practice parameter: Screening and diagnosis of autism: Report of the Quality Standards Subcommittee of the American Academy of Neurology and the Child Neurology Society. *Neurology, 55*, 468–479.

Fitzgerald, M. (2004). *Autism and creativity: Is there a link between autism in men and exceptional ability?* London: Brunner-Routledge.

Frith, U. (1989). *Autism: Explaining the enigma.* Oxford, England: Blackwell.

Gillberg, C., & Coleman, M. (2000). *The biology of the autistic syndromes* (3rd ed.). London: MacKeith Press.

IDEA. (2002). *Data Notes for IDEA, Part B.* Retrieved April 22, 2005, from IDEAdata Web side: http://www.ideadata.org/docs/bdatanotes2002.doc

Kanner, L., & Eisenberg, J. (1956). Early infantile autism 1943–1955. *American Journal of Orthopsychiatry, 26*, 55–65.

M.I.N.D. Institute. (2002). *Report to the Legislature on the principal findings from The Epidemiology of Autism in California: A Comprehensive Pilot Study.* Davis: University of California-Davis.

Rutter, M. (1978). Diagnosis and definition. In M. Rutter & E. Schopler (Eds.), *Autism: A reappraisal of concepts and treatments* (pp. 1–25). New York: Plenum Press.

U.S. Department of Education. (2002). *Twenty-fourth annual report to Congress on the implementation of the Individuals With Disabilities Education Act.* Washington, DC: Author.

Wing, L., & Potter, D. (2002). The epidemiology of autistic spectrum disorders: Is the prevalence rising? *Mental Retardation and Developmental Disabilities Research Reviews, 8*, 151–162.

Address correspondence to Morton Ann Gernsbacher, Department of Psychology, University of Wisconsin-Madison, 1202 W. Johnson St., Madison, WI 53706; e-mail: MAGernsb@wisc.edu.

From *Current Directions in Psychological Science,* Vol. 14, no. 2, February 2005, pp. 55-58. Copyright © 2005 by The Association for Psychological Science. Reprinted by permission. **www.blackwell-synergy.com**

Savior Parents

Rescuing an ailing child can become a crusade and a career

ELIZABETH WEILL

Jannine and John Cody were packing to move from Sheppard Air Force Base in Wichita Falls, Texas, to Brooks Air Force Base in San Antonio in 1985 when a military doctor gave them some devastating news. Their 6-week-old daughter Elizabeth was missing part of her 18th chromosome. To explain what that meant, the doctor showed Jannine a textbook with a horrifying picture and caption that she still keeps in her files. It read, "They are probably the most seriously afflicted among carriers of chromosome abnormalities. They maintain the froglike position observed in infants and are reduced to an entirely bedridden and vegetative life." The young mother was incredulous. "That just didn't jibe with what I was seeing," Cody vividly recalls. "It had been raining for a week, everything was wet, the packers were angry. I had a 3-year-old, a 6-week-old and a mother-in-law to deal with. I was on total overload, so I said to myself, O.K., this doesn't quite fit; she doesn't seem like a vegetable. I'll deal with that later."

Elizabeth's first year included three surgeries to fix a cleft palate and a cleft lip. By age 2, she had slipped far behind on the growth charts. Her pediatrician seemed to think that was inevitable, but her mother demanded that Elizabeth's symptoms be treated, a radical notion at the time. She took her daughter to an endocrinologist, who put Elizabeth on daily injections of human growth hormone, a therapy that caused her to grow like a weed and blossom developmentally as well. When Elizabeth had difficulty learning to speak, Cody pushed for her to see a neurologist, who determined that the problem had more to do with the impairment of her hearing than with her intelligence. The 3-year-old was fitted with a hearing aid and began learning sign language.

The journey to save Elizabeth took both mother and daughter to unexpected places. Cody went back to college and earned a Ph.D. in human genetics at age 42. Her dissertation topic: syndromes of the 18th chromosome. Today this former homemaker and president of her local embroiderers' guild conducts genetic research at the University of Texas Health Science Center. Her work has helped raise Elizabeth's IQ into the normal range and has provided a model for helping the approximately 500 other kids in the U.S. with the same defect. Cody also set up the Chromosome 18 Registry and Research Society—a foundation that connects affected families with one another and funds research.

This month Cody will reap a huge personal reward for her efforts: Elizabeth will graduate from high school. A few years ago, Cody sat watching Elizabeth's pep squad perform at a football game, wearing red, white and blue, the school colors. "Suddenly I'm watching, and I realize I can't pick her out of the crowd. She wasn't so bad!" says Cody. "I just burst into tears. I never ever thought I would see the day when she'd just be one of the girls in high school, out there on the field with all the other kids. It was amazing."

Being a parent brings out the most extreme traits in all of us—capacities for love, fear, persistence you never knew you had—and those traits are only magnified when a kid is in danger. You stay up all night when your daughter spikes a 101° fever. You drive across town in five minutes flat when your son falls out of a tree. But parenting a child who has a serious genetic disease transcends that entirely, as movies like *Lorenzo's Oil* have shown. It turns Clark Kents into Supermen and former science-phobes into experts in molecular biology. "For a long time in the pediatric community, [the attitude was] if you have a major chromosomal abnormality, you're going to not grow well, you're going to be developmentally delayed, you're going to be mentally retarded, and there's not a darn thing we can do about it," says Dr. Daniel Hale, a pediatric endocrinologist who works closely with Cody. These days the situation is different. At the molecular level, genetic diseases are better understood, and new avenues are opening for dealing with them, thanks in part to the advocacy of parents like Cody who embrace the notion that kids with chromosomal abnormalities have a right to reach their fullest potential.

"I'm a person, NOT A DISEASE!" insists Sam Berns, age 7

Particular Clark Kents, of course, turn into particular superheroes because of varying talents and inclinations. Leslie Gordon and Scott Berns, for example, were both multidegree doctors—she has an M.D. and a Ph.D., he has an M.D. and a master's in public health—when a doctor friend diagnosed progeria in their 21-month-old son Sam, now 7 (the rare disease causes accelerated aging and often leads to death by early adolescence). The next day, Gordon took a leave from her training in pediatric ophthalmology. Within nine months, she created the Progeria Research Foundation to bring attention to and research funds for the disease, which affects just 1 in 4 million babies. "There was nothing out there. Zero," says Gordon from her home in Foxboro, Mass., her voice brimming with fierce enthusiasm. "I was surprised because as a doctor, you train, you train, you train, and when you get out there you realize there are holes."

Gordon and Berns are committed to the idea that Sam, who inhabits the body of a 70-year-old, should just be a kid. Currently he's obsessed with baseball, school and drums, and when a new friend informs him he has no hair, he says, "Tell me something I don't know. Let's go play." Gordon, in just over five years, has started a tissue bank, raised serious money and lured top scientists into studying her son's disease. In October 2002, she, along with an international team, succeeded in isolating the progeria gene. Progeria, it turns out, is caused by a tiny point mutation in a child's DNA, a one-letter typo in the chromosomal book. But even after that research triumph—the culmination of an 11-month, white-hot burn of constant phone and e-mail conversations—Gordon did not take a break. Sam, she reasons, has no time to waste. A stroke could hit at any time, and the same is true for the more than 50 other kids with progeria whom Gordon has come to know and love. "Somebody called me a barracuda once, and I said thank you," Gordon says. "You can't hand a child a paper saying we found the gene, and here, you're cured. Isolating the gene was the end of Chapter One. We now have a gene that leads to a protein defect that researchers can sink their teeth into. Fantastic labs can ask fantastic questions. We can pull in a lot more terrific researchers, ask better questions and start moving toward treatment."

Taking on the responsibility of finding a cure for your child's rare genetic disease can be both comforting and painful, like all parental obligations, except in this case the stakes aren't seeing a child's soccer game vs. working out, but seeing your child's future birthdays vs. (perhaps) not blaming yourself if you don't.

"You don't want to ever have to tell your kids someday that you didn't try your best," says Brad Margus, a Harvard M.B.A. and the former owner of a Florida shrimp-processing company who switched careers after discovering that two of his four boys had a rare, degenerative disease. "Being a dad, you're expected by your kids to be able to fix anything, right? So they're counting on you to do something about it," says Margus, who is now CEO of Perlegen Sciences, a Silicon Valley biotech firm.

Margus' nightmare started when he and his wife Vicki still had three boys in diapers, and his second eldest, Jarrett, then 18 months, developed difficulty walking and his speech slurred. At first doctors thought the cause was mild cerebral palsy. Then around his 18-month mark, Margus' next eldest boy, Quinn, started developing the same symptoms as Jarrett's, which suggested that the problem was genetic. The boys endured blood tests, spinal taps, muscle biopsies. After spending $60,000 and turning up nothing, the Marguses took their sons to see Dr. Jean Aicardi, a world-famous French neurologist who happened to be visiting Miami Children's Hospital. "In the first five minutes, he saw our kids and said, 'It looks an awful lot like ataxia-

telangiectasia,' which we couldn't even pronounce. 'I assume you've tested for this?' All it takes is a $20 blood test. The local doctors just looked at their feet." The Marguses recognized the name (it's pronounced ay-*tack*-see-uh teh-*lan*-jick-*tay*-sha), but all they knew was that A-T was really bad. At home that night they read that about 40% of kids with A-T get cancer by age 12; 100% deteriorate neurologically, so they're in wheelchairs as early as age 8; most die of lung problems or cancer by their late teens or early 20s. "You kind of go through a grief process," Margus says. "Your kids aren't dead, but the kids you thought you had are gone."

"You don't want to ever have to tell your kids that YOU DIDN'T TRY your best."

Like progeria, A-T is what might be called a superorphaned disease. It affects so few kids—just 400 in the U.S.—that scientists and drug companies don't bother with it. So Margus began applying his business brain to the problem of how to find a cure. He broke it down into smaller problems, assembling a list of things he needed to learn about: molecular biology, how the government funds research, how you capture the interest of top-notch scientists, what lobbying is all about. He decided his approach would be to pollinate as many excellent labs as possible, funding postdocs to work under superstars and hoping that whenever researchers discovered something relevant, they might at least ask themselves, Could this help Brad's kids? "Early on, you're naive enough that you don't know how challenging the problem really is, so you give it a shot." The result? Margus has raised more than $15 million to date, and he funded the research that isolated the A-T-mutated gene nine years ago.

Still, Margus sounds distinctly sad. Sure, he has raised a lot of money and even made a savvy career switch that puts him in regular contact with executives from five of the top 10 pharmaceutical companies. Yet, in his mind, "so far we haven't done squat." His kids, now 13 and 15, are deteriorating daily. This summer he hopes to move his family from Florida to California, where he spends most of his time, but first he will need to retrofit a house "for two teenagers in power wheelchairs who can't control their motor skills very well, so they take out huge chunks of drywall." When his boys ask their father about his work, Margus is honest. "Quinn is quite tough on me," Margus says. "He asks what those researchers are doing. And candidly, I have to say that we've failed. We've set up a center at Johns Hopkins, so at least there's one place in the world that's accumulating a lot of data on the kids. But as far as a treatment or cure or even slowing the progression of the disease, we still haven't done it."

The struggles of parents like Brad Margus and Leslie Gordon are less lonely than they were in the pre-Internet era. Numerous websites help such parents reach out and learn from one another; among them are sites created by the Genetic and Rare Diseases Information Center at the National Institutes of Health and the Genetic Alliance, an advocacy group. This June in San Antonio, Jannine Cody is convening the first World Congress on Chromosome Abnormalities. More than 1,000 parents, doctors and researchers are expected to attend. Sessions will range from "Neurological and Anatomical Imaging" to "Potty/Sleep Solutions." The event is the culmination of 15 years of work, with twin goals of building stronger advocacy groups for children with chromosomal abnormalities and establishing a nucleus of scientists dedicated to addressing their problems. "Somebody ought to give that lady a MacArthur," says Dr. Hale.

On a recent afternoon, Elizabeth Cody comes bounding down the stairs to greet her mother, who has just returned from work. There is nothing froglike or vegetative about the bright-eyed 19-year-old, who flops onto the sofa and expresses relief that her mother has remembered to bring home a chart showing exactly which part of her 18th chromosome is missing. "A boy at my school used to make fun of me, so I wanted to show him this," Elizabeth explains. After graduation in May, Elizabeth plans to attend a local community college, and then become a teacher's assistant in a hearing-impaired classroom and perhaps move out to California. One thing she can count on: her mother will be cheering all the way.

Index

Index

Test Your Knowledge Form

We encourage you to photocopy and use this page as a tool to assess how the articles in *Annual Editions* expand on the information in your textbook. By reflecting on the articles you will gain enhanced text information. You can also access this useful form on a product's book support Web site at *http://www.mhcls.com/online/*.

NAME:

DATE:

TITLE AND NUMBER OF ARTICLE:

BRIEFLY STATE THE MAIN IDEA OF THIS ARTICLE:

LIST THREE IMPORTANT FACTS THAT THE AUTHOR USES TO SUPPORT THE MAIN IDEA:

WHAT INFORMATION OR IDEAS DISCUSSED IN THIS ARTICLE ARE ALSO DISCUSSED IN YOUR TEXTBOOK OR OTHER READINGS THAT YOU HAVE DONE? LIST THE TEXTBOOK CHAPTERS AND PAGE NUMBERS:

LIST ANY EXAMPLES OF BIAS OR FAULTY REASONING THAT YOU FOUND IN THE ARTICLE:

LIST ANY NEW TERMS/CONCEPTS THAT WERE DISCUSSED IN THE ARTICLE, AND WRITE A SHORT DEFINITION:

We Want Your Advice

ANNUAL EDITIONS revisions depend on two major opinion sources: one is our Advisory Board, listed in the front of this volume, which works with us in scanning the thousands of articles published in the public press each year; the other is you—the person actually using the book. Please help us and the users of the next edition by completing the prepaid article rating form on this page and returning it to us. Thank you for your help!

ANNUAL EDITIONS: Child Growth and Development 07/08

ARTICLE RATING FORM

Here is an opportunity for you to have direct input into the next revision of this volume.
We would like you to rate each of the articles listed below, using the following scale:

1. **Excellent: should definitely be retained**
2. **Above average: should probably be retained**
3. **Below average: should probably be deleted**
4. **Poor: should definitely be deleted**

Your ratings will play a vital part in the next revision.
Please mail this prepaid form to us as soon as possible.
Thanks for your help!

RATING	ARTICLE
	1. Brave New Babies
	2. Treating the Tiniest Patients
	3. Reading Your Baby's Mind
	4. Brain Research and Early Childhood Development: A Primer for Developmentally Appropriate Practice
	5. Culture and Language in the Emergence of Autobiographical Memory
	6. Gender Bender
	7. Language and Children's Understanding of Mental States
	8. A Deeper Sense of Literacy
	9. Parental School Involvement and Children's Academic Achievement
	10. The Trouble with Boys
	11. The Preschool Promise
	12. Children's Capacity to Develop Resiliency
	13. Friendship Quality and Social Development
	14. Loneliness and Peer Relations in Childhood
	15. The Power of Make-Believe
	16. Gender and Group Process: A Developmental Perspective
	17. Taming Wild Girls
	18. Girls Just Want to Be Mean
	19. A Profile of Bullying at School
	20. The Case for Staying Home
	21. Contemporary Research on Parenting: The Case for Nature *and* Nurture
	22. Stress and the Superdad
	23. Physical Discipline and Children's Adjustment: Cultural Normativeness as a Moderator
	24. A Nation of Wimps
	25. Why Our Kids Are Out of Control
	26. Siblings' Direct and Indirect Contributions to Child Development
	27. The Environment of Childhood Poverty
	28. Childhood for Sale
	29. The Culture of Affluence: Psychological Costs of Material Wealth
	30. Watch and Learn

RATING	ARTICLE
	31. Forensic Developmental Psychology: Unveiling Four Common Misconceptions
	32. How Many Fathers Are Best for a Child?
	33. The Pediatric Gap
	34. Attention Deficit Hyperactivity Disorder in Very Young Children: Early Signs and Interventions
	35. Childhood's End
	36. Children of the Fallen
	37. When Does Autism Start?
	38. Three Reasons Not to Believe in an Autism Epidemic
	39. Savior Parents

(Continued on next page)

BUSINESS REPLY MAIL
FIRST CLASS MAIL PERMIT NO. 551 DUBUQUE IA

POSTAGE WILL BE PAID BY ADDRESEE

McGraw-Hill Contemporary Learning Series
2460 KERPER BLVD
DUBUQUE, IA 52001-9902

NO POSTAGE
NECESSARY
IF MAILED
IN THE
UNITED STATES

ABOUT YOU

Name _____ Date _____

Are you a teacher? ☐ A student? ☐
Your school's name _____

Department _____

Address _____ City _____ State _____ Zip _____

School telephone # _____

YOUR COMMENTS ARE IMPORTANT TO US!

Please fill in the following information:
For which course did you use this book?
_____

Did you use a text with this ANNUAL EDITION? ☐ yes ☐ no
What was the title of the text?
_____

What are your general reactions to the *Annual Editions* concept?
_____

Have you read any pertinent articles recently that you think should be included in the next edition? Explain.
_____

Are there any articles that you feel should be replaced in the next edition? Why?
_____

Are there any World Wide Web sites that you feel should be included in the next edition? Please annotate.
_____

May we contact you for editorial input? ☐ yes ☐ no
May we quote your comments? ☐ yes ☐ no